The Cognitive Early Warning Predictive System Using the Smart Vaccine

The New Digital Immunity Paradigm for Smart Cities and Critical Infrastructure

The Cognitive Early Warning Predictive System Using the Smart Vaccine

The New Digital Immunity Paradigm for Smart Cities and Critical Infrastructure

Dr. Rocky Termanini

CRC Press
Taylor & Francis Group
Boca Raton   London   New York

CRC Press is an imprint of the
Taylor & Francis Group, an **informa** business
AN AUERBACH BOOK

CRC Press
Taylor & Francis Group
6000 Broken Sound Parkway NW, Suite 300
Boca Raton, FL 33487-2742

© 2016 by Taylor & Francis Group, LLC
CRC Press is an imprint of Taylor & Francis Group, an Informa business

No claim to original U.S. Government works

Printed on acid-free paper
Version Date: 20151020

International Standard Book Number-13: 978-1-4987-2651-1 (Hardback)

Visit the Taylor & Francis Web site at
http://www.taylorandfrancis.com

and the CRC Press Web site at
http://www.crcpress.com

Contents

Preface

I saw the light of the future when I first read Ray Kurzweil's best-seller book *The Singularity Is Near: When Humans Transcend Biology*. One cubic inch of nanotube circuitry, once fully developed, would be up to one hundred million times more powerful than the human brain.

Nanobots, nano programs, will be able to travel through the bloodstream, then go in and around our cells and perform various functions, such as removing toxins, sweeping out debris, and correcting DNA errors, repairing and restoring cell membranes, reversing atherosclerosis, modifying the levels of hormones, neurotransmitters, and other metabolic chemicals and a myriad of other tasks. For each aging process, down to the level of individual cells, cell components. Wow—This is heavy!

Then I started passionately reading chapter after chapter and got more adsorbed in knowing what he meant by the physics of the impossible. I started to wonder if we will ever get a chance, in our lifetimes, to understand the anatomy of our future and how we can go forward and backward in time and be older than our parents. I know it is going to happen, because it is based on real science. I was thunderstuck by his scientific prophecies and visionary futurism about our brains. Ray Kurzweil shook the tree of the scientific community when he revealed his *law of accelerating returns*, which crystal balls the reality of the exponential increase in technologies, like computers, genetics, nanotechnology, robotics, and artificial intelligence. He says this will lead to a technological singularity in the year 2045, the time when progress will be so transformed that people will augment their minds and bodies with genetic alterations, nanotechnology implants, and artificial intelligence. What amazes me about Kurzweil is his argumentation skills and the depth of his scientific knowledge: "If you have a different impression of the world today, I would want you to know that I am technically correct. If the rest of the world fails to think that's enough, the rest of the world is wrong!"

I have always been fascinated by the magic of artificial intelligence (AI) and its rough edges. It is not stepping into science fiction as many believe. It is the science of reality and the mirror of human intelligence and will surpass humans' ability to comprehend it. On the contrary, Ray Kurzweil gained the respect of the world not because of his visionary countdown to the "singularity," but he became a magical storyteller with his scientific revelations. He is the inventor of the flatbed scanner, inventor of the first optical character recognition, the first inventor of the first commercial text-to-speech synthesizer, the Kurzweil K250 music synthesizer, and in 2002 he was inducted into the National Inventors Hall of Fame, established by the U.S. Patent Office. Kurzweil doesn't believe in half measures, he takes 180 to 200 vitamin supplements a day.

He is a "restless genius" as described by the *Wall Street Journal*.

This brings me to the core of my own singularity concept which is replicating the Human Immune System in the Digital World; I call it "Digital Immunity (DI)." Cybertechnology is galloping forward in leaps and bounds—just imagine, the Internet is not even 30 years old (still in its infancy) and yet, its domination in the world is much more than all the inventions and discoveries for the last 1000 years. The Internet has brought us great things, but malware will always remain its evil shadow. Sudden assailments have toppled societies and shaken civilizations. The element of surprise became a very potent change agent, and, perhaps, the most powerful weapon of all. And the mythic success of the Trojan Horse victory set a high bar for surprise and world-changing attacks that followed through the eons.

My interest in building Digital Immunity goes back to 2001, right after the attack on the World Trade Center in New York. I was wondering how the United States, with all its technological might, could not foresee or envision this provocative attack, while the terrorists were dancing and playing the war drums. As it was eloquently expressed by Senator Thomas Kean, head of the 9/11 Commission, "a failure of imagination.…" One interesting key the Commission unearthed was that "Terrorism wasn't the chief security concern of the Bush or Clinton administrations." Amazing!

In 2002, I joined MERIT International Security Consultants with a focus on cybersecurity. Working with Joe Rodriguez, a veteran and former Newark officer, was a great inspiration and stimulus for my research. The idea of Digital Immunity started to gel in my mind, and I spent many hours studying the Human immune System with unceasing interest and jumped into the cold waters of immunology. On May 12, 2004, I gave a presentation at the Society of American Military Engineers in New Jersey, which made me aware that the country was not ready for any cyber war. It was a 2-day conference where top presenters from the military talked about conventional arms with a sprinkle of low-tech creativity. I was the very last presenter and only given 15 minutes. To my surprise, my concept of DI turned out to be the most interesting and eye-popping presentation, with my scenario "The Electronic Pearl Harbor" Using Virus Rain™ and how the Smart Vaccine™ like the (B cells) is systematically winning the battle. I knew then that the country was in need of new technology to protect its infrastructures and eradicate cybercrime and terrorism.

Every time I give a presentation on Digital Immunity and the Smart Vaccine, I surprise the audience. Everyone is pleasantly stupefied with this compelling ingenious concept. I have even presented the Smart Vaccine to New Jersey congressmen and State Police, and the Secret Service, but stunningly they could not assimilate the potentiality of the idea. In December 2010, Joe Rodriguez and I applied for a federal grant issued by the Department of the Navy (BAA 11-007) and the reply came, "innovative idea but too far advanced to implement." Ironically, Stuxnet sabotaged Iran's nuclear program in June 2010. Whoever made this diabolical bomb had a long list of targets yet to come. We submitted a couple of ARPA (Advanced Research Projects Agency) proposals, but the response was "it is way ahead of its time. ..." In 2009, we met with Department of Homeland Security (DHS) representatives at the New Jersey Institute of Technology (NJIT). I remember I told the DHS representative (a retired brigadier general William Marshall): "What would happen to us if immunization never existed today? We would be walking zombies dead at 30." It is heartbreaking to see DHS and DoD spending billions of dollars on throwaway grants and loose balloons and giving glamorous consulting companies so much money in return for well-bound 1000-page reports worth only their weight. I have yet to see a spark of innovation coming from these people. Unfortunately, projects are awarded to companies that spend a fortune promoting their services while entertaining chief information officers (CIOs) and chief security officers (CSOs) in return for winning a bid.

In 2012, I was invited to present the Smart Vaccine at the International Security National Resilience (ISNR) Conference in Abu Dhabi, United Arab Emirates (UAE). I got the chance to meet Dr. Bastaki, CEO of the ICTFund organization. He encouraged me to pursue this hi-tech project which is badly needed for a booming nation like the UAE.

In 2003, President Bush published a surprising document highlighting the importance of protecting the country's critical infrastructures. The document was titled "The Physical Protection of Critical Infrastructures and Key Assets" in which he said, "Much work remains, however, to insure that we sustain these initial efforts over the long term. This National Strategy for the Physical Protection of Critical Infrastructures and Key Assets represents the first milestone in the road ahead. Consistent with the National Strategy for Homeland Security, this document identifies a clear set of goals and objectives and outlines the guiding principles that will underpin our efforts to secure the infrastructures and assets vital to our public health and safety, national security, governance, economy, and public confidence. It provides a unifying structure, defines roles and responsibilities, and identifies major initiatives that will drive our near-term protection priorities. Most importantly, it establishes a foundation for building and fostering a cooperative environment in which government, industry, and private citizens can work together to protect our critical infrastructures and key assets."

In October 2014, President Obama's proclamation over the security of critical infrastructures resonated how important the issue is: "The security of our Nation is my top priority, and my Administration is dedicated to preserving and fortifying the systems that support our daily lives. Guided by our Cybersecurity Framework, we are working to protect our critical infrastructure from cyber threats, while promoting an open and reliable cyberspace. In the face of a diverse set of physical risks to our infrastructure—from extreme weather and the impacts of climate change to health pandemics, accidents, and acts of terrorism—we are taking steps to reduce our vulnerabilities. And because the majority of our critical infrastructure is owned and operated by private companies, we are encouraging the private sector to recognize their shared responsibility. As part of our National Infrastructure Protection Plan, we are finding new ways we can strengthen our public-private partnerships to bolster our systems and networks and to better manage risks."

My aspiration for writing this book is to tell everyone that the present cybersecurity industry is not strong enough to win the battle against cybercrime much less for the escalating cyberterrorism. Antivirus Technology (AVT) has hit a plateau of stagnation and it is time to shift to a new paradigm. Looking at the horrific staggering statistics of cyber malware (no one can really provide definitive statistics), we definitely need a cutting-edge holistic approach to "intelligently" secure the country's critical infrastructure, and more importantly outsmart those cybercriminals every time.

Look, for example, at how Dubai City redefined the term "metropolis" by pushing the envelope of urban innovation ahead of every city in the world. Today, it is considered the magnet of technovation, and will certainly be one of the best models of smart cities with Digital Immunity as part of its success and glamour. It amazes me how a small country like the UAE has more appreciation for the prowess of the Smart Vaccine than Google, Amazon, and Microsoft.

Another influencing reason for writing this book is to bring into focus the importance of nanotechnology (NT) and artificial intelligence. These two emerging technologies have started to exhibit their potentialities to reinvent the cybersecurity domain. If we need to catch up with cybercrime, we need to harness these two pioneering domains and redraw our security blueprints. Digital Immunity is the convergence of these two emerging technologies and will usher the beginning of a cybersecurity renaissance.

The adversary countries have their own electronic armies, and other cybercrime communities will be turning to AI and NT for the next generation of cybernetic malware.

Horst Ludwig Störmer, the German physicist Nobel Laureate, described NT as follows: "Nanotechnology has given us the tools ... to play with the ultimate toy box of nature—atoms and molecules. Everything is made from it.... The possibilities to create new things appear limitless."

Robert A. Freitas, Jr., the pioneer of nanomedicine, described it as "The net effect of these nanomedical interventions will be the continuing arrest of all biological aging, along with the reduction of current biological age to whatever new biological age is deemed desirable by the patient, severing forever the link between calendar time and biological health. Such interventions may become commonplace several decades from today. Using annual checkups and cleanouts, and some occasional major repairs, *your biological age could be restored* once a year to the more or less constant physiological age that you select. You might still eventually die of accidental causes, but you'll live at least ten times longer than you do now."

It is amazing what we will be able to do with NT and AI in the domain of Smart Security. That is why we designed Digital Immunity as the cognitive shield for smart cities. Here is a glimpse of what nanobiology is doing to enhance the quality of our lives, as explained by Ray Kurzweil: "When nanotechnology is mature, it's going to solve the problems of biology by overcoming biological pathogens, removing toxins, correcting DNA errors, and reversing other sources of aging. We will then have to contend with new dangers that it introduces, just as the Internet introduced the danger of software viruses. These new pitfalls will include the potential for self-replicating nanotechnology getting out of control and the integrity of the software controlling these powerful, distributed nanobots. We'll actually accomplish most of that with biotechnology, methods such as RNA interference for turning off destructive genes, gene therapy for changing your genetic code, therapeutic cloning for regenerating your cells and tissues, smart drugs to reprogram your metabolic pathways, and many other emerging techniques. But whatever biotechnology doesn't get around to accomplishing, we'll have the means to do with nanotechnology."

During the development of the Digital Immunity System, known as the CEWPS/Smart Vaccine, I met very interesting scientists and researchers who are working diligently on great pioneering projects to enhance the quality of human life and, in particular, overcome the mysteries of diseases and how the brains of the criminals dynamically process relatively fine-grained level plans for malware and vandalism. On Facebook I met Dr. Randal Koene, a neuroscientist who is pioneering, like myself, by uploading his brain knowledge data onto a "Virtual Brain" computer to reprogram data for mental diagnosis and intelligence enhancement. This Virtual Brain will provide neuroscientists and clinicians with an incredible opportunity to replicate the functions of the brain in the way they are encoded in neural ensembles.

The replication of human immunity is not science fiction. It is creativity in motion. I am writing this book for the younger generation, which has been nurtured on videogame milk and smartphone cookies. I am designing Digital Immunity for visionary whiz kids who are way ahead of their time, and can see the world as a brighter and smarter place. They will take this product and use their intelligence to make it of equal intelligence. I am writing this book for the young Kurzweils, the Hawkings, and the Einsteins, who will erect the new pillars of *human intelligence*.

I am providing the architecture and the foundation design for the Cognitive Early Warning Predictive System (CEWPS™) for the Smart City and Smart City Cloud. The next step will be putting together a tiger team to assemble all the smart components into the new paradigm—Digital Immunity.

A smart city is a multiplexed metropolis where a smart grid will offer ubiquitous data services will make cities more livable, more efficient, more sustainable, and perhaps, more democratic. But, more importantly, smart cities will use the smart grid to protect all the vital information hubs and home area networks from malicious exploits and "zero-day" black holes. Smart cities need two things: a Digital Nervous System and a Digital Immune System. The former will facilitate the dynamics of data, and the latter will protect the city's data. As American author Jane Jacobs wrote in her influential 1961 book *The Death and Life of Great American Cities*, "Cities have the capability of providing something for everybody, only because, and only when, they are created by everybody." To achieve this wonderful utopia, smart cities will be blessed with smart security that will protect all the information arteries just like in our body's immune system. The Smart Vaccine is the holy grail of Digital Immunity. Often I was told this topic is ahead of its time, well I don't think so. We are already immersed in the future right now.

Finally, I hope my points were well taken. I humbly express my gratitude and gratefulness to all the people who worked with me to make this happen.

Acknowledgments

I humbly express my gratitude to all the people who have supported me in this new journey, to the ones who gave me a listening ear, to the ones who vehemently argued with me, to the ones who stood in awe listening to my science fiction, and to the ones who have fought with me tooth and nail:

My wife Lina

My daughter Nadia, Attorney at Law

Dr. Zafer Termanini, Orthopedic Surgeon

My sister Mia Termanini, Business Consultant

Irene Corpuz, Security Head, Abu Dhabi, United Arab Emirates

Dr. Issa Bastaki, President of the University of Dubai, Dubai, United Arab Emirates

Saeed Salem Al Hanki, Major General, Ministry of Interior, Abu Dhabi, United Arab Emirates

Meshaal Bin Hussain, Director EA/CERT, Dubai, United Arab Emirates

Ahmad Hassan, Director of Risk Management and Compliance, DU, Dubai, United Arab Emirates

Ms. Amna Almadhoob, Senior Security and Researcher, AMX Middle East, Bahrain

Dr. Adel Al Alawi, Professor, University of Bahrain, Bahrain

John Casgrove, President of Cosgrove Computer Systems, El Segundo, California

Michael Krieger, Attorney, Los Angeles, California

Joe Rodriguez, President of M.E.R.I.T. Investigative Services

Stan Stahl, PhD, President of the Information Group, Los Angeles, California

And I thank the rest of my visionary friends for their gracious assistance.

Rocky Termanini

BIG INSPIRATION FROM THE HUMAN IMMUNE SYSTEM

Immune Universe

Our body is a multicellular organism made up of perhaps 100 trillion cells. The cells in our body are fairly complicated smart machines. Each one has a nucleus, energy production equipment, a data repository of information, DNA code, and protein builder. Our body has two complex systems that protect our existence. The first one is the nervous system followed by the immune system.

In order to understand the sophistication and complexity of the Human Immune System (HIS), we need to link 5 million data center in the world (like Amazon) into one cohesive grid, managed by 5 billion professionals working harmoniously together 24/7 all year around the clock, without the slightest conflict or confusion. Of course it is an imaginary vision but it gives you an idea on the magnitude of the morphology of our immune system.

The Human Immune System is the Pentagon of the human body. Its main mission is to monitor and protect and keep people healthy. HIS is a layered defense system that quickly responds to any foreign invasion. HIS is run and managed by experienced generals who guide millions of troops into a highly sophisticated and strategic war.

So what makes the Human Immune System so miraculous? Well, first, it self-protects the body from invading germs, which are called *antigens*. It smartly knows the type of attack, time, and location. While the defending cells are hurrying to the attack location to set the right ambush and booby traps, the other cells are alerting some killer cells to devour the germs. Another group of cells carry supplies to the front. And then there are the *memory cells* that document the attack and the chemistry of the attacking virus. The immune system knows how to mobilize with amazing scalability billions of ready-to-fight warrior cells. Like with any army, the immune system has a *paramedic unit* available to repair and heal wounded cells.

Holding Hands: The Nervous System and the Immune System

The Human Immune System can be systematically represented as shown in Figure 1.1. It can be replicated into the Digital Immune System (DIS) to proactively and intelligently defend the Digital World (Figure 1.1). But let's learn a little about our immune system first.

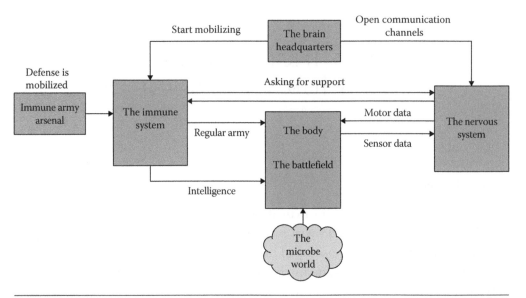

Figure 1.1   The immune system and the nervous system are two federated (symbiotic) systems that bring together their recourses against any virus attack. The brain is the commander in chief and responds to the help request from the immune system. The nervous system offers the necessary services.

The immune system and the nervous system are in fact interlinked in several ways. One well-known connection involves the adrenal glands. In response to stress messages from the brain, the adrenal glands release hormones into the blood. In addition to helping a person respond to emergencies by mobilizing the body's energy reserves, these *stress hormones* can stifle the protective effects of antibodies and lymphocytes (the white cells—B cells and T cells). Lymphocytes can travel throughout the body using the *blood vessels*. The cells can also travel through a system of *lymphatic vessels* that closely parallel the body's veins and arteries. Cells and fluids are exchanged between blood and lymphatic vessels, enabling the lymphatic system to monitor the body for invading microbes. The lymphatic vessels carry *lymph*, a clear fluid that bathes the body's tissues.

Biological links between the immune system and the central nervous system exist at several levels. Hormones and other chemicals such as neuropeptides, which convey messages among nerve cells, have also been found to *speak* to cells of the immune system—and some immune cells even manufacture typical neuropeptides. In addition, networks of nerve fibers have been found to connect directly to the lymphoid organs.

Figure 1.2 shows how closely interlocked systems facilitate the duplex (two-way) flow of information. It has been suggested that immune cells may function in a sensory capacity, detecting the arrival of foreign invaders and relaying chemical signals to alert the brain. The brain, for its part, may send signals that guide the traffic of cells through the lymphoid organs.

Another link between the immune system and the nervous system is that the hormones and other chemicals that transfer messages among nerve cells communicate with the cells of the immune system. Indeed, some immune cells are able to

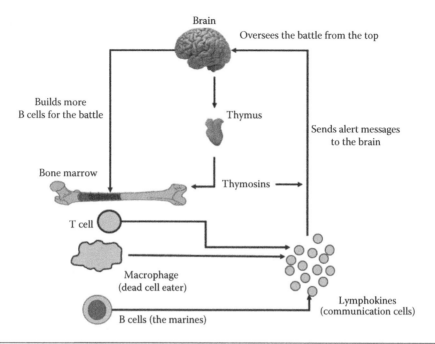

Figure 1.2   The interlocked organs facilitating a duplex (two-way) flow of information. Immune cells, it has been suggested, may function in a sensory capacity, detecting the arrival of foreign invaders and relaying chemical signals to alert the brain. The brain, for its part, may send signals that guide the traffic of cells through the lymphoid organs.

manufacture typical nerve cell products, and some lymphokines acting as "catalysts" can transmit information to the nervous system. Moreover, the brain may send messages directly down nerve cells to the immune system. Networks of nerve fibers have been found to connect to the lymphoid organs.

Anatomy of the Human Immune System

The organs of our immune system are positioned throughout our body.

They are called the *lymphoid organs* because they are home to lymphocytes—the white blood cells that are key operatives of the immune system. Within these organs, the lymphocytes grow, develop, and are deployed as shown in Figure 1.3a.

Bone marrow, the soft tissue in the hollow center of bones, is the ultimate source of all blood cells, including the immune cells.

The *thymus* is an organ that lies behind the breastbone; T cells mature in the thymus; *lymphocytes* known as *T lymphocytes*, or just *T cells*, mature there.

The *spleen* is a flattened organ at the upper left of the abdomen. Like the lymph nodes, the spleen contains specialized compartments where immune cells gather and confront antigens.

In addition to these organs, clumps of lymphoid tissue are found in many parts of the body, especially in the linings of the digestive tract and the airways and lungs, gateways to the body. These tissues include the *tonsils*, *adenoids*, and *appendix*.

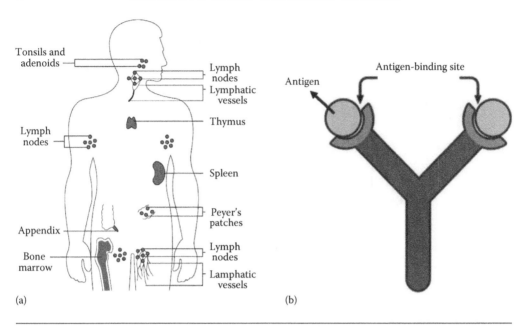

(a)   (b)

Figure 1.3 (a) Consider the lymphatic system as a network of factories to produce the B cells. The white cells are designed to protect the body from intruding microbes. (b) Antibodies are proteins that are produced by the body to fight the intrusion of foreign molecules such as toxins or other poisons. The antibodies are designed to bind very tightly to their adversaries (antigens).

Pyramid of the Immune System

The immune system stockpiles a tremendous arsenal of cells. Some staff the general defenses, while others are trained on highly specific targets. To work effectively, however, most immune cells require the active cooperation of their fellows. Sometimes, they communicate through direct physical contact and sometimes by releasing versatile chemical messengers.

The major responsibility for carrying out the activities of the immune system is done by small white blood cells called *lymphocytes* and count over 1 trillion. The two major classes of lymphocytes are B cells, which grow to maturity independent of the thymus, and T cells, which are processed in the thymus. Both B cells and T cells recognize specific antigen targets.

Each B cell is programmed to make one specific antibody. One B cell will make an antibody to block a common cold virus. Another B cell will produce an antibody that zeros in on pneumonia bacterium.

Antibodies are Y-shaped proteins, the body's building blocks formed from amino acids. Proteins are made from amino acids using information encoded in genes in DNA as shown in Figure 1.3b.

The main responsibility of B cells is to produce *antibodies*. These antibodies will go after roaming antigens and handcuff them. T cells, in contrast, will penetrate living body cells (like a SWAT team) and go after the attacking virus that commandeered the cell. B cells mainly produce antibodies as defense by offense weapons. They roam around a lymph node, waiting for a macrophage (cells that carry antigens) to bring an antigen or for an invader such as bacteria to arrive. When an antigen-specific antibody on a B cell matches up with an antigen, a remarkable transformation occurs.

Once an antibody recognizes a particular antigen, it will attach itself to a specific marker on the cell surface of the antigen so that the latter can be targeted for destruction. In many ways, the binding of an antibody to an antigen can be likened to the insertion of a key in a lock.

The antigen binds to the antibody receptor, the B cell swallows it, and with the help of a helper T cell, the B cell starts to produce identical copies of the needed antibody at an astonishing pace—up to 10 million copies an hour.

A given antibody matches an antigen (*antibody generate*) much as a key matches a lock. The fit varies: sometimes it is very precise, while at other times, it is little better than that of a skeleton key. To some degree, however, the antibody interlocks with the antigen and thereby marks it for destruction.

Bacteria will divide every 20 minutes in a perfect growing environment. This kind of exponential growth has the potential to be very deadly, very quickly, as bacteria kill their host cell within the human body. Luckily, bacteria hit their carrying capacity in the human body at a relatively low manageable level for the immune system to fight off due to competition resulting from such limiting factors as space and food. In some people, bacteria in the intestines and colon can lay dormant for years until set off by antibiotics.

Mounting an Immune Response

Infections remain the most common cause of human disease. Produced by bacteria, viruses, parasites, and fungi, infections may range from relatively mild respiratory illnesses such as the common cold, to debilitating conditions like chronic hepatitis, to life-threatening diseases such as AIDS and meningitis.

To fend off the threatening horde, the body, as devised, astonishingly intricates defenses. Microbes attempting to enter the body must first find a chink in the body's external protection. The skin and the mucous membranes that line the body's portals not only pose a physical barrier, they are also rich in scavenger cells and IgA antibodies.

Next, invaders must elude a series of nonspecific defenses—those cells and substances equipped to tackle infectious agents without regard for their antigenic peculiarities. Many potential infections are cut short when microbes are intercepted by patrolling scavenger cells or disabled by complement or other enzymes or chemicals. Virus-infected cells, for instance, secrete interferon, a chemical that rouses natural killer cells.

How to Recognize the Enemy: Antigens

In order to recognize and respond to the antigens that are their specific targets, both B cells and T cells carry special receptor molecules on their surface. For the B cell, this receptor is a prototype of the antibody that the B cell is prepared to manufacture, anchored in its surface. When a B cell encounters a matching antigen in the blood or other bodily fluid, this antibody-like receptor allows the B cell to interact with it very efficiently.

Infection Symptoms

Clinically, infections manifest themselves through the five classic symptoms of the inflammatory response—redness, warmth, swelling, pain, and loss of function. Redness and warmth develop when, under the influence of a powerful chemical substance secreted by B cells and complement components, small blood vessels in the vicinity of the infection become dilated and carry more blood. Swelling results when the vessels, made leaky by yet other immune secretions, allow fluid and soluble immune substances to seep into the surrounding tissue and immune cells to converge on the site.

Immunity: Natural and Acquired

As long ago as the fifth century BC, Greek physicians noted that people who had recovered from the plague would never get it again—they had acquired immunity. This is because, whenever T cells and B cells are activated, some of the cells become *memory* cells. Then, the next time that an individual encounters that same antigen, the immune system is primed to destroy it quickly.

The degree and duration of immunity depend on the kind of antigen, its amount, and how it enters the body. An immune response is also dictated by heredity; some individuals respond strongly to a given antigen, others weakly, and some not at all.

Infants are born with relatively weak immune responses. They have, however, a natural *passive* immunity; they are protected during the first few months of life by antibodies they receive from their mothers. The antibody IgG, which travels across the placenta, makes them immune to the same microbes to which their mothers are immune. Children who are nursed also receive IgA from breast milk, which protects the digestive tract.

The Immune System and the Nervous System

Biological links between the immune system and the central nervous system exist at several levels. One well-known pathway involves the adrenal glands, which, in response to stress messages from the brain, release corticosteroid hormones into the blood. In addition to helping a person respond to emergencies by mobilizing the body's energy reserves, these *stress hormones* decrease antibodies and reduce lymphocytes in both number and strength.

In addition, the brain may directly influence the immune system by sending messages down nerve cells. Networks of nerve fibers have been found to connect to the thymus gland, spleen, lymph nodes, and bone marrow. Moreover, experiments show that immune function can be altered by actions that destroy specific brain areas.

The image that is emerging is of closely interlocked systems facilitating a two-way flow of information, primarily through the language of hormones. Immune cells, it has been suggested, may function in a sensory capacity, detecting the arrival of foreign invaders and relaying chemical signals to alert the brain. The brain, for its part, may send signals that guide the traffic of cells through the lymphoid organs.

We Are Born with Immunity

Innate *natural* immunity is the initial immunity that comes at birth. White blood cells do not have experience fighting all the foreign invaders. Innate immunity, unlike acquired immunity, has no memory of attack episodes and does not remember specific foreign antigens and does not provide any ongoing protection against future infection.

Innate immunity offers nonspecific defense mechanisms that come into play immediately or within hours of an antigen's appearance in the body. These mechanisms include physical barriers such as skin, chemicals in the blood, and an army of defending cells that attack foreign cells in the body. The innate immune response is activated by chemical properties of the antigen (Figure 1.4).

Acquired (Also Called Adaptive) Immunity

Acquired (adaptive or specific) immunity is not present at birth. It is learned. As a person's immune system encounters invading germs (antigens), the body's immunity system learns the best way to attack each antigen and begins to develop a memory for that antigen. Acquired immunity is also called *specific immunity* because it plans its attack on a specific fight that took place earlier. Its hallmarks include its ability

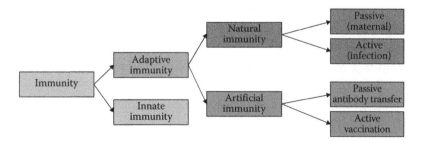

Figure 1.4   The Human Immune System is created during birth (called innate immunity). During its lifetime, we realize that the body cannot defend itself. Active vaccination adds additional artificial immunity to the body through in order to defeat the attacking pathogen.

Table 1.1   While We are Impressed with the Anatomy and Mechanics of the Immune System, Digital Immunity Is Pretty Much a Mirror Image of the Human Immune System (This table illustrates how both systems are run by autonomic control.)

FUNCTIONALITY	HUMAN IMMUNITY	DIGITAL IMMUNITY
Early warning capability	Messages sent to B cells	Alerts sent to vaccine factory
Defense technology	Acquired immunity (two layers)	Autonomic on-demand Smart Vaccine inoculation
Defense sophistication	B cells, T cells, memory cells	Autonomic Smart Vaccine agents
Broadcast attack	Yes	Early warning alerts
Reaction under attack	Totally sympathetic	Total mobilization
Issue early warning	Yes	Radar grid
Capture viruses	Antibodies capture antigens	Viruses fall in the honeypots
Reverse engineer viruses	Yes, recognized and destroyed	Viruses undergo autopsy
Virus/attack analysis	B cells	Bayesian reasoning
Disposition of virus	T cells eat pathogens	Viruses are catalogs in KB
Disposition of attack	Memory cells are active	Attack episodes are catalogued
Vaccine emergency calls	Dispatched	Dispatched
Infested cell status	Isolated from healthy cells	Infested system is repaired back to normal

to learn, adapt, and remember. Acquired immunity takes time to develop after initial exposure to a new antigen. However, because a memory is formed, subsequent responses to a previously encountered antigen are more effective.

Adaptive immunity is carried out by B cells and T cells. The white blood cells are responsible for acquired immunity. Typically, an acquired immune response begins when antibodies, produced by B cells (lymphocytes), encounter an antigen. Dendritic cells, cytokines, and the complement system (which enhances the effectiveness of antibodies) are also involved. Table 1.1 shows the fascinating similarity between Human and digital immunity.

Vaccinations

Simplistically speaking, vaccination is the process of artificial induction of immunity in an effort to protect against infectious disease that invaded the body. Vaccination is to prime the immune system with an antigen that causes the generation of antibody immune response. Stimulating immune responses (*immunogen*) with an infectious agent is known as *immunization*.

Vaccination is a very effective method to boost immunity among healthy people before they contract the disease.

Understanding the difference between vaccines, vaccinations, and immunizations can be tricky. Let's explain further:

- A *vaccine* is a product that produces immunity from a disease and can be administered through needle injections, by mouth, or by aerosol.
- A *vaccination* is the process of injecting a killed or weakened organism that produces immunity in the body of the person against that organism.

- An *immunization* is the step that follows vaccination, which protects (makes the person immune) against disease.
- *Inoculation* is the process of injecting a sample of the diluted disease into the arm of the patient.

All these procedures are done as part of the artificial induction of immunity. We can also call it *acquired immunity*.

Benefits of Vaccination

Vaccination is a national responsibility to keep citizens healthy and extend their longevity. In the United States, every president has been promoting different health programs. The Centers for Disease Control and Prevention (CDC) is one of the major operating components of the U.S. Department of Health and Human Services. As the nation's health protection agency, the CDC saves lives and protects people from health threats. Vaccination has become the most effective method to fight death-threatening and vaccine-preventing diseases.

Glossary: The Human Immune System

For ergonomic reasons, this immune system glossary has been placed in the same chapter to minimize flipping and wasting energy; it is a compliment of the National Institute of Allergy and Infectious Diseases glossary:

Adenoids: See *Tonsils.*
Adrenal gland: A gland located on each kidney that secretes hormones regulating metabolism, sexual function, water balance, and stress.
Allergen: Any substance that causes an allergy.
Antibody: A molecule (also called an *immunoglobulin*) produced by a mature B cell (plasma cell) in response to an antigen. When an antibody attaches to an antigen, it helps the body destroy or inactivate the antigen.
Antigen: A substance or molecule that is recognized by the immune system. The antigen can be from foreign material such as bacteria or viruses.
Antiserum: A serum rich in antibodies against a particular microbe.
Appendix: Lymphoid organ in the intestine.
Artery: A blood vessel that carries blood from the heart to other parts of the body.
Autoantibody: An antibody that reacts against a person's own tissue.
Autoimmune disease: Disease that results when the immune system mistakenly attacks the body's own tissues. Examples include multiple sclerosis, type 1 diabetes, rheumatoid arthritis, and systemic lupus erythematosus.
B cell or B lymphocyte: A small white blood cell crucial to the immune defenses. B cells come from bone marrow and develop into blood cells called plasma cells, which are the source of antibodies.

Bacteria: Microscopic organisms that are composed of a single cell. Some cause disease.

Basophil: A white blood cell that contributes to inflammatory reactions. Along with mast cells, basophils are responsible for the symptoms of allergy.

Blood vessel: An artery, vein, or capillary that carries blood to and from the heart and body tissues.

Cell: The smallest unit of life; the basic living unit that makes up tissues.

Chemokine: A small protein molecule that activates immune cells, stimulates their migration, and helps direct immune cell traffic throughout the body.

Clonal anergy: The process of switching off the ability of potentially harmful T or B cells to participate in immune responses. Clonal anergy is essential for generating the tolerance of T and B cells to the body's *self* tissue antigens.

Clonal deletion: The genetically controlled process of eliminating immune cells that could destroy the body's own cells and tissues. The elimination process removes immature T and B lymphocytes that have receptors for cells with *self* MHC or HLA antigens, and could therefore attack and destroy the body's own cells.

Clone: A group of genetically identical cells or organisms descended from a single common ancestor, or, to reproduce identical copies.

Complement: A complex series of blood proteins whose action *complements* the work of antibodies. Complement destroys bacteria, produces inflammation, and regulates immune reactions.

Complement cascade: A precise sequence of events, usually triggered by antigen–antibody complexes, in which each component of the complement system is activated in turn.

Cytokines: Powerful chemical substances secreted by cells that enable the body's cells to communicate with one another. Cytokines include lymphokines produced by lymphocytes and monokines produced by monocytes and macrophages.

Cytotoxic T lymphocyte (CTL): A subtype of T cells that carries the CD8 marker and can destroy body cells infected by viruses or transformed by cancer.

Dendritic cell: An immune cell with highly branched extensions that occurs in lymphoid tissues, engulfs microbes, and stimulates T cells by displaying the foreign antigens of the microbes on their surfaces.

Deoxyribonucleic acid (DNA): A long molecule found in the cell nucleus. Molecules of DNA carry the cell's genetic information.

Enzyme: A protein produced by living cells that promotes the chemical processes of life without itself being altered.

Eosinophil: A white blood cell containing granules filled with chemicals damaging to parasites and enzymes that affect inflammatory reactions.

Epithelial cells: Cells that make up the epithelium, the covering for internal and external body surfaces.

Fungus: A member of a class of relatively primitive vegetable organisms. Fungi include mushrooms, yeasts, rusts, molds, and smuts.

Gene: A unit of genetic material (DNA) inherited from a parent that controls specific characteristics. Genes carry coded directions a cell uses to make specific proteins that perform specific functions.

Genome: A full set of genes in a person or any other living thing.

Graft rejection: An immune response against transplanted tissue.

Graft-versus-host disease: A life-threatening reaction in which transplanted cells attack the tissues of the recipient.

Granule: A membrane-bound organelle (specialized part) within cells where proteins are stored before secretion.

Granulocyte: A phagocytic white blood cell filled with granules. Neutrophils, eosinophils, basophils, and mast cells are examples of granulocytes.

Growth factors: Chemicals secreted by cells that stimulate the proliferation of or changes in the physical properties of other cells.

Helper T cells: A subset of T cells that carry the CD4 surface marker and are essential for turning on antibody production, activating cytotoxic T cells, and initiating many other immune functions.

Hepatitis: The name of several viruses that cause liver diseases. These viruses include hepatitis A, hepatitis B, and hepatitis C.

Histocompatibility testing: A test conducted before transplant operations to find a donor whose MHC molecules are similar to the recipient's; helps reduce the strength of transplant rejection.

Human immunodeficiency virus (HIV): The virus that causes AIDS.

Human leukocyte antigen (HLA): A protein on the surfaces of human cells that identifies the cells as *self* and, like MHC antigens, performs essential roles in immune responses. HLAs are used in laboratory tests to determine whether one person's tissues are compatible with another person's and could be used in a transplant. HLAs are the human equivalent of MHC antigens; they are coded for by MHC genes.

Immune response: Reaction of the immune system to foreign substances. Although normal immune responses are designed to protect the body from pathogens, immune dysregulation can damage normal cells and tissues, as in the case of autoimmune diseases.

Immunoglobulin: One of a family of large protein molecules, also known as antibodies, produced by mature B cells (plasma cells).

Immunosuppressive: Capable of reducing immune responses.

Inflammation: An immune system reaction to *foreign* invaders such as microbes or allergens. Signs include redness, swelling, pain, or heat.

Inflammatory response: Redness, warmth, and swelling produced in response to infection; the result of increased blood flow and an influx of immune cells and their secretions.

Innate: An immune system function that is inborn and provides an all-purpose defense against invasion by microbes.

Interferon: A protein produced by cells, which stimulates antivirus immune responses or alters the physical properties of immune cells.

Interleukins: A major group of lymphokines and monokines.

Lymph: A transparent, slightly yellow fluid that carries lymphocytes, bathes the body tissues, and drains into the lymphatic vessels.

Lymph node: A small bean-shaped organ of the immune system, which is distributed widely throughout the body and linked by lymphatic vessels. Lymph nodes are garrisons of B and T cells, dendritic cells, macrophages, and other kinds of immune cells.

Lymphatic vessels: A body wide network of channels, similar to the blood vessels, which transports lymph to the immune organs and into the bloodstream.

Lymphocyte: A small white blood cell produced in the lymphoid organs and essential to immune defenses. B cells, T cells, and NK T cells are lymphocytes.

Lymphoid organ: An organ of the immune system where lymphocytes develop and congregate. These organs include the bone marrow, thymus, lymph nodes, spleen, and various other clusters of lymphoid tissue. Blood vessels and lymphatic vessels are also lymphoid organs.

Lymphokines: Powerful chemical substances secreted by lymphocytes. These molecules help direct and regulate the immune responses.

Macrophage: A large and versatile immune cell that devours invading pathogens and other intruders. Macrophages stimulate other immune cells by presenting them with small pieces of the invaders.

Major histocompatibility complex (MHC): A group of genes that controls several aspects of the immune response. MHC genes code for *self* markers on all body cells.

Mast cell: A granulocyte found in tissue. The contents of mast cells, along with those of basophils, are responsible for the symptoms of allergy.

Memory cells: A subset of T cells and B cells that have been exposed to antigens and can then respond more readily when the immune system encounters those same antigens again.

Microbe or microorganism: A microscopic living organism. Examples include bacteria, protozoa, and some fungi and parasites. Viruses are also called microbes.

Molecule: The smallest amount of a specific chemical substance. Large molecules such as proteins, fats, carbohydrates, and nucleic acids are the building blocks of a cell, and a gene determines how each molecule is produced.

Monoclonal antibody: An antibody produced by a single B cell or its identical progeny that is specific for a given antigen. Monoclonal antibodies are used as research tools for binding to specific protein molecules and are invaluable in research, medicine, and industry.

Monocyte: A large phagocytic white blood cell which, when entering tissue, develops into a macrophage.

Monokines: Powerful chemical substances secreted by monocytes and macrophages. These molecules help direct and regulate the immune responses.

Natural killer (NK) cell: A large granule-containing lymphocyte that recognizes and kills cells lacking self-antigens. These cells target recognition molecules are different from T cells.

NK T cell: A T cell that has some characteristics of NK cells. It produces large amounts of cytokines when stimulated and is activated by fatty substances (lipids) bound to non-MHC molecules called CD1d.

Neutrophil: A white blood cell that is an abundant and important phagocyte.

Organ: A part of the body that has a specific function, such as the lungs.

Organism: An individual living thing composed of one or more cells.

Parasite: A plant or animal that lives, grows, and feeds on or within another living organism.

Passive immunity: Immunity resulting from the transfer of antibodies or antiserum produced by another person.

Pathogen: A disease-causing organism or virus.

Phagocyte: A large white blood cell that contributes to immune defenses by ingesting microbes or other cells and foreign particles.

Phagocytosis: Process by which one cell engulfs another cell or large particle.

Plasma cell: A large antibody-producing cell that develops from B cells.

Platelet: A cellular fragment critical for blood clotting and sealing off wounds.

Serum: The clear liquid that separates from the blood when it is allowed to clot. This fluid contains the antibodies that were present in the whole blood.

Spleen: A lymphoid organ in the abdominal cavity that is an important center for immune system activities.

Stem cell: An immature cell from which other cells derive. Bone marrow is rich in the kind of stem cells that become specialized blood cells.

T cell or T lymphocyte: A small white blood cell that recognizes antigen fragments bound to cell surfaces by specialized antibody-like receptors. "T" stands for the thymus gland, where T cells develop and acquire their receptors.

T cell receptor: Complex protein molecule on the surfaces of T cells, which recognizes bits of foreign antigen bound to self-MHC molecules.

Tissue: A group of similar cells joined to perform the same function.

Tissue typing: See histocompatibility testing.

Tolerance: A state of immune nonresponsiveness to a particular antigen or group of antigens.

Toll-like receptor (TLR): A family of proteins important for first-line immune defenses against microbes.

Tonsils and adenoids: Prominent oval masses of lymphoid tissues on either side of the throat.

Toxin: An agent produced in plants and bacteria, normally very damaging to cells.

Vaccine: A preparation that stimulates an immune response that can prevent an infection or create resistance to an infection. Vaccines do not cause disease.

Vein: A blood vessel that carries blood to the heart from the body tissues.

Virus: A particle composed of a piece of genetic material—RNA or DNA—surrounded by a protein coat. Viruses can reproduce only in living cells.

Websites

http://health.howstuffworks.com/human-body/systems/immune/immune-system7.htm.
http://techland.time.com/2013/07/17/your-future-brain-machine-implant-ultrasonic-neural-dust/.
http://www.niaid.nih.gov/topics/immunesystem/.
http://www.niaid.nih.gov/topics/immunesystem/pages/glossary.aspx.
http://www.niaid.nih.gov/topics/immunesystem/pages/nervoussystem.aspx.
http://www.sciencedirect.com/science/article/pii/S2090123214000290.

PART I

2
The Story of the Smart Vaccine

The World of Vaccine

In the beginning there was water, and then man discovered many wonderful deadly things.

On Sunday, February 15, 2015, CBS's *60 Minutes* discussed the challenges of finding a vaccine for the deadly Ebola virus. Everyone should see how scary a loose virus wiped out complete villages and communities. The present drugs did not help. The vaccine is the only solution to this deadly disease (http://www.cbsnews.com/news/zmapp-and-the-fight-against-ebola/). The show reverberates the problem that our digital world is suffering from. We need a new vaccine for our growing and unpredictable cyberattacks.

Around 250 years ago, scientists discovered, after the invention of microscope, that we live together with many tiny creatures, which we cannot see with the naked eye. These creatures are present everywhere—from the air we inhale, to the water we drink, to any object that comes in contact with the surface of our body. It was also discovered that these creatures penetrate the human body.

Of all the inventions and discoveries in the world, we should consider that the vaccine had the most influential bang on the human race. Not the exploration of space, not B1 Stealth Bomber, not walking on the moon, not even the Internet comes close. Nothing comes close to the discovery of the vaccine. Simply because it is a life saver.

The word *vaccine* was devised by Edward Jenner to denote cowpox. He used it in 1798 in the long title of his *Inquiry into the…Variolae vaccinae…known as the Cow Pox*, in which he described the protective effect of cowpox against smallpox. In 1881, to honor Jenner, Louis Pasteur proposed that the terms should be extended to cover the new protective inoculations than being developed.

Then Comes Pasteur

One day, a mother brought her son, Joseph, to Pasteur. Joseph had been bitten by a mad dog. He had 14 wounds all over his body. The dog had rabies. Everyone felt sorry for the boy. They said, "The child is sure to die." Even Pasteur had no hope. But he had decided to save the boy.

Pasteur had prepared a serum from a rabbit. The rabbit had died of rabies. He injected the serum into the boy's body, at first in small quantities. Slowly, he increased the dosage. On the ninth day, Joseph showed improvement. He was out of danger. In 3 months' time, Joseph walked out of the hospital. He then became a perfectly healthy child. The year was 1885. Many had been bitten by mad dogs. But no one had escaped death.

Since 1885, thousands of lives have been saved by antirabies treatment. The world has to thank Louis Pasteur. Louis Pasteur is considered to be the greatest scientist of France, by the people of France. The first vaccine was developed in the late eighteenth century, but people recognized the importance of immunity long before that.

Here is another revelation: During the plague of Athens in 430 BC, the Greeks realized that people who had previously survived smallpox did not contract the disease a second time. In fact, these survivors were often called upon to attend to those afflicted with smallpox, according to a 1998 article in the *International Journal of Infectious Diseases*.

In the tenth century, Chinese healers began blowing dried smallpox scabs into the noses of healthy patients, who then contracted a mild form of the disease—and the patients who recovered became immune to smallpox. This practice, which was called variolation or inoculation, spread to Europe and the New England in the 1700s.

The human body is home to trillions of bacteria, which outnumber our own cells 10 to 1. In the gastrointestinal tract, these microbes are often beneficial, helping with digestion and synthesizing vitamins B and K. But research has also shown that our gut bacteria help our immune system and keep us healthy in various ways.

For example, the beneficial bacteria prevent pathogenic (disease-causing) bacteria from taking root in our epithelial and mucosal tissues. And these commensal bacteria also train the immune system to better distinguish between disease-causing pathogens and harmless antigens, which may help prevent the development of allergies.

Similarly, the *good* bacteria may influence the immune system's sensitivity to antigens, potentially helping to prevent autoimmune diseases, conditions in which the immune system attacks the body's own tissues. The bacteria also produce useful antibodies and trigger the expression of intestinal proteins, which cause the immune system to repair internal injuries.

For decades, scientists have known that exposure to sunlight—specifically ultraviolet radiation (UVR)—can suppress the immune system's (IS) response to bacterial, viral, and fungal infections. To suppress the Human Immune System, it takes UVR doses that are only 30%–50% of what is required to cause barely detectable sunburn, according to a 2010 article in the *Journal of Investigative Dermatology*.

At the same time, however, sunlight causes the body to produce vitamin D. A recent study in *Nature Immunology* suggested that T cells do not mobilize if they detect only small amounts of vitamin D in the bloodstream. Additionally, other research suggests that vitamin D might induce the production of antimicrobial peptides in the skin—these compounds help defend the body against new infections.

The immune system is constantly at work to protect you from diseases and fight infections you already have, so you might expect that the system's soldiers—the white blood cells—would make up a large portion of your blood. But this is not the case. White blood cells account for only 1% of the cells in the 5 L of blood in an adult's body. But not to worry, there are more than enough white blood cells to get the job done: In each microliter of blood, there are between 5,000 and 10,000 white blood cells.

Made in China, Too!

The story of vaccines did not begin with the first vaccine—Edward Jenner's use of material from cowpox pustules to provide protection against smallpox. Rather, it began with a long history of infectious disease in humans, and in particular, with early uses of smallpox material to provide immunity to that disease.

Evidence exists that the Chinese employed smallpox inoculation (or variolation, as such use of smallpox material was called) as early as 1000 CE. It was practiced in Africa and Turkey as well, before it spread to Europe and America.

Edward Jenner's innovations, began with his successful 1796 use of cowpox material to create immunity to smallpox, which quickly made the practice widespread. His method underwent medical and technological changes over the next 200 years, and eventually resulted in the eradication of smallpox.

Louis Pasteur's 1885 rabies vaccine was the next to make an impact on human disease. And then, at the dawn of bacteriology, developments rapidly followed. Antitoxins and vaccines against diphtheria, tetanus, anthrax, cholera, the plague, typhoid, tuberculosis, and more were developed through the 1930s as shown in Figure 2.1.

Figure 2.1 Edward Jenner and Louis Pasteur are greater than any emperor, king, or president. They made the water of life to give patients their life again. They are indeed an incredible tour de force. They fought the Reaper and they won! Pasteur created the rabies vaccine while Jenner gave us the smallpox vaccine. Ironically, though Pasteur and Jenner knew that the vaccines worked, no one in the world of science then knew how it worked!

The middle of the twentieth century was an active time for vaccine research and development. Methods for growing viruses in the laboratory led to rapid discoveries and innovations, including the creation of vaccines for polio. Researchers targeted other common childhood diseases such as measles, mumps, and rubella, and vaccines for these diseases reduced the disease burden greatly.

Innovative techniques now drive vaccine research, with recombinant DNA technology and new delivery techniques leading scientists in new directions. Disease targets have expanded, and some vaccine research is beginning to focus on non-infectious conditions such as addiction and allergies.

More than the science behind vaccines, these timelines cover the cultural aspects of vaccination as well, from the early harassment of smallpox variolators (the intimidation of a prominent minister described in the 1721 Boston Smallpox Epidemic entry) to the establishment of vaccination mandates, to the effect of war and social unrest on vaccine-preventable diseases. Edward Jenner, Louis Pasteur, and Maurice Hilleman, pioneers in vaccine development, received particular attention as well.

Why Was the Term *Vaccine* Selected?

Selection of the term *vaccine* was not coincidence. When a dear parent or a close friend ends up with a "terminal" disease, we get intimidated to the core, and we look at all the technological advances in military and space in disdain and anger. Eventually, man with vaccine will conquer the most virulent enemy of human race.

Our cyber world has been bombarded with attacking vicious pathogens and runaway malware. It is hit-and-run and no evidence and no witnesses. Our conventional arms are good for jungles and deserts but not for cyberspace. We are getting crippled by successive invasions and we need to resort to the vaccination approach as our best proactive defense.

Why Was the Term *Smart* Selected?

I selected the term *smart* for its cognitive ability and residual intelligence to determine what the next move is. We used the term *smart* because immunity battles are something that fascinate and rivet the mind, but they are a slaughter house that requires smart commanders, smart vaccinators, and smart paramedics to overcome the assault. Next to the nervous system, the immune system is the most complex system in the human body. Here are some of the most fascinating maneuvers of immune cells when the early warning alarm sounds.

Regardless of the type of host cell, all viruses follow the same basic massacring steps in what is known as the *lytic cycle*, which has six stages. In the first stage, called *penetration*, the virus attaches to a host cell. In the second stage, it injects its own nucleic acids and genetic instructions into a host cell. In the third stage, the viral acids form a circle in the center of the cell and its genetic material recruits the host cell's enzymes. In the fourth stage, the host cell then mistakenly copies the viral acids instead of its own nucleic acids. In the fifth stage, the viral DNA organize themselves as viruses inside the host cell. In the sixth stage, when the number of viruses inside becomes too much for the cell to hold, the membrane splits, and the viruses are then free to infect other cells.

> *Cognition*: The immune system (IS) is an incredible learning machine, capable of recognizing new patterns. It has been proven that the immune system is a cognitive system; IS has beliefs, knowledge, and view about concrete things in our bodies, which gives IS the ability to abstract, filter, and classify the information to take the proper decisions. The immune system has a cognitive ability to differentiate between healthy and unhealthy cells. The immune system is by nature a highly distributed, adaptive, and self-organized system that maintains a memory of past encounters and has the ability to continuously learn about new encounters; the immune system as a whole is being interpreted as an intelligent agent. The immune system, along with the central nervous system, represents the most complex biological system in nature.

Because a virus is merely a set of genetic instructions surrounded by a protein coat, and because it does not carry out any biochemical reactions of its own, viruses can live for years or longer outside a host cell. Some viruses can *sleep* inside the genetic instructions of the host cells for years before reproducing.

When something dies, its immune system (along with everything else) shuts down. In a matter of hours, the body is invaded by all sorts of bacteria, microbes, parasites, etc. None of these things is able to get in when your immune system is working, but the moment your immune system stops, the door is wide open. Once you die, it only takes a few weeks for these organisms to completely dismantle your body and carry it away, until all that is left is a skeleton. Obviously, your immune system is doing something amazing to keep all of that dismantling from happening when you are alive.

One anomaly that is not so obvious is that we sometimes see the immune system because it prevents us from doing things that would be otherwise beneficial. For example, organ transplants are much harder than they should be because the immune system often rejects the transplanted organ.

> *Scalability*: The immune system has a big arsenal of leukocytes (B cells) to take on any massive surprise attacks. The lymphoid organs (the spleen, bone marrow, and thymus) are always ready to generate new B cells and T cells.
>
> *Responsiveness*: An infected person sneezes near you. You inhale the virus particle, and it attaches to cells lining the sinuses in your nose. The virus then attacks the cells lining the sinuses and rapidly reproduces new viruses. The host cells break, and new viruses spread into your bloodstream and also into your lungs. Because you have lost cell lining your sinuses, fluid flows into your nasal passages and give you a runny nose. Viruses in the fluid that drip down your throat attack the cells that line your throat and give you a sore throat. Viruses in your bloodstream can attack muscle cells, which cause muscle aches.

Mobilization Trickery: The immune system responds to the infection, and in the process of fighting, it produces chemicals called *pyrogens* that cause the body's temperature to increase. This *fever* actually helps you to fight the infection by slowing down the rate of viral reproduction, because most of the body's chemical reactions have an optimal temperature of 98.6°F (37°C). If the temperature rises slightly above this, the reactions slow down. This immune response continues until the virus is eliminated from the body. However, if you sneeze, thousands of new viruses can spread into the environment to await another host.

Magical Analogy between Human Immunity and Digital Immunity

There is a fascinating analogy between Human Immunity and Digital Immunity. We both immunities have been tabulated by functionality as shown in Table 2.1. All the functionalities of Digital immunity are stored in Knowledge Bases of the system.

The immune system is made up of a network of cells, tissues, and organs that work together to protect the body. The cells involved are white blood cells, or leukocytes, which come in two basic types that combine to seek out and destroy disease-causing organisms or substances.

Leukocytes are produced or stored in many locations in the body, including the thymus, spleen, and bone marrow. For this reason, they are called the lymphoid organs. There are also clumps of lymphoid tissue throughout the body, primarily as lymph nodes, that house the leukocytes.

Table 2.1   The Amazing Similarity between Human Immunity and Digital Immunity—All Information Is Catalogued and Stored in the Knowledge Base (KB)

FUNCTIONALITY	HUMAN IMMUNITY	DIGITAL IMMUNITY
Early warning capability	Messages sent to B cells	Alerts sent to vaccine factory
Defense technology	Acquired immunity (two layers)	Autonomic on-demand Smart Vaccine inoculation
Defense sophistication	B cells, T cells, memory cells	Autonomic Smart Vaccine agents
Broadcast attack	Yes	Early warning alerts
Reaction under attack	Totally sympathetic	Total mobilization
Issue early warning	Yes	Radar grid
Capture viruses	Antibodies capture antigens	Viruses fall in the honeypots
Reverse-engineer viruses	Yes, recognized and destroyed	Viruses undergo autopsy
Virus/attack analysis	B cells	Bayesian reasoning
Disposition of virus	T cells eat pathogens	Viruses are catalogued in KB
Disposition of attack	Memory cells are active	Attack episodes are catalogued
Vaccine emergency calls	Dispatched	Dispatched
Infested cells status	Isolated from healthy cells	Infested system repaired back to normal

The leukocytes circulate through the body between the organs and nodes via lymphatic vessels and blood vessels. In this way, the immune system works in a coordinated manner to monitor the body for germs or substances that might cause problems.

The two basic types of leukocytes are as follows:

1. *Phagocytes*: Cells that chew up invading organisms
2. *Lymphocytes*: Cells that allow the body to remember and recognize previous invaders and help the body destroy them

The two kinds of lymphocytes are *B lymphocytes* (*B cells*) and *T lymphocytes* (*T cells*). Lymphocytes start out in the bone marrow and either stay there and mature into B cells or they leave for the thymus gland, where they mature into T cells. B cells and T cells have separate functions: B cells are like the body's military intelligence system, seeking out their targets and sending defenses to lock onto them. T cells are like the soldiers, destroying the invaders that the intelligence system has identified. Here is how it works.

When antigens (attacking germs) are detected, several types of cells work together to recognize them and respond. These cells trigger the B cells to produce antibodies (specialized proteins that lock onto specific antigens).

Once produced, these antibodies continue to exist in a person's body, so that if the same antigen is presented to the immune system again, the antibodies are already there to do their job. So if someone gets sick with a certain disease, like chickenpox, that person typically does not get sick from it again.

This is also how vaccination prevents certain diseases. A vaccination (as a mock attack) introduces a diluted antigen in the body, in a way that does not make the person sick, but does allow the body to produce antibodies that will then protect the person from future attack by the germ or substance that produces that particular disease.

Although antibodies can recognize an antigen and lock onto it, they are not capable of destroying it without help. That is the job of the T cells, which are called *killer cells*. Antibodies can also neutralize toxins (poisonous or damaging substances) produced by different organisms. Finally, antibodies can activate a group of proteins called *complement* that assists in killing bacteria, viruses, or infected cells.

Here Is Digital Immunity

Digital Immunity has the pivotal responsibility of being available throughout a city's smart grid. Digital Immunity is actually an autonomic operating environment built with federated subsystems that are constantly communicating with one another. We have deliberately included in the book different views of the CEWPS to give the reader a better understanding of the Digital Immune System. Some views are more complex than others. Some views emphasize information flow; while others focus on the architecture and structure of the system. Figure 2.2 shows an analogy with the Human Immune System.

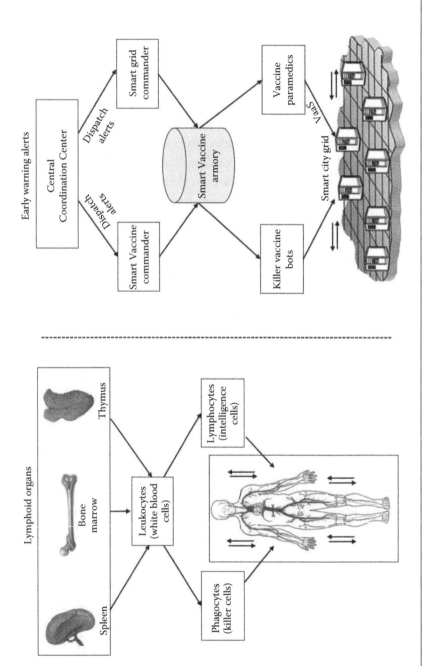

Figure 2.2 An amazing analogy between the Human Immune System and the Digital Immune System. Both systems are fully autonomic. Both systems are self-protecting and self-healing. Both are a marvel of engineering.

The Central Coordination Center (CCC) is where all the wires and information pipelines end up at the top. The CCC is like the brain of the CEWPS, overseeing all activities from its dynamic dashboard (DD). It is connected to the Smart City command control to early warning alerts and notifications. The CCC is also connected to smart grid central where all the critical systems are connected.

This is the advantage of having a superconductive smart grid. It acts like a super-highway to transfer messages in real time and with precision. The smart grid always tries to be ahead of danger and massive attacks.

The CCC commander is also in constant communication with the Smart Vaccine Commander (SVC) who controls the Smart Vaccine Grid (tightly coupled with the city's smart grid); the Smart Vaccine army; the Vaccine Knowledge Base (VKB) that has all the signatures and instructions of the vaccines; the Attack Knowledge Base (AKB); and the Virus Knowledge Base (ViKB). Again, like the battle in the human body, B cells and T cells combine their skills to circle and kill the attackers. The Virus Knowledge Base collects all the killer agents after they are quarantined and keeps parts of the agents for forensic analysis.

The vaccine paramedics (not shown in Figure 2.2 but will be described later) are also special vaccine agents that will remove the parts of the attacking viruses and repair the damage caused by the attack.

CEWPS Digital Immunity has several important security duties in The Smart City, which are as follows:

1. It *creates a smart (cognitive) barrier* that prevents malicious viruses from entering the smart grid.
2. If a virus does get into the grid, the Smart Vaccine Grid (SVG) will eventually *detect and localize* it before contamination spreads to the other systems.
3. In the worst case, the attack will infect a honeypot trap on the grid, and the Smart Vaccine grid will *capture* it and will get reverse engineered at home.

Microcosm of the Smart Vaccine

One astonishing characteristic of the Human Immune System (HIS) that we did not know about is that the B cells in the HIS behave like the Marines at Camp Pendleton, where during peace, the B cells like first-class Marines train and retrain and learn from their mistakes and previous battles so they can fight better in the next battle.

We envision that in the near future, software technology will build smart city centric operating systems (OSs), which will be designed to manage smart grids and future versions of the Smart Vaccine. These OSs will be running in real-time mode performing transactional smart grid services (SGS) similar to cloud Amazon Web Services as shown in Figure 2.3.

At present, we do not have small city centric (SCC) operating systems. We do not have smart grid services either. We do expect in the near future to have working prototypes and platforms to usher the generation of the new computing environment.

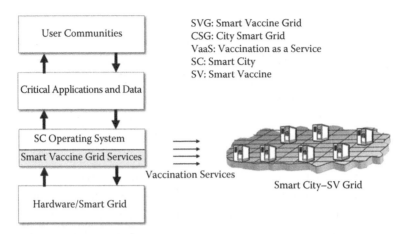

Figure 2.3   Operating system software companies will soon develop a new OS designed specifically for The Smart City, and Digital Immunity (Smart Vaccine grid services) will be integrated into it. The new OS will include Grid Computing, Cloud Computing, and Autonomic Computing. The Vaccination Services (VaaS) will replace Antivirus Technology (AVT).

But most importantly, CEWPS Digital Immunity will be an integral part of the Smart City centric operating system (as shown in the diagram). Like in the Human Immune System that is a part of the marvelous human engine, CEWPS Digital Immunity will be welded within the Smart City smart grid. Digital Immunity will be totally transparent to users, while their machines will be protected by the cognitive Smart Vaccine grid (SVG).

If one of the smart grid critical systems were to be hit by a preempted attack, the SCC operating system would instantiate an emergency response request to the Smart Vaccine Commander (SVC) who will mobilize the army of vaccinators, the vaccine paramedics, and the virus killers to defend the grid and later to remedy the attacked system.

Like their biological siblings, cybergerms (malware) are everywhere. They are in every machine, data center, cloud, network, city, and country, regardless whether we are connected to the Web or not. We infect our machines through e-mails, chats, file swapping, and social media happy hours. Many of these cybergerms sneak into the machine and go into dormant mode waiting to be activated. But the majority of them are active at the entry time, and antivirus software will respond before the viruses dump their payloads.

Awesome Morphology of the Virus

Viruses are programmed to deceive users before attacking their systems. Cyberterrorists have a huge arsenal of trickery tools to bypass or fool intrusion checkpoints. They have a depot of cyber missiles and cyber grenades to use in vicious attacks. We have selected a few types of camouflaging-type viruses for illustration. We also rated the types by technological sophistication on a scale from 1 to 10.

Self-replicating (*3 on the scale*): Like in the Human Immune System, viruses are tricky and malevolent. They are designed to inflict damage in different ways. In fact, in 1949, the scientist John von Neumann theorized that a self-replicated program was possible. Today, we have worms that replicate themselves while traveling from one machine to another. A doctoral student named Fred Cohen was the first to describe self-replicating programs designed to modify computers as viruses. The name has stuck ever since. In the spring of 1999, a man named David L. Smith created a computer virus based on a Microsoft Word macro. He built the virus so that it could spread through e-mail messages. Smith named the virus *Melissa*, saying that he named it after an exotic dancer from Florida.

Mass-mail destruction (2 on the scale): The ILOVEYOU virus initially traveled the Internet by e-mail, just like the Melissa virus. The subject of the e-mail said that the message was a love letter from a secret admirer. An attachment in the e-mail was what caused all the trouble. The original worm had the file name of LOVE-LETTER-FOR-YOU.TXT.vbs given by Onel de Guzman. Microsoft's visual basic script (VBS) extension pointed to the language that the hacker used to create the worm: Visual Basic Scripting. An antivirus software could trap this attack without difficulty.

Hardware activator (7 on the scale): The hackers who designed Stuxnet aimed it at the centrifugal pumps of a nuclear enrichment plant. This is the most dangerous type of attack because it is aimed at critical infrastructures and not mass mailing. This type of virus is highly educated and highly autonomous. No antivirus software could intercept this malicious attack. It does not have any history to learn from, even a SCADA computer system that has a sophisticated security system could not recognize the danger before the attack.

Robobots (9 on the scale): These are the autonomic self-propelled, self-navigating viruses (similar to drones) that can ram into any system and destroy its content. Many of these attacking cybergerms are remotely activated from another machine.

Nanoattack vector (NAV) (over 10 on the scale): This is a futuristic type of an autonomic attack component installed as the hardwired electronic chip of a USB. None of the present antivirus systems could detect it, stop it, or quarantine it. Once the USB is inserted, it will download and execute an attack vector in binary code, and it will be too late for the antivirus software to recognize and catch it.

Smart Vaccine Transactional Messages and Services

Digital Immunity has a very well-structured organizational chart showing the hierarchy of the Smart Vaccine family. It is like the white blood cells (leukocytes); no one cell can do all the fighting. Each Smart Vaccine agent (SVA) has a specific responsibility that supports and complements other responsibilities. All SVAs communicate with a repertoire of commands or *messages* while delivering their services. The subject of Smart Vaccine services (SVS) will be covered later in this chapter.

The Smart Vaccine Army

At the top of the organization, is the Smart Vaccine commander, followed by the Smart Vaccine intelligence officer, the Smart Vaccine vaccinator, the Smart Vaccine

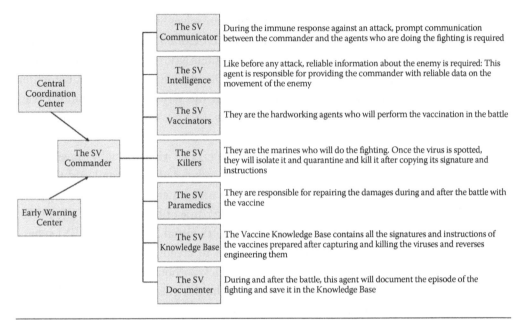

Figure 2.4 The hierarchy of the Smart Vaccine team and responsibilities of its agents. The commander's messages, attack alerts, vaccination requests, vaccination in progress status, vaccination outcome, and documentation are working concurrently over the Smart Vaccine Grid. It is a real war.

communicator, Smart Vaccine documenters, Smart Vaccine paramedics, Smart Vaccine Knowledge Base keeper, and Smart Vaccine killers. The Smart Vaccine Commander (SVC) oversees the whole battlefield to protect the critical systems from any improvised attack (Figure 2.4). The following is a description of each agent.

Smart Vaccine commander: It gets the directives from the Central Coordination Center commander. Its responsibilities cover total security monitoring and response for the entire smart grid.

Smart Vaccine vaccinator (SVV): It gets orders from the Smart Vaccine commander (SVC) to perform vaccination services for a particular critical system. There are thousands of SVVs that are dedicated to perform vaccination-as-a-service throughout the city's smart grid.

Smart Vaccine intelligence officers: These agents have the responsibility to roam around the smart grid and collect intelligence information for the Smart Vaccine commander and the CCC. They also communicate with the early warning command for alerts.

Smart Vaccine communicator: This agent is responsible for signaling other Smart Vaccines during the attack. It is responsible for communicating with the other SVVs and the paramedics.

Smart Vaccine killers: These are the heavy-duty agents that are responsible for quarantining the attacking worm or virus and deleting it after getting a copy of its code and signature.

Smart Vaccine paramedics: As the name implies, these agents will repair the damage after the attacking virus is destroyed. If the damage cannot be fixed, then the system administrator will be notified.

Smart Vaccine Knowledge Base keeper: These agents work as librarians and are responsible for the storage and retrieval of the proper vaccines, as instructed by the intelligence officers and the vaccinators.

Smart Vaccine documenters: These agents are responsible for collecting documentation on the attacking virus and how the attack was executed and how the battle was won. These agents act like the m cells, which is one of the highlights of the immune system.

Cognitive Early Warning Predictive System (CEWPS)/ Smart Vaccine Speaks Web Service Language

Web services are an intercommunication messaging technology. Life is very simple, but we made it complicated. Similarly, the concept of Web services (WS) is simple and common sense, but the IT folks made it complicated. CEWPS/SV will use Web services to store vaccination messages and critical system activities.

Figure 2.5 illustrates the basic mechanics of Web services:

1. The SV commander invokes a request on the status of the battle and its outcome.
2. The critical system requests some information from the Knowledge Engine.

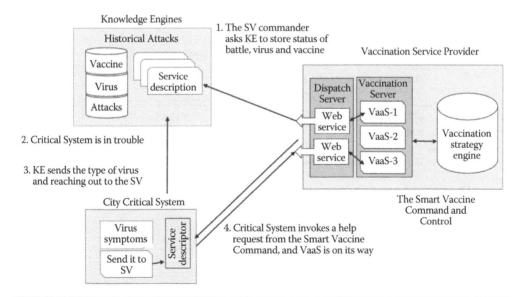

Figure 2.5 The Smart Vaccine Command and Control runs the show. 1. The SVC asks the knowledge engine to store the results of the previous attack. 2. The Critical System indicates it has been compromised. 3. The Critical System reaches out to the SV. 4. The Critical System describes to SV the attack and how it happened.

3. The Knowledge Engine sends the critical system information on the type of virus and its corresponding vaccine.

4. The critical system invokes a vaccination service from the Smart Vaccine Commander.

Web Services Will Have a Big Role

SOAP provides the envelope for protection and integrity of the message. It uses http (Internet protocol) as a rail to transfer messages from one node to another node as shown in Figure 2.6.

Smart Vaccine Transactional Services (SVS)

Familiarity with Web services will definitely help the reader understand SVS. For those readers who are not familiar with WS, a simple overview on the subject is provided. Figure 2.7 speaks for itself.

The Smart Vaccine services are divided into three groups as follows:

Group-1: *Smart Vaccine services to smart city grid services*—The human body cannot operate or even live with the connectivity of the nervous system. All its endpoints (trillions) are recognized, and their locations are stored in the brain (the human central knowledge engine). Critical systems are attached to the grid with an adapter. They are called *nodes* and are recognized (by location and characteristics) and monitored by the Smart City central grid command (Figure 2.8).

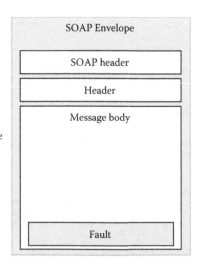

• Envelope
  • Element that identifies the XML document as a SOAP message
• Header
  • Element that contains header information
• Body
  • Element that contains call and response information
• Fault
  • Element containing errors and status information

Figure 2.6 SOAP document structure. In CEWPS/Smart Vaccine language, all message envelopes that travel on the SOAP highway will have the sender address, the receiver address, the information inside the envelope, and what to do in case the envelope is lost or it is the wrong address.

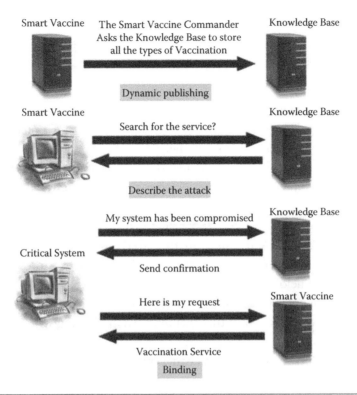

Figure 2.7 Exchange of messages between the Critical System after it was hit by an attack, and the Smart Vaccine Commander. Web Services are used to give a ride to the vaccination services (VaaS).

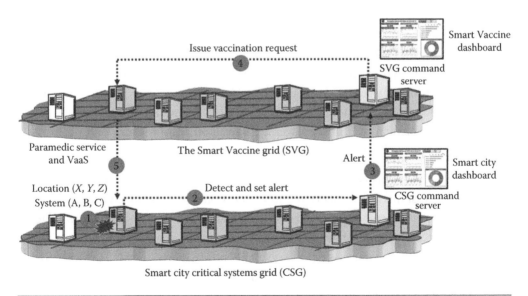

Figure 2.8 Grid-to-grid scenario. A simple scenario of how the Smart Vaccine grid communicates with the Smart City grid. In reality, the Smart Vaccine grid is a subset of the Smart City grid. By analogy, blood vessels and nerves run and work together.

By design, all critical systems in the city are connected to the city's smart grid (CSG) and the Smart Vaccine Grid (SVG). They are recognized and monitored by the CSG command server by location and platform characteristics. They are displayed on the dashboard. The scenario described in Figure 2.8 is as follows:

1. A preempted attack takes place on a critical system on the grid. This will happen since malware is also getting more sophisticated and potent. So system (A, B, C) is crippled and calling for help.
2. The City Smart Grid (CSG) command server receives a request for repair (RfR). The dashboard shows the location and characteristics of the critical system.
3. The RfR is routed to the Smart Vaccine Grid command. The location and properties of the attacked system are displayed on the SVG dashboard.
4. The SVG command sends a request for vaccination (RfV) to the grid Smart Vaccine (in the field) with the necessary data about the attacked system.
5. Smart Vaccine paramedics and vaccination-as-a-service (VaaS) are rushed to the attacked system. Later in this chapter, we describe how the Smart Vaccine eradicates the virus.

Group-2: *Preventive vaccination*—Whenever the smart grid is attacked by an attacking virus, the Smart Vaccine rushes to vaccinate the remaining critical systems as shown in Figure 2.9. It is also like subscribing to a fitness program to keep all the critical systems in healthy operating mode; regular *preventive* vaccinations are necessary whenever a virus is caught on the grid and a vaccine agent is created to eradicate it. Then, vaccine agents rush to all the systems on the grid and vaccinate them as precaution.

Group-3: *Defense by offense vaccination*—This is the most noble duty of the Smart Vaccine. Like in the human body, whenever there is a virus attack on a critical system, the Smart City Grid (SCG) command will be aware of the attack, and its dashboard will display the attacked system location. Smart Vaccine Grid (SVG) command goes on alert, and the proper vaccine agent (vaccinator) will rush to the attacked system for help. Figure 2.10 shows in detail the magnificent fight between the Smart Vaccine and the attacking virus (Figure 2.10). Let's go over each step.

1. The attacking virus is activated after a backdoor Trojan sneaked in. Instantly, city grid instantiates an alert request. The honeypot had the virus trapped before. It was reverse engineered (autopsy) and stored in the Virus Knowledge Base (ViKB). The antidote was built and stored in the Vaccine Knowledge Base (VaKB). The early warning system sends a query request to both the ViKB and VaKB for a match and gets the matched antidote.
2. The Smart Vaccine Commander is informed and is in charge.
3. In the battlefield, the Smart Vaccine vaccinator gets the antidote and carries it to the crippled system for vaccination.

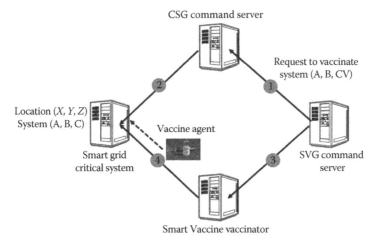

CSG command server

Request to vaccinate
system (A, B, CV)

Location (X, Y, Z)
System (A, B, C)

Vaccine agent

Smart grid
critical system

SVG command
server

Smart Vaccine vaccinator

1. The attacking virus is activated after a backdoor Trojan sneaked in. Instantly, city grid instantiates an alert request. The honeypot had the virus trapped before. It was reveres engineered (autopsy), and stored in the Virus Knowledge Base (ViKB). The antidote was built and went to the Vaccine Knowledge Base (VaKB). The early warning system send a query request to both (ViKB) and (ViKB) for a match, and gets the matched antidote.
2. The Smart Vaccine commander is informed and is in charge.
3. Right in the battlefield, the Smart Vaccine vaccinator gets the antidote and carries it to the crippled system for vaccination.
4. Antidote was loaded in the crippled system, and was back to normal. All other critical systems on the city grid got vaccinated with the antidote.
5. First line of defense (the Smart Vaccine intelligence) was sent for more information the origin of the attack, in case there are other copies of the virus. Mutation could be possible.

Figure 2.9 Preventive vaccination scenario: Whenever the smart grid gets attacked, the Smart Vaccine rushes to vaccinate the remaining critical systems.

4. Antidote was loaded in the crippled system and was back to normal. All other critical systems on the city grid got vaccinated with the antidote.

5. The first line of defense (Smart Vaccine intelligence) was sent for more information about the attack, in case there are other copies of the virus. Mutation could be possible.

6. The Smart Vaccine is starting to appraise the level of the attack and the damage.

7. The Smart Vaccine commander ordered the vaccinators to inoculate the critical systems with the created vaccine, just in case the worm might spread to the other systems.

8. The inoculation process started for all the systems on the grid.

9. Like in the human body, the B cells dismember the virus and retain the part as a memory token for the next similar attack. The attack vector and payload will be documented and packaged, ready to send to the Virus Knowledge Base. CEWPS is an extremely intelligent and cognitive system with several autonomous subsystems as specific service providers. During the attack, the Smart Vaccine commander orders service instances and each service instance has a start and finish. Some instances are stateless, and others are stateful.

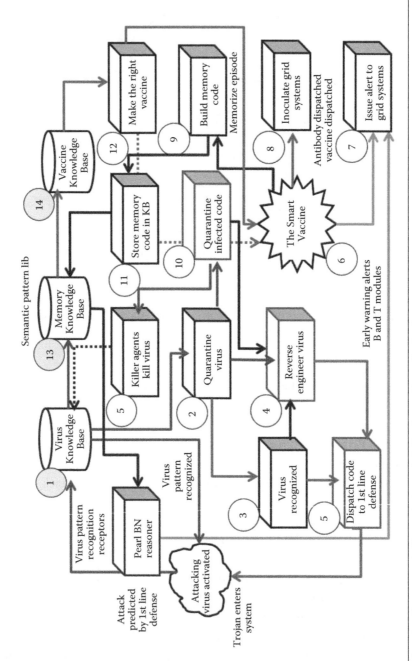

Figure 2.10 Defense by offense scenario: The vaccinator combats the virus and keeps its signature.

10. The Smart Vaccine killer agents will finish the virus completely by deleting the attack vector and calling upon the Smart Vaccine paramedics to fix any damage caused by the attack.
11. Once the anatomy of the virus is known and the attack vector code has been reverse engineered, it will be packaged and be ready to store in the memory Knowledge Base.
12. The proper vaccine code has already been assembled and is ready to be executed by the Smart Vaccine.
13. The memory Knowledge Base is the repository that stores all the attack vectors as documentation and reference for future attacks.
14. The Vaccine Knowledge Base is the repository that stores all the prepared vaccines for the attack.

As can be seen, a viral attack is a complex operation and needs to be matched by a very intelligent commanding agent with lots of hands-on experience. This is why we call it the Smart Vaccine. The Antivirus Technology does not have the intelligence of the Smart Vaccine. While viral attacks are becoming intelligent and more potent, only the Smart Vaccine with his highly scalar intelligence will be to take down the virus and nullify the attack.

A Summary of the Smart Vaccine Transactional Services and Messages

Grid-to-Grid Messages

- SendCSGAlert city smart grid (CSG)
- SendSVGAlert smart vaccine grid (SVG)

Alert Messages

- ForecastAttack
- SendAlert
- ReceiveAlert

Vaccine Registry Messages

- PublishVaccine
- StoreVaccine
- AnalyzeVaccine

Vaccination Messages

- QueryVaccine
- GetVaccine
- StartVaccinate
- AbortVaccinate
- EndVaccinate

Virus Registry Messages

- StoreVirus
- QueryVirus
- RetrieveVirus

Offense Messages

- RecognizeVirus
- QuarantineVirus
- DecomposeVirus
- DecompileVirus
- DisassenbleVirus
- TerminateVirus

Memory Messages

- BuildMemoryCode
- StoreMemoryCode
- QueryMemoryCode

Preventive Vaccination (Nonattack Situation)

- CheckSchedule
- UpdateSchedule

Websites

http://anatomylist.com/tag/immunity+system.
http://kidshealth.org/parent/general/body_basics/immune.html.
http://science.howstuffworks.com/life/cellular-microscopic/virus-human3.htm.
http://www.ncbi.nlm.nih.gov/pmc/articles/PMC4070499/.
http://www.ncbi.nlm.nih.gov/pubmed/25003131.
http://www.thebody.com/content/art1788.html.

3

CRITICAL INFRASTRUCTURES OF SMART CITIES

Why Did Cities Exist?

Aleppo is considered by many historians to be the oldest city in the world. The city today rests on four previous cities and civilizations. Its unique charm is in its chronic age and resilience to atrocious wars and continuous onslaughts. Since inscription, the layout of the old city in relation to the dominant citadel has remained basically unchanged. Conservation efforts within the old city have largely preserved the attributes of the Outstanding Universal Value. However, the setting is distinctly vulnerable due to the lack of control mechanisms in the planning administration, including the absence of a buffer zone. The historical and traditional handicrafts and commercial activities continue as a vital component of the city sustaining its traditional urban life.

It is just as holy as the Jerusalem and the Vatican because the Prophet Zechariah's shrine has been there for a modest 2300 years. If you want to learn about the history of civilization, you have to visit this invincible city.

Aleppo will never turn into a smart city simply because retrofitting and modernizing the city is an gargantuan effort. Converting the people of Aleppo into smart citizens is another monumental task, as the people will not trade their residual culture for a disruptive technology. Aleppo will remain thriving on orderly chaos. The corollary of this phenomenon is that none of the old cities in the world will suffer from retrofitting to become a true smart city.

What Is a Smart City?

A smart city is a holistic environment where human infrastructures are gracefully integrated with physical infrastructure. A smart city is run like a tight ship, where central command oversees all activates. The Internet has played a pivotal role in the making of smart cities. Using power sensors, wireless networks, and Web- and mobile-based applications, smart cities are becoming a reality. The term *smart city* is in fact very ambiguous and confusing, simply because the concept is used all over the world with different nomenclatures, context, and meanings. As of 2014, there is not a complete smart city. There is not even a quarter smart city, simply because it is almost impossible to implement at one stage. It will take at least a decade to implement, provided that the government has allocated the money and the right people to manage the project.

In a sense, The Smart City is not an autonomous robot, but a mechanism that works with humans in order to create a healthier and more productive lifestyle for the people that live in it. On September 12, 2013 *Time* magazine had an issue titled "Number of City Dwellers to Double in 2050," which was an eye-opener and shocker. It meant we are adding the equivalent of seven New York cities to the planet every single year. As our planet becomes more urban, our cities need to get smarter. To handle this large-scale urbanization, we will need to find new ways to manage complexity, increase efficiency, reduce expenses, and improve the quality of life.

With this rapid growth ahead of us, imagine if our cities could talk—if they could give us live status updates on traffic patterns, pollution, parking spaces, water, power, and light. Imagine how that kind of information could improve the economic and environmental health of a city for residents, merchants, and visitors. Imagine how it could improve working conditions and productivity for the people who maintain the city.

What Is a Critical Infrastructure?

First, the term *critical* is an interesting one. It means that there is a red line coming up, warning you not to step beyond it. The term has profound repercussions that need to be respected and observed. Adding this adjective to the word infrastructure makes it somewhat very important but fragile.

So, the critical infrastructures (CIs) are those vulnerably fragile items that constitute the backbone of our nation's economy, security, and health. We know it as the power we use in our homes, the water we drink, the transportation that moves us, and the communication systems we rely on to stay in touch with friends and family.

Ironically, the term *critical infrastructure* was born and became priority number one, right after the 9/11 attack on the World Trade Center.

Critical infrastructures are the assets, systems, and networks, whether physical or virtual, which are so vital that their incapacitation or destruction would have a debilitating effect on security, national economic security, national public health or safety, or any combination thereof.

Critical Infrastructure Frameworks for Smart Cities

To start with, no city is smart unless it has secured its critical infrastructures.

The main components of a smart city are smart infrastructures, smart governance, smart management, smart citizens, smart living, smart economy, smart environment, and smart connectivity. For example, A380 is the most complex avionic marvel that has ever been built. It is equipped with 100,000 different wires, totaling 330 miles in length, that perform 1,150 separate functions. The smart city is another engineering marvel. When a city has all its vital activities operating autonomously and being weaved into one cohesive framework, then we can have a smart city (Figure 3.1).

The key success factor in developing a smart city is *connectivity* where all of its components are pathologically and holistically connected in *real time* to the city's

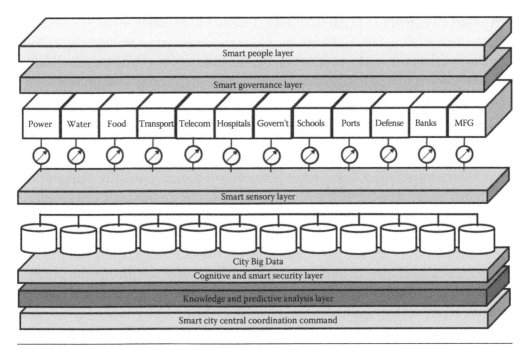

Figure 3.1 The monolithic structure of the happy smart city. Sensors collect information from smart people and all other smart establishments. CEWPS is one of the foundation layers that is incorporated in the structure.

centralized command center. Therefore, one of the most important prerequisites is to have a smart grid that ties all the pieces together. It is pretty much like the nervous system in the human body. A smart city is just as smart as its sensors. Data sensors collect live data and transmit the data to a processing center to become knowledge, saved semantically in a Knowledge Base. Then based on the Reasoning Engine, action sensors will respond back to the infrastructure. The environment of The Smart City is totally autonomic, self-correcting, and self-optimizing.

By definition, a *critical infrastructure* is a vital entity that supports the life of the city. Any damage or destruction to this entity will have a debilitating effect on the performance of the city.

There are two categories of infrastructures. The first category is the human infrastructure, which includes health, food, banking, and education. The second category is the physical, which includes energy, telecom, transport, and water.

A smart city works on implementing a blueprint that guarantees the people smart mobility, smart governance, a smart environment, smart living, and a smart economy.

A smart city is a cohesive environment that monitors all of its critical infrastructures, including roads, bridges, tunnels, rails, subways, airports, seaports, communications, water, power, and even major buildings, through a cognitive early warning predictive security system.

A smart city connects its physical infrastructure, IT infrastructure, social infrastructure, and the business infrastructure to leverage the collective intelligence of the city.

A smart city strives to make itself more efficient, sustainable, equitable, and livable. A smart city combines information and communication technology throughout all its organizations in order to speed up bureaucratic processes and help to identify new, innovative solutions to city management complexity, in order to improve sustainability and livability.

Securing the Critical Infrastructures for Smart Cities: The Plan

The National Infrastructure Protection Plan (NIPP) (http://www.dhs.gov/nationalinfrastructure-protection-plan) is the overall proactive security blueprint for the United States. The NIPP is the responsibility of the Department of Homeland Security (DHS). It outlines how government and private sector participants in the critical infrastructures community work together to manage risks and achieve security and resilience outcomes. The NIIP establishes a vision, mission, and goals that are supported by a set of core tenets focused on risk management and partnership to influence future critical infrastructures security and resilience planning at the international; national; regional; state, local, tribal, and territorial (SLTT); and owner and operator levels.

The NIIP builds upon the critical infrastructures risk management framework introduced in the 2006 NIPP. Effective risk management requires an understanding of the criticality of assets, systems, and networks, as well as the associated dependencies and interdependencies of critical infrastructures. To this end, the National Plan encourages partners to identify critical functions and resources that impact their businesses and communities to support preparedness planning and capability development. In addition to cooperative public and private support, the National Plan receives supplemental help from the National Cybersecurity and Communications Integration Center (NCCIC) and the National Infrastructure Coordinating Center (NICC).

The NIPP report offers the reader its own definition to some key concepts throughout the plan, which are given in the following:

- *Critical infrastructures*: Defined as "all systems and assets, whether physical or virtual, so vital to the United States that the incapacity or destruction of such systems and assets would have a debilitating impact on security, national economic security, national public health or safety, or any combination of those matters."
- *Security*: Defined as "reducing the risk to critical infrastructure by physical means or defensive cyber measures to intrusions, attacks, or the effects of natural or man-made disasters."
- *Resilience*: Defined as "the ability to prepare for and adapt to changing conditions and withstand and recover rapidly from disruptions, it includes the ability to withstand and recover from deliberate attacks, accidents, or naturally occurring threats or incidents."

- *Risk*: Defined as "the potential for an unwanted outcome resulting from an incident, event, or occurrence, as determined by its likelihood (a function of threats and vulnerabilities) and the associated consequences."
- *Risk management*: Defined as "the process of identifying, analyzing, and communicating risk and accepting, avoiding, transferring, or controlling it to an acceptable level at an acceptable cost."

The NIPP has identified 16 critical infrastructure sectors, but there is more hard work ahead apart from listing them in the following:

1. *Chemical*: The chemical sector is an integral component of the U.S. economy, relying on and supporting a wide range of other critical infrastructure sectors. The sectors can be divided into five main segments, based on the end product produced:
   a. Basic chemicals
   b. Specialty chemicals
   c. Agricultural chemicals
   d. Pharmaceuticals
   e. Consumer products
2. *Energy*: The U.S. energy infrastructure fuels the economy of the twenty-first century.
3. *Health care and public health*: The health care and public health sector protects all sectors of the economy from hazards such as terrorism, infectious disease outbreaks, and natural disasters. Because the vast majority of the sector's assets are privately owned and operated, collaboration and information sharing between the public and private sectors is essential to increasing resilience of the nation's health care and public health critical infrastructures. The sector plays a significant role in response and recovery across all other sectors in the event of a natural or man-made disaster.
4. *Dams*: The dams sector is composed of assets that include dam projects, hydropower generation facilities, navigation locks, levees, dikes, hurricane barriers, mine tailings, other industrial waste impoundments, and other similar water retention and water control facilities. The dams sector is a vital part of the nation's infrastructure and provides a wide range of economic, environmental, and social benefits, including hydroelectric power, river navigation, water supply, wildlife habitat, waste management, flood control, and recreation. There are over 87,000 dams in the United States; approximately 65% are privately owned, and safety offices regulate more than 77% of state dams.
5. *Commercial facilities*: Facilities associated with the commercial facilities sector operate on the principle of open public access and masses of people, such as arenas, stadiums, aquariums, zoos, parks, museums, and convention centers. The majority of the facilities in this sector are privately owned and operated. We all

watched horror movies where monsters cause massive people to be stamped out. Terrorists are using these facilities for political mass killing. Guarding these facilities with cameras and guards has become an operating necessity.

6. *Food and agriculture*: The food and agriculture sector is almost entirely under private ownership and is composed of an estimated 2.2 million farms, 900,000 restaurants, and more than 400,000 registered food manufacturing, processing, and storage facilities. This sector accounts for roughly one-fifth of the nation's economic activity.

7. *Government facilities*: This sector includes a wide variety of buildings, located in the United States and overseas. These facilities include general-use office buildings and special-use military installations and armories, embassies, courthouses, central post office, and national laboratories, including restricted zones for nuclear testing.

8. *Information technology*: Despite illicit but affluent technology espionage and smuggling, this sector is central to the nation's security, economy, and public health and safety. Businesses, governments, academia, and private citizens are increasingly dependent upon information technology sector functions. These virtual and distributed functions produce and provide hardware, software, and information technology systems and services and—in collaboration with the communications sector—the Internet. The sector's complex and dynamic environment makes identifying threats and assessing vulnerabilities difficult and requires that these tasks be addressed in a collaborative and creative fashion.

9. *Nuclear reactors and waste*: Nuclear power accounts for approximately 20% of our nation's electrical generation, provided by 100 commercial nuclear reactors licensed to operate at 62 nuclear power plants. This sector includes the following:
   a. Nuclear power plants
   b. Nonpower nuclear reactors used for research, testing, and training
   c. Manufacturers of nuclear reactors or components
   d. Radioactive materials used primarily in medical, industrial, and academic settings
   e. Nuclear fuel cycle facilities
   f. Decommissioned nuclear power reactors
   g. Transportation, storage, and disposal of nuclear and radioactive waste

10. *Transportation systems*: The transportation systems sector consists of seven key categories:
   a. *Aviation*: This includes 450 commercial airports and 19,000 civil and limitary airports and heliports.
   b. *Highway infrastructure and motor carriers*: This includes 4 million miles of roadway, almost 600,000 bridges, and some 400 tunnels in 35 states.
   c. *Maritime transportation system*: This consists of about 95,000 miles of coastline, 361 ports, 25,000 miles of waterways, and 3.4 million square miles of exclusive economic zone.

   d. *Mass transit and passenger rail*: This includes service by buses, commuter rail transit trolleys and streetcars, and long-distance railroad trains such as Amtrak and Alaska.
   e. *Pipeline systems*: These include approximately 2.2 million miles of natural gas distribution pipelines, about 168,900 miles of hazardous liquid pipelines, and more than 109 liquefied natural gas processing and storage facilities.
   f. *Freight rail*: This consists of 7 major carriers, more than 100 smaller railroads, over 140,000 miles of active railroad, over 1.3 million freight cars, and roughly 20,000 locomotives. Further, over 12,000 trains are operated daily. The Department of Defense has designated 30,000 miles of track and structure as critical to mobilization and resupply of U.S. forces.
   g. *Postal and shipping*: 707,000 career employees work for this entity. The postal service delivers to nearly 153 million addresses in every state, city, and town in this country. It moves over 206 billion envelops/year. An incredible crawling slug!

11. *Water and wastewater systems*: This sector is vulnerable to a variety of attacks, including contamination with deadly agents, physical attacks such as the release of toxic gaseous chemicals, and cyberattacks. If these attacks were realized, the result could be large numbers of illnesses or casualties and/or denial of service that would also impact public health and economic vitality. Critical services such as firefighting and health care (hospitals), and other dependent and interdependent sectors, such as energy, food and agriculture, and transportation systems, would suffer negative impacts from a denial of service in the water and wastewater systems sector. There are approximately 160,000 public drinking water systems and more than 16,000 publicly owned wastewater treatment systems in the United States. Approximately 84% of the U.S. population receives their potable water from these drinking water systems, and more than 75% of the U.S. population's sanitary sewerage is treated by these wastewater systems.

12. *Financial services*: The financial services sector represents a vital component of our nation's critical infrastructure. Large-scale power outages, recent natural disasters, and an increase in the number and sophistication of cyberattacks demonstrate the wide range of potential risks facing the sector.

13. *Communications*: This sector is an integral component of the U.S. economy, underlying the operations of all businesses, public safety organizations, and government. Over the last 25 years, the sector has evolved from predominantly a provider of voice services into a diverse, competitive, and interconnected industry using terrestrial, satellite, and wireless transmission systems. Just imagine the Internet goes down in the country as a result of a major blackout of power.

14. *Critical manufacturing*: This is crucial to the economic prosperity and continuity of the United States. If you think Boeing is not important, then travel by mule-drawn wagon. Direct attack on or disruption of certain elements of the

manufacturing industry could disrupt essential functions at the national level and across multiple critical infrastructures sectors.

15. *Defense industrial base*: The defense industrial base sector is the worldwide industrial complex that enables research and development, as well as design, production, delivery, and maintenance of military weapons systems, subsystems, and components or parts, to meet U.S. military requirements. Take for example, *Area 51*. The intense secrecy surrounding the base has made it the frequent subject of conspiracy theories and a central component to unidentified flying object (UFO) folklore.

16. *Emergency services sector (ESS)*: This is the Homeland Security initiative that covers prevention, preparedness, response, and recovery elements. ESS represents the nation's first line of defense in the prevention and mitigation of risk from both intentional and unintentional man-made incidents as well as from natural disasters. ESS also serves as the primary protector for the other 15 critical infrastructures sectors. The primary mission of ESS is to save lives, protect property and the environment, assist communities impacted by disasters, and aid in the recovery from emergencies.

U.S. Computer Emergency Readiness Team (US-CERT)

Originally, the grandfather, CERT started in academia as research in computer science. Then DHS renamed it US-CERT. It was the first Internet security incident center, and it is still here 25 years later. Only now, the grandson CERT got bigger, smarter, and more arrogant with his expertise from incident response to a comprehensive, proactive approach to securing networked systems. CERT is part of the Software Engineering Institute, which is based at Carnegie Mellon University in Pittsburgh, Pennsylvania, and was founded by Andrew Carnegie and Andrew W. Mellon. It is considered the world's leading trusted authority dedicated to improving the security and resilience of computer systems and networks and is a national asset in the field of cybersecurity.

As described on the US-CERT website (see the "Websites" listing in the back of the chapter), its full mission is, through its 24/7 operations center,

- To accept triages and collaboratively respond to incidents
- To provide technical assistance to information system operators
- To disseminate timely notifications regarding current and potential security threats and vulnerabilities
- To leverage the Protected Critical Infrastructure Information Program that provides advice to the private sector
- US-CERT is part of the DHS National Cybersecurity and Communications Integration Center (NCCIC)

US-CERT strives to be a trusted global leader in cybersecurity—collaborative, agile, and responsive in a dynamic and complex environment.

Challenges of US-CERT for Smart Cities

It is clear that the US-CERT alone cannot handle a national response during a massive cyberattack on infrastructures, as indicated by the U.S. Government Accountability Office (GAO), which is an independent, nonpartisan agency that works for the congress. Often called the *Congressional watchdog*, the GAO investigates how the federal government spends taxpayer dollars (http://www.gao.gov/products/GAO-08-588).

The US-CERT has been under the gun of GAO to report credible cyber threat predictive analyses. The US-CERT has a larege reservoir of talent and experienced domain experts, but it is unfortunately shackled by a heavy load of national responsivities and stringent performance acceptance criteria (PAC).

Challenges of Cybersecurity in Smart Cities

The management of smart city cybersecurity is a Himalayan challenge that all technology providers underestimate, which is smart city security. We have lots of running rabbits in this grueling race. It is estimated that $40 billion will be spent on smart city technologies by 2016. We examined one survey on the 10 best smart cities in the world. Interestingly enough, Vienna, Toronto, Paris, New York, London, Tokyo, Berlin, Copenhagen, Hong Kong, and finally Barcelona turned out to be the best smart cities in the world. The survey was based in the following criteria: "The survey selected cities that use information and communication technologies (ICT) to be more intelligent and efficient in the use of resources, resulting in cost and energy savings, improved service delivery and quality of life, and reduced environmental footprint—all supporting innovation and the low-carbon economy." New York is the only city in the United States that has all the qualities to be called a smart city.

Unfortunately, the survey did not factor security into the criteria, which would have pushed Tokyo to the top as the best smart city. Tokyo is already bundled with intensive electronic technologies that smart cities need.

Another remarkable country that is racing toward smart cities and setting a model to other developing countries is the United Arab Emirates (UAE). The country, born in 1971 (over 40 years old), with superb leadership and harmony among the seven emirates, it has managed to turn sand into gold. Today, Abu Dhabi (capital) and Dubai have become global attractions. You can see ultimate modernization and high-tech urbanization to the highest level. Physical security and cybersecurities were first on the agenda.

The UAE Is Setting a Good Example

The United Arab Emirates first established the UAE National Electronic Security Authority (NESA) as the federal authority responsible for developing, supervising, and monitoring the implementation of UAE cybersecurity strategies, policies, and standards. NESA seeks to safeguard the UAE online environment and contribute to the collective achievement of national goals. NESA also published the first edition of the "National Cyber Security Strategy (NCSS)," "Critical Information Infrastructure Policy (CIIP)," and the "UAE Information Assurance (IA) Standards" that collectively work toward enhancing UAE national security by improving the protection of national information and communications infrastructure (ICT). Then, the UAE set up a computer emergency response center in Dubai.

The *UAE Computer Emergency Response Center (aeCERT)* is a miniature copy of US-CERT. It is recognized as a trusted, authoritative organization dedicated to improving the security and resilience of computer systems and networks. The aeCERT is managed by top-notch domain experts and is considered a national asset in the field of cybersecurity and regularly partners with government, industry, law enforcement, and academia to develop advanced methods and technologies to counter large-scale, sophisticated cyber threats. aeCERT is the cybersecurity coordination center for the UAE. It is established by the Telecommunications Regulatory Authority (TRA) as an initiative to facilitate the detection, prevention, and response of cybersecurity incidents on the Internet. Its mission is to sustain a resilient and vigilant ICT infrastructure against a broader set of cybersecurity threats and to build a secure and safe cyber culture in the United Arab Emirates.

The United Arab Emirates Power Grids: A Must See

The United Arab Emirates is progressing with gigantic leaps and bounds to become a model country with the most advanced infrastructures. Power generation is a *federated* infrastructure that every emirate controls rather than at the central federal level.

It is worth mentioning that the UAE's appetite for power is three times the global average. The need for power in the emirates was growing at a rate of 9% each year, while the world energy demand was rising at around 3% on average. According to the statistical Annual Report for Electricity and Water, 2011–2013, the UAE's present power consumption is about 85.17 billion KWh, which can increase to 40,000 MW by 2020.

The rapid industrialization of the Arabian Gulf, in particular in the UAE, has led to a sharp rise in electricity demand, plus the growing urbanization and lifestyle improvements that came with the growing economic prosperity, and was enhanced further by the resurgent construction boom that has now returned to the region.

Each emirate (state) is responsible for the power consumption. But all the emirates will be connected with one national grid, which will amalgamate the power generation, transmission, and distribution networks of the seven emirates into a single national grid.

The Emirates National Grid (ENG) is expected to be connected with the Gulf Cooperation Council (GCC) grid, linking the UAE with Qatar, Bahrain, Saudi Arabia, Kuwait, and Oman (Figure 3.2).

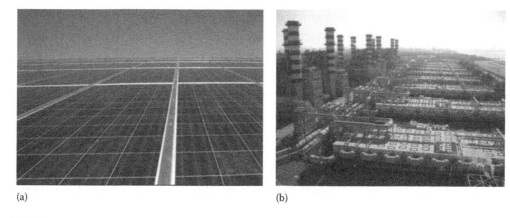

(a)   (b)

Figure 3.2   Smart city builders have to consider the new technologies to generate power. Dubai— the largest city in the United Arab Emirates (UAE)—has leapfrogged the world with its innovative technologies. (a) It uses solar energy (photovoltaic power) and (b) desalinization to generate electricity (steam power) plus the water supply for the city.

One important note to mention is that the Arabian Gulf countries including Saudi Arabia have started to focus on solar energy (*photovoltaic power*)—as shown in the picture. Dubai has been built at the leading edge of technology in every domain and will be setting an example of a smart city to the rest of the world.

Statistics from the Dubai Electricity and Water Authority (DEWA) show the impressive demographic demand of power and water: 10,356 MW of power capacity and 470 million of water imperial barrels of drinking water.

The transition of Dubai to smart city requires a new security paradigm to protect an ultracomplex city with three downtowns. Several cities in the Gulf region are considering to use Digital Immunity (DI) with the implementation of Cognitive Early Warning Predictive System (CEWPS™)–Smart Vaccine. The Gulf countries are spending their own oil money (at one time, used to invest the money outside the country) on accelerated urbanization to build smart cities, smart government, smart universities, and smart homes. The Gulf countries have emerged as the focal point for mega projects managed by global technology companies. They realized that a smart power grid is the backbone of The Smart City.

Smart Cities Cannot Live without Smart Grids

Paradoxically, as cyberspace provides a world without borders, Internet connectivity has made suburbia a part of the city. People who started to work in remote locations and virtually are connected to business. Telecommuting has provided people convenience, comfort, and safety. The information highway has become critical and vulnerable. The increasing production of information in cities raises issues of privacy, access, and inclusion. Who will own the brains of smart cities? *Fast Company* magazine (December 2010 issue) sees a battle for control between *hacktivists* pushing for self-serve governance and companies providing opaque systems based on proprietary technology. Achieving balance depends on an agenda of openness, transparency, and inclusiveness led by a central trusted agency and driven by open standards. Smart grids are modernized electricity grids with smart sensory components connected to information highways and hierarchical control units monitoring signal and data traffic and relaying it to central command. In order to deliver sustainable and scalable energy to consumers, smart grids are in fact an *open* grid that can easily integrate all sorts of renewable energy supplies, like solar, wind, and cogeneration plants.

Smart grids are more reliable, with fewer and shorter blackouts. They allow electric vehicles to be charged when demand on the network is low, and their combined battery storage can be used to support the network when demand is high. Consumers need no longer be passive receivers of power, but instead can take charge of their energy use and make meaningful decisions that will benefit both the environment and their hip pockets. Household appliances can be programmed or directly controlled by the network to run when it is most cost-effective.

In a smart city, power is managed more efficiently and effectively, lowers the ratio of electricity consumption per economic output, reduces overall greenhouse gas emissions with demand management, and encourages energy efficiency, improves reliability, and reduces recurring costs while making prudent investments.

A smart grid performs three important functions. First, it modernizes power systems through self-healing designs, automation, remote monitoring and control, and establishment of microgrids. Second, it informs and educates consumers about their energy usage, costs, and alternative options, to enable them to make decisions autonomously about how and when to use electricity and fuels. Third, it provides safe, secure, and reliable integration of distributed and renewable energy resources. All these add up to an energy infrastructure that is more reliable, more sustainable, and more resilient. Thus, a smart grid sits at the heart of The Smart City, which cannot fully exist without it.

Smart cities depend on a smart grid to ensure resilient delivery of energy to supply their many functions, present opportunities for conservation, improve efficiencies, and, most importantly, enable coordination between urban officialdom, infrastructure operators, those responsible for public safety. The Smart City depends on how the city *organism* works together as an integrated whole and survives when placed under extreme conditions. Energy, water, transportation, public health and safety, and other aspects of a smart city are managed in concert to support smooth operation of critical infrastructure while providing for a clean, economic, and safe environment to live, work, and play.

A Smart City Runs on a Smart Grid

Consider the human body as a smart city with four intrinsic attributes that add to the marvel of the human body. The first attribute we know is the connectivity of all the parts together, although each part works independently and autonomously managing its own operating responsibility. The second attribute is that each part has its own sensors to prepare the part for defense, for attack, and for self-repair. The third attribute is that each part is able to communicate with the other parts for help, for food supplies, and for exchange of information due to injuries. The fourth attribute is that each part of the body is intelligent enough to respond to the outside world with the proper sensors. The nervous system is the smart grid of our body. It carries sensor signals to the brain for action. The brain will respond by sending motor signals to the parts. Let us not forget the fifth important attribute which is the Human Immune System (HIS) that detects attacks of intruders and mobilize armies to defeat these intruders. Now we understand the pivotal importance of the smart grid to The Smart City as shown in Figure 3.3.

Here is one example of how cost-effective efficiency can be achieved in a smart city: Water utilities are typically one of the largest consumers of energy in a city; savings can be achieved by lessening their consumption of electricity as the electric utility nears its peak condition when energy is most expensive. By coordinating with the electric utility and shifting water pumping to nonpeak hours, the water utility can reduce its energy consumption (and ultimately its bill), help the electric utility avoid problems, and allow other more critical and less flexible functions (such as hospitals) to maintain uninterrupted supply. In the same sense, electric trains can be accelerated more slowly to reduce power consumption while maintaining schedules. Building owners and the public can also participate in demand response programs to the same end. Building on all the combined data points and analysis of the smart grid, the smart city represents the next step in the process.

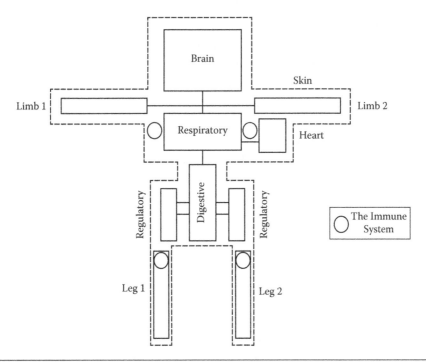

Figure 3.3 A rough draft of the human body as a smart grid that connects all the parts of the body with nerves. There are three distinct characteristics: interconnected, instrumented, and intelligent.

How to Inject Resilience in the Smart Grid

Merriam–Webster defines *resilience* as the ability of a substance or object to spring back into shape or elasticity. Under extreme conditions, the most critical function of a smart city would be predictability. This is the most difficult attribute of the smart grid. The City Coordination Center (CCC) should be prepared to manage the grid before and during the incoming danger. The issue of cyberattacks and defense by offense will be discussed later in Chapter 13. The smart grid would maintain the load in a predictable and more manageable fashion so that critical city infrastructure and functions are maintained (among them are police, fire, hospitals), supported by microgrids. Self-healing automation would restore power rapidly to areas where alternate routes are available. Local generation would be exploited to support immediate needs. The community (industry, commercial, residential) would respond automatically, to reduce their energy needs, to lessen the burden of restoration. Transportation and traffic systems would coordinate with the energy systems to support critical transportation arteries and modes. Through it all, timely logistics information would be gathered and supplied to the public by all means available, but particularly through social media networks. Conservation, efficiency, and safety will all be greatly enhanced through the availability of accurate logistical information.

Testing the smart grid for resilience is a big challenge. Three things have to be factored into resilience. First, a qualified staff is required to manage the SGC during extreme conditions. Second, the public should be aware and be given notice on how to handle the incoming problem. Third, the SGC should know the red zone of resilience prior to breakdown.

Complete smart cities do not exist yet in their entirety anywhere in the world, but some cities such as Dubai are heading toward a smart city. The secret sauce is the way the ruler of the city is managing the city with a very competent and loyal team. Technology is the means, but the human factor in crafting the right plan is the most important ingredient in developing a smart city.

Smart cities, like the smart grid, will evolve slowly, but surely, over the next two decades. They will more fully harness, integrate, and utilize information to be shared between departments, infrastructure operators, and citizens. Cities will partner with vendors to create integrated solutions, and the smart grid will become only a part of a greater, more responsive urban ecosystem. Ultimately, with The Smart City, we are all in it together.

Smart Grid Success Formula

The first step toward building a smart city is leadership, followed by a team of innovators and risk-taking technology pioneers. This team will craft a blueprint for a holistic efficient, livable, and sustainable city and drive collaboration between best-in-class global and local players across the whole smart city value chain. The main focus will be on integration of operation and information, hardware and software to improve the overall efficiency of the city. Figure 3.4 shows the systematic planning effort required to build a city's Smart Grid.

Cyber-Cognitive Early Warning Model

As the old saying goes, "History shows that those who do not learn from *history* are doomed to repeat." Radar was secretly developed by several nations before and during World War II. The term RADAR was coined in 1940 by the U.S. Navy as an acronym for *RAdio Detection and Ranging*. Radar becomes a crucial operating necessity in aviation. It is used to detect aircraft, ships, spacecraft, guided missiles, motor vehicles, weather formations, and terrain. Unfortunately, radar operators were sleeping on the job when the Japanese attacked Pearl Harbor. It could have saved the *Titanic*. History does lie.

Radar, however, is an object-detection system that uses radio waves to determine the range, altitude, direction, or speed of objects. The radar dish or antenna transmits pulses of radio waves or microwaves that bounce off any object in their path. The object returns a tiny part of the wave's energy to a dish or antenna that is usually located at the same site as the transmitter.

Cyberattacks cannot be detected by radar. Cyber missiles are stealth. Conventional weapons cannot protect smart grids. You need new technology. We will show you how to defend the smart grids.

Holy Grail of the Smart Grid

To protect the smart grid, you need another smart grid to shield from malicious attacks. In other words, to protect the City Smart Grid (CSG), we need the Smart Vaccine Grid (SVG). If you have a city with 1000 critical systems, it will be impossible to protect all of them at the same time unless they are *pathologically* (physically and logically) connected to a smart grid. Again, back to the human body, just imagine that each part has its own brain and nervous system. We would not be able to function normally. In any city, the water system is independent from the power network that is independent from the telephone network for a good reason.

In Figures 3.5 and 3.6, we show how Digital Immunity (DI) works by using the grid layering concept. Digital Immunity is the smart protection layer to the Smart Vaccine. The CEWPS is the powerhouse of Digital Immunity for the city's smart grid. CEWPS has the main responsibilities to recognize all the incoming attacks ahead of time, to warn all the critical systems on the city's smart grid (CSG), and to order the Smart Vaccine Commander (SVC) to manage the vaccination missions. Digital Immunity is constantly in a dynamic state of alert and is achieved with the

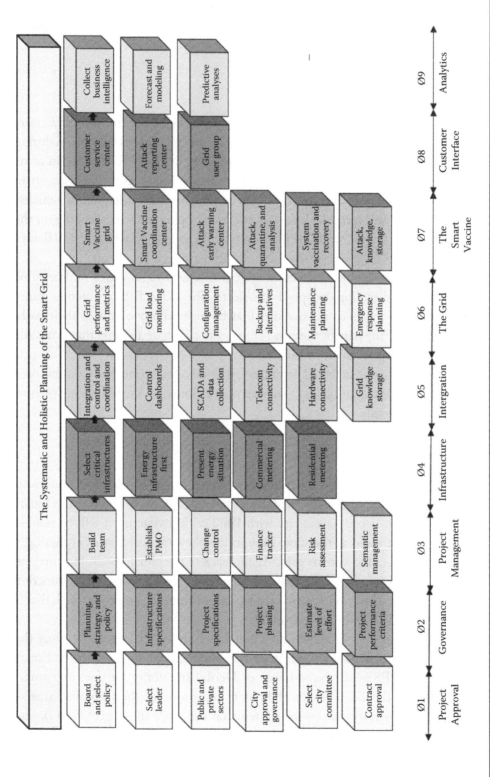

Figure 3.4 The systematic and holistic planning phases to deploy the city's smart grid. There are nine contiguous phases that have to be successfully completed before we get the smart grid.

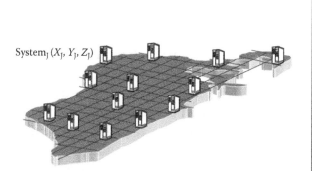

- Energy
- Water
- Agriculture and food
- Information and telecom
- Government
- Public health
- Emergency services
- Transportation
- Defense industries
- Banking and finance
- Chemical plants
- Postal and shipping
- Education

Figure 3.5 The first layer of the smart grid determines the perimeter (area covered under the grid) and then localizes the nominated critical infrastructures and their systems. Each system will be identified on the grid as a node. Then each node will be connected to the metering system and to the dashboard of the city's smart grid coordination center (SGC).

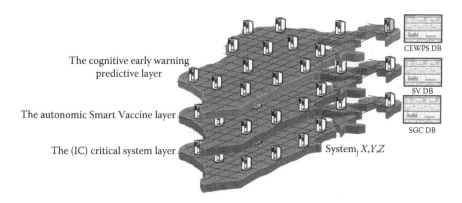

Figure 3.6 This is the high-rise architecture of Digital Immunity. CEWPS and its Smart Vaccine will be the technological solution to fully detect and eradicate all attacks. The critical systems will also be connected to the Smart Vaccine layer and will be under the real-time protection of the cognitive early warning layer. All the grids have their own dashboard and are interconnected.

Smart Vaccine Grid (SVG) that sits at the top of the City Smart Grid (CSG) and is managed by the Smart Vaccine Commander (SVC) and its army of vaccinators that are ready to combat any foreign agents that hurt the critical systems.

Two Technologies to Build the Smart Grid

Like in any conventional war, there are a couple of crucial requirements that determine victory. The first is to know the landscape of the battlefield, and the second is to know the location of the enemy relative to the landscape. The army that has information on these two requirements will be able to control the timing of the attack.

First Technology: Spatial Data Infrastructures (SDI)

Most human activity depends on location-based or geospatial information, that is, knowing where things are and how they relate to one another. These geospatial data are collected by The Smart City to locate the critical infrastructures and assign a set of coordinates to them on the smart grid.

A spatial data infrastructure (SDI) is an incredible network of data repositories (can be on the cloud) to promote data sharing and consumption. SDI implements a framework of geographic data, which is derived from geographic information system (GIS) that is another prominent technology designed to capture, store, manipulate, analyze, manage, and present all types of spatial or geographical data and metadata. Users can be registered online to have access to SDI storage. A GIS is often used to create an account for SDI. From the diverse literature on SDI, we found it useful to distinguish five major categories:

1. Spatial data
2. Technologies (hardware, software, and clouds)
3. Laws and policies
4. People (data providers, service providers, and user)
5. Standards for data acquisition, representation, and transfer

Due to its nature (size, cost, number of interactors), an SDI is usually government related. The National Spatial Data Infrastructure (NSDI) is the (SDI) in the United States. On the European side, INSPIRE is the SDI, and ultimately the United Nations Spatial Data Infrastructure (UNSDI) will be ready for specialized agencies and member countries. In the Middle East, there are two SDIs worth mentioning: Israel-SDI and Abu Dhabi Spatial Data Infrastructure (AD-SDI).

Second Technology: Geographic Information Systems (GIS)

Smart cities need smart grids which in turn need smart locations. To build smart locations by coordinates, geospatial technologies are used to calculate geospatial data about the most crucial infrastructures such as power plants, hospitals, government building, schools, and manufacturing plants. The GIS is the right technology to capture, store, manipulate, analyze, manage, and present all types of spatial or geographical data. A little interesting blip of history about GIS is worthwhile: GIS was used as early as 1832 as one of the first applications of spatial analysis in epidemiology. French geographer Charles Picquet, in his research *"Rapport sur la marche et les effets du choléra dans Paris et le département de la Seine,"* represented the 48 districts of the city of Paris by a halftone color gradient according to the percentage of deaths by cholera per 1000 inhabitants. In 1854, John Snow depicted a cholera outbreak in London using points to represent the locations of some individual cases, an early successful use of a geographic methodology in epidemiology.

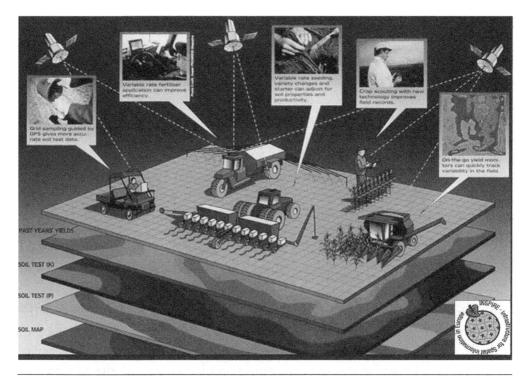

Figure 3.7 A descriptive 3D picture of the multiple benefits of a spatial data infrastructure (SDI). All GIS data will be filtered and stored in an SDI database before all the critical infrastructures are identified for the smart grid.

There are a variety of methods that can be used to enter data into a GIS, where it is stored in a digital format. One way is positions from a global navigation satellite system (GNSS) like global positioning system (GPS) can also be collected and then imported into a GIS. Another method is satellite remote sensing that collects raster data that will be further processed using grid of tiny cells. A value is stored in each of these cells to represent the nature of the corresponding location on the ground (Figure 3.7).

After entering data into a GIS, the data usually require editing, streamlining, and homogenizing for consistency. For vector data, the data must be made *topologically correct*, which means the coordinates of the vector should be known, before it can be used for some advanced analysis. A line is drawn as a vector with a pair of coordinates. A building is equivalent to a square with four coordinates. For a road network, lines must connect with nodes at an intersection. Errors such as undershoots and overshoots must also be removed.

GIS Benefits GIS is encroaching into new fields, and the core GIS software has become available on an open platform interfacing with other enterprise systems. The software that runs on network, cloud, or mobile devices includes analytical and sophisticated graphical tools and an ad hoc reporting system. The website "Geospatial Analysis" set up by Dr. Michael de Smith and Prof. Paul Longley, University College London, and Prof. Mike Goodchild, UC Santa Barbara (http://www.spatialanalysisonline.com) provides a reasonably comprehensive guide to the subject. One thing worth mentioning is that geospatial intelligence, based on GIS spatial analysis, has also become a key element for security. GIS as a whole can be described as conversion to a vectorial representation or to any other digitization process. So, a GIS must be able to convert geographic data from one structure to another. In so doing, the implicit assumptions behind different ontologies and classifications require analysis. Object ontologies have gained increasing prominence as a consequence of object-oriented programming and sustained work by Barry Smith and his coworkers. GIS has also become the foundation to a new technique called *spatial intelligence* which, when openly delivered via the intranet, democratizes access to geographic and social network data.

Third Technology: Digital Orthoimagery (DOI)

Digital orthoimagery will be one of the most important geospatial Knowledge Bases used during the development of smart cities. Orthoimagery is a set of pictures of the Earth captured by aircraft equipped with digital or film cameras and processed to fit the Earth with high precision. DOI was traditionally used to provide an accurate visual grid-based map for measuring distances and has enough clarity to represent roads, structures, vegetation, and other features on the ground. But more importantly, during the emergence of smart cities, DOI became an indispensable *locality* tool for the critical infrastructures. First, a virtual grid covers the whole city. Then, all critical infrastructures from power plants, hospitals, emergency facilities, schools, banks, water system, airports, and transportation systems are identified on the grid by relative coordinates. The grid of the city might have 10,000 tiles, and each tile would be equivalent to an area of 1 km × 1 km. Each critical item would have coordinates (X, Y, Z), a criticality index, and many indicators related to connectivity, backup, security, and other blocks of data. Figure 3.8 illustrates how orthoimagery can be used to identify the locality of critical systems in the New Jersey area. All items are semantically stored in a Knowledge Base that is in turn connected to a Reasoning Engine for predictive analyses (this topic will be discussed in detail later).

Quantitative Assessment of Vulnerability of Critical Infrastructures

The objective of these doctrinal guidelines is to enable the user to produce sound and commensurable quantitative estimates of the vulnerability of the nation's critical infrastructure systems, assets, and resources. Adhering to these guidelines will allow the user to quantify risks so that they can be effectively compared across the critical infrastructure sectors.

The Department of Homeland Security (DHS) has been diligently trying to evaluate quantitatively the vulnerability of a cyberattack on the critical infrastructures and the consequence of miscellaneous attacks. In this section, we will look at the different

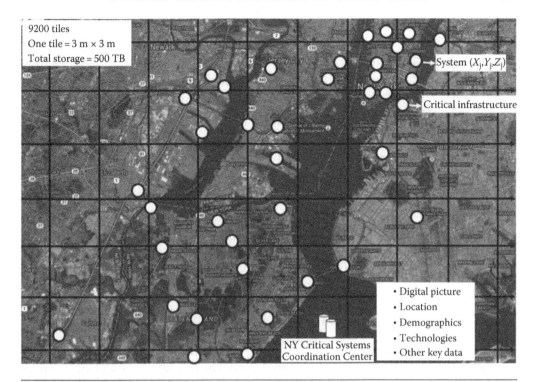

Figure 3.8 A descriptive 3D picture of the most critical infrastructures in the New York and New Jersey area. All data will be filtered and stored in a CEWPS (Smart Vaccine Knowledge Base). This is a great use of orthoimagery for the smart grid.

approaches that have been developed by the DOD, and DHS, as well as many universities which have been funded by the U.S. federal government. The Department of Homeland Security asked the Institute for Defense Analyses (IDA) to provide doctrinal guidelines for operationalizing a framework for quantifying risk, with a specific focus on quantitatively estimating the vulnerability of assets and systems comprising the nation's critical infrastructure.

In 2010, the Department of Homeland Security published an interesting document on terms and definitions called the *DHS Risk Lexicon* (2010 edition). This is the second edition of the DHS Risk Lexicon and represents an update of the version published in September 2008. More than 70 terms and definitions were included in the first edition; the 2010 edition includes 50 new terms and definitions in addition to the revised definitions of 23 of the original terms.

It was produced by the DHS Risk Steering Committee (RSC). The RSC, chaired by the Undersecretary for the National Protection and Programs Directorate and administered by the Office of Risk Management and Analysis (RMA), has produced a DHS Risk Lexicon with definitions for terms that are fundamental to the practice of homeland security risk management and analysis. The RSC created the Risk Lexicon Working Group (RLWG) to represent the DHS risk community of interest (COI) in the development of this professional risk lexicon.

The RSC is the risk governance structure for the DHS, with membership from across the department. All terms in the DHS Risk Lexicon were completed using this process and represent the collective work of the DHS risk COI. The DHS Risk Lexicon terms and definitions will be included as part of the DHS Lexicon, and future additions and revisions will be coordinated by the RSC and RLWG in collaboration with the DHS Lexicon Program.

The Lexicon is a 69-page document containing in detail all the security and vulnerability terms with examples (https://www.dhs.gov/xlibrary/assets/dhs-risk-lexicon-2010.pdf). We reviewed it and extracted some of its content that applies to this book.

Vulnerability, when used in a critical infrastructure homeland security context, is difficult to define because (1) various homeland security decision makers define and use metrics for vulnerability in different ways to support their decisions, and (2) cascading consequences, interdependencies, and systems issues can lead to computational complexities that make the idea and valuation of isolated vulnerabilities of little or no use to decision makers:

$$\text{Risk} = \frac{\text{Threat} \times \text{Vulnerability}}{\text{Countermeasures}} \times \text{Impact}$$

The risk equation that we use is quite simple: risk equals impact multiplied by probability weighed against the cost (risk = impact × probability/cost). Impact is the effect on the organization should a risk event occur. Probability is the likelihood (threat) the event could occur within a given time frame. Cost (countermeasures) is the amount it takes to mitigate or reduce the risk to an acceptable level.

Simplistically, we can say: risk is the *probability* that a *threat* will *exploit* a *vulnerability* to cause harm to an *asset*. This is represented by $R = f(T, V, A)$ where T = threat, V = vulnerability, and A = asset.

Vulnerability can also be defined as the conditional probability of success given an attack for a given scenario:

$$\text{Probability (Success|Attack)} = P(S|A)$$

Risk Computation

Commonly defined, *risk* is the potential for an unwanted outcome resulting from an incident, event, or occurrence, as determined by its likelihood and the associated consequences. Quantitatively, risk is estimated as the expected value of loss from one or more scenarios times the likelihood or frequency of those scenarios. A scenario describes an incident (attack, accident, or natural disaster) and what specifically is being attacked or affected. The probability or frequency of a scenario and the associated consequences are calculated with respect to a domain, which defines the extent of the effects of calculations. The domain is defined either geographically, or functionally (e.g., cascading, interdependent effects), or both. The domain also includes the time horizon (for example, immediate, 1 week, and 5 years).

As an example, consider a set of attack scenarios comprising cyberterrorists, using Stuxnet-like worm, to attack a grid of power plants that supplies energy to 5 million people in the metropolitan city, and the consequence estimates that include astronomical loss of the business, major logistic chaos, and a severe economic impact until conditions are normalized. Another example could be a set of scenarios involving hurricanes that strike the East Coast from June through November of a given year, and the domain could be the national electrical grid and the costs and economic consequences due to the associated large-scale power outages.

To compute a probabilistic risk assessment, a set of attack scenarios is specified. For each attack scenario, a probability of occurrence is determined and the *E*xpected *V*alue of the *C*onsequences (EVC) given the attack occurrence is calculated. The following relationship is a mathematical formula for a probabilistic risk assessment:

$$\text{Risk (Scenario } S, \text{Domain } D)$$

$$= \sum_{\text{Scenarios } S} P \text{ (Scenario } S, \text{Domain } D) * \text{EVC (Scenario } S, \text{Domain } D)$$

In case a quantitative risk metric is given to restrict the condition of the attack, then the risk of the attack becomes conditional. This is called the *conditional risk* associated with that attack. The conditional risk, defined as the expected value of loss given that the scenario occurs, is calculated as follows:

Conditional Risk = Probability that an attack is successful given that it occurs
× Consequences of the attack given that it is successful

or symbolically

Risk = P (successful Attack) * Impact of successful attack

When dealing with layered defenses, for example, in the power grid, then the probability of an attack successfully penetrating the outer layer of defense is not a condition of successfully penetrating any previous layer. For all layers of defense contained within this outer layer, the probabilities are a condition of the sequence of previously penetrated layers.

For example, in a two-layer defense—F_1 (firewall-1) and F_2 (firewall-2)—the joint probability of successfully penetrating both F_1 and F_2 is $P(F_1) \times P(F_2|F_1)$. That is, the unconditional probability of successfully penetrating F_1 is multiplied by the probability of successfully penetrating F_2, given that F_1 has been successfully penetrated. This general formula can be extended to accommodate multiple layers.

Supervisory Control and Data Acquisition (SCADA)

The SCADA system represents a wide range of protocols and technologies for monitoring and managing equipment and machinery in various sectors of critical infrastructure and industry. This includes, but is not limited to, power generation, manufacturing, oil and gas, water treatment, and waste management. The SCADA technologies and protocols are a concern related to national security because the disruption of these critical services would result in the failure of the related infrastructure and loss of life. The SCADA system will be discussed in detail in Chapter 10.

Stuxnet as Enemy Number 1 for Smart Grids

Stuxnet is the work of the devil impersonated by a group trying to destroy the nuclear reactors of Iran.

Response Planning and Preparedness

Can Infrastructures Be Secured by Smart Cities?

This is how deep the risk ocean is. Smart city planners cannot build a smart grid with vulnerable infrastructures. The risk is high and the emergency response during a calamity becomes another disaster. It is important to note that every event related to critical infrastructure is unique, leaving planners to face more unknowns than knowns, when it comes to response.

Response   The capabilities necessary to save lives, protect property and the environment, and meet basic human needs after an incident has occurred. But each time an infrastructure element fails, "it causes the emergency managers to reconsider all of their emergency response plans." Infrastructure failure is a moving target.

The situation is further compounded by the privatization of roughly 85% of the nation's most critical infrastructure systems. Infrastructure may encompass varied forms. The U.S. government classified the national infrastructures into 16 categories. In contemplating this extremely wide range of possible sources of calamity, emergency managers must work through a delicate dance with private owners of infrastructure.

When the infrastructure is becoming fatigued, the private sector has a financial interest to ensure its critical components are sound. While the public sector is notoriously underfunded and behind on its upgrades in many jurisdictions, it is obvious from the risk assessment that the public side is more vulnerable and has higher risk.

Responding to a critical infrastructure disaster is not just a two-way street—public to private. It is an every-way street. It is in the nature of critical systems to be enmeshed and intertwined with a whole host of other systems and processes. A burst dam causes a flood, which takes down power, which kills the phones. Meanwhile roads wash away. The ripple effect can be staggering to emergency responders.

Infrastructure Disaster Preparedness   The acid test of preparedness is painful. Learning from past experience will definitely help in disaster preparedness. But how do we test the preparedness for the smart grid for the first time?

The first thing we need to know is the sources of smart grid disaster risk. The second thing is to make the appropriate investments now to mitigate risk in the future. And the third thing is to establish a level of trust ahead of time between the public and private sectors. The deployment of the smart grid requires leadership and tremendous knowledge in disaster causality.

It is interesting that when we compare preparedness to human immunity we find the same pattern.

The National Response Framework (NRF) (http://www.fema.gov/media-library/assets/documents/97352) is a guide on how the nation responds to all types of disasters and emergencies. It is built on scalable, flexible, and adaptable concepts identified in the National Incident Management System (NIMS) to align key roles and responsibilities across the nation. This framework describes specific authorities and best practices for managing incidents that range from the serious but purely local to large-scale terrorist attacks or catastrophic natural disasters. The National Response Framework describes the principles, roles and responsibilities, and coordinating structures for delivering the core capabilities required to respond to an incident and further describes how response efforts integrate with those of the other mission areas.

NRF incident annexes describe coordinating structures, in addition to the Emergency Support Functions (ESF), which may be used to deliver core capabilities and support response missions that are unique to a specific type of incident. Incident annexes also describe specialized response teams and resources, incident-specific roles and responsibilities, and other scenario-specific considerations. NRF incident annexes address the following contingencies or hazards:

- Biological incidents
- Catastrophic incidents
- Cyber incidents
- Food and agriculture incidents
- Mass evacuation incidents
- Nuclear/radiological incidents
- Terrorism incidents, law enforcement and investigations

National Operations Center (NOC): In the event of an act of terrorism, natural disaster, or other emergency, the National Operations Center is the principal operations center for the Department of Homeland Security.

National Response Coordination Center (NRCC): When activated, the NRCC is a multiagency coordination center located at FEMA headquarters.

National Military Command Center (NMCC): DOD's NMCC is the nation's focal point for continuous monitoring and coordination of worldwide military operations.

Strategic Information and Operations Center (SIOC): The SIOC acts as the FBI's worldwide EOC.

Operations Research

Operations research (OR), also known as the *science of better*, can be described as a scientific approach leading to effective solutions of problems in the management of complex systems including distributed and preemptive cyberattacks. OR is used to produce powerful results in business, industry, and government to decrease cost, increase revenue or return on investment, manage and reduce risk, improve quality, increase throughput while decreasing delays, and improve utilization of limited resources. In practice, operations research is a team effort, requiring close collaboration between decision makers, OR analysts, and other stakeholders. Operations research comes with a rich portfolio of tools to solve practically any operational problem. Of course in our case, we will focus on the development of better predictive models to combat complex cyberattacks.

- Optimization through linear and nonlinear programming and integer programming
- Network scheduling
- Dynamic programming
- Waiting line or queuing theory
- Game theory
- Inventory control models
- Simulation
- Sequencing theory
- Markov and stochastic processes
- Decision analysis and utility/value theory
- Definition of key performance and effectiveness measures
- Life cycle cost estimation and return on investment
- Development of asset maintenance and enhancement strategies
- Creation of resource allocation, operations plans, and budgets

Modeling the Grid Using Queuing Theory

In the mainframe era, computer performance management (CPM) and capacity planning (CP) were a great challenge for the data processing department or data centers. The Internet was not born yet, and the phone companies were making fortunes by charging premium price for telecommunication networks and phone lines. Remote users had to use modem and slave terminals to connect to the central computer. There was no other choice. In fact, the Internet revolution started—like any other societal revolution, due to the abuse of the data processing department where users were at the mercy of the operation managers. Big corporations, airline companies, retailers and government, and health care institutions had centralized data centers and controlled the information world. Remote users had dumb terminals and they would connect to the data center through slow modem. The response time was not impressive, and users were lucky to get their reports on time.

Today, with cyber freedom, users are in the driving seat, and the age of central data processing has become "dinosaurish." Ironically speaking, Internet service providers (ISP) have the control of delivering Internet services, and instead of using large water-cooled mainframes, they use server blades by the millions. The Internet inventors (Vinton Cerf, Tim Berners-Lee, Robert Kahn, Leonard Kleinrock, Ray Tomlinson, Bob Metcalfe) could not believe the monster they created. Refer to the following site for a historical review of the Internet: http://en.wikipedia.org/wiki/History_of_the_Internet.

However, all scientific applications, mathematical formulas, and analytical methods remained the same, and the term operations research (OR) adopted a new term, *management science and analytics.* Queuing theory (QT) remained the elegant science used to combat unpleasant waiting lines, traffic queues and gridlocks, and emergency response, and of course in Telecom. Now that the smart grid is the backbone of smart cities, and its performance has become pivotal.

Smart Grid Information Traffic Analysis

The smart grid is an incredible information highway that connects all the critical infrastructures and a big variety of commercial and residential applications that are all running simultaneously. Traffic needs to be constantly monitored and evaluated. As there are different traffic types with different quality of service requirements in the smart grid, we differentiated five classes of traffic:

Class 1: *Level 1 Transactions*—These are assigned to high-priority real-time traffic such as security Smart Vaccine messages, alerts, warning messages, real-time monitoring, and control with SCADA systems.

Class 2: *Level 2 Transactions*—These include systems that critically control processes on the smart grid.

Class 3: *Level 3 Transactions*—Surveillance cameras and emergency connectivity through mobile base stations are some sample applications.

Class 4: *Level 4 Transactions*—These include metering data and event notification.

Class 5: *Level 5 Transactions*—These include broadband voice telephony, multimedia transactions, and social media.

The smart grid is tied to 16 critical infrastructures, each critical infrastructure could have a dozen computer systems and each computer system may have several applications with several users per application. The smart grid is a nebulous service facility. As a result, modeling the smart grid for performance becomes necessary.

Using the smart metering system, customer will be able to be informed about the current price of electric energy. Whenever the energy is too expensive, they can turn

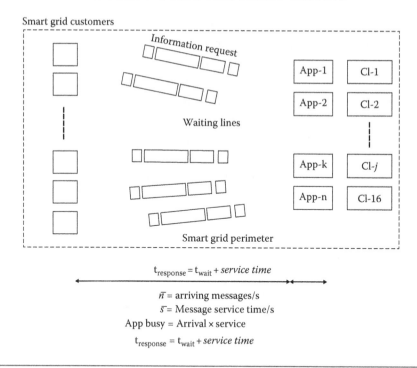

Figure 3.9   Simplistic view of the smart grid service model characterized as a multiserver with each application belongs to a unique Critical Infrastructure (CI) with its own waiting line.

off some electrical appliances to reduce their total energy consumption. So by using the smart grid, customers are able to manage their electrical use to minimize their costs.

The smart grid can be described as a multiservice facility serving transactions coming from five different sources. The smart grid is represented in the simple diagram in Figure 3.9.

Analytics of a Cyberattack on the Smart Grid

Queuing theory (QT) is the favorite mathematical tool for the people who work in modeling the performance of cybersecurity. We will use it to model cyberattacks, predict insider threats, construct preemptive attack scenarios, and most importantly, formulate strategies on how to predictively *respond* to surprise attacks and eliminate them altogether. Unfortunately, we are not there yet. The diagram in Figure 3.10 demonstrates the difference between a reactive response and a predictive response.

The top layer shows *scenario-1*, which is the conventional attack: the criminal plans the attack, rehearses it, and assesses the risk. Then he or she conducts the attack from his Internet Protocol (IP) stealth station. The victim organization, depending on the severity of the attack, will suffer physical damages and will endure agonizing morale problems on the top of confusion. In the case of an infrastructure, the damage will initially be in the

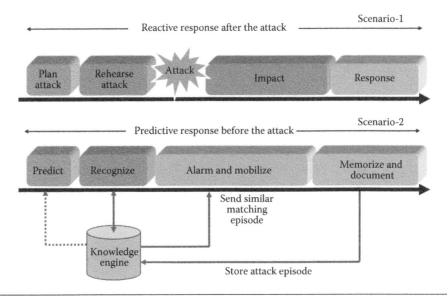

Figure 3.10   Reactive response versus predictive response.

computer which will lose control of the physical operation, and the damage will be transferred to the physical facility.

The lower layer shows *scenario-2*, which shows the predictive approach utilized in the Cognitive Early Warning Predictive System (CEWPS) that replicates the Human Immune System. The whole pivotal concept is that postmortem is not appealing anymore and premortem, by predictive analyses, is the only way to save the world from malware. The whole book will be explaining this concept and how it will work.

Queuing Formulas

Partial Universal Queuing Equations Used in CEWPS

These are universal formulas used by industrial engineers, system performance analysts, transportation planners, intersection traffic light designers, and by emergency departments and paramedics to optimize arrival time. Predictive analysts also resort to these formulas to study Big Data access time. We are using these formulas to determine the arrival time of the Smart Vaccine to the location of the attack. Then we will be able to calibrate the performance with many assumptions until we meet the optimum results.

λ is the arrival rate of the attack
μ is the service rate of the vaccinator
ρ is the λ/μ utilization of the Smart Vaccine commander
C is the number of vaccinators used
M is the random arrival/service rate (Poisson)
D is the deterministic service rate (constant rate)

M/D/1 Case (Random Arrival, Deterministic Service, and One Service Channel)

$$\text{Expected average queue length:} \; E(m) = \frac{(2\rho - \rho 2)}{2\,(1-\rho)}$$

$$\text{Expected average total time:} \; E(v) = 2 - \frac{\rho}{2}\mu(1-\rho)$$

$$\text{Expected average waiting time:} \; E(w) = \frac{\rho}{2}\mu(1-\rho)$$

M/M/1 Case (Random Arrival, Random Service, and One Service Channel)

The probability of having zero vehicles in the system: $P_o = 1 - \rho$.

The probability of having n attacks on the smart grid: $P_n = \rho_n P_o$.

$$\text{Expected average queue length:} \; E(m) = \frac{\rho}{(1-\rho)}$$

$$\text{Expected average total time:} \; E(v) = \frac{\rho}{\lambda}(1-\rho)$$

$$\text{Expected average waiting time:} \; E(w) = E(v) - \frac{1}{\mu}$$

M/M/C Case (Random Arrival, Random Service, and C Service Channel)

Expected average queue length:

$$E(m) = P_o \frac{\rho^{c+1}}{cc!}\frac{1}{(1-\rho/c)^2}$$

$$\text{Expected average number in the systems:} \; E(n) = E(m) + \rho$$

$$\text{Expected average total time:} \; E(v) = \frac{E(n)}{\lambda}$$

$$\text{Expected average waiting time:} \; E(w) = E(v) - \frac{1}{\mu}$$

Glossary: Smart Grid

AMI: Advanced metering infrastructure is a term denoting electricity meters that measure and record usage data at a minimum, in hourly intervals, and provide usage data to both consumers and energy companies at least once daily.

AMR: Automated meter reading is a term denoting electricity meters that collect data for billing purposes only and transmit these data in one way, usually from the customer to the distribution utility.

Ancillary services: Services that ensure reliability and support the transmission of electricity from generation sites to customer loads. Such services may include load regulation, spinning reserve, nonspinning reserve, replacement reserve, and voltage support.

Appliance: A piece of equipment, commonly powered by electricity, used to perform a particular energy-driven function. Examples of common appliances are refrigerators, clothes washers and dishwashers, conventional ranges/ovens and microwave ovens, humidifiers and dehumidifiers, toasters, radios, and televisions. Note: Appliances are ordinarily self-contained with respect to their function. Thus, equipment such as central heating and air-conditioning systems and water heaters, which are connected to distribution systems inherent to their purposes, are not considered appliances.

Capital cost: The cost of field development and plant construction and the equipment required for industry operations.

Carbon dioxide (CO_2): A colorless, odorless, nonpoisonous gas that is a normal part of Earth's atmosphere. Carbon dioxide is a product of fossil-fuel combustion as well as other processes. It is considered a greenhouse gas as it traps heat (infrared energy) radiated by Earth into the atmosphere and thereby contributes to the potential for global warming. The global warming potential (GWP) of other greenhouse gases is measured in relation to that of carbon dioxide, which by international scientific convention is assigned a value of one (1).

Carbon footprint: A carbon footprint is the measure of the environmental impact of a particular organization's operation, measured in units of carbon dioxide.

Carbon neutral: To be considered carbon neutral, an individual or organization must reduce its carbon footprint to zero.

Carbon offset: Credits achieved through financial support of projects that reduce the emission of greenhouse gases.

Carbon trading: Practice of purchasing carbon offsets in order to advertise a building, organization or event as being *carbon neutral*. Practice is regulated in countries that signed the Kyoto Protocol. Carbon trading in the United States is not overseen by industry-wide standards or certification.

Climate change: A term used to refer to all forms of climatic inconsistency, but especially to significant change from one prevailing climatic condition to another.

In some cases, *climate change* has been used synonymously with the term *global warming*; scientists, however, tend to use the term in a wider sense inclusive of natural changes in climate, including climatic cooling.

Compressed air energy storage: A way to store massive amounts of renewable power by compressing air at very high pressures and storing it in large underground caverns, depleted wells, or aquifers.

Congestion: A condition that occurs when insufficient transfer capacity is available to implement all of the preferred schedules for electricity transmission simultaneously.

Demand-side management (DSM): This demand-side management category represents the amount of consumer load reduction at the time of system peak due to utility programs that reduce consumer load during many hours of the year. Examples include utility rebate and shared savings activities for the installation of energy-efficient appliances, lighting and electrical machinery, and weatherization materials. In addition, this category includes all other Demand-side management activities, such as thermal storage, time-of-use rates, fuel substitution, measurement and evaluation, and any other utility-administered Demand-side management activity designed to reduce demand and/or electricity use.

Distributed generator: A generator that is located close to the particular load that it is intended to serve. General, but nonexclusive, characteristics of these generators include an operating strategy that supports the served load and interconnection to a distribution or subtransmission system.

Distribution: The delivery of energy to retail customers.

Distribution system: The portion of the transmission and facilities of an electric system that is dedicated to delivering electric energy to an end user.

Electric generation industry: Stationary and mobile generating units that are connected to the electric power grid and can generate electricity. The electric generation industry includes the *electric power sector* (utility generators and independent power producers) and industrial and commercial power generators, including combined heat-and-power producers, but excludes units at single-family dwellings.

Electric generator: A facility that produces only electricity, commonly expressed in kilowatt-hours (kWh) or megawatt hours (MWh). Electric generators include electric utilities and independent power producers.

Electric grid: A network of synchronized power providers and consumers that are connected by transmission and distribution lines and operated by one or more control centers. When most people talk about the power *grid*, they are referring to the transmission system for electricity.

Electric power: The rate at which electric energy is transferred. Electric power is measured by capacity and is commonly expressed in megawatts (MW). A megawatt (MW) is 1 million watts.

Electric power grid: A system of synchronized power providers and consumers connected by transmission and distribution lines and operated by one or more control centers. In the continental United States, the electric power grid consists of three systems: the Eastern Interconnection, the Western Interconnection, and the Texas Interconnection. In Alaska and Hawaii, several systems encompass areas smaller than the state (e.g., the interconnect serving Anchorage, Fairbanks, and the Kenai Peninsula; individual islands).

Electric system reliability: The degree to which the performance of the elements of the electrical system results in power being delivered to consumers within accepted standards and in the amount desired. Reliability encompasses two concepts, adequacy and security Adequacy implies that there are sufficient generation and transmission resources installed and available to meet projected electrical demand plus reserves for contingencies. Security implies that the system will remain intact operationally (i.e., will have sufficient available operating capacity) even after outages or other equipment failure. The degree of reliability may be measured by the frequency, duration, and magnitude of adverse effects on consumer service.

Electric utility: Any entity that generates, transmits, or distributes electricity and recovers the cost of its generation, transmission, or distribution assets and operations, either directly or indirectly, through cost-based rates set by a separate regulatory authority (e.g., State Public Service Commission), or is owned by a governmental unit or the consumers that the entity serves. Examples of these entities include investor-owned entities, public power districts, public utility districts, municipalities, rural electric cooperatives, and state and federal agencies.

Electricity congestion: A condition that occurs when insufficient transmission capacity is available to implement all of the desired transactions simultaneously.

Electricity demand: The rate at which energy is delivered to loads and scheduling points by generation, transmission, and distribution facilities.

Energy efficiency, electricity: Refers to programs that are aimed at reducing the energy used by specific end-use devices and systems, typically without affecting the services provided. These programs reduce overall electricity consumption (reported in megawatt hours), often without explicit consideration for the timing of program-induced savings. Such savings are generally achieved by substituting technologically more advanced equipment to produce the same level of end-use services (e.g., lighting, heating, motor drive) with less electricity. Examples include high-efficiency appliances, efficient lighting programs, high-efficiency heating, ventilating and air-conditioning (HVAC) systems or control modifications, efficient building design, advanced electric motor drives, and heat recovery systems.

Energy savings: A reduction in the amount of electricity used by end users as a result of participation in energy-efficiency programs and load management programs.

Energy service provider: An energy entity that provides service to a retail or end-use customer.

FERC: The Federal Energy Regulatory Commission is a federal agency with jurisdiction over interstate electricity sales, wholesale electric rates, hydroelectric licensing, natural gas pricing, oil pipeline rates, and gas pipeline certification. FERC is an independent regulatory agency within the Department of Energy and is the successor to the Federal Power Commission.

Fuel cell: A device capable of generating an electrical current by converting the chemical energy of a fuel (e.g., hydrogen) directly into electrical energy. Fuel cells differ from conventional electrical cells in that the active materials such as fuel and oxygen are not contained within the cell but are supplied from outside. It does not contain an intermediate heat cycle, as do most other electrical generation techniques.

Generation: The process of producing electric energy by transforming other forms of energy; also, the amount of electric energy produced, expressed in kilowatt-hours.

Global warming: An increase in the near surface temperature of Earth. Global warming has occurred in the distant past as a result of natural influences, but the term is today most often used to refer to the warming some scientists predict will occur as a result of increased anthropogenic emissions of greenhouse gases.

Greenhouse gases: Those gases, such as water vapor, carbon dioxide, nitrous oxide, methane, hydrofluorocarbons (HFCs), perfluorocarbons (PFCs), and sulfur hexafluoride, which are transparent to solar (short-wave) radiation but opaque to long-wave (infrared) radiation, thus preventing longwave radiant energy from leaving Earth's atmosphere. The net effect is a trapping of absorbed radiation's surface.

Intermittent electric generator or intermittent resource: An electric generating plant with output controlled by the natural variability of the energy resource rather than dispatched based on system requirements. Intermittent output usually results from the direct, nonstored conversion of naturally occurring energy fluxes such as solar energy, wind energy, or the energy of free-flowing rivers (that is, run of river).

Interruptible load: This demand-side management category represents the consumer load that, in accordance with contractual arrangements, can be interrupted at the time of annual peak load by the action of the consumer at the direct request of the system operator. This type of control usually involves large-volume commercial and industrial consumers. Interruptible load does not include direct load control.

Line loss: Electric energy lost because of the transmission of electricity. Much of the loss is thermal in nature.

Load (electric): The amount of electric power delivered or required at any specific point or points on a system. The requirement originates at the energy-consuming equipment of the consumers.

Load control program: A program in which the utility company offers a lower rate in return for having permission to turn off the air conditioner or water heater for short periods of time by remote control. This control allows the utility to reduce peak demand.

NERC: North American Electric Reliability Corporation, an institution that oversees and regulates the reliability of the North American electrical grids.

Off peak: Period of relatively low system demand. These periods often occur in daily, weekly, and seasonal patterns; these off-peak periods differ for each individual electric utility.

On peak: Periods of relatively high system demand. These periods often occur in daily, weekly, and seasonal patterns; these on-peak periods differ for each individual electric utility.

Outage: The period during which a generating unit, transmission line, or other facility is out of service.

Peak demand or peak load: The maximum load during a specified period of time.

Peaker plant or peak load plant: A plant usually housing old, low-efficiency steam units, gas turbines, diesels, or pumped-storage hydroelectric equipment normally used during the peak-load periods.

Peaking capacity: Capacity of generating equipment normally reserved for operation during the hours of highest daily, weekly, or seasonal loads. Some generating equipment may be operated at certain times as peaking capacity and at other times to serve loads on an around-the-clock basis.

Rate base: The value of property upon which a utility is permitted to earn a specified rate of return as established by a regulatory authority. The rate base generally represents the value of property used by the utility in providing service and may be calculated by any one or a combination of the following accounting methods: fair value, prudent investment, reproduction cost, or original cost. Depending on which method is used, the rate base includes cash, working capital, materials and supplies, deductions for accumulated provisions for depreciation, contributions in aid of construction, customer advances for construction, accumulated deferred income taxes, and accumulated deferred investment tax credits.

Rate case: A proceeding, usually before a regulatory commission, involving the rates to be charged for a public utility service.

Rate features: Special rate schedules or tariffs offered to customers by electric and/or natural gas utilities.

Rate of return: The ratio of net operating income earned by a utility is calculated as a percentage of its rate base.

Rate of return on rate base: The ratio of net operating income earned by a utility, calculated as a percentage of its rate base.

Rate schedule (electric): A statement of the financial terms and conditions governing a class or classes of utility services provided to a customer. Approval of the schedule is given by the appropriate ratemaking authority.

Ratemaking authority: A utility commission's legal authority to fix, modify, approve, or disapprove rates as determined by the powers given the commission by a state or federal legislature.

Rates: The authorized charges per unit or level of consumption for a specified time period for any of the classes of utility services provided to a customer.

Reliability (electric system): A measure of the ability of the system to continue operation while some lines or generators are out of service. Reliability deals with the performance of the system under stress.

Renewable energy resources: Energy resources that are naturally replenishing but flow limited. They are virtually inexhaustible in duration but limited in the amount of energy that is available per unit of time. Renewable energy resources include biomass; hydrothermal; geothermal; solar, wind, and ocean thermal; wave action; and tidal action.

Solar energy: The radiant energy of Sun, which can be converted into other forms of energy, such as heat or electricity.

Smart grid: A generic label for the application of computer intelligence and networking abilities to a dumb electricity distribution system.

Tariff: A published volume of rate schedules and general terms and conditions under which a product or service will be supplied.

Thermal energy storage: The storage of heat energy during utility off-peak times at night, for use during the next day without incurring daytime peak electric rates.

Thermal limit: The maximum amount of power a transmission line can carry without suffering heat-related deterioration of line equipment, particularly conductors.

Time-of-day pricing: A special electric rate feature under which the price per kilowatt-hour depends on the time of day.

Time-of-day rate: The rate charged by an electric utility for service to various classes of customers. The rate reflects the different costs of providing the service at different times of the day.

Transmission and distribution loss: Electric energy lost due to the transmission and distribution of electricity. Much of the loss is thermal in nature.

Transmission (electric) (verb): The movement or transfer of electric energy over an interconnected group of lines and associated equipment between points of supply and points at which it is transformed for delivery to consumers or is delivered to other electric systems. Transmission is considered to end when the energy is transformed for distribution to the consumer.

Utility generation: Generation by electric systems engaged in selling electric energy to the public.

Utility-sponsored conservation program: Any program sponsored by an electric and/or natural gas utility to review equipment and construction features in buildings and advise on ways to increase the energy efficiency of buildings. Also included are utility-sponsored programs to encourage the use of more energy-efficient equipment. Included are programs to improve the energy efficiency in the lighting system or building equipment or the thermal efficiency of the building shell.

Wind energy: Kinetic energy present in wind motion that can be converted to mechanical energy for driving pumps, mills, and electric power generators.

Websites

http://en.wikipedia.org/wiki/Area_51.
http://www.cert.org/.
http://www.dewa.gov.ae/default.aspx.
http://www.dhs.gov/protected-critical-infrastructure-information-pcii-program.
http://www.emergencymgmt.com/safety/Crumbling-Infrastructure-Challenge-Emergency-Managers.html?page=2.
http://www.fastcoexist.com/1679127/the-top-10-smart-cities-on-the-planet.
http://www.gao.gov/assets/670/662901.pdf.
http://www.gao.gov/products/GAO-08-588.
http://www.nationaldefensemagazine.org/archive/2011/June/Pages/WhoisResponsiblefor Cybersecurity.aspx.
http://www.sciencedirect.com/science/article/pii/S2090123214000290.
http://www.sdimedia.com/location/israel/.
http://www.symantec.com/content/en/us/enterprise/other_resources/b-istr_appendices_v19_221284438.en-us.pdf.
https://www.smartgrid.gov/lexicon/6/letter_a
https://www.us-cert.gov/ncas.

4

STATE OF THE ART OF ANTIVIRUS AND CEWPS TECHNOLOGIES

Historical Synopsis

During the mainframe era, the antivirus never existed. At the very least, users were not involved in cleaning their terminals. The Central Data Processing Department had to take the system down and do the cleaning. Terms like *corrupt files, tracking cookies, worms,* and *Trojans* never existed. In fact the term *virus* was not born yet until the days of the first PCs in 1982. On MS-DOS, contamination took place through floppy disks only.

While there is some contention about who actually made the first overtly harmful computer virus, it is fairly well accepted (though sometimes challenged) that Bernd Fix developed the first antivirus software in 1987. Fix, a German astrophysicist and amateur computer programmer (at the time), developed software to combat the first computer virus *in the wild*, which means that the virus had escaped the confines of the lab or network in which it was created (which was only done via floppy disk at that time).

Virus Hall of Infamy

The first PC virus, *Brain*, appeared in 1986. It was a boot sector virus that works by modifying the first sector on floppy disks. The infected floppy executes and loads its code into memory, as soon as it is loaded. It does not have to be a system disk: any disk will do. The software called BIOS detects the disk in drive A and automatically loads whatever infected code is in the boot sector. The user realizes they have tried to boot from a floppy disk by mistake when they see the message "*Nonsystem disk or disk error, replace and press any key when ready.*" They then remove the disk and continue working, suspecting nothing about what has just happened. The malicious code is already in the RAM waiting for the kill.

You may have heard of the newly discovered *Flame* virus in recent days. According to the *Washington Post* (June 19, 2012), "The United States and Israel jointly developed a sophisticated computer virus nicknamed Flame that collected intelligence in preparation for cyber sabotage aimed at slowing Iran's ability to develop a nuclear weapon."

Security experts think it is likely that a government created the Flame virus—not to target average citizens but to be utilized for cyber espionage. From the investigation of Kaspersky Lab, it was discovered that the virus has an MD5 (message-digest 5) encryptor function that generates a 128-bit (16-byte) hash to hide the virus that was built to disrupt Iran's ability to develop a nuclear weapon. The sophisticated virus has been circulating almost exclusively in the Middle East and appears to be targeted at Iran.

In 2010, a computer virus called *Stuxnet* made headlines for making the centrifuges in Iran used to enrich uranium spin out of control. Now there is Flame and Roel Schouwenberg of Kaspersky Labs—the security firm that discovered the virus—claims it makes Stuxnet look like child's play. "Flame is 20 times the size of Stuxnet, which again shows the kind of manpower and man hours that has been put into this project," Schouwenberg said.

Flame basically turns computers into spies—giving them the ability to log keystrokes, take screenshots of a machine, and even enable the microphone to record conversations.

No one knows for sure who created the virus but if the United States was involved, Flame was likely the work of the National Security Agency (NSA), whose mission is to eavesdrop on communications.

The following is a list of notorious attacks that created major global disruption, which caused severe financial damages:

Melissa: Named after a stripper in Miami, this macro virus caused the most damage in 1999. In its wake, Melissa caused so much e-mail traffic that companies such as Intel and Microsoft were forced to close down their e-mail services. At the heart of the virus was a Word document, called List.DOC, which was sent as an attachment and, once opened, provided access to porn sites. The virus is said to have infected up to 20% of computers worldwide.

SQL Slammer: Also known as *Sapphire*, in January 2003, this virus targeted Microsoft's SQL Server and Desktop Engine database software, initiating distributed denial-of-service (DDoS) attacks on various targets. Within minutes of infecting the first server, Slammer began doubling its number of infected machines every few seconds. The effects of this virus had an impact on real-world situations. The Bank of America suffered ATM outages, the city of Seattle was unable to take 911 calls for a period, and customers traveling via Continental Airlines experienced ticketing and check-in issues. The virus is estimated to have caused around $1 billion of damages in total.

Sasser/Netsky, May 2004: Commonly known as one of the most famous outbreaks ever to make the news, Sasser and Netsky are famous not only for their astonishing effectiveness but also for the fact that they have been traced back to a then 17-year-old German teenager named Sven Jaschan. Sasser and Netsky are separate viruses, and it was the similarities in the code that initially linked them both to the same individual.

Storm Worm, 2007: Originally distributed in e-mail messages containing the subject *230 dead as storm batters Europe*, the Storm Worm (as it became known) is a nasty Trojan horse that would further infect a user's machine with malware once active. While Storm Worm is the name that has stuck, the virus has been seen masquerading behind other news-inspired subject lines. E-mails infected with the worm contained an executable attachment. Once run, further malware may be installed, and the infected computer will become part of a botnet—a network of remotely controllable PCs (Zombies). By September 2007, it was believed that anywhere 1–10 million computers were infected and part of the Storm botnet, but due to the way that computers communicate, gauging the size is impossible without access to the control server.

CryptoLocker: In early September 2013, several antivirus and information security companies began receiving reports of a new piece of malware that was spreading across the net quickly. The so-called CryptoLocker virus belonged to the group of malware called *ransomware*. It threatens to hijack your computer or data and hold it for ransom unless a payment is made to the creators of the virus. While this type of malware has always been fairly common, with plenty of examples espousing fake messages from the Federal Bureau of Investigation (FBI) or the CIA or the NSA, CryptoLocker stood apart because of its ability to follow through on the promise of making your files completely inaccessible unless the ransom was paid.

What makes CryptoLocker different from most older ransomware malware is its use of asymmetric key cryptography. This form of encryption, long the gold standard for most common encryption applications, uses a key pair composed of a public key and a private key. The public key is used to encrypt the data, while the private one decrypts it. CryptoLocker uses a public key generated from a unique ID to encrypt all files on your computer that end in popularly used extensions, including images, PDF files, and documents.

Anatomy of a Biological (Human) Virus

Not to be amused by it, the *Curse of the Pharaohs* until today is still being observed by some strong believers who trust that it brings a biological causality. The curse also referred to as the *Egyptian Curse* believed to be affecting any person with greedy curiosity. Ironically, this solemn invisible damn does not differentiate between thieves and archaeologists. A priori stories about the unfortunate fatalities described bad luck, followed by illness or death. Since the mid-twentieth century, many authors and documentaries have argued that the curse is *real* in the sense of being created by scientifically explicable causes such as dormant virus, bacteria, or radiation. However, the modern origins of Egyptian mummy curse tales shifted from magic to science to explain curses. Interestingly enough, the virus existed since the dawn of life, but it was considered a religious taboo caused by wrath of gods. So far, the people who died from the curse could not lie. The people who survive it did view it as *unadulterated clap trap*. We will leave it to the discretion of the reader.

Originally, the term *virus* came from Latin referring to *poison* and other noxious substances. In biology, a virus is an infective microorganism that typically consists of a nucleus that contains a DNA or RNA strand surrounded by protein shell to bond to host cell. A virus is too small to be seen by light microscopy and is able to multiply only within the living cells that will harbor them as host. Viruses are also referred to as pathogen (suffering generator) because they are infectious agents and produce diseases. We may consider a pathogen as a ticking bomb that will explode and empty its payload when the environment is suitable. Diseases are caused by *opportunistic* pathogens that penetrate the human body, as predators, and create havoc. They multiply and create clones and strategically proliferate and start attacking healthy cells. History has recorded incredible pathogenic fights between smallpox, influenza, mumps, measles, AIDS, and Ebola diseases. The human body has an incredible immune system that demonstrated superiority in defense by offense. This book is about how we can replicate the Human Immune System and apply it to the digital world. Learning about our virus world will give us great advantage to defeat the digital counterpart.

Figure 4.1 shows how a virus looks under the microscope. The autonomy of a virus consists of three parts: (1) the genetic material made from either DNA or RNA, (2) a protein coat that protects these genes, and (3) an envelope that surrounds the protein coat when they are outside a cell. The shapes of viruses can be helical and spherical. The average virus is about one-hundredth the size of the average bacterium. Most viruses are too small to be seen directly with an optical microscope.

It was noticed during the eighteenth century that people who had suffered from the less virulent cowpox were immune to smallpox. People did not have any idea about the vaccine. Incidentally, a farmer by the name of Benjamin Jesty at Yetminster had

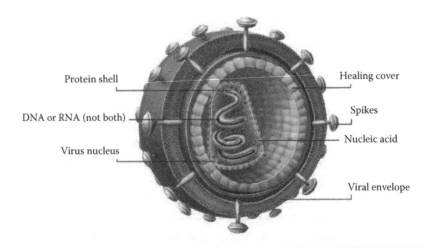

Figure 4.1   Viruses are not plants, animals, or bacteria, but they are the quintessential parasites of the living kingdom. Although they may seem like living organisms because of their prodigious reproductive abilities, viruses are not living organisms in the strict sense of the word.

suffered the disease and transmitted it to his own family in 1774. The mild version of smallpox acted as inoculation and saved the lives of his sons.

It was Edward Jenner, a doctor in Berkeley, who established the procedure by introducing a material from a cowpox vesicle on Sarah Nelmes, a milkmaid, into the arm of a boy named James Phipps. Two months later, he inoculated the boy with smallpox and the disease did not develop. Louis Pasteur is another vaccination pioneer who risked his life with rabies, but in the end he created the water of life with his vaccine.

Unlike human cells or bacteria, viruses do not contain the chemical machinery (*enzymes*) needed to carry out the chemical reactions for life. Instead, viruses carry only one or two enzymes that decode their genetic instructions. So, a virus must have a *host cell* (bacteria, plant, or animal) to live and make more viruses. Outside of a host cell, viruses cannot function. For this reason, viruses tread the fine line that separates living things from nonliving things. Most scientists agree that viruses are alive because of what happens when they infect a host cell.

Figure 4.2 shows a sequence diagram of how a virus miraculously attacks the healthy body cells (host cells). It is an incredible holy war that goes on in our body. More advances in immunology and nanobiology have made us healthier. This is why

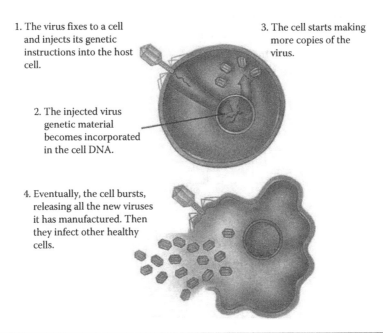

1. The virus fixes to a cell and injects its genetic instructions into the host cell.

2. The injected virus genetic material becomes incorporated in the cell DNA.

3. The cell starts making more copies of the virus.

4. Eventually, the cell bursts, releasing all the new viruses it has manufactured. Then they infect other healthy cells.

Figure 4.2   Once inside the host cell, the viral enzymes begin making copies of the viral genetic instructions and new viral proteins using the virus's genetic instructions and the cell's enzyme machinery. The new copies of the viral genetic instructions are packaged inside the new protein coat to make new viruses. Once the new viruses are made, they leave the host cell in one of two ways: (1) They break the host cell open after they destroy the host cell. (2) They pinch out from the host cell membrane and break away with a piece of the cell membrane surrounding them. This is how enveloped viruses leave the cell. In this way, the host cell is not destroyed. Once free from the host cell, the new viruses can attack other cells. Because one virus can reproduce thousands of new viruses, viral infections can spread quickly throughout the body.

replicating the same concept in the digital world will make us catch up with cyber malware. We are on the right track.

Anatomy of a Digital Virus

A digital virus is the most important diabolical invention of the twenty-first century. It is the mastery of a new breed of creative *nerds of the third kind*, who can hatch an ingenious piece of code to create a technological holocaust for millions of people. These goons can do it for money or for political or religious reasons. They surpass the intelligence of a rocket scientist and challenge the perseverance of a rock climber. Hackers and hacking syndrome will be discussed throughout the book. Figure 4.3 illustrates the temple of critical infrastructure terrorism showing an assortment of malware that would make any terrorist drool while selecting his next apocalyptic mayhem.

Hackers are truly nasty cyber snipers, who sit behind their magic tunes and with pleasure shoot at a company, or a complete city, or even the whole nation. An act of soft violence, hackers come in two categories: *category-1*—the smart hacker and *category-2*—the smarter hacker. The business is immorally prosperous carrying a price tag of $100 billion a year. It is not an underground business anymore. Companies use it to spy on one's competitors. Governments resort to it to bring down hostile regimes. Hacking ushers the dawn of the information war. The repertoire of malware is more impressive than the Louvre Museum!

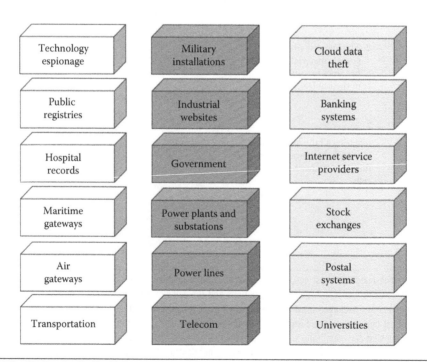

Figure 4.3   The temple of critical infrastructure terrorism.

Simplistically, the sky is the limit when it comes to building a potent virus. Nobody knows how many types of viruses exist in the digital world. It is like the classic saying "if you can measure it, you can control it."

Anyone can write an evil code and throw it onto the information highway. According to the Internet World Stats, at www.internetworldstats.com, the population of Internet users in the world, as of September 2014 was 2,802,478,934! This roughly comes out as 2.4 of the world's population of 7,181,858,619. The yearly penetration rate into the Internet is truly impressive with 39%. With such an accelerated adoption rate, viral pollution is running almost at the same rate.

A virus is a software drone (often called a *bot*) masqueraded as an e-mail from a friend, a picture, a brochure, a video, or a message about winning a lottery. Once it is in the host computer, it will find a good place to incubate in hiding, and sneak into the target file before unleashing its malicious code as instructed by the hacker who is monitoring the attack from his or her remote dashboard. Often, the virus will go to the registry of the operating system and hide there with its encrypted name.

In order for the virus to replicate itself, it must be permitted to execute code and write to memory. For this reason, many viruses attach themselves to executable files that may be part of legitimate programs. If a user attempts to launch an infected program, the virus code may be executed simultaneously.

Shopping for a Malice Act

Type 1: The Virus

Residential virus: A virus smart enough to bluff the operating system and execute its attack vector with a salute.

Nonresidential virus: It is just as smart as its sibling, but it looks for a specific file to install its attack vector that will detonate later and leave without notice.

Boot sector virus: This virus infects diskettes and hard drives. Boot sector viruses often spread to other computers by the use of shared infected disks and pirated software applications.

Program viruses: Active when the program file (usually with extensions .BIN, .COM, .EXE, .OVL, and .DRV) carrying the virus is opened. Once active, the virus will make copies of itself and will infect other programs on the computer.

Macro virus: Programmed as a macro embedded in a document, usually found in Microsoft Word or Excel. Once it gets in to your computer, every document you produce will become infected. It is a relatively new type of virus and may slip by your antivirus software if you do not have the most recent version installed. Melissa is another example of this type of virus.

Multipartite virus: A hybrid of a boot sector and program viruses. It infects program files and when the infected program is active it will affect the boot record.

Polymorphic virus: A virus that can encrypt its code in different ways so that it appears differently in each infection. These viruses are more difficult to detect.

Bacteria virus: A virus known as *Rabbit*. It is a program that does not directly damage the system; instead, it replicates itself until it monopolizes the CPU, memory, or disk space. This constitutes a denial-of-service attack.

Bomb virus: A bomb is actually a type of Trojan horse that can be used to release a virus or bacteria. Bombs work by causing an unauthorized action at a specified date and time or when a particular condition occurs. There are two types of bombs: logic and time. Logic bombs are set to go off when a particular event occurs. Time bombs go off at a specified time or date or after a set amount of time elapses.

Industrial spy virus: Edward Snowden pioneered the leakage of classified information from the National Security Agency (NSA) to the mainstream media. The U.S. government has set up an intricate secret network to spy on the U.S. citizens and abroad. Cyber spying has become a normal activity among the nations, although Snowden revealed that NSA documents were not related to industrial spying. Some of the Asian countries excelled not only in *organized spying* but also in stealing precious engineering and computer documents.

Russian security researchers from Kaspersky Lab claim the NSA has found a way to hide spying software deep inside hard drives, giving the agency free reign to eavesdrop on your computer activity. U.S. citizens remain perplexed about the NSA spying rational (https://www.rt.com/news/312567-nsa-spy-un-internet/).

The autonomic (Intelligent)Virus: Figure 4.4 shows the main components of a typical intelligent and autonomic virus.

The *kernel* is the commander of the virus; it sets the execution rules and makes sure they are done completely and properly. Under its command, the *replicator* as first officer (copilot) will spread copies of the mutated virus throughout the network. The *communicator* relays to the headquarter's dashboard, all the collected information, and how effective the virus performed. This information is very valuable in the design of more sophisticated version of the virus. The *navigator* is the component that communicated with TCP/IP and assigns itself a legitimate address to fool the scrutiny of the firewall and intrusion detection system (IDS).

Type 2: The Worm—A worm is a small piece of software that uses computer networks and security holes to replicate itself. A copy of the worm scans the network for another machine that has a specific security hole. It copies itself to the new machine using the security hole and then starts replicating from there as well. Stuxnet is the worm that attacked the nuclear plant in Iran.

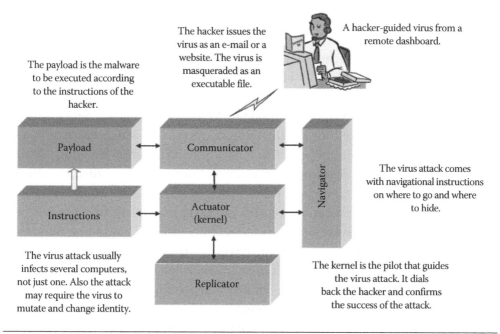

The hacker issues the virus as an e-mail or a website. The virus is masqueraded as an executable file.

A hacker-guided virus from a remote dashboard.

The payload is the malware to be executed according to the instructions of the hacker.

The virus attack comes with navigational instructions on where to go and where to hide.

The virus attack usually infects several computers, not just one. Also the attack may require the virus to mutate and change identity.

The kernel is the pilot that guides the virus attack. It dials back the hacker and confirms the success of the attack.

Figure 4.4 A virus is a software robot (called a *bot*) that carries instructions (payload) to be executed once the target is reached. It travels in stealth mode on the Internet (TCP/IP) and navigates its way until it reaches its destination. Then, it starts executing the instructions without being discovered. It mutates into another virus and starts all over.

Type 3: The Trojans—Named after the wooden horse from Greek mythology, *Trojan horses* are nonreplicating programs that appear to be benign but actually have a hidden malicious purpose. Some Trojan horses are intended to replace existing files with malicious versions, whereas other Trojan horses add another application to a system without overwriting existing files. Trojan horses *are often difficult to detect because they appear to be performing a useful function.*

Type 4: The Zombies—A computer that has been implanted with a daemon (a program that runs in the background and performs a specified operation at predefined times or in response to certain events that put it under the control of a malicious hacker without the knowledge of the computer owner. Zombies are used by malicious hackers to launch DoS attacks. The hacker sends commands to the zombie through an open port. On command, the zombie computer sends an enormous amount of packets of useless information to a targeted website in order to clog the site's routers and keep legitimate users from gaining access to the site. The traffic sent to the website is confusing and the computer receiving the packets steals CPU cycles and other applications running on the computer will come to a screeching halt.

Mainframe Legacy

In the golden days of the mainframe, there were three reputable companies who were selling, specifically IBM-centric support and services in performance management (not necessarily antivirus scanners) and removers. The three companies were Candle Corporation, Boole & Babbage, and BGS. BGS, which was located in Waltham, Massachusetts, wrote capacity-planning software for the IMB MVS systems. It was acquired by Houston-based BMC Software in March 1998. Boole & Babbage, which was located in Sunnyvale, California, was also acquired by BMC in November 1998. Candle Corporation headquarters were in Santa Monica, California, and were famous for its elite product *Omegamon*, which was acquired by IBM in June 2004 and became an integral part of IBM Business Systems. In early 2002, these three companies, among others, could not compete against the emerging Internet companies and became part of the group of defunct companies. New companies have started to focus on security as a first priority issue much more than performance. Scalability was not a critical factor; companies could hog thousands of blade serves into huge farms. With the change in the computing landscape post-911, cybersecurity became the real national and business concern. The Internet has created the *globalization effect* and the United States could not maintain its lead in cybersecurity. New companies have emerged to offer a life jacket to the computing world. Today, there are a dozen of reputable AVT vendors that have stolen the thunder from Silicon Valley. In fact, we all rely on one of these antivirus products:

- McAfee from the United States
- Symantec from the United States
- Sophos from England
- F-Secure from Finland
- Kaspersky from Russia
- Imperva from Israel
- Bitdefender from Romania
- Trend Micro from Japan
- Avast from Czechoslovakia

Introducing the Current Antivirus Vendors

McAfee: Presently, it is part of Intel Security. In 1987, in the United States, John McAfee founded the *McAfee* company (now part of Intel Security), and at the end of that year, he released the first version of VirusScan. In the autumn of 1988, in the United Kingdom, Alan Solomon founded S&S International and created his *Dr. Solomon's Antivirus Toolkit* (although he launched it commercially only in 1991—in 1998, Dr. Solomon's company was acquired by McAfee).

Symantec: In May 1990, Symantec acquired Peter Norton Computing, a developer of various utilities for DOS. In 2009, Symantec's Norton products included a slew of utility and file management products: Norton 360, Norton AntiVirus (for Windows and Mac), Norton Internet Security (for Windows and Mac),

Norton SystemWorks (which now contains Norton Utilities), Norton Save & Restore, Norton Ghost, Norton pcAnywhere, Norton Smartphone Security, Norton Partition Magic, Norton Online Backup, and Online Family. Most significantly, on May 19, 2010, Symantec acquired VeriSign's authentication business unit, which included the Secure Sockets Layer (SSL) Certificate, public key infrastructure (PKI), VeriSign Trust, and VeriSign Identity Protection (VIP) authentication services.

Kaspersky: This is a Russian company, founded by Eugene Kaspersky, Vadim Bogdanov, and Alexey De Mont De Rique. The antivirus software was released by KAMI in Russia in 1991.

F-Secure: This is a Finnish company, which boasts one of the best antivirus programs. It is streamlined, fast, and effective. With advanced protection technology and additional integrated security features, F-Secure protects against viruses, spyware, worms, and Trojans. F-Secure can also locate and eliminate rootkits. This antivirus software also protects against viruses spread through e-mails, cookies, or malware that attempts to infiltrate the PC registry. F-Secure antivirus uses heuristics and proactive protection against zero-hour threats that go undetected by the current virus signatures.

Trend Micro: This is a Japanese company founded in 1988, originally in Los Angeles by Steve Chang. Trend Micro competes in the threat and breach detection industry. In the antivirus industry, Trend Micro competes against F-Secure, Kaspersky, McAfee, Sophos, and Symantec.

Sophos: This is a privately owned British–American computer antivirus software company and is coheadquartered in Abingdon, England, and Burlington, Massachusetts. Sophos competes in the antivirus industry against F-secure, Kaspersky, McAfee, and Symantec.

Bitdefender. This is a Romanian company with very high marks. Its elite AVT software *Total Security 2015* boasts one of the top malware protection engines in the industry.

Imperva. This is an American company founded in November 2002 by Shlomo Kramer and headquartered in Redwood Shores, California. Imperva is one of the visionary ATV companies that markets Web security-as-a-service, as well as directly protects critical applications and data assets in physical and virtual data centers. Imperva has a client base of over 3000 customers in more than 75 countries. Imperva has a dedicated research team: the Application Defense (ADC) Center that actively researches current threats and hacker trends.

The Limping Antivirus Industry

The first canonical rule is that "Malware is running on Steroids, Security is running on Diesel." In cyberspace crime pays, and it pays well. The criminal mind is phenomenally creative and visionary and often is hired by law enforcement. Crime will *not* be eliminated because it is part of the human psycho-infrastructure. There is a strong biological basis for criminality. CBS hit television show *Criminal Minds* talks about criminals. "Those who kill in the spur of the moment tend to have a poorly functioning prefrontal cortex, the area that regulates emotion and impulsive behavior. In contrast, serial killers and others who carefully plan their crimes exhibit good prefrontal functioning! Criminals carry *criminal gene* in their DNA!

We are not talking about newbies and first timers who were the pioneers of hacking. We are talking about heavyweight professionals who turned into cyberterrorists, cyber Zodiacs, and cyber Mansons. We all remember the ingenious parachute escape from flight NW 305 in November 1971. Well, most bank robbers today can funnel millions of dollars into their private accounts from their remote PCs. But the focus here is on these ruthless Hellraisers who have a specific devilish plan in mind: going after critical and precious infrastructure. This is an honorable terrorism. A Stuxnet-like Trojan could trigger massive blackout, similar to the one that hit the northeast in 2003. Organized cybercrime is global and well funded. The Hall of Infamy is adorned with the Russian Business Network (RBN), the Chinese Mafia, the Romanian Mafia, and a bottomless list of syndicates specializing in cyberterrorism. Check the Epilogue at the end of the book. Figure 4.5 overwhemingly shows how cyberterrorism surpassed Antivirus Technology (AVT), even in probability of occurrence.

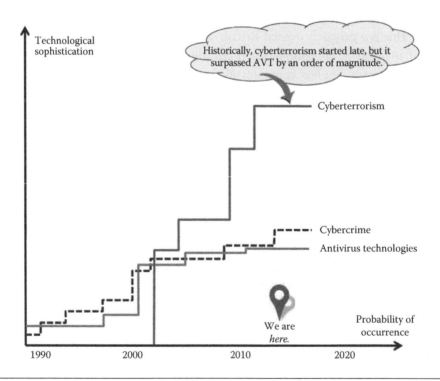

Figure 4.5 Cyberterrorism, although it started late, has surpassed Antivirus Technology in sophistication. The gap between AV Technologies and cyberterrorism is as high as the Golden Gate Bridge.

The Flat Tire of AVT, No Runflat

There are valid reasons for AVT limitations:

- The dynamic proliferation of malicious programs was written by cyber vandals. AVT providers could not keep up with this viral explosion. Many computer programmers are becoming professional hackers, hired by the underground or even competing companies for spying and stealing trade secrets.
- Antivirus users do not regularly implement the upgrades issued by the vendors. Often the antivirus software vendors do not have the updates ready and users decide to change brands.
- Antivirus software are not compatible and do not follow any standards. Users have hard time replacing one AVT with another. AVT software cannot coexist on the same PC.
- The *zero-day* malware is called such because the software vendor has just been aware of the flaw and had zero day to fix it. A zero-day attack is purposely planned to intimidate the software vendor. That is exactly what happened to Microsoft.
- These *paparazzi* hackers, serial cyber banditos, and "1%er" gang went after Microsoft Internet Explorer (IE) and defamed it with zero-day sharpshooting attacks. IE became very vulnerable and lost its shirt. Estimates for Internet Explorer's overall market share range from 27.4% to 54.13%, as of October 2012. The half-cooked IE limped through half a dozen of unfortunate stumbles and serious sinkholes. Zero-day hackers were claimed to be the real champions in the emergence of Firefox and later Google Chrome. The diagram below shows the timeline of this aggravating malware. The crucial time is T_4-T_3 that represents the recovery time from the zero-day virus. Many users ignore this period and have given up on updates. Many users found Firefox and Chrome faster and easier to install. However, Microsoft decided to integrate IE with Windows, which makes it extremely difficult to remove (Figure 4.5).
- Microsoft has not been able to come up, until today, with a robust browser to gain back its loyal users.
- AVT software generally has good intentions, but not all antivirus software are reliable. Immediately after scanning the drives, the software tries to delete the infected user and system files, and by removing them, Windows stops functioning properly.
- The new generation of viruses has the ability to mutate and take another identity with new signature. The virus signature is like a fingerprint in that it can be used to detect and identify specific viruses. The signature is a unique string of bits or the binary pattern with an encrypted hash. Antivirus software uses the virus signature to scan the presence of malicious code. Once the virus takes a new identity, its trail disappears and tracking the virus becomes a real challenge as shown in Figure 4.6.

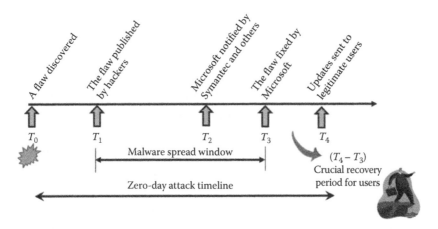

Figure 4.6   Timeline of the notorious zero-day exploit, the Achilles of Microsoft IE.

Since innovation is driven by technology, Microsoft has taken the lead and set the pace to establish its kingdom. The whole world at one time depended on Windows. The chart in Figure 4.7 shows that 90% of all desktops were under the gravitational force of Microsoft.

However, Microsoft did not pay attention to the Internet genie coming out of the bottle, until it was too late. Bill Gates was publicly denouncing the Web as just a fad. Microsoft penetrated the Internet with its *half-cooked* Internet Explorer in 1995, which underwent 11 major updates and was still very vulnerable and in fact has been an annoying speed bump to progress. Antivirus companies have been marching at Microsoft's drumbeat and cautiously trying not to step on the turf of the software giant. Hardware vendors also paid homage to Microsoft. Software companies that challenged Microsoft were either doomed or acquired. From July 1987 to late 2014, Microsoft has bought or acquired 166 companies. For example, Skype was bought for 8.5 billion and later Nokia for 7.2 billion (http://en.wikipedia.org/wiki/List_of_mergers_and_acquisitions_by_Microsoft).

Microsoft has never been a security elite company and that is why Antivirus Technology (AVT) providers have been under the gravitation of Microsoft in order to survive. Most of them survived because they did not advance beyond Microsoft marching orders. Consumers were lured, we all remember that, to buying an antivirus software that came with their new PCs and laptops as the ultimate *life jacket*. The state of the health of system security stagnated, although the AVT kitchen was huffing and puffing with lots of cooking and boiling, but AVT providers did not offer innovative solutions to address the escalating cybercrime/cyberterrorism. There were lots of updates and new covers. Zero-day attacks were big time and it was party time for the Black Hat community. Microsoft lost the lead and the Bill Gates era passed into oblivion. Apple, Google, and Amazon took the lead in software and stunned the market with awesome innovations. Microsoft became the fifth behind Apple, Google, Oracle, and CISCO, dragging its feet with imitated gadget. Microsoft fooled everyone with

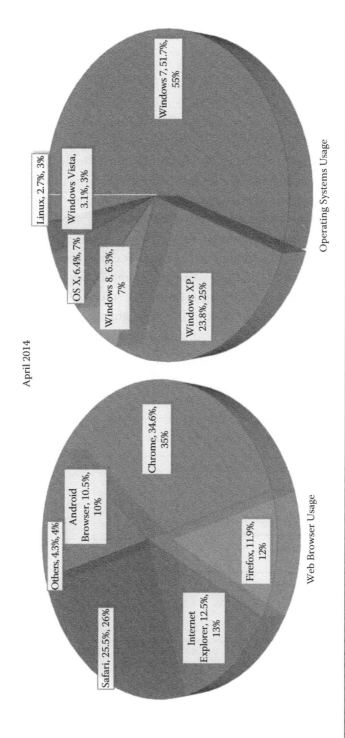

Figure 4.7   Statistics show that Microsoft is losing its grip. (From Shareaholic, www.shareholic.com.)

its phony promises. Windows has lost its shine and became fragile and brittle. With the emergence of tablets, even Amazon threw its hat in the ring with its fire tablet. Security technology hit a cul-de-sac and consumers have decided to switch to tablets.

Two-Generation Leap

Figure 4.8 clearly shows the progression of the AVT industry and the quantum leap of the new system, CEWPS. From the beginning of the antivirus software industry of 1986 until the present time, there has been substantial progress and sophistication among all the competing AVT vendors. Their contribution is in fact monumental to say the least. However, looking at the state of the art of malware, we realize that AVT is losing its grip on malware and in fact, it has reached the plateau of stagnation. In general, AVT software is not designed as an expert system. It does not have any artificial intelligence (AI) components. AVT software does not have any autonomic computing or self-managing capabilities of distributed computing resources, adapting to unpredictable changes while hiding intrinsic complexity to operators and users. The first characteristic is self-configuring to adapt to dynamically changing environments. The second characteristic is self-healing for business resilience by discovering, analyzing, and acting to prevent disruptions. The third characteristic is self-optimizing to achieve operational efficiency by tuning resources and balancing workloads to

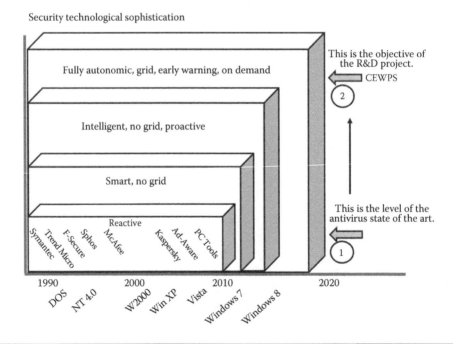

Figure 4.8   CEWPS is two generations ahead of the present Antivirus Technology (AVT). To win the war on cyberterrorism, we have to leap two generations into the artificial intelligence domain. That is why CEWPS was developed. Technology pioneers such as Google, Amazon, Apple, Microsoft, and IBM should be part of this new paradigm shift.

maximize the use of system resources. The fourth characteristic is self-protecting by anticipating, detecting, identifying, and protecting against attacks. The present AVT software does not operate on an intelligent grid. Each user PC has to have a copy. AVT vendors made killing by selling static copies and forced customers to a yearly subscription to download updates. Vendors use every dirty trick to scare users. Often, users are hijacked unaware that a copy of an unknown antivirus sneaks into their PC. To add insult to injury, the downloaded antivirus immobilizes the original antivirus and imposes control over the user. The software licensing trauma left a bitter taste in the user's mouth. Microsoft made its billions with its monopoly of shrink-wrap and click-wrap licenses. Software license contracts were written for the benefit of the vendors and shoved down the user's throat. Users had to click "yes"; otherwise, they could not install the software, despite having paid for it. AVT vendors copycatted all this mischief and drummed up agreements with Dell, IBM, HP, and the rest of the pack to amalgamate software and PC and fool the user as a great deal.

InfoSec Community Forums in November 2012 published an article titled "The Shortcomings of Anti-Virus Software" authored by Daniel Wesemann where he systematically showed how corrupt the AVT vendors are.

None of the AVT software has an early warning component to alert the user about an attack forecast—pretty much like the weather forecast. This feature is very complex and requires a Reasoning Engine with a Knowledge Base where all historical attacks are semantically stored. Another feature that is missing from all the AVT software is the forensic tracking. To delete or quarantine an attack causes a serious problem: it modifies or eradicates evidence. The alert is not enough; a detailed explanation on the removed threat and why it was eradicated will be beneficial. In other words, if the AV software removes a registry key to release a DLL, why could not the AV log tell us where this registry key was and when it was created? This would give a strong indication on how far back we have to investigate and determine what data were compromised. The same holds true for the actual threat files that get deleted or quarantined: a full MAC (modify/access/create) time stamp in the logs could be very beneficial to have. The MD5 message-digest algorithm could be added to verify the data integrity before and after the attack.

Based on all the evidence presented, the new system, CEWPS, has been designed to cover all the deficiencies of the present AVT software (Figure 4.8).

Winning the war on cyberterrorism requires a totally new way of looking at digital security. Building a cognitive immune defense system like the Human Immune System will take security to the highest level. This approach will offer two robust advantages:

1. An early warning alert capability to increase the preparedness of the public, the government, and private business
2. A responsive vaccination capability to inoculate critical infrastructure systems (CISs) with the Smart Vaccine, which is autonomically released in case of a surprise intrusion or stealth attack

We need to look at the solution with a holistic vision. We cannot rely on after-the-attack forensic techniques to recover damage and endure emotional distress. Rather than thinking tactically and reacting to new threats, we need to think strategically by building a smarter environment to alert and quickly defend our critical infrastructures and systems.

The digital world, without system immunity, will have the same destiny of the human world without immunity protection. Our critical infrastructures systems will become very vulnerable with regular crippling attacks. Furthermore, the attacking viruses will become more smart and potent as technology brings advances and new tools.

The Smart Vaccine (SV) in the heart of the Cognitive Early Warning Predictive System (CEWPS) kicks off a new generation in cybersecurity beyond the most sophisticated Antivirus Technology of today:

- A semantic Attack Knowledge Engine (AKE), which uses ontology to classify and store all the historical attack episodes for early warning prediction. Also the knowledge engine stores causality attack rules.
- Reverse engineering and forensic analysis component to study the anatomy of the most complex attacks and the impact. This will enable CEWPS to calculate the probability of risk and to know how to eradicate future attacks.
- The word *predictive* in CEWPS is very meaningful in AI because our prediction is based on well-established cognitive science (Bayesian network modeling). Early warning, on the other hand, is a descriptive term that can be visual, audible, or based on a hunch.
- The *Reasoning Engine (RE)* in CEWPS operates in a three-state cycle: match rules, select rules, and execute rules. The rules are logical premises, modus ponens with semantic properties, and relational constructs leading to a conclusion. Reasoning rules are logically chained to represent a specific violent situation.
- A Reasoning Engine using Bayesian logic to perform unbiased inference determines the likelihood of future attacks, based on the occurrence in the past.
- CEWPS operates on a *smart grid*, like the nervous system, to facilitate the communication and transfer of early warning alerts, inoculation outcome, and navigation commands between the Smart Vaccine and the central command. The advantage of the grid is that it allows central command to broadcast alert instructions and allow systems to interact and alert one another. None of the AVT software, at this time, operates on a smart grid. This is one of the crucial components that gives CEWPS a tremendous operating advantage. Chapter 5 will discuss the CEWPS grid component in detail. The nervous system is an incredible microcosm made of multilevel interconnected grids with millions of miles of "nervous system" highways that transmit directionally sensory and motor intelligent signals.

One of the reasons why CEWPS runs on an intelligent grid is because grid technology offers a tremendous security advantage for smart cities. Here are some more benefits.

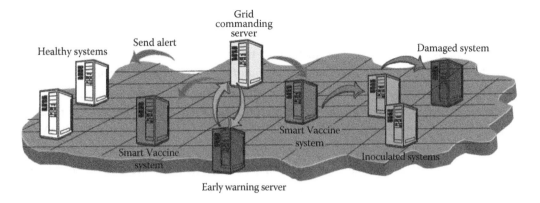

Figure 4.9 Collaboration between the City Grid Commander and the Smart Vaccine Commander. The damaged system triggers a whole new phenomenon of vaccination service. All systems will be served with the same vaccine. No system will stay behind. The attack will be saved in the Attack Knowledge Base. Being humans, we learn and gain knowledge from our mistakes.

An intelligent grid allows critical systems to collaborate and exchange information. If one system (node) is down, then the rest of the systems will compensate and offer temporary help until the damaged system is repaired. The grid server that oversees the operation of the grids makes sure that all systems are running normally. Figure 4.9 shows how all systems collaborate on the CEWPS grid.

The Smart Vaccine is a *cognitive* system. It extracts critical answers through perception, reasoning, intuition, and previous knowledge.

The CEWPS Cockpit Is Fully Autonomic

CEWPS is like the Human Immune System that is equipped with a set of autonomic components with its most creative radar-like feature of *predictive cognition.*

Let's explain what predictive cognition means.

Predictive depicts one of the most relevant concepts in cognitive neuroscience, which emphasizes the importance of *looking into the future*, namely, prediction, preparation, anticipation, prospection, or expectations in various cognitive domains. Predictive processing is the type of processing that incorporates information from the past, the present, but even the future. Predictive processing is the conjugate of cognitive processing, which supports perception and motor and cognitive control.

Cognition is all mental abilities and processes related to knowledge. It includes attention, working memory, judgment and evaluation, reasoning and computation, problem solving and decision making, and comprehension and production of language. Simply speaking, cognition is responsible for information processing before it is stored as knowledge in the brain. Looking at cognition from a different angle, we can say experience (the biological process created by external sensation or internal reflection) is received by cognition and converted into *knowledge* and stored as the neurological description of experience. Furthermore, knowledge later is split as conscious and unconscious categories, concrete or abstract, intuitive or conceptual.

The success in smart cities is in its end-to-end integration with its infrastructure. In fact, smart cities utilize an *On-Demand Operating Environment* (*ODOE*) to achieve better infrastructure management and Digital Immunity. In fact, the main purpose of ODOE is to optimize the management of infrastructures. The same applies to CEWPS that uses ODOE, which fits like a hand in a glove. CEWPS is fully integrated within the Smart City on-demand environment, where the Smart Vaccine offers its magic vaccination services whenever the central command instructs it to do so. So what is a CEWPS On-Demand Operating Environment? And how does it work?

To transform a city such as Dubai into a smart city is a true integration challenge for an On-Demand Operating Environment. All infrastructures have to be integrated, automated, and self-managed.

CEWPS is designed specifically to protect the infrastructures in smart cities. The architecture of the CEWPS environment includes autonomic computing, grid computing, Artificial Intelligence, knowledge engineering, and on-demand computing, all bundled with service-oriented architecture (SOA). Let's review the diagram in Figure 4.10 and see how it works.

This layer is the brain of the CEWPS operating environment. It is the cockpit where all the components are autonomic and self-configuring. The early warning

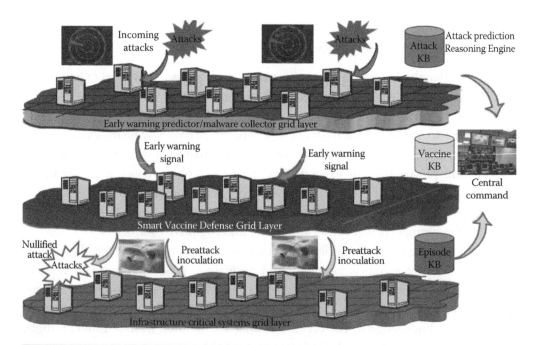

Figure 4.10 The logical view of CEWPS in motion. The Central Coordination Center (CCC) invokes intelligence messages (instances) that are in an active state. The Smart Vaccine Commander also invokes order (state) instances to its team. The vaccination session data will all be reserved at the Attack Knowledge Base.

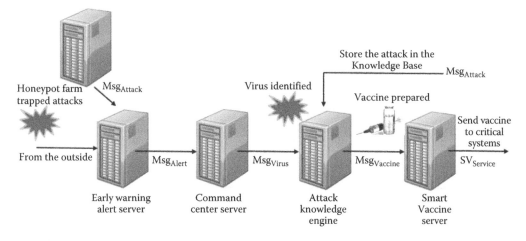

Figure 4.11   The Central Coordination Center (CCC) receives information from the early warning alert server. The CCC also gets advice from the Attack Knowledge Base on what to do next. Next, the Smart Vaccine Commander gets its marching orders.

predictor (EWP) is always on the alert constantly evaluating the situation. It gets signals from honeypots and constantly inquires from the Reasoning Engine about possible future attacks. The Knowledge Base (KB) *semantically* stores all the historical attack episodes. The knowledge engine (called inference) examines all these historical *a priori* attack cases and applies causality rules to generate forecast and prediction alerts.

The early warning layer communicates with the Smart Vaccine Defense and the infrastructure critical system layers through a whole portfolio of service-oriented messages.

The Smart Vaccine Defense Grid Layer is the most innovative and intelligent layer. The Smart Vaccine receives regular intelligence signals and alerts before any eminent attack. All SV servers are pathologically connected and are ready to inoculate the critical systems with the right vaccine. If the vaccine is not available, then the SV servers would issue a vaccine service request to the vaccine registry for discovery. Most importantly, the central command would issue alert messages to all the critical systems prior to the attack. At the same time, the SV servers would rush to inoculate the critical system with the right vaccine prior to the attack. The diagram in Figure 4.11 offers a further explanation on the flow and processing of messages (data and instructions) in CEWPS.

Inoculation Missions of the Smart Vaccine

The Smart Vaccine is the life saver of the critical systems that reside on the grid. The Smart Vaccine constantly receives instructions from the grid central command before it delivers the vaccination services to the proper systems. The diagram in Figure 4.12 shows the type of vaccination services that are delivered.

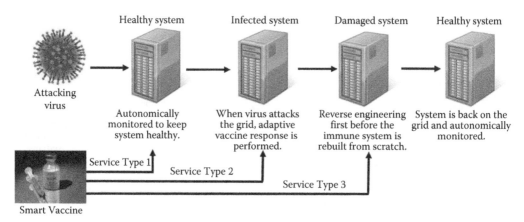

Figure 4.12   The Smart Vaccine has three vaccination services: The first is to scan healthy systems and make sure they are fully vaccinated and immune against attacks. The second is to help the infected system quarantine the virus and collect all information about the attack. The third is to isolate the *partially* damaged system, switch it to the backup system, and rebuild its destroyed immunity from scratch.

Analytic Thinking Reduces Belief in Conspiracy Theories

Cognition Magazine (volume 133, issue 3), from Elsevier, published an interesting paper on the relationship between analytic thinking and conspiracy. We think the same logic would apply to cyberterrorism theories. The paper states:

> Belief in conspiracy theories has been associated with a range of negative health, civic, and social outcomes, requiring reliable methods of reducing such belief. Thinking dispositions have been highlighted as one possible factor associated with belief in conspiracy theories, but actual relationships have only been infrequently studied. In Study 1, we examined the association between belief in conspiracy theories and a range of measures of thinking dispositions with a population sample of 990. Results indicated that a stronger belief in conspiracy theories was significantly associated with lower analytic thinking and open-mindedness and greater intuitive thinking. In Studies 2–4, we examined the causational role played by analytic thinking in relation to conspiracist ideation. In Study 2 with a sample population of 112, we showed that a verbal fluency task that elicited analytic thinking reduced belief in conspiracy theories. In the third, Study 3 with 189 samples, we found that an alternative method of eliciting analytic thinking, which related to cognitive disfluency, was effective at reducing conspiracist ideation in a student sample. In Study 4, we replicated the results of Study 3 with a sample population of 140 in relation to generic conspiracist ideation and belief in conspiracy theories about the July 7, 2005, bombings in London. Our results highlight the potential utility of supporting attempts to promote analytic thinking as a means of countering the widespread acceptance of conspiracy theories.

The Immune System and the Nervous System

According to the National Institute of Allergy and Infectious Diseases (NIAID), there is clear evidence that our immune system and nervous system are tightly coupled in several ways. One well-known connection involves the adrenal glands. In response to stress messages from the brain, the adrenal glands release hormones into the blood. In addition to helping a person respond to emergencies by mobilizing the body's energy reserves, these *stress hormones* can stifle the protective effects of antibodies and lymphocytes.

Another link between the immune system and the nervous system is that the hormones and other chemicals that convey messages among nerve cells also *speak* to the immune system cells. Indeed, some immune cells are able to manufacture typical nerve cell products, and some lymphokines can transmit information to the nervous system. Moreover, the brain may send messages directly down nerve cells to the immune system. Networks of nerve fibers have been found to connect to the lymphoid organs.

The neuroimmune system, as the name implies, is the area where the immune system interacts with the nervous system. The nervous system grid is the information highway that carries crucial signals to navigate the immune cells during the attack.

Psychoneuroimmunology studies the interactions between human behavior and the immune system. Believe it or not, there are regulating components, under the name of *endocrines* that provide chemical balance and stability to the nervous system. For example, the brain modulates the immune system hardwiring sympathetic and parasympathetic nerves (autonomic nervous system). Reciprocally, the immune system modulates brain activities such as sleep and body temperature. From fever to stress, the influence of one system on the other has evolved in an intricate manner to help sense danger and to mount an appropriate adaptive response.

CEWPS (the Digital Immune System) incorporates similar features and capabilities, and its three grids are tightly coupled and interact heavily with perfect collaboration. Chapter 5 will discuss the details of the system and how it works.

The Running Mind of the Hacker "Catch Me If You Can"

Breakthroughs in molecular biology are making it possible for researchers to examine DNA and explore how genetics may affect the brains of criminals. Neurolaw experts are troubled by the potential human rights issues presented here. Should those with brains predisposed to violence be given lighter sentences or, conversely, be locked away to prevent them from causing further harm? Should an accused killer be forced to have a brain scan? And if a child or young adult's brain scan indicates a violent disposition, should he be relegated to a detention or prevention program? So far brain scans have not conclusively given a scientific validity or findings. However, neuroscientific theories, as intriguing and promising as they are, must be proven beyond any reasonable doubt. And the controversy goes on with its slippage, while crime proliferates and gradually is migrating into the cyberworld. The cliché "my brain made me do it" is becoming elusive and justified in cybercrime.

For as long as evil has existed, people have wondered about its source, and you do not have to be too much of a scientific reductionist to conclude that the first place to look is the brain. There is not a thing you have ever done, thought, or felt in your life that is not ultimately traceable to a particular Web work of nerve cells firing in a particular way, allowing the machine that is you to function as it does. So if the machine is busted—if the operating system in your head fires in crazy neurons—are you fully responsible for the behavior that follows?

Glossary: Technical Terms about Computer Viruses and Antiviruses

ActiveX: This technology is used, among other things, to improve the functionality of Web pages (adding animations, video, 3D browsing, etc.). ActiveX controls are small programs that are inserted in these pages. Unfortunately, as they are programs, they can also be targets for viruses.

Address Book: A file with WAB extension. This is used to store information about other users such as e-mail addresses.

Administrator: A person or program responsible for managing and monitoring an IT system or network, assigning permissions, etc.

Administrator rights: These rights allow certain people to carry out actions or operations on networked computers.

ADSL: This is a kind of technology that allows data to be sent at very high speed across an Internet connection. It requires a special ADSL modem.

Adware: Programs that display advertising using any means: pop-ups, banners, changes to the browser home page or search page, etc. Adware can be installed with the user consent and awareness, but sometimes it is not. The same happens with the knowledge or lack of knowledge regarding its functionalities.

Algorithm: A process or set of rules for calculating or problem solving.

Alias: Although each virus has a specific name, very often it is more widely known by a nickname that describes a particular feature or characteristic of the virus. In these cases, we talk about the virus *alias*. For example, the virus CIH is also known by the alias Chernobyl.

ANSI (American National Standards Institute): A voluntary organization that sets standards, particularly for computer programming.

Antidebug/antidebugger: These are techniques used by viruses to avoid being detected.

Antivirus/antivirus program: These are programs that scan the memory, disk drives, and other parts of a computer for viruses.

API (Application Programming Interface): This is a function used by programs to interact with operating systems and other programs.

Armoring: This is a technique used by viruses to hide and avoid detection by the antivirus.

ASCII: A standard code—American Standard Code for Information Interchange—for representing characters (letters, numbers, punctuation marks, etc.) as numbers.

ASP (Active Server Page): These are particular types of Web pages that allow a site to be personalized according to user profiles. This acronym can also refer to application service provider.

Attributes: These are particular characteristics associated with a file or directory.

Autoencryption: The way in which a virus codifies (or encrypts) part or all of itself, making it more difficult to analyze or detect to analyze.

AutoSignature: This is normally a short text including details like name and address that can be automatically added to new e-mail messages.

Backdoor: This is a program that enters the computer and creates a backdoor through which it is possible to control the affected system without the user realizing.

Banker Trojan: A malicious program, which uses different techniques, steals confidential information to the customers of online payment banks and/or platforms.

Banner: An advert displayed on a Web page, promoting a product or service that may or may not be related to the host Web page and that in any event links directly to the site of the advertiser.

Batch files/BAT files: Files with a BAT extension that allow operations to be automated.

BBS (bulletin board system): A system or service on the Internet that allows subscribed users to read and respond to messages written by other users (e.g., in a forum or newsgroup).

BHO (Browser Helper Object): A plugin that automatically runs along with the Internet browser, adding to its functionality. Some are used for malicious ends, such as monitoring the Web pages viewed by users.

BIOS (Basic Input/Output System): A group of programs that enable the computer to be started up (part of the boot system).

Bit: This is the smallest unit of digital information with which computers operate.

Boot/master boot record (MBR): Also known as the boot sector, this is the area or sector of a disk that contains information about the disk itself and its properties for starting up the computer.

Boot disk/system disk: Disk (floppy disk, CD-ROM, or hard disk) that makes it possible to start up the computer.

Boot virus: A virus that specifically affects the boot sector of both hard disks and floppy disks.

Bot: A contraction of the word *robot*. This is a program that allows a system to be controlled remotely without either the knowledge or consent of the user.

Bot herder: A person or group that controls the botnet. They are also known as *bot master* or *zombie master*.

Botnet: A network or group of zombie computers controlled by the owner of the bots. The owner of the botnets sends instructions to the zombies. These commands can include updating the bot, downloading a new threat, displaying advertising, or launching denial-of-service attacks.

Browser: A browser is the program that lets users view Internet pages. The most common browsers are Internet Explorer, Netscape Navigator, Opera, etc.

Buffer: This is an intermediary memory space used to temporarily save information transferred between two units or devices (or between components in the same system).

Bug: This is a fault or error in a program.

Bus: Communication channel between different components in a computer (communicating data signals, addresses, control signals, etc.).

Byte: This is a unit of measurement of digital information. One byte is equal to 8 bits.

Cache: This is a small section of the computer's memory.

Category/type (of virus): As there are many different types of viruses, they are grouped into categories according to certain typical characteristics.

Cavity: Technique used by certain viruses and worms to make them more difficult to find. By using this technique, the size of the infected file does not change (they only occupy cavities in the file affected).

Chat/Chat IRC/Chat ICQ: These are real-time text conversations over the Internet.

Client: IT system (computer) that requests certain services and resources from another computer (server), to which it is connected across a network.

Cluster: Various consecutive sectors of a disk.

CMOS (complementary metal-oxide semiconductor): This is a section of the computer's memory in which the information and programs needed to start up the system are kept (BIOS).

Code: Content of virus files—virus code, written in a certain programming language. It can also refer to systems for representing or encrypting information.
In its strictest sense, it can be defined as a set of rules or a combination of symbols that have a given value within an established system.

Common name: The name by which a virus is generally known.

Companion/companion virus/spawning: This is a type of virus that does not insert itself in programs but attaches itself to them instead.

Compressed/compress/compression/decompress: Files, or groups of files, are compressed into another file so that they take up less space.

Cookie: This is a text file that is sometimes sent to a user visiting a Web page to register the visit to the page and record certain information regarding the visit.

Country of origin: This generally refers to the country where the first incidence of virus was first recorded.

Cracker: Someone who tries to break into (restricted) computer systems.

CRC (CRC number or code): A unique numeric code attached to files that acts as the file ID number.

Crimeware: All programs, messages, or documents used directly or indirectly to fraudulently obtain financial gain to the detriment of the affected user or third parties.

CVP (Content Vectoring Protocol): Protocol developed in 1996 by Check Point that allows antivirus protection to be integrated into a firewall server.

Cylinder: Section of a disk that can be read in a single operation.

Damage level: This is a value that indicates the level of the negative effects that a virus could have on an infected computer. It is one of the factors used to calculate the threat level.

Database: A collection of data files and the programs used to administer and organize them. Examples of database systems include Access, Oracle, SQL, Paradox, and dBase.

DDoS/distributed denial of service: This is a denial-of-service (DoS) attack where multiple computers attack a single server at the same time. Compromised computers would be left vulnerable, allowing the attacker to control them to carry out this action.

Debugger: A tool for reading the source code of programs.

Deleted items: A folder in e-mail programs that contains messages that have been deleted (they have not been eliminated completely from the computer). After deleting a message containing a virus, it is advisable to delete it from this folder as well.

Detection updated on: The latest date when the detection of a malware was updated in the virus signature file.

Dialer: This is a program that is often used to maliciously redirect Internet connections. When used in this way, it disconnects the legitimate telephone connection used to hook up to the Internet and reconnects via a premium rate number. Often, the first indication a user has of this activity is an extremely expensive phone bill.

Direct action: This is a specific type of virus.

Directory/Folder: Divisions or sections used to structure and organize information contained on a disk. The terms folder and directory really refer to the same thing. They can contain files or other subdirectories.

Disinfection: The action that an antivirus takes when it detects a virus and eliminates it.

Distribution level: This is a value that indicates the extent to which a virus has spread or the speed at which it is spreading. It is one of the factors used to calculate the threat level.

DNS (domain name system): System to enable communication between computers connected across a network or the Internet. It means that computers can be located and assigns comprehensible names to their IP addresses.

DNS servers are those computers in which these names are handled (resolved) and associated with their corresponding IPs.

DoS/denial of service: This is a type of attack, sometimes caused by viruses, that prevents users from accessing certain services (in the operating system, Web servers, etc.).

Download: This is the process of obtaining files from the Internet (from Web pages or FTP sites set up specifically for that purpose).

Driver/controller: A program, known as a controller, used to control devices connected to a computer (normally peripherals like printers and CD-ROM drives).

Dropper: This is an executable file that contains various types of virus.

Dynamic link library (DLL): A special type of file with the extension DLL.

EICAR: European Institute for Computer Antivirus Research. An organization that has created a test to evaluate the performance of antivirus programs, which is known as the EICAR test.

ELF files: Executable and Linking Format. These are executable files (programs) belonging to the Unix/Linux operating system.

Emergency disk/rescue disk: A floppy disk that allows the computer to be scanned for viruses without having to use the antivirus installed in the system, but by using what is known as the *command line antivirus*.

Encryption/self-encryption: This is a technique used by some viruses to disguise themselves and therefore avoid detection by antivirus applications.

EPO (Entry Point Obscuring): A technique for infecting programs through which a virus tries to hide its entry point in order to avoid detection. Instead of taking control and carrying out its actions as soon as the program is used or run, the virus allows it to work correctly for a while before the virus goes into action.

Exceptions: This is a technique used by antivirus programs to detect viruses.

Exploit: This can be a technique or a program that takes advantage of a vulnerability or security hole in a certain communication protocol, operating system, or other IT utility or application.

Extension: Files have a name and an extension, separated by a dot: NAME. EXTENSION. A file can have any NAME, but the EXTENSION (if it exists) has a maximum of three characters. This extension indicates the type of file (text, Word document, image, sound, database, program, etc.).

Family/group: Some viruses may have similar names and characteristics. These viruses are grouped into families or groups. Members of the group are known as variants of the family or the original virus (the first to appear).

FAT (File Allocation Table): This is a section of a disk that defines the structure and organization of the disk itself. It also contains the *addresses* for all the files stored on that disk.

File/document: Unit for storing information (text, document, images, spreadsheet, etc.) on a disk or other storage devices. A file is identified by a name, followed by a dot and then its extension (indicating the type of file).

Firewall: This is a barrier that can protect information in a system or network when there is a connection to another network, for example, the Internet.

FireWire: A high-speed communication channel, used to connect computers and peripherals to other computers.

First appeared on: The date when a particular virus was first discovered.

First detected on: The date when the detection of a certain malware was first included in the virus signature file.

Flooding: Programs that repeatedly send a large message or text to a computer through messaging systems like MSN Messenger in order to saturate, collapse, or flood the system.

Format: Define the structure of a disk, removing any information that was previously stored on it.

Freeware: All software legally distributed free of charge.

FTP (File Transfer Protocol): A mechanism that allows files to be transferred through a TCP/IP connection.

Gateway: A computer that allows communication between different types of platforms, networks, computers, or programs.

GDI (Graphics Device Interface): A system that allows the Windows operating system to display presentations on-screen or in print.

Groupware: A system that allows users in a local area network (LAN) to use resources like shared programs; access to the Internet, intranet, or other areas; e-mail; and firewalls and proxies.

Hacker: Someone who accesses a computer illegally or without authorization.

Hacking tool: Program that can be used by a hacker to carry out actions that cause problems for the user of the affected computer (allowing the hacker to control the affected computer, steal confidential information, scan communication ports, etc.).

Hardware: Term referring to all physical elements in an IT system (screen, keyboard, mouse, memory, hard disk, microprocessor, etc.).

Header (of a file): This is the part of a file in which information about the file itself and its location is kept.

Heuristic scan: This term, which refers to problem solving by trial and error, is used in the computer world to refer to a technique used for detecting unknown viruses.

Hijacker: Any program that changes the browser settings to make the home page or the default search page different from the one set by the user.

Hoax: This is not a virus, but a trick message warning of a virus that does not actually exist.

Host: This refers to any computer that acts as a source of information.

HTTP (Hypertext Transfer Protocol): This is a communication system that allows Web pages to be viewed through a browser.

IFS (Installable File System): System used to handle inbound/outbound information transfers between a group of devices or files.

Identity theft: Obtaining confidential user information, such as passwords for accessing services, in order that unauthorized individuals can impersonate the affected user.

IIS (Internet Information Server): This is a Microsoft server, designed for publishing and maintaining Web pages and portals.

IMAP (Internet Message Access Protocol): This is a system or protocol that allows access to e-mail messages.

In circulation: A virus is said to be in circulation, when cases of it are actually being detected somewhere in the world.

In the wild: This is an official list drawn up every month of the viruses reported causing incidents.

Inbox: This is a folder in e-mail programs that contains received messages.

Infection: This refers to the process of a virus entering a computer or certain areas of a computer or files.

Interface: The system through which users can interact with the computer and the software installed on it. At the same time, this software (programs) communicates via an interface system with the computer's hardware.

Interruption: A signal through which a momentary pause in the activities of the microprocessor is brought about.

Interruption vector: This is a technique used by a computer to handle the interruption requests to the microprocessor. This provides the memory address to which the service should be provided.

IP (Internet Protocol)/TCP–IP: An IP address is a code that identifies each computer. The TCP/IP is the system, used in the Internet, that interconnects computers and prevents address conflicts.

IRC (Chat IRC): These are written conversations over the Internet in which files can also be transferred.

ISDN (Integrated Services Digital Network): A type of connection for digitally transmitting information (data, images, sound, etc.).

ISP (Internet Service Provider): A company that offers access to the Internet and other related services.

Java: This is a programming language that allows the creation of platform-independent programs, that is, they can be run on any operating system or hardware (multiplatform language).

Java Applets: These are small programs that can be included in Web pages to improve the functionality of the page.

JavaScript: A programming language that offers dynamic characteristics (e.g., variable data depending on how and when someone accesses, user interaction, and customized features) for HTML Web pages.

Joke: This is not a virus, but a trick that aims to make users believe they have been infected by a virus.

Kernel: This is the central module of an operating system.

Key logger: A program that collects and saves a list of all keystrokes made by a user. This program could then publish the list, allowing third parties to access the data (the information that the user has entered through the keyboard: passwords, document texts, e-mails, key combinations, etc.).

LAN (local area network): A network of interconnected computers in a reasonably small geographical area (generally in the same city or town or even building).

Links/hyperlinks: These are parts of a Web page, e-mail, or document (text, images, buttons, etc.), which when clicked on, they take the user directly to another Web page or section of the document.

Link virus: This is a type of virus that modifies the address where a file is stored, replacing it with the address of the virus (instead of the original file). As a result, when the affected file is used, the virus activates. After the computer has been infected, the original file will be unusable.

Logic bomb: This is a program that appears quite inoffensive, but which can carry out damaging actions on a computer, just like any other virus.

Loop: A set of commands or instructions carried out by a program repeatedly until a certain condition is met.

Macro: A macro is a series of instructions defined so that a program, say Word, Excel, PowerPoint, or Access, carries out certain operations. As they are programs, they can be affected by viruses. Viruses that use macros to infect are known as macro viruses.

Macro virus: A virus that affects macros in Word documents, Excel spreadsheets, PowerPoint presentations, etc.

Malware: This term is used to refer to all programs that contain malicious code (*malicious software*) or contain malicious code, whether it is a virus, Trojan, or worm.

Map: This is the action of assigning a shared network disk a letter in a computer, just as if it were another drive in the computer itself.

MAPI: Messaging Application Programming Interface. A system used to enable programs to send and receive e-mail via a certain messaging system.

Mask: This is a 32-bit number that identifies an IP address in a certain network. This allows the TCP/IP communication protocol to know if an IP address of a computer belongs to one network or another.

Means of infection: A fundamental characteristic of a virus. This is the way in which a virus infects a computer.

Means of transmission: A fundamental characteristic of a virus. This is the way in which a virus spreads from one computer to another.

Microprocessor/processor: This is the integrated electronic heart of a computer or IT system, for example, Pentium (I, II, III, IV), 486, and 386.

MIME (Multipurpose Internet Mail Extensions): This is the set of specifications that allows text and files with different character sets to be exchanged over the Internet (e.g., between computers in different languages).

Modem: A peripheral device, also known as modulator–demodulator, used to transmit electronic signals (analogical and digital). It is designed to enable communication between computers or other types of IT resources. It is most often used for connecting computers to the Internet.

Module: In IT parlance, this is a set or group of macros in a Word document, Excel spreadsheet, etc.

MS-DOS (Disk Operating System): This operating system, which predates Windows, involves the writing of commands for all operations that the user wants to carry out.

MSDE (Microsoft Desktop Engine): A server for storing data, which is compatible with SQL Server 2000.

MTA (message transfer agent): This is an organized mail system that receives messages and distributes them to the recipients. MTAs also transfer messages to other mail servers. Exchange, sendmail, qmail, and Postfix, for example, are MTAs.

Multipartite: This is a characteristic of a particular type of sophisticated virus, which infects computers by using a combination of techniques used by other viruses.

Mutex (mutual exclusion object): Some viruses can use a mutex to control access to resources (e.g., programs or even other viruses) and prevent more than one process from simultaneously accessing the same resource.

By doing this, they make it difficult for antiviruses to detect them. These viruses can *carry* other malicious codes in the same way that other types, such as polymorphic viruses, do.

Network: Group of computers or other IT devices interconnected via a cable, telephone line, or electromagnetic waves (satellite, microwaves, etc.), in order to communicate and share resources. The Internet is a vast network of other subnetworks with millions of computers connected.

Newsgroup: An Internet service through which various people can connect to discuss or exchange information about specific subjects.

Nuke (attack): A nuke attack is aimed at causing the network connection to fail. A computer that has been nuked may block.

Nuker: Person or program that launches a nuke attack, causing a computer to block or the network connection to fail.

OLE (Object Linking and Embedding): A standard for embedding and attaching images, video clips, MIDI, animations, etc., in files (documents, databases, spreadsheets, etc.). It also allows ActiveX controls to be embedded.

Online registration: System for subscribing or registering via the Internet as a user of a product or services (in this case, a program and associated services).

Operating system (OS): A set of programs that enables a computer to be used.

Overwrite: This is the action that certain programs or viruses take when they write over a file, permanently erasing the content.

P2P (peer to peer): A program—or network connection—used to offer services via the Internet (usually file sharing), which viruses and other types of threats can use to spread. Some examples of this type of program are KaZaA, Emule, and eDonkey.

Packaging: An operation in which a group of files (or just one) is put into another file, thus occupying less space. Packaging is similar to file compression, but is the usual way of referring to this in Unix/Linux environments. The difference between packaging and compression is in the tools used. For example, a tool called tar is normally used for packaging, while zip or gzip—WinZip—is used for compressing.

Parameter: A variable piece of data indicating how a program should behave in any given situation.

Partition: A division of a computer's hard disk that enables the operating system to identify it as if it were a separate disk. Each partition of a hard disk can have a different operating system.

Partition table: An area of a disk containing information about the sections or partitions that the disk is divided into.

Password: This is a sequence of characters used to restrict access to a certain file, program, or other areas, so that only those who know the password can enter.

Password stealer: A program that obtains and saves confidential data, such as user passwords (using key loggers or other means). This program can publish the list, allowing third parties to use the data to the detriment of the affected user.

Payload: The effects of a virus.

PDA (personal digital assistant): A pocket-sized, portable computer (also called palmtops). Like other computers, they have their own operating system, have programs installed, and can exchange information with other computers, the Internet, etc. Well-known brands include Palm and Pocket PC.

PE (Portable Executable): PE refers to the format of certain programs.

Permanent protection: This is the process that some antivirus programs carry out of continually scanning any files that are used in any operations (albeit by the user or the operating system). It is also known as sentinel or resident.

Phishing: Phishing involves massive sending of e-mails that appear to come from reliable sources and that try to get users to reveal confidential banking information. The most typical example of phishing is the sending of e-mails that appear to come from an online bank in order to get users to enter their details in a spoof Web page.

Platform: Refers to an operating system, such as, Windows, Unix, or Linux.

Plugin: A program that adds new functionality to an existing system.

Polymorphic/polymorphism: A technique used by viruses to encrypt their signature in a different way every time and even the instructions for carrying out the encryption.

POP (Post Office Protocol): This is a protocol for receiving and sending e-mails.

Pop-up menu: List of options that is displayed when clicking on a certain item or area of a window in a program with the secondary mouse button (usually the right). These options are shortcuts to certain functions of a program.

Pop-up windows: A window that suddenly appears, normally when a user selects an option with the mouse or clicks on a special function key.

Port/communication port: Point through which a computer transfers information (inbound/outbound) via TCP/IP.

Potentially unwanted program (PUP): Program that is installed without express permission from the user and carries out actions or has characteristics that can reduce user control of privacy, confidentiality, use of computer resources, etc.

Prepending: This is a technique used by viruses for infecting files by adding their code to the beginning of the file. By doing this, these viruses ensure that they are activated when an infected file is used.

Preview pane: A feature in e-mail programs that allows the content of the message to be viewed without having to open the e-mail.

Privacy policy: This is the document that sets out the procedures, rules, and data security practices of a company to guarantee the integrity, confidentiality, and availability of data collected from clients and other interested parties in accordance with applicable legislation, IT security needs, and business objectives.

Proactive protection: Ability to protect the computer against unknown malware by analyzing its behavior only and therefore not needing a virus signature file periodically updated.

Process killer: A program that ends actions or processes that are running (active) on a computer, which could pose a threat.

Program: Elements that allow operations to be performed. A program is normally a file with an EXE or COM extension.

Programming language: Set of instructions, orders, commands, and rules that are used to create programs. Computers understand electronic signals (values 0 or 1). Languages allow the programmer to specify what a program must do without having to write long strings of zeros and ones, but using words (instructions) that are more easily understood by people.

Protocol: A system of rules and specifications that enables and governs the communication between computers or IT devices (data transfer).

Proxy: A proxy sever acts as a middleman between an internal network, such as an intranet, and the connection to the Internet. In this way, one connection can be shared by various users to connect to an Internet server.

Quick Launch bar: The area next to the Windows Start button or menu, which contains shortcut icons to certain items and programs: e-mail, the Internet, antivirus, etc.

RAM (random-access memory): This is a computer's main memory, in which files or programs are stored when they are in use.

Recycle bin: This is a section or folder on the hard disk where deleted files are stored (provided they have not been permanently deleted).

Redirect: Access one address via another.

Remote control: The action of gaining access to a user's computers (with or without the user's consent) from a computer in a different location. This access could pose a threat if it is not done correctly or for legitimate purposes.

Rename: Action whereby a file, directory, or other element of a system is given a new name.

Replica: Among other things, the action by which a virus propagates or makes copies of itself, with the aim of furthering the spread of the virus.

Resident/resident virus: A program or file is referred to as resident when it is stored in the computer's memory, continuously monitoring operations carried out on the system.

Restart: Action whereby the computer is temporarily stopped and then immediately starts again.

Ring: A system governing privilege levels in a microprocessor and controlling the operations that can be performed and its protection. There are various levels: Ring0 (administrator), Ring1 and Ring2 (administrator with less privileges), and Ring3 (user).

ROM (read-only memory): This is a type of memory that under normal circumstances cannot be written on, and therefore, its content is permanent.

Root directory: This is the main directory or folder on a disk or drive.

Rootkit: A program designed to hide objects such as processes, files, or Windows registry entries (often including its own). This type of software is not malicious in itself but is used by hackers to cover their tracks in previously compromised systems. There are types of malware that use rootkits to hide their presence on the system.

Routine: Invariable sequence of instructions that make up part of a program and can be used repeatedly.

Scam: Any illegal plot or fraud in which a person or group of persons are tricked into giving money, under false promises of economic gain (trips, vacations, lottery prizes, etc.).

Scanning ports, IP addresses: The action of identifying the communications ports and/or IP addresses of a computer and getting information about their status. This action can sometimes be considered an attack or threat.

SCR files: These files, which have the extension SCR, could be Windows screensavers or files written in script languages.

Screensaver: This is a program that displays pictures or animations on the screen. These programs were originally created to prevent images from burning onto the screen when the computer was not used for a while.

Script/script virus: The term *script* refers to files or sections of code written in programming languages like Visual Basic Script (VBScript) and JavaScript.

Sector: This is a section or area of a disk.

Security patch: Set of additional files applied to a software program or application to resolve certain problems, vulnerabilities, or flaws.

Security risk: This covers anything that can have negative consequences for the user of the computer (e.g., a program for creating viruses or Trojans).

Sent items: A folder in e-mail programs that contains copies of the messages sent out.

Server: IT system (computer) that offers certain services and resources (communication, applications, files, etc.) to other computers (known as clients), which are connected to it across a network.

Service: The suite of features offered by one computer or system to others that are connected to it.

Services applet: An applet in Windows XP/2000/NT, which configures and monitors system services.

Shareware: Evaluation versions of a software product that allow users to try out a product for a period of time before buying it. Shareware versions are normally free or significantly cheaper than complete versions.

Signature/identifier: This is like the virus passport number. A sequence of characters (numbers, letters, etc.) that identify the virus.

SMTP (Simple Mail Transfer Protocol): This is a protocol used on the Internet exclusively for sending e-mail messages.

Software: Files, programs, applications, and operating systems that enable users to operate computers or other IT systems. These are the elements that make the hardware work.

Spam: Unsolicited e-mail, normally containing advertising. These messages, usually mass mailings, can be highly annoying and waste both time and resources.

Spammer: A program that allows the mass mailing of unsolicited, commercial e-mail messages. It can also be used to mass-mail threats like worms and Trojans.

Spear phishing: This attack uses phishing techniques but is aimed at a specific target. The creator of this type of attack will never use spam to obtain a massive avalanche of personal user data. The fact that it is targeted and not massive implies careful preparation in order to make it more credible and the use of more sophisticated social engineering techniques.

Spyware: Programs that collect information about users' browsing activity, preferences, and interests. The data collected are sent to the creator of the application or third parties and can be stored in a way that it can be recovered at another time. Spyware can be installed with the user consent and awareness, but sometimes it is not. The same thing happens with the knowledge or lack of knowledge regarding data collected and the way it is used.

SQL (Structured Query Language): A standard programming language aimed at enabling the administration and communication of databases. It is widely used in the Internet (e.g., Microsoft SQL Server, MySQL, etc.).

Statistics: A sample of malware has statistics whenever its infection percentage is among the 50 most active threats.

Status bar: A section that appears at the bottom of the screen in some Windows programs with information about the status of the program or the files that are in use at the time.

Stealth: A technique used by viruses to infect computers unnoticed by users or antivirus applications.

String: A sequence of characters (letters, numbers, punctuation marks, etc.).

Subtype: Each of the subgroups into which a type is divided, in this case, a group of viruses or threats within the same category or type, with certain characteristics in common.

Symptoms of infection: These are the actions or effects that a virus could have when it infects a computer including trigger conditions.

System services: Applications that normally run independently when a system is started up and that close, also independently, on shutting down the system. System services carry out fundamental tasks such as running the SQL server or the Plug & Play detector.

Targeted attack: Attacks aimed specifically at a person, company, or group that are normally perpetrated silently and imperceptibly. These are not massive attacks as their aim is not to reach as many computers as possible. The danger lies precisely in the customized nature of the attack, which is designed especially to trick potential victims.

Task list: A list of all programs and processes currently active (normally in the Windows operating system).

Technical name: The real name of a virus, which also defines its class or family.

Template/global template: This is a file that defines a set of initial characteristics that a document should have before starting to work with it.

Threat level: This is a calculation of the danger that a particular virus represents to users.

Title bar: A bar on top of a window. The title bar contains the name of the file or program.

Track: A ring on a disk where data can be written.

Trackware: All programs that monitor the actions of users on the Internet (pages visited, banners clicked on, etc.) and create a profile that can be used by advertisers.

Trigger: This is the condition that causes the virus to activate or to release its payload.

Trojan: Strictly speaking, a Trojan is not a virus, although it is often thought of as such. Really they are programs that enter computers appearing to be harmless programs, install themselves, and carry out actions that affect user confidentiality.

TSR (terminate and stay resident): A characteristic that allows certain programs to stay in memory after having run.

Tunneling: A technique used by some viruses to foil antivirus protection.

Updates: Antiviruses are constantly becoming more powerful and adapting to the new technologies used by viruses and virus writers. If they are not to become obsolete, they must be able to detect the new viruses that are constantly appearing. To do this, they have what is called a virus signature file.

UPX: This is a file compression tool (Ultimate Packer for eXecutables) that also allows programs compressed with this tool to be run without having to be decompressed.

URL (uniform resource locator): Address through which to access Internet pages (or other computers).

Vaccination: An antivirus technique that allows file information to be stored and possible infections detected when a change is noted in the file.

Variant: A variant is a modified version of an original virus, which may vary from the original in terms of means of infection and the effects that it has.

Virus: Viruses are programs that can enter computers or IT systems in a number of ways, causing effects that range from simply annoying to highly destructive and irreparable.

Virus constructor: A malicious program intended to create new viruses without having any programming skills, as it has an interface that allows to choose the characteristics of the created malware: type, payload, target files, encryption, polymorphism, etc.

Virus signature file: This file enables the antivirus to detect viruses.

Volume: This is a partition of a hard disk or a reference to a complete hard disk. This term is used in many networks where there are shared disks.

Vulnerability: Flaws or security holes in a program or IT system, often used by viruses as a means of infection.

WAN (wide area network): A network of interconnected computers over a large geographical area, connected via telephone, radio or satellite.

Windows desktop: This is the main area of Windows that appears when you start up the computer. From here you can access all tools, utilities, and programs installed on the computer, via shortcut icons, options in the Windows Start menu, the Windows taskbar, etc.

Windows Explorer: Program or application available in Windows to administer the files available on the computer. It is very useful for getting an organized view of all directories.

Windows Registry: This is a file that stores all configuration and installation information of programs installed, including information about the Windows operating system.

Windows Registry Key: These are sections of the Windows Registry that store information regarding the system's settings and configuration.

Windows System Tray: Area in the Windows taskbar (usually in the bottom right corner of the screen), which contains the system clock, icons for changing system settings and viewing the status of the antivirus protection, etc.

Windows taskbar: This is a bar that appears at the bottom of the screen in Windows. The bar contains the Start button, the clock, icons of all programs resident in memory at that moment, and shortcuts that give direct access to certain programs.

WINS (Windows Internet Name Service): A service for determining names associated with computers in a network and allowing access to them. A computer contains a database with IP addresses (e.g., 125.15.0.32) and the common names assigned to each computer in the network (e.g., SERVER1).

Workstation: One of the computers connected to a local network that uses the services and resources in the network. A workstation does not normally provide services to other machines in the network in the same way a server does.

Worm: This is similar to a virus, but it differs in that all it does is make copies of itself (or part of itself).

Write access/permission: These rights or permissions allow a user or a program to write to a disk or other type of information storage unit.

Write protected: This is a technique used to allow files on a disk or other storage device to be read but to prevent users from writing on them.

WSH (Windows Script Host): The system that enables you to batch process files and allows access to Windows functions via programming languages such as Visual Basic Script and JavaScript (script languages).

XOR (OR exclusive): An operation used by many viruses to encrypt their content.

Zip: A particular format of compressed file corresponding to the WinZip application.

Zombie: A computer controlled through the use of bots.

Zoo (virus): Those viruses that are not in circulation and that only exist in places like laboratories, where they are used for researching the techniques and effects of viruses.

Websites

http://www.cs.ox.ac.uk/people/leslieann.goldberg/papers/virus.pdf.
http://www.cwjobs.co.uk/careers-advice/it-glossary/cyber-crime-timeline.
http://www.digitalcraft.org/?artikel_id=295 http://www.google.com/patents/US7231667.
http://www.pandasecurity.com/usa/homeusers/security-info/glossary/.

5

ARCHITECTURE OF EARLY WARNING PREDICTIVE SYSTEM FOR SMART CITIES

Digital Immunity: A New Dawn

We all remember the famous business metric "If you can measure it, you can control it." Well, the Internet has become a mega–gravitational force establishing new rules and regulations. We are riding the Internet whether we like it or not. Cybercrime and cyber terrorism have been making drastic black holes in our societal fabric and thriving on profound immorality and political poisoning. The World Trade Center disaster was above all a *failure of imagination* as lamented by Senator Thomas Keen during the 9/11 Commission Report.

Since necessity is the mother of invention and in order to control or at least to manage global malware, we need to have a holistic and scientific strategy (a new prescription because the present one is going flat) that focuses on collaborative efforts among government, industry, and academia R&D. Like the Human Immune System, the Cognitive Early Warning System (CEWPS) is the counterpart in the digital world, championed by the magical agent called the Smart Vaccine. If vaccination has been contributing to the longevity of mankind, then CEWPS will extend to the longevity of healthy systems. The Smart Vaccine (SV) offers unique *adaptive* vaccination services that are the true life jackets of a city's systems. The Smart Vaccine is actually from the third kind with a much higher level of intelligence to beat the best hacking brains. Does it sound like science fiction huh? So let's start with the design of the CEWPS Knowledge Base.

Smart Cities Are Like the Human Body

The closest analogy of The Smart City (SC) ecosystem that comes to my mind is the human body, which is holistically administered by the brain and by federated systems (organs) that perform autonomically with perfect precision. No waterway on Earth is as complete, as commodious, or as populous as that wonderful river of life called the *Stream of Blood*. The violin, the trumpet, the harp, the grand organ, and all the other musical instruments are mere counterfeits of the human voice.

Another marvel of the human body is the self-regulating process (so-called auto-nomic) by which nature keeps the body temperature in health at 98°. Whether in India, with the temperature at 130°, or in the arctic regions, where the records show 120° below freezing point, the body temperature remains the same, practically steady at 98° despite the extreme to which it is subjected. It was said that "All roads lead to Rome!," but modern science has discovered that all roads of real knowledge lead to the human body.

And you think cities are crowded now? For the first time in history, more than 50% of the world's population lives in cities. By 2030, more than 5 billion people will live in urban settings. But before we get to that kind of population density, we have to optimize our cities. We need to make them smarter, safer, and above all more secure. Yes, tech-nology can help. Modern cities compete with each other to attract businesses, talent, skills, and taxpayers. As a result, administrations are becoming entrepreneurial, valuing innovation, technology, marketing, and communication. The smart city (SC) ecosystem is a broad partnership between the public and private sector. City planners and develop-ers, nongovernmental organizations, IT system integrators, software vendors, energy and utility providers, the automotive industry, and facility control providers, as well as technology providers for mobile technology, cloud computing, networking, and system-to-system (S2S) and radio frequency identification (RFID) have a role to play.

Again, like the human body, component connectivity is one of the principal pre-requisites for building smart city. Smart city live by their smart grids, that is, their nervous system. It allows cities to breathe, to facilitate exchange of information, and to respond promptly to danger. In case of a massive cyberattack on the city, the smart grid will be the best savior. The grid will help isolate the attack and the infected sec-tion of the city. By design, integrating CEWPS into the smart grid will offer several advances. For one thing, it will predict and deter the attack and alert everyone on the grid. Even if part of the grid is crippled by the attack, CEWPS will be able to reach out to all the other critical systems and offer vaccination help.

Keeping the city thriving on quality living is critical. Transportation strategies have an impact on public safety, the environment, energy, rapid response services, the abil-ity to do business, and critical deliveries have to fit precisely in this gigantic jigsaw puzzle while keeping the general quality of life. Real-time traffic flow information, coupled with Telco, Global Positioning Systems (GPS), machine-to-machine com-munication, Wi-Fi, and RFID technologies, as well as data analytics and prediction techniques, can all be used to enhance private and public travel. Smart cities live by their sensors that collect information about traffic conditions at critical city spots and send via wireless or GPS communication to centralized control systems. These data can, for example, contribute to the optimization of synchronized traffic lights as shown in Figure 5.1.

By definition, smart city implies smart government, smart citizens, smart tech-nologies, and more importantly, smart future. Predicting the future has always been a human endeavor since the beginning of time. History tells us interesting stories

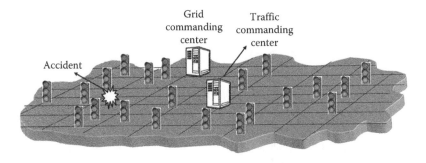

Figure 5.1 The city's smart grid is a big contributor to optimize the flow of traffic by synchronizing the traffic lights when the traffic is heavy or there is an accident in a congested area of the city. The traffic command center knows the location of the lights and the hourly estimated flow. The traffic is monitored remotely, especially around school crossings, and traffic data are relayed to the city directorate for predictive analyses.

about how the future was predicted. Romans, Egyptians, and Greeks had high priests who influenced the rules with predictions about calamities, sickness, and wars. Temples were holy places where mysterious rituals were performed by priests, which included sorcery, exorcism, and astrology. Today, we consider all these rituals nonsense and without true scientific basis.

CEWPS Is the Electronic Shield of Smart Cities

CEWPS, shown in Figure 5.2, which surrounds The Smart City, will be able to identify the attack and build the proper vaccine to eradicate it. CEWPS has several crucial responsibilities, not only to destroy the attacking virus but also to preserve a copy of the virus and keep its structure in the Virus Knowledge Base (ViKB) for future attacks. More importantly, CEWPS will notify the city's Coordination Command Center (CCC) about the attack, its nature, its expected impact, and its whereabouts. The CCC will broadcast alerts to all the critical systems, using its smart grid. One thing to remember is that CEWPS has its own grid also referred to as the Smart Vaccine Grid (SVG), while The Smart City has its own Smart Grid (SG). The CEWPS Central Coordination Center exchanges information with the city's Coordination Command. CEWPS and The Smart City CCC has to quickly draw up an emergency response plan covering all possible situations of the attack.

The most prominent feature in CEWPS is its intelligent early warning predictive system. It is the radar of the city. It is a complex artificial intelligence system that operates like the human brain. Before we describe its anatomy, we would like to enrich your knowledge with two important terms: *causality* and *prediction*.

What Is Causality?

Let's first examine what causality or causal inference means. Causality is the relationship between an event (the cause) and a second event (the effect), where the second

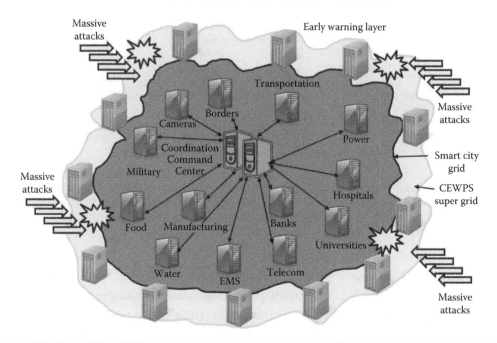

Figure 5.2 Smart cities can come in any form or shape. In this configuration, the Cognitive Early Warning Predictive System shields the critical infrastructures from massive distributed malware. If the attack succeeds to penetrate the grid, the Coordination Command Center (CCC) will order the Smart Vaccine Commander to send its army to inoculate the critical systems with the proper vaccine.

event is understood to be the consequence of the first. Causality governs the relationship between events. There are however two cases of causality. The first case is called *necessary causes*: If x is a necessary cause of y, then the presence of y necessarily implies the presence of x. The presence of x, however, does not imply that y will occur. The second case is called *sufficient causes*: If x is a sufficient cause of y, then the presence of x necessarily implies the presence of y. However, another cause, z, may alternatively cause y. Thus, the presence of y does not imply the presence of x.

What Is Prediction?

By definition, a prediction of this kind might be inductively valid if the predictor is a knowledgeable person in the field and is employing sound reasoning and accurate data. But as a rule, predicting an event $E(t_f)$ to happen in the future (t_f) is perfectly valid, if previously, one or several similar events did occur at the same place and time $E(t_{f-1})$, $E(t_{f-2})$, $E(t_{f-3})$.

The probability that event $E(t_f)$ will occur, provided that event $E(t_{f-1})$ did occur. Using probability formalism, we can write $P(E(t_f)|E(t_{f-1}))$.

In summary, we can deduce causal mechanisms from past data. Causality is an ingredient of the CEWPS Reasoning Engine.

Anatomy of CEWPS and Its Main Components

The CEWPS comes with an arsenal of offensive and defensive systems. It is designed specifically to defend, by offense, smart city, and large metropolitan areas. CEWPS is in fact an incredible *brain* that controls a multitude of autonomic subsystems, which are connected through CEWPS sensory and motor grid. This book often describes CEWPS with different configurations, depending on the subject and the content. CEWPS has nine subsystems headed by the Central Coordination Command, which acts as the "nerve center" and control hub. In fact, all the subsystems are dynamic components with a specific set of responsibilities and unique skill sets to support the Smart Vaccine in the battlefield. Figure 5.3 shows the nine interlinked operating subsystems. Here's an explanation of each component.

Component 1: The Central Coordination Command (CCC)

The CCC is the nerve center of CEWPS. It is an incredible hub of transactional traffic, orchestrating autonomically all CEWPS activities, inspecting performance readings from the operating components, routing alert messages, and dispatching service

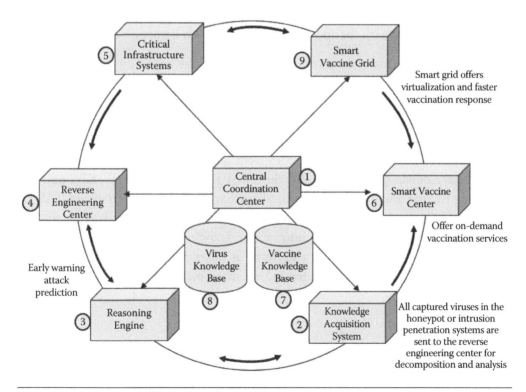

Figure 5.3   The topology of CEWPS is unique: All nine of the components are equally critical. However, they receive commands from the Central Coordination Center. During an attack, all the components are mobilized and work together. The main focus is to protect the critical systems from the attack through vaccination and, at the same time, capture the virus and determine its identity and save it for the next attack.

requests to the Smart Vaccine Commander (SVC). The CCC also relies heavily on its Causality Reasoning Engine, which provides significant intelligence information on incoming attacks.

CEWPS comes with dynamic steering dashboard equipped with 3D visualization feature to see everything before deciding on the next action. The dashboard offers visibility to trap attacks before they penetrate the city's smart grid. CCC regularly receives performance data from the city's smart grid.

The CEWPS main dashboard has the highest administrative authority over the following information:

1. Connectivity of all the subscribed infrastructure critical systems
2. Control of the security thresholds and risk proximities before and during the attack
3. Maintenance and administration of the infrastructure critical systems key performance indicators
4. Registry and authorization of all the vaccination services
5. Monitoring the vaccination in progress
6. Monitoring the attack in progress
7. Authentication and authorization of the attack alerts
8. Communication with the operation centers of the infrastructure critical systems

Figure 5.4 shows the main screen of the dashboard. There are 60 dynamic subscreens to provide the status of CEWPS–Smart Vaccine activities. The administrator can add dynamically additional screens or run an ad hoc SQL query on demand.

There is also another layout of the CEWPS dashboard with more details in the "CEWPS Screens Layout" section at the end of this chapter.

CEWPS draws its predictive analytics from its Attack Knowledge Base (AKB), the Vaccine Knowledge Base (VaKB), the Virus Knowledge Base (ViKB), and the Reasoning Engine. Building a synergistic alliance with AVT providers gives CEWPS higher credibility and, more importantly, feeds CEWPS with a steady fresh flow of malware data ready to be converted into vaccine knowledge.

CEWPS is also equipped with a network of *smart honeypots* to capture cyberattacks, which will be reverse engineered to help make matching vaccines.

CEWPS Component 2: The Knowledge Acquisition Component

Where Wisdom, Experience, and Knowledge Are Distilled   Let's define some basic terms that will be heavily used throughout the book. By analogy, we can compare the acquisition process to our sense system, which is made of sensory cells that collect external data for distillation, filtration, and conversion into stimuli stored in the brain.

What Is Experience?   Experience is in fact a conscious event that creates a brain process and gets stored internally in sensory cortex of the brain. Once an experience episode

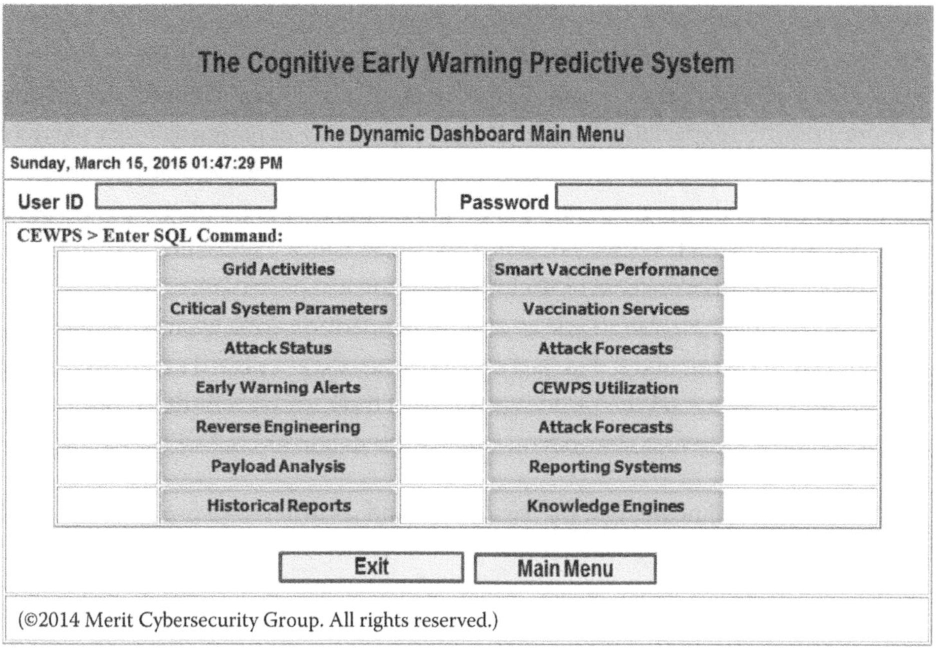

The Cognitive Early Warning Predictive System

The Dynamic Dashboard Main Menu

Sunday, March 15, 2015 01:47:29 PM

User ID   Password

CEWPS > Enter SQL Command:

Grid Activities		Smart Vaccine Performance
Critical System Parameters		Vaccination Services
Attack Status		Attack Forecasts
Early Warning Alerts		CEWPS Utilization
Reverse Engineering		Attack Forecasts
Payload Analysis		Reporting Systems
Historical Reports		Knowledge Engines

Exit   Main Menu

Figure 5.4 The main dashboard of CEWPS, showing all the features of the system. Staff of the Central Coordination Center have administrative privileges, but biometrics and two-factor authentication apply to everyone. Behind the main screen, there are 60 subscreens to collect and request vital data. The system is also equipped with an SQL query feature to interrogate any of the Knowledge Bases of the system.

gets into the brain, a memory record is created and ready to be stored. There are three types of memory records: The first is the sensory stage, which is the front end. The registration of information during perception occurs in the brief sensory stage that usually lasts for only a fraction of a second. It is your sensory memory that allows a perception such as a visual pattern, a sound, or a touch to linger for a brief moment after the stimulation is over. Second, after that first flicker, the sensation is stored in short-term memory, which has fairly limited capacity; it can hold about seven items for no more than 20 or 30 seconds at a time. Third, long-term memory can store unlimited amounts of information indefinitely. People tend to more easily store material on subjects that they already know something about, since the information has more meaning to them and can be mentally connected to related information that is already stored in their long-term memory. That is why someone who has an average memory may be able to remember a greater depth of information about one particular subject. Most people think of long-term memory when they think of *memory* itself. Biologically, information must first pass through sensory stage and short-term memory before it can be stored as a long-term memory.

So, experience E_j is an event or an episode that we participate in or live through. We all learn from experience, regardless if they are ugly, bad, or happy ones. Experience is cumulative and gets transformed into knowledge later. Experience is gained by repeated trials. We all experience it in life. Quantitatively speaking, experience is a function of time $f(t)$ with a start time $E_j t_1$ and a finish time $E_j t_2$. Experience duration is expressed as $t_2 - t_1$. Since experience can have many modes such as physical, emotional, mental, spiritual, vicarious, or virtual, the parameter j represents the experience mode. So, E_j represents experience for a particular mode m. When we add the time duration to a particular experience including its mode, we get the following.

$E_j t_{j\,m}$ m is the mode (1 = physical, 2 = mental,...). Once experience is stored in the brain, it gets magically converted into knowledge.

CEWPS considers a cyberattack as an independent discrete event that has a start and finish. But knowing about the past cyberattacks E_{j-1} (a priori) can definitely help forecast incoming attacks. CEWPS is a smart machine, and it is built for one purpose: to catch cyberattacks before they occur. That is the magic of CEWPS.

What Is Knowledge?   Knowledge, on the other hand, is different from experience. It is the derivative of experience.

$$K_t = \frac{d}{dt}(E_t)$$

Knowledge can be defined as "the fact or condition of knowing something with familiarity gained through experience or association." The knowledge engine takes disparate experience episodes $E_j t_{j.m}$ and converts them into knowledge patterns and catalogs them in the brain for subsequent neural response. Intelligence is another human characteristic, but it refers to the fast ability of retrieving knowledge, connecting pieces of knowledge together, or processing knowledge quickly.

CEWPS stores a priori knowledge extracted from previous cyberattacks on the smart grid. Attackers already know that there is a smart grid, and they design their attack vector to penetrate the grid from the weakest side and hide until the time comes for spreading to the center of the grid.

Six Stages of Cybercrime   No one has ever analyzed a cyberattack on a smart grid in a smart city. Let's not forget that the smart grid is not only a power grid. It is a resilient and secure platform that connects all the infrastructure critical systems together. Smart grids are the new paradigm where technology and security vendors are jockeying to learn about it and introduce their new products. Smart grid cyberattacks will usher the beginning of the new cyber war, and we had better be ready for it. CEWPS is designed to defend smart grids, which are the backbone of a future smart city.

As we described earlier, a cyberattack is an unknown event where its occurrence can be represented as a Bayesian network model (BNM) as conditional dependencies in probability distributions. We can deduce from experience that all cyberattacks follow the same six stages as shown in Figure 5.5.

So, the attack on the smart grid has to be well studied, engineered, and executed. The smart grid is equipped with the Smart Vaccine Grid (SVG) which is totally new

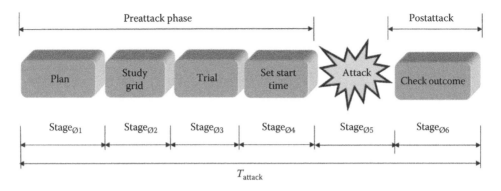

Figure 5.5   Most cyberattacks share the same pattern. There are six stages to a cyberattack. The attack is just as good as its plan. The success of one will trigger successive attacks with "augmented" learning from the previous ones. Skipping one stage makes the attack less successful.

to terrorists. One way for them to penetrate the grid is with the cooperation of an internal help—someone who can pass some key access information to the terrorists. If they succeed to penetrate any of the critical systems with an admin password and open a port, then they can upload a backdoor Trojan with a worm that carries a malicious payload. Generally, most cyberattacks on large installations or critical infrastructures occur through some internal help. The terrorists will also try to target insecure installations on the grid, but their trail could be detected. The cyberterrorists most likely studied the grid (stage 2) and tried different hacks (stage 3) and have decided on the final target. Nowadays, cyberattacks are driven mostly by political and religious motifs. Cyberterrorism is planned and executed by expert cyber hackers who know where the most vulnerable spots are in the major cosmopolitan city in the world. Each country has its electronic army, which is equipped with the latest symmetrical technologies. Cyberterrorists learn from their success and failures and will try to launch several "distractive" attacks at different locations on the city grid. Most likely organized electronic armies have similar technologies as CEWPS, where they model attacks and develop new payloads. In other words, smart cities are attacked by smart attacks.

The FBI, the Dutch Korps Landelijke Politiediensten, UK Interpol, the French Sûreté, and the German Bundeskriminalamt have automated fingerprint identification systems (AFIS) that they share among themselves in order to catch serial cyberterrorists. Often cybercriminals at one time had a security job with the government or big institution, then they were lured to join a terrorist organization like ISIS for money and women. There are many Crime Service Providers (CSP) that exist under a fictitious business name, and attract anti-government activists and hacktivists. CEWPS will be a great help for law enforcement agencies to use advanced technologies to hunt cybercriminals and cyberterrorists. CEWPS collects also crime data from many global sources, even Big Data will be used in predictive reasoning to generate cybercrime analytics.

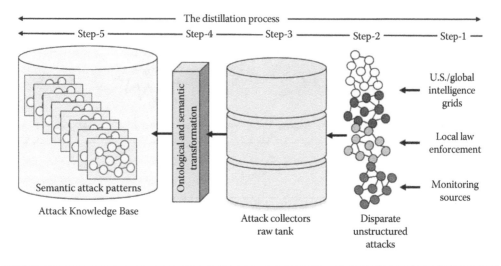

Figure 5.6   The unstructured raw data is collected from many sources (Big Data is a potential feeder of attack data). Then the collected raw data go through an ontology and semantic engine and transform into uniform patterns stored in the attack Knowledge Base. The pattern is a data model that represents an attack with all its attributes.

Cybercrime Raw Data Distillation Process   There is an invaluable "deep web" of disparate crime data that could be collected and distilled. In order for CEWPS to be effectively successful as an early warning predictive machine, it needs first a reliable and rich Attack Knowledge Base (AKB) and second an intelligent Reasoning Engine. The distillation process of raw crime data will create the Attack Knowledge Base in five basic steps as shown in Figure 5.6. The Causality Reasoning Engine (CRE) will be discussed in the next section.

Step 1: The raw data feeders: U.S./global intelligence agencies and the local law enforcement agencies have to feed fresh and all historical data. The millions of crime case will enrich the Knowledge Base and enhance the performance of the inference engine.

Step 2: Raw input data: Since cybercrime records are coming from many different law enforcement agencies, research organizations, or other crime repositories, obviously, data would be disparate, redundant, structured with different formats, or even processed by different software systems. Each country, for example, has its own proprietary finger or face identification system. The data collector will homogenize the data.

Figure 5.7 shows the graphical representation of a typical premeditated cybercrime "episode" with all its attributes. It is not a pure Directed Acyclic Graph (DAG) because the attributes (variables) did not come with conditional probabilities. They need to be converted into a uniform Bayesian network model with conditional probabilities and interdependencies before they can be used for reasoning inference.

Step 3: Raw data cleansing: All unedited cybercrime episodes will be routed to an intermediate repository for cleaning and filtering. This process is pretty much like an iron mill where iron will be smelted and cast or even like the oil refinery.

The Domain of a Cyberattack

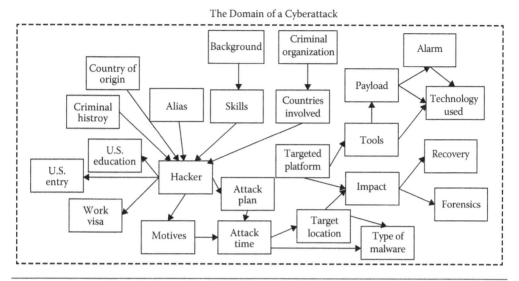

Figure 5.7   Attributes of a cyberattack represented graphically as a network of activities. It is considered a nonstandard raw model, which will be transformed into a semantic pattern used in reasoning and attack prediction. All priori (from the earlier) episodes will also be stored as semantic patterns.

Step 4: Ontological and semantic transformation: In this step, we try to convert all the raw crime data into knowledge records. First, let's define two important words: ontology and semantics.

Ontology: It has a lot of Greek history, but here it has a different meaning. In the context of knowledge, it refers to the technology that creates a knowledge model. CEWPS uses ontology to convert unstructured cybercrime episodes into a crime knowledge model ready for reasoning. In simple terms, it is a network of attributes centered around a common subject.

Ontology components are as follows:

1. Instances or objects
2. Classes, types, kinds
3. Attributes, properties, predicates, features
4. Relationships—how one variable relates to another; parent-to-child relationship

Semantics is the technology that converts a pattern from the Attack Knowledge Base into a semantic framework called a *document*. The Web Ontology Language (OWL) and Resource Description Framework (RDF) are the two dominating languages that enable the encoding, exchange, and reuse of structured metadata. The two languages are application of XML, which impose needed structural constraints to provide unambiguous methods of expressing semantics.

In summary, step 4 is the conversion of the mishmash of all the cybercrime cases to a standardized format (semantic attack pattern) to facilitate reasoning and causal prediction using Bayesian network modeling technique.

Ontology and Semantic Technologies   Two techniques will be utilized in the Knowledge Base to prepare the data for the next stage. Ontology is the technique of converting a cyberattack into a knowledge model. OWL will do the conversion. The second technique is called semantics, which uses the RDF language to store it in the AKB.

CEWPS comes with two knowledge engines that include databases. The first one is the Attack Knowledge Base (AKA virus DB) and the second is the Vaccine Knowledge Base (VaKB). The two knowledge engines are CEWPS components 7 and 8 as shown in Figure 5.3.

Step 5: The AKB is a well-organized, centralized, and dynamic repository designed with the Web Ontology Language (OWL) and Resource Description Framework (RDF/XML) knowledge building languages. AKB uses special cybercrime taxonomy codes for the first time. CEWPS also complies with the standards of the World Wide Web Consortium (W3C) to build the cybercrime knowledge patterns.

The activities shown in Figure 5.7 need to be converted into knowledge model. Data attributes will be converted "semantically" into equivalent meaningful data elements. Then, the new semantic model will be stored in the Attack Knowledge Base (AKB). Semantic translation links the activities into edges and vertices, following a logical sequence that describes the premeditated attack by a terrorist. In the end, we converted the raw model into a Bayesian Network Model as shown in Figure 5.8.

Let's remember that in a Bayesian network graph, each feature is represented with a node (box) in the graph, and an arrow from one node X to another node Y in the graph

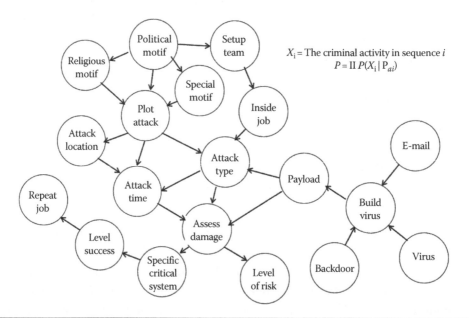

X_i = The criminal activity in sequence i
$$P = \Pi\, P(X_i \mid P_{ai})$$

Figure 5.8 This graph represents a knowledge model of a cyberattack. It is also called a Bayesian network model. All cyberattacks can be transformed into this model. Ontology is the technique that is used to convert a cyberattack into a knowledge model. Web Ontology Language does the conversion. The semantic Resource Description Framework (RDF) stores it in the Attack Knowledge Base (AKB). The vertices (circles) represent the variables (criminal activity), and the arcs (arrows) represent the causal relationship between the activities.

represents the probabilistic dependence of *Y* on *X* (not shown here; see supplementary information S1 for further details). Note that the direction of an arrow between two nodes does not necessarily reveal causality or hierarchy but merely shows a probabilistic relationship between the two corresponding features.

The CEWPS Attack Knowledge Base is actually a very smart engine with high-level autonomicity and intelligence. It is an *expert library* that contains significant archival crime episodes from around the world. Cyberterrorism is the biggest global supply chain in the world with a monitory flow of $16 billion per year. Cybercrime and its older brother cyberterrorism are the most affluent profession in the world. Forty-nine law enforcement agencies will be the regular crime data feeders into CEWPS AKB. CEWPS will have the biggest crime *refinery* in the world. The AKB engine will be running 24/7 trying to convert data into knowledge. Like crude oil, raw crime episodes go into an extensive distillation process to convert into a uniform structure. The formatted episode data will then be routed into the AKB and will be transformed into a *knowledge model* before it goes into the inference engine for predictive induction.

CEWPS Component 3: The Reasoning Engine

The Reasoning Engine (RE) is the *smart guy* component of CEWPS, often referred to as the knowledge-based system. CEWPS refers to it as the early warning predictor (EWP). The early warning predictor is an inference reasoning engine that relies on the Bayesian network model (BNM) to generate probabilistic attack forecast. Some of the benefits of using BNM are as follows:

1. They are graphical models, capable of displaying relationships clearly and intuitively.
2. They are directional, thus being capable of representing cause–effect relationships.
3. They can handle uncertainty.
4. They handle uncertainty through the established theory of probability.
5. They can be used to represent indirect, in addition to, direct causation.

Bayesian network is a set of local conditional probability distributions. Together with the graph structure, they are sufficient to represent the joint probability distribution of the domain

$$\Pr(X_1, X_2, \ldots, X_n) = \prod_{i=1}^{n} \Pr(X_i | \mathrm{Pa}_i)$$

where Pa_i is the set containing the parents of X_i in the Bayesian network.

We Can Forecast the Weather, Why Can't We Predict Crime?   Let's take a look at other forecast systems such as weather and stock forecasting systems. Weather forecasting is the application of science and technology to predict the state of the atmosphere for a given location. Weather forecasts are made by collecting in the first step quantitative weather data from weather satellites about the current state of the atmosphere on a given place and using scientific methods of atmospheric processes to project how the atmosphere will change. In the second step, data are loaded into a mathematical weather model to generate credible prediction results.

Anatomy of the Reasoning Engine?   The Reasoning Engine (RE) is an AI-based system. It is commonly known as the *reasoning inference engine* (IE). This type of engine is the *holy grail* of artificial intelligence science. It is highly educated and a fast-learner machine. Let's take a look at its anatomy as shown in Figure 5.9.

An inference engine cycles through three sequential steps: *match rules*, *select rules*, and *execute rules*. The execution of the rules will often result in new facts or goals being added to the Knowledge Base, which will trigger the cycle to repeat. This cycle continues until no new rules can be matched.

In the first step, match the rules, the inference engine finds all of the rules that are triggered by the current contents of the Knowledge Base. In forward chaining, the engine looks for rules where the antecedent (left-hand side) matches some facts in the Knowledge Base. In backward chaining, the engine looks for antecedents that can satisfy one of the current goals.

In the second step, select the rules, the inference engine prioritizes the various rules that were matched to determine the order to execute them.

In the third step, execute the rules, the engine executes each matched rule in the order determined in step 2 and then iterates back to step 1 again. The cycle continues until no new rules are matched.

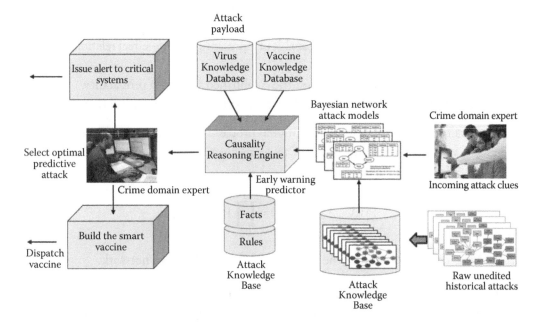

Figure 5.9   The Causality Reasoning Engine is the heart of the CEWPS. It extracts information from the Attack Knowledge Base (AKB) and Vaccine Knowledge Base (VaKB) and applies the proper facts and rules to generate probabilistic forecasts.

The Attack Knowledge Base represents facts about the cyberattacks, cybercriminal profiles, victims, and impact of the attack. The world was represented as classes and subclasses, and instances and assertions were replaced by values of object instances. The rules worked by querying and asserting values of the objects.

CEWPS Component 4: Reverse Engineering Center (REC)

Reverse Engineering Center is responsible for decomposing all attacking unknown viruses and learning everything about their code and technologies. The pathology reports on captured and quarantined viruses will be cataloged and stored in the Virus Knowledge Base (ViKB). Information coming from other forensic centers will also be stored in ViKB. Meanwhile, the corresponding antivirus vaccine will be stored in the Vaccine Knowledge Base (VaKB). The Central Coordination Center (CCC) will receive daily bulletins from the reverse engineering center (REC). The Smart Vaccine center (SVC) is getting ready for its fast response vaccination services.

Tools of reverse engineering are categorized into debuggers or disassemblers, hex editors, and monitoring and decompiling tools. Profession cybercriminals possess libraries of Reverse Engineering. They can't live with them.

1. *Disassemblers*: A disassembler is used to convert binary code into assembly code and also used to extract strings, imported and exported functions, libraries, etc. The disassemblers convert the machine language into a user-friendly format. There are different disassemblers that specialize in certain things.
2. *Debuggers*: This tool expands the functionality of a disassembler by supporting the CPU registers, the hex duping of the program, view of stack, etc. Using debuggers, the programmers can set break points and edit the assembly code at run time. Debuggers analyze the binary in a similar way as the disassemblers and allow the reverser to step through the code by running one line at a time to investigate the results.
3. *Hex editors*: These editors allow the binary to be viewed in the editor and changed as per the requirements of the software. There are different types of hex editors available that are used for different functions.
4. *Portable executable and resource viewer*: The binary code is designed to run on a Windows-based machine and has a very specific data that tell how to set up and initialize a program. All the programs that run on Windows should have a Portable Executable that supports the Dynamic Link Libraries, which the program needs to borrow from.

CEWPS Component 5: Smart City Critical Infrastructure

The Smart City Critical Infrastructures (SCCI) is part of CEWPS environment because the critical infrastructures (i.e., critical systems) are wired inside the Smart Vaccine Grid (SVG).

In the domain of terrorism, the term *critical infrastructure* became of paramount importance. In fact, certain national infrastructures are so vital that their incapacity or destruction would have a debilitating impact on the defense or economic security of the United States. This is the reason we included the critical infrastructures as a part of the CEWPS environment. These infrastructures include the following:

1. Telecommunications
2. Electrical power systems
3. Gas and oil storage and transportation
4. Banking and finance
5. Transportation
6. Water supply systems
7. Emergency services (including medical, police, fire, and rescue)
8. Continuity of government
9. Chemical and manufacturing plants
10. Postal services and shipping
11. Agriculture
12. Banking services
13. Academia and universities

More details on how CEWPS protects the critical infrastructures will be covered in the smart grid section.

CEWPS Component 6: The Smart Vaccine Center

The Smart Vaccine center is the *Marines* of CEWPS. We can also refer to it as a mobile emergency hospital. It receives marching orders from CCC to perform its vaccination services to all the critical systems on the smart grid. The Smart Vaccine negotiates with the critical system to take the vaccine on time before any attacks. The vaccine will immunize the critical system against a particular attack. The vaccine has already been approved by the reverse engineering center and CCC and stored in the Vaccine Knowledge Base (VaKB). The Smart Vaccine army is described in detail in Chapter 2.

CEWPS Component 7: The Vaccine Knowledge Base (VaKB)

The VaKB is the intelligent *pharmacy* that has all prescriptions of all possible vaccines that were manufactured for previous attacks. It works very closely with the Causal Reasoning Engine. Further explanation will be provided in the next section.

CEWPS Component 8: The Virus Knowledge Base (ViKB)

The ViKB is the repository (we call it the morgue) that contains all the attack payloads, attack anatomy, the originating source, cause of death, and the expected target.

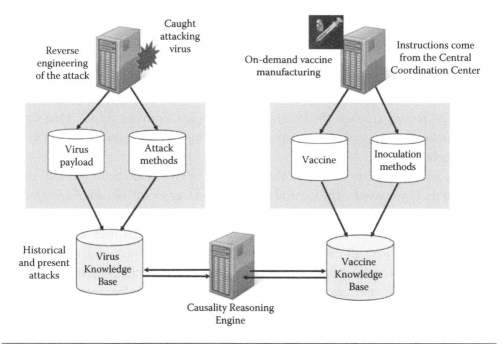

Figure 5.10   The parallelism between virus reverse engineering (once it is caught by honeypots) and vaccine processing is uncanny and fascinating. Using Bayesian visualization reasoning, CEWPS comes up with amazing predictions to vaccinate the critical systems before the attack spreads to the other critical systems.

It is also the documentation (battle report) library of the attack episodes. It works very closely with the Causality Reasoning Engine (CRE) during the analysis and prediction of future attacks.

Figure 5.10 shows the compelling matching process between the virus and the vaccine. The matching is necessary because of the "specificity" of the virus. Not all vaccination services are successful, simply because the right vaccine was not matched. Often there will be situations where the virus is new (not available in the Virus Knowledge Base), and its matching vaccine is not ready, then the infected system will provide samples of the virus, and a vaccine will promptly be fabricated for the rest of the critical systems on the grid. The prediction process for future attacks will continue regardless.

CEWPS Component 9: CEWPS Smart Grid

Let's assume the state of New Jersey decided to use the Smart Vaccine Grid (SVG) to protect all the critical systems of all the power grid. The first thing to do is to identify the location of the power plants. The NJ Geospatial RDBMS can be used to identify the location (coordinates) of the power plants across the state. In case the power plant data are not available, the New Jersey Geographic Information System (GIS) (https://njgin.state.nj.us/) and the Digital Orthoimagery databases can be tapped to capture the information, or the US Energy Information Administration (http://www.eia.gov/state/?sid=NJcan) can provide the locality of New Jersey power plants, their characteristics, generating capacity, consumption, and the demography of the consumers, and most importantly, the hardware/software used at each plant.

One should set up the Smart Vaccine Grid (SVG), which will connect all the power plant systems together, including SCADA systems that are used to collect and monitor the physical process through the Programmable Logic Controller (PLC). One should also remember that the power plants are already tied to their own power grid and should not be touched.

Figure 5.11 shows how the Smart Vaccine Grid (SVG) will be tied to all the critical systems of the power plants. The Central Coordination Center will be pathologically connected in real time to the Smart Vaccine Grid (SVG). The CEWPS screen in Figure 5.11 shows how the State of New Jersey counties and subcounties has been mapped into a grid-centric screen with all the critical systems that control the major infrastructures in the state. The grid has 2D coordinates to facilitate the location of any particular system. Each critical system is recognized by a location code and type of infrastructure. CEWPS was using infrastructure data from the State of New Jersey during its development.

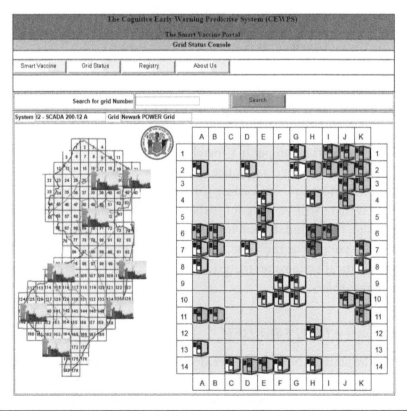

Figure 5.11 This is one of the most unique features of CEWPS. On the left, we see the grid of the state New Jersey with some of the critical power plant identified by the number of their respective subgrids. On the right, we see the grid of Newark with all the critical systems identified by 2D coordinates. In case of an attack, the grid will blink and show the target system. All city attacks would show on the screen with its entry location. The smart vaccine team got the call and is ready to respond.

The New Jersey Grid   New Jersey is rich in Critical Infrastructure and Key Resources (CIKR), situated in or near the most densely populated real estate in the country. The U.S. Critical Infrastructure Protection (CIP) program has an ongoing and robust organizational structure with identified roles and responsibilities in two functional areas: risk mitigation and field operations. Both branches support structured sector working groups (SWGs) comprised of private and public sector partners that meet regularly. The mission of the bureau is to ensure the protection, preparedness, and resiliency of New Jersey's CIKR through the implementation of the National Infrastructure Protection Plan (NIPP).

The State of New Jersey has a total population of 8.9 million people (ranked as the 11th in the nation). However, it is the most densely populated state in the union. New Jersey is growing grayer and more ethnic, and its residents are increasingly abandoning the suburbs and rural pockets in favor of cities. New Jersey is located in one of the most important industrial regions of the U.S. eastern corridor. It is one of the most dynamic hubs centered between New York City, Washington DC, and Philadelphia.

Having said that, New Jersey has great vulnerability and susceptibility to massive cyberattacks from the inside and outside. Our dependence on electric energy has increased by 800% from 1960 to 2013. There have been 25 blackouts in the northeastern and eastern regions of the United States with millions of people subjected to a traumatic experience. The most notable one is the northeast blackout of 2003 on August 14, where a wide-area power failure in the northeastern United States and central Canada affected over 55 million people. Protecting the critical infrastructures is like protecting a house of cards. There is a tremendous risk that needs to be evaluated and controlled (Figure 5.12). Risk is generated by threat, which is as defined by the International Standards Organization 73 as "The combination of the probability of an event and its consequence."

During the design of CEWPS, we looked at the risk issue and how it can be best managed; we realized that the only way it can be mitigated—not completely eliminated—is to incorporate a Smart Grid like the human nervous system. There are several unique advantages to the smart grid. For one thing, it is an incredible piece of middleware to transfer services, data, and alerts. More importantly, a smart grid (SG) is the best medium to inform adjacent systems during an attack. Also, it will detect failures and attacks and will provide failover mechanism as shown in Figure 5.13.

Connectivity of Critical Systems to a City's Smart Grid   The main purpose of having the smart grid is to allow the critical infrastructure systems (CIS) to be in real-time binding with the Central Coordination Center. The smart grid would be the main transport of vaccination services, attack outcome status, system-to-system (S2S) messaging, and important administrative instructions to the Smart Vaccine Commander (SVC).

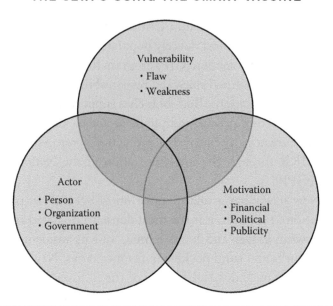

Figure 5.12   Any attack includes the three threat sources. The circles are not geometrically equal in area. Motivation is the main driver. Cyberterrorists have access to key data on the Web, which is confidential and should be removed. Having cameras on every corner and entrance of government venues helps both the cyberterrorists and law enforcement agencies.

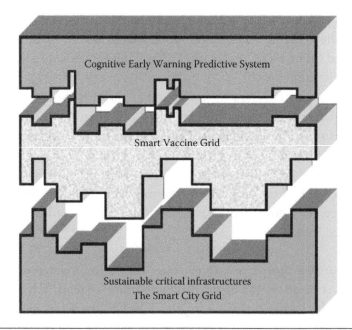

Figure 5.13   The Smart City is a replica of the human nervous system. There are three contiguous components that are virtually amalgamated together. CEWPS as the top component, a Smart Vaccine Grid as the middle component, and Sustainable Critical Infrastructures as the bottom component.

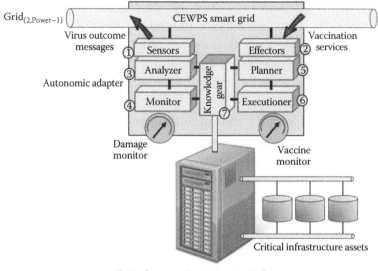

Figure 5.14   Each critical system, like an appliance, is connected to the Smart Vaccine Grid (SVG), which is the nervous system of CEWPS. Connection is made through the autonomic adapter (AA), which has all the expert components to carry vaccination services, and relay to the Smart Vaccine Commander (SVC) the attack outcomes.

The autonomic adapter (AA) engine (see Figure 5.14) is the smart interface between the critical infrastructure system and the smart grid. It carries on its back the following important mechanisms:

- Delivery of the vaccination services to the CIS, which is also called the client system
- Sending out attack outcome status to the Central Coordination Center
- Authentication of grid users
- Vaccination schedules and provisions
- Security bulletins and alerts
- Attack data from infected systems
- Connectivity between system-to-system

The autonomic adapter (AA) engine includes seven functional components as shown in Figure 5.14.

1. *The Sensors*: They collect information about the attack, the nature of the attacking virus, and the damage and sends this information through the smart grid to the Central Coordination Center (CCC) for immediate response. At the same time, the collected information is sent to the knowledge gear to be converted to knowledge.
2. *The Effectors*: As the name indicates, it describes vaccination services due to an attack. Effectors work very closely with the Smart Vaccine Commander during vaccination.

3. *The Analyzer*: It provides the mechanism to evaluate the situation (normal versus attack) based on performance and security metrics and rules.
4. *The Monitor*: It monitors the sensors that provide real-time signals from the CIS according to the rules of the analyzer.
5. *The Planner*: It packages a list of vaccination services for the attack and passes them to the commander.
6. *The Executioner*: It receives the vaccination services from the planner and passes them to the critical infrastructure systems.
7. *The Knowledge Gear*: It gathers activity sensor and effector data from all of the four functional components of the AA and gets converted into knowledge and can be discussed between the four components and the Smart Vaccine Commander.

Critical Infrastructures in Smart Cities

What Is Criticality?   It is also appropriate to clarify the subject of criticality, because it is very closely related to threat, risk, and attacks. Criticality is a relative measure of the consequences of a failure mode and its frequency of occurrences. To say that the power grid is highly critical means that a blackout will create a very grave impact. The power grid is very complex and has many interconnections and components. Failure can either be human, mechanical, electrical, or in the design of the system. The resultant failure therefore can be either catastrophic, critical, or marginal. Failure mode is defined as the way in which a failure is observed. It describes the way the failure occurs and its impact on equipment operation. A failure mode deals with the present, whereas a failure cause happened in the past and a failure effect deals with the future. Let's analyze the situation numerically.

The formula of criticality due to a failure is

$$C_m = \beta\alpha\lambda_p t$$

Criticality mode = (probability of next higher failure) × (failure mode ratio)

× (part failure rate) × (duration of applicable mission phase)

Total item criticality (C_r) is a joint probability of the item under all the failure modes:

$$C_r = \sum_{n=1}^{j} (\beta\alpha\lambda_p t)^n$$

where
   C_r is the criticality probability
   n is the initial failure mode of the item being analyzed where n = 1, 2, 3, 4,...,j
   j is the number of failure modes for the item being analyzed

Criticality of any critical infrastructure can be computed with the given formula $C_r = \Sigma_{n=1}^{j}(\beta\alpha\lambda_p t)_n$

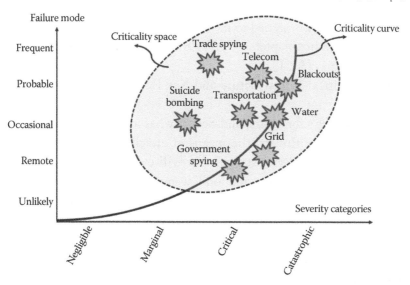

Figure 5.15 Most of the attacks on infrastructures are considered *critical* and associated with high failure probability. Smart cities cannot afford to have infrastructures with high levels of vulnerability. Predictive Analytics comes in handy to offer predictable future scenarios.

Severity is an attribute associated with the damage caused by the cyberattack. There are four levels of severity: negligible, marginal, critical, and catastrophic (Figure 5.15).

A Smart City Is Idealistic Hype   Let's start with a realistic note: a smart city is idealistic hype, although the term is very attractive, but it will not happen soon. It is a moving target with so many uneasy-to-control variables. For one thing, smart city needs an inexhaustible approved budget but, above all, a stable government led by credentialed visionary leader. Building a smart city and setting up a *base city* take at least 20 years. No one started a smart city from scratch, which is a futile endeavor, if not impossible. According to the United Nations, there are 196 capital cities of sovereign on Earth. None of them is a true smart city. My personal observation is that Dubai is steadfastly moving toward a smart city. It has the money, the plan, and the leadership. So, a smart city is nothing but a cross-pollinated booming urbanite with some inherent beauty. It can be on the ocean, in the ocean, or in the middle of the desert. The term *smart cities* is a bit ambiguous. Some people choose a narrow definition—that is, cities that use information and communication technologies (ICT) to deliver services to their citizens. My favorite definition of a smart city is that it is a booming metropolis with resilient and future-ready infrastructures, bundled with intelligent information and communication technologies (ICT) to secure the use of its key resources and managed by a team of smart citizens and smart government. But the most influencing variable in The Smart City polynomial is its ability to secure itself from physical human-provoked attacks and catastrophes. A smart city should have a mechanism to defend itself, mitigate danger, and eliminate it.

Protecting the Critical Infrastructure and Key Resources (CIKR) in The Smart City requires a brand-new approach to cybersecurity and a new set of technologies. CEWPS was specifically designed to meet the crucial security requirements in smart cities. As we have seen in Chapter 3, CEWPS is two generations ahead of the present Antivirus Technologies (AVT).

What are the Critical Infrastructure and Key Resources that smart cities have to worry about?

The National Strategy for Homeland Security has identified 13 critical sectors. As we learn more about the threats, the means of attack, and the various criteria that make targets lucrative for terrorists, this list will evolve. The critical infrastructure sectors consist of, first, agriculture and food, water, public health, emergency services, government; second, the defense industrial base, information, and telecommunications; and third, energy, transportation, banking and finance, chemicals and hazardous materials, and postal and shipping.

Smart cities should be characterized by optimum urban performance reflected in 13 critical sectors. But smart cities are more than the sum of those sectors. We can say that smart city is a digitally intelligent city. In other words, it is the balanced hybrid mixture of networked infrastructures and human capital. CEWPS (call it the *holy grail*) would only qualify to protect the 13 critical sectors of the city.

What Is a Critical Infrastructure   We keep using the term *critical infrastructure* everywhere. But what does it mean in terms of a smart city?

In a smart city, energy, water, transportation, public health and safety, and other key services are managed in concert to support smooth operation of critical infrastructure while providing for a clean, economic, and safe environment in which to live, work, and play. Timely logistics information will be gathered and supplied to the public either by the cloud, secure information highways, or social media networks.

The energy infrastructure is arguably the single most important feature in any city. If unavailable for a significant enough period of time, all other functions will eventually cease. This is why CEWPS utilizes the smart grid to offer on-demand vaccination services to immunize the power grid as well as the other critical infrastructure system.

Critical infrastructure is a term coined by governments to represent the backbone of The Smart City's economy, security, and health. People are aware of it as the power they use at homes, the water they drink, the transportation that moves them, and the communication systems they rely on to stay in touch with friends and family. The corollary of this can be stated as "smart city cannot exist without a smart grid protecting its critical infrastructures."

How did a particular infrastructure become critical? This is an interesting question. Infrastructures were born with cities. The oldest infrastructures were aqueducts and roads. The Egyptians built canals and irrigations systems. They did not make so many roads. Roads were not so important because they relied on the Nile for transportation. The Romans build aqueducts, roads, and bridges. As cities became more and more populated, the infrastructures became more important, and additional sections were added to the old ones.

Engineering, medicine, and the military became the most important elements of civilization survival. The first one is to build healthy city, the second one is to maintain healthy citizens, and the third one is to defend the city. George Stephenson invented the steam locomotive engine in 1820, Karl Benz invented the modern car in 1879, and the Wright Brothers invented the airplane in 1903. All these three inventions brought to the modern world three new infrastructures. Thomas Edison gave us the grace of electricity in 1879, Alexander Graham Bell gave us the telephone in 1876, Thomas John Watson, Sr. gave us the International Business Machines computer in 1953, and then Leonard Kleinrock and Vinton Cerf gave us the Internet, and that was the beginning of the electronic *Big Bang* that we are living in today.

The reality of living defies predictions and forecasts. Today, 54% of the world's population lives in urban areas, a proportion that is expected to increase to 66% by 2050. Just 10 years ago, the number of Internet users was 910 million with a world population of 6.4 billion. These numbers have jumped to a whopping 3.1 billion with a world population of 7.2 billion. Cities are becoming more crowded and noisier, with more crime and poverty. But governments are fighting all these miseries by seriously considering jumping on the *smart city bandwagon*. The strategy is to utilize innovation and ability to solve social problems and use ICTs to improve this capacity. The intelligence lies in the ability to solve problems of these communities and is linked to technology transfer when a problem is solved. In this sense, intelligence is an inner quality of any territory, any place, city, or region where innovation processes are facilitated by ICTs. What varies is the degree of intelligence, depending on the person, the system of cooperation, and digital infrastructure and tools that a community offers its residents. Take for example Tokyo, it tops the population list and remains the world's largest city with 38 million dwellers. Amazingly, Tokyo is rated as the third most impressive smart city on Earth. The website (http://freshome.com/2013/02/07/10-most-impressive-smart-cities-on-Earth) describes the article "10 Most Impressive Smart Cities On Earth" authored by Rick Delgado on February 7, 2013. This is the secret.

After months of rolling blackouts due to lack of nuclear power, the need for the Japanese to innovate has never been greater. Japan's biggest companies are behind the Smart City revolution taking place around the globe and are using Tokyo as their proving ground. Panasonic, Sharp, Mitsubishi, and many other big names are working very hard to infuse smart technology into this massive city.

CEWPS Screen Layout   CEWPS/SV system will have around 150 dynamic screens and 100 online reports categorized by component. Selective main screens are shown in Figures 5.16 and 5.17.

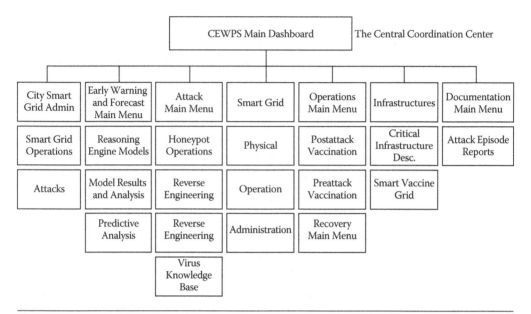

Figure 5.16   The CEWPS main dashboard and main operations screens. Each block is equipped with dynamic reporting capability. Each block will have additional subblocks (now shown). Administrators are well trained on how to respond to a preemptive massive attack.

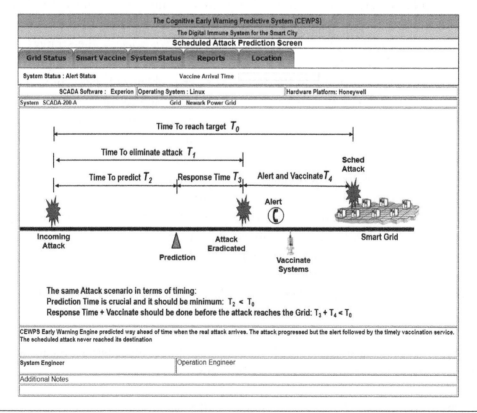

Figure 5.17   This is a real-time of what happens in the battlefield. The uniqueness of CEWPS comes in its accurate prediction. As soon as the virus reaches the grid, the smart vaccine army will be ready to protect the critical system. The cognitive smart vaccine grid (SVG) is of paramount importance in the victory. (©2014 Merit Cybersecurity Group. All rights reserved.)

Glossary with Bibliography[*]

Accommodation (Piaget and Inhelder, 1969): A process to which Piaget referred in his theory of cognitive development, whereby an individual's existing understanding is modified from a new experience.

Adaptable hypermedia systems (De Bra, 1998): Systems in which users can explicitly set preferences or establish profiles through filling out forms to provide information for the user model, which is then used to determine the presentation of information.

Adaptable systems (Streitz, 1988): Systems in which users have the ability to diagnose their own progress and modify student/user models as needed.

Adaptation model (Wu, Houben, and De Bra, 2000): The component of an adaptive hypermedia system that allows the system to modify information presentation so that reading and navigation style conform to user preferences and knowledge level and that specifies the way in which the user's knowledge modifies the presentation of information.

Adaptive multimedia presentation (De Bra, 1998): A type of content adaptation in which the selection of the presentation medium is based on the needs of the user but which does not yet allow for the adaptation of individual elements of multimedia content.

Adaptive navigation (Brusilovsky, 1998): Adaptive hypermedia techniques that modify the links accessible to a user at a particular time; link adaptation.

Adaptive presentation (Brusilovsky, 1998): Techniques that modify the contents of a page based on the user model; content adaptation.

Adaptive systems (Streitz, 1988): Systems that modify the student/user model to adjust to progress and characteristics of users.

Adaptive text presentation (Brusilovsky, 1998): A type of content adaptation in which the user model determines a page's textual content. While there are various techniques for adaptive text presentation, they look similar from the perspective of *what can be adapted*, that is, those with varying user models see different textual content as the content for the same page.

Adaptive tutoring systems (ATS) (Streitz, 1988): What many refer to as intelligent tutoring systems, though Streitz is reluctant to ascribe intelligence to technical systems.

Aesthetic entry point (Gardner, 1999a): A way to introduce a topic that engages the senses through works of art that relate to the subject matter being studied. Also, concepts and examples have their own aesthetic properties, which can be examined and discussed in conjunction with the topic at hand.

Assimilation (Piaget and Inhelder, 1969): A process of adaptation to interactions with the environment through which individuals add new experiences to their base of knowledge according to Piaget's theory of cognitive development.

---

[*] From http://www.brainjolt.com/multi-intelligent-e-learning/glossary/.

Asynchronous learning (Jackson, 2001): Directed study or *self-study* that does not occur in real time or in a live instructor-led setting.

Asynchronous Web technology (Harasim, 1999): A type of computer-mediated communication that involves the use of the World Wide Web to provide information in non-real time.

Behaviorism (Graham, 2000): A major school of thought on the nature of learning and the properties of knowledge that was dominant in the 1950s and 1960s and focused on the observation of behavior and the adaptation of organisms to the environment. Behaviorist learning theories view knowledge as objective, given, and absolute.

Bodily kinesthetic intelligence (Gardner, 1999b): A biopsychological potential that involves using one's body for processing information in order to solve problems or build products.

Bug catalog (Psotka, Massey, and Mutter, 1988): A set of errors compiled and analyzed by an intelligent tutoring system to indicate where a particular learner is having difficulty.

Categorization (Bruner, Goodnow, and Austin, 1956): The basis of a cognitive learning theory developed by Jerome Bruner, a cognitive psychologist and educator. According to Bruner's theory, people interpret the world in terms of similarities and differences among various events and objects. While engaged in categorizing, people employ a coding system based on a hierarchical arrangement of categories that are related to each other, with successively more specific levels.

CGI (NCSA, 1998): Common Gateway Interface; a standard for external gateway programs to interface with information servers such as Hypertext Transfer Protocol (HTTP) servers used for the World Wide Web.

Classicism (Eliasmith, 1998): An approach to modeling thinking from the field of cognitive science that employs symbolic processing to model thought processes, also referred to as symbolism.

Cognitive constructivism (Chen, 2000): A school of thought within constructivism that postulates that learning occurs as a result of the exploration and discovery by each individual learner. In the view of cognitive constructivists, knowledge is a symbolic, mental representation in the mind of each individual.

Cognitive psychobiology (Hebb, 1949): Interdisciplinary field of study involving biological neural studies. D.O. Hebb is considered by many to be the father of cognitive psychobiology.

Cognitive science (Audi, 1995): The interdisciplinary study of mind and intelligence, which attempts to further an understanding of intelligent activities and the nature of thought. The major contributing disciplines to the field include philosophy, psychology, computer science, linguistics, neuroscience, and anthropology.

Cognitivism (Gardner, 1985): Major school of thought that employs an information processing approach to learning and uses a model based on the input–output information processing architecture of digital computers. Though cognitivist learning theories are based on active mental processing on the part of learners, such theories still maintain the behaviorist perspective on knowledge, considering knowledge to be both given and absolute.

Computational system (Gardner, 1985): A term used in cognitive science to denote a system that uses discrete mathematics to model cognitive agents and the process of cognition.

Computer-assisted (-aided) instruction (Lawler and Yazdani, 1987): Usually refers to sequentially ordered *linear programs*. CAI generally follows a step-by-step procedural approach to the presentation of subject matter, based on the principles of behaviorist psychology.

Computer-based instruction (CBI) (Psotka et al., 1988): Using computers for training and instruction. However, the term "CBI" usually refers to instruction that does not use technology from artificial intelligence. Production rules and expert systems are generally not used for sequencing the elements of information that are presented to the student. This approach generally produces linear sequences of information, and such CBI programs are referred to as *linear programs*.

Computer-based learning environments (Lawler and Yazdani, 1987): Systems that use a constructivist approach based on Piaget's theory of active learning, with the objective of providing an environment in which students can develop their own authentic knowledge. Examples of computer-based learning environments are Papert's *Mindstorms* (Papert, 1980/1999) and Lawler's *Microworlds* (Lawler, 1984).

Computer-based training (CBT) (Beck, Stern, and Haugsjaa, 1996): Developed in the 1950s, CBT bases its training approach on behaviorist psychology theory. CBT *teaches* courses by presenting knowledge to be learned through a step-by-step procedure, leading students from one item to be learned to the next.

Computer-mediated communication (Harasim, 1999): The passing of messages or sharing of information through networking tools, such as e-mail, conferencing, newsgroups, and websites.

Connectionism (Eliasmith, 1998): An approach to modeling thinking developed in the field of cognitive science that views thought processes as connections between nodes in a distributed network.

Constructionism (Resnick, 1998): A term coined by an Masssachusetts Institute of Technology researcher to connote the combination of constructivist learning theories with the creation and development of individually designed learning projects.

Constructivism (Houghton Mifflin, 2001): Major school of thought on the nature of knowledge that views knowledge as a constructed entity developed by each individual. According to constructivist theory, information is transmitted but knowledge cannot be transmitted from teacher to student, parent to child, or any one individual to another; rather, knowledge is (re)constructed by each individual in his/her own mind and is relative, varying through time and space.

Constructivist learning theory (Chen, 2000): The theory, originally based on the research of Jean Piaget, holds that learning is the result of an individual's mental construction. The theory posits that individuals learn by actively constructing their own understanding, incorporating new information into the base of knowledge they have already constructed in their own minds.

Content adaptation (Brusilovsky, 1998): Techniques that adapt the content of a page based on the user model; also known as adaptive presentation.

Course management system (Jackson, 2001): A type of online learning system, categorized in terms of its functions of content delivery, assessment, and administration.

Deconstruction (Rorty, 1995): An analytical method to uncover multiple interpretations of text developed by Jacques Derrida, a French philosopher, in the 1960s.

Differential equations (van Gelder, 1998): A branch of mathematics used in dynamic systems theory to describe a multidimensional space of potential thoughts and behaviors, traversed by a path of thinking followed by an agent under certain environmental and internal pressures.

Direct guidance (Brusilovsky, 1998): An adaptive navigation technique providing a link to the page that the system determines to be the most suitable next stop along the path to the user's information goal. Usually provided via the "next" button, direct guidance offers a guided tour based on user needs.

Domain model (Wu et al., 2000): The component of an adaptive hypermedia application that describes the structure of the information content of the application. The domain model specifies the relationship between the concepts handled by the application and the connection between the concepts and the information fragments and pages.

Dynamic (dynamical) systems theory (van Gelder, 1998): The theoretical approach that uses differential equations to describe a multidimensional space of potential thoughts and behaviors, traversed by a path of thinking followed by an agent under certain environmental and internal pressures. Some cognitive scientists view dynamic systems theory as a promising approach to modeling human thinking.

Educational adaptive hypermedia (Brusilovsky, 1998): One of the six major application domains within existing adaptive hypermedia systems. Educational hypermedia constitutes one of the earliest application areas and is still the most widely encountered application domain for adaptive hypermedia systems. Most educational hypermedia systems limit the size of the hyperspace by focusing on a specific course or topic for learning. User modeling-based adaptive hypermedia techniques are useful in educational hypermedia systems since knowledge level varies widely among users, the knowledge of an individual user can expand very quickly, and novice users need navigational assistance even in a limited hyperspace.

Educational hypermedia (Brusilovsky, 1998): One of the six major application domains within existing adaptive hypermedia systems. Educational hypermedia constitutes one of the earliest application areas and is still the most widely encountered application domain for adaptive hypermedia systems. Most educational hypermedia systems limit the size of the hyperspace by focusing on a specific course or topic for learning. User modeling-based adaptive hypermedia techniques are useful in educational hypermedia systems since knowledge level varies widely among users, the knowledge of an individual user can expand very quickly, and novice users need navigational assistance even in a limited hyperspace.

Entry point framework (Gardner, 1999a): An educational methodology that accommodates individual differences by providing multiple ways to introduce a topic. While certain entry points activate particular intelligences, a one-to-one correspondence does not exist between entry points and intelligences.

Epistemology (Heylighen, 2000): The branch of philosophy that studies knowledge and attempts to answer basic questions about knowledge, such as what distinguishes true or adequate knowledge from false or inadequate knowledge.

Existential/foundational entry point (Gardner, 1999a): A way to introduce a topic that allows individuals to approach a topic through addressing fundamental questions, such as the meaning of life. Philosophical issues invite certain learners to engage on a deep level, which piques and holds their interest in studying a particular topic.

Expert model (Beck et al., 1996): An intelligent tutoring system component that provides a representation of the knowledge in a way that a person who is skilled in the subject matter represents such knowledge. In recent intelligent tutoring systems, the expert model is a runnable program with the facility to solve problems in the subject matter domain. The expert model is used to compare the learner's solution to the expert's solution; in this way, the intelligent tutor identifies specific points that the learner does not yet understand or topics the learner has not yet mastered.

Explanation variants (Brusilovsky, 1998): Content adaptation method that involves storing variations of sections of information and presenting each individual with the particular variation that best fits the individual's user model.

Formative evaluation (Tessmer, 1996): The evaluation of a working prototype or, in some cases, a rough draft of a system.

g Factor (Jensen, 1998): The theory that there exists a single, monolithic, and measurable, general mental ability in humans referred to as g.

Generative topics (Perkins, 1998): Topics that are central to one or more disciplines or subjects, accessible and interesting to students, as well as connected to teachers' passions.

Global guidance (Brusilovsky, 1998): A method for adaptive navigation support that helps the user follow the shortest and most direct path to reach the information goal by telling the user which link to follow next or sorting links from a given node according to their relevance to the overall goal.

Global orientation (Brusilovsky, 1998): A method for adaptive navigation support, offering annotation landmarks and hiding nonrelevant information so that users understand the structure and position in hyperspace.

Hands-on entry point (Gardner, 1999a): A way to introduce a topic that engages learners in constructing experiments with physical materials or through computer simulations. Other hands-on approaches invite learners to learn by building or manipulating a physical manifestation of some aspect of the topic they are studying.

Hypermedia (Wu et al., 2000): Technology that focuses on information nodes and the connections between the nodes.

Instrumentalism (Dewey, 1938/1963): Naturalistic understanding and philosophy that was developed by John Dewey based on the underlying belief that thought is the product of the interaction between an organism and the environment and knowledge, guiding and controlling the interaction between the organism and the environment.

Intelligences (Gardner, 1999b): Biopsychological potentials for processing information, solving problems, and developing products valued by the culture in which the person resides.

Intelligent computer-aided instruction (Sleeman and Brown, 1982): Sleeman and Brown consider intelligent computer-aided instruction to be the same as intelligent tutoring systems.

Intelligent educational systems (IES) (Goodyear, 1991): Systems that advise learners and treat them as collaborators rather than directing them in an authoritarian manner. IES provide learner models that can be inspected and modified by the learners themselves.

Intelligent tutoring systems (ITS) (Psotka et al., 1988): An advanced form of intelligent computer-aided instruction (ICAI) and computer-based instruction (CBI) that attempts to individualize instruction by creating a computer-based learning environment. The environment performs in a manner similar to a human teacher, working with students to indicate when they make errors, offering suggestions on how best to proceed, recommending new topics to study, and collaborating with students on the curriculum. Such systems should be able to analyze student responses and keep track of the preferences and skills of each individual learner, customizing materials to fit the needs of individual students.

Interpersonal entry point (Gardner, 1999a): A way to introduce a topic that engages learners with each other so that they can interact, cooperate, work together, or alternately debate and argue with each other. Students learn from each other through group projects, in which each student contributes to the overall effort.

Interpersonal intelligence (Gardner, 1999b): A biopsychological potential that involves a person's ability to understand the intentions, motivations, and desires of other people and, therefore, to relate effectively with other people.

Intrapersonal intelligence (Gardner, 1999b): A biopsychological potential to understand oneself and to construct an effective working model of personal capabilities and difficulties as well as to employ such knowledge for managing one's life.

Knowledge-based tutoring systems (KBTS) (Streitz, 1988): Systems that incorporate knowledge about the subject matter, principles of teaching, characteristics of individual learners, and human–computer interaction.

Learning management system (Jackson, 2001): Online learning system categorized by function, similar to course management systems, which contain content delivery, assessment, and administration functions with an integrated view of all active courses, with assessment and goal-tracking facilities.

Learning objects (Innes, McGreal, and Roberts, 2000): Components, lessons, modules, courses, or programs that are individually structured digital or non-digital entities, for use or reference in online learning systems.

Legacy systems (Brinson et al., 2001): Existing applications or systems within an organization that are not Web based or are not integrated with the Web.

Linguistic intelligence (Gardner, 1999b): A biopsychological potential that involves the ability to learn and use spoken and written language to process information and achieve specific goals.

Link adaptation (Brusilovsky, 1998): Adaptive hypermedia techniques that modify the links accessible to a user at a particular time; adaptive navigation.

Local guidance (Brusilovsky, 1998): A method for adaptive navigation support that offers suggestions for the most relevant link to follow for the next step, based on the user's preferences, knowledge, and background.

Local orientation (Brusilovsky, 1998): A method for adaptive navigation support that helps users understand their location in hyperspace and nearby information, offering information about nodes available from the current location or limiting navigation possibilities, focusing on the most relevant links.

Logical entry point (Gardner, 1999a): A way to introduce a topic that allows learners to deduce the cause and effect of certain occurrences and apply deductive reasoning to understand the relationships among various factors involved in the study of a particular topic.

Logical–mathematical intelligence (Gardner, 1999b): A biopsychological potential that involves the ability to conduct logical analysis of problems as well as scientific investigations and to carry out mathematical operations.

Logical positivism (Thagard, 1996): School of thought in philosophy that was widely accepted in the early 1950s, which questioned the value of systematic inquiry into the operation of the mind.

Marxism (Wilson, 1997): The philosophy developed by Karl Marx (1818–1883) that truth can be discerned by analyzing economic structures.

Modernity (Wilson, 1997): A period during the Enlightenment when the worldview was based on using rational, empirical, and objective approaches to discern the truth.

Multimedia technologies (Cisco, 2001): A number of different media-based technologies provide delivery services for online learning. These technologies include live, streaming video, audio, and slides; on-demand prerecorded video and/or audio with accompanying graphics; browser-based Web conferencing combined with audio conferencing; interactive graphics, slide shows, audio and video clips, and Web pages.

Multiple representations (Gardner, 1999a): An educational methodology that is used to convey the definitive aspects of an idea or topic, by modeling them through abstract or natural representation systems. The form of the representation may be closely tied to the physical subject, such as a photographic record, map, or chart, or may provide a formal model. Contrary to established approaches, Gardner argues for a family of representations rather than a single representation that is considered to be the best. Multiple representations allow students to choose elements from known reference areas to represent and model the new topic. The use of multiple representations allows students to understand on a deeper level through developing models of the new subject matter.

Musical intelligence (Gardner, 1999b): A biopsychological potential that involves the ability to perform, compose, and appreciate musical patterns.

Narrative entry point (Gardner, 1999a): A way to introduce a topic that engages students in learning through relating stories. Linguistic, intrapersonal, and interpersonal intelligences are activated through verbal storytelling, with additional intelligences activated through symbolic narrative forms, including movies and mime.

Naturalist intelligence (Gardner, 1999b): A biopsychological potential that involves the ability to recognize and classify many species that constitute the flora and fauna of a person's environment.

Neopragmatist (Rorty, 1979): A philosophical approach adopted by Richard Rorty, similar to the pragmatist view, based on the belief that as humans, we create ourselves and our worlds and that human understanding is based on our interpretation of the world through a variety of paradigms rather than on an objective structure of the mind.

Numerical entry point (Gardner, 1999a): A way to introduce a topic that offers students who like to deal with numbers and numerical relations the opportunity to learn through measurement, counting, listing, and determining statistical attributes of the topic being studied.

Ongoing assessment (Perkins, 1998): Asks the question: how will you and your students know what they understand? Students reflect on their own learning experiences throughout the process, and there are multiple ways for students to demonstrate to the teacher and to themselves what they understand.

Online learning (Harasim, 1999): Educational technology using computer-mediated communication facilities that generally arise from the use of the Internet and Web technology.

Overlay model (Beck et al., 1996; Psotka et al., 1988): The standard type of student model in which a student's knowledge is considered to be a subset of that of a subject matter expert. A technique for student modeling that involves measuring the student's performance against the standard of an expert's model.

Page variants (Brusilovsky, 1998; De Bra, 1998): Content adaptation technique of fragment variants in which a fragment is an entire page. Multiple versions of particular pages exist and are selected based on variables in the user model. Users receive structurally different explanations of concepts based on user model attributes. Easy to implement, this technique offers a variant for each user stereotype.

Papert's principle (Minsky, 1985): Papert's belief that major steps in mental growth are based on acquiring new ways to organize and use what a person already knows, not just on learning new skills.

Perceptron (Rosenblatt, 1958): A system invented by Frank Rosenblatt in 1957 through research in connectionism with which Rosenblatt demonstrated learning by a machine when the Mark I Perceptron *learned* to recognize and identify optical patterns.

Performances of understanding (Perkins, 1998): Asks the question: what will students do to build and demonstrate their understanding? Students can build and demonstrate their understanding through presentations, portfolios, and other approaches to demonstrate to the teacher and to themselves what they have learned.

Pragmatism (Dewey, 1938/1963): A school of thought developed by William James (1842–1910) and adopted by John Dewey. Dewey then developed a theory of knowledge based on pragmatism that encompassed a view of the world as one in which active manipulation of the environment is involved throughout the process of learning.

Primacy effect (Gardner, 1999a): A psychological effect that means that students are particularly apt to remember the starting point in a learning experience.

Postmodernism (Wilson, 1997): A philosophy based on a belief in the plurality of meaning, perspectives, methods, and values, and an appreciation of alternative interpretations. Postmodernists distrust theories that purport to explain why things are the way they are, believing in the existence of multiple truths based on various perspectives and ways of knowing.

Psychoanalytic movement (Wilson, 1997): School of psychology begun by Sigmund Freud (1856–1939), understanding an individual's psyche through an examination of the unconscious.

Self-directed learning (Harasim, 1999): Self-paced, asynchronous online learning with the learner proceeding at his/her own pace through course materials.

Situated learning (Brown, Collins, and Duguid, 1989): Instruction that places an emphasis on the context in which learning occurs and provides students with opportunities to construct new knowledge and understanding in real-life situations, thereby seeking to avoid the decontextualized nature of typical classroom learning.

Social constructivism (Chen, 2000): A school of thought that stresses the collaborative efforts of groups of learners as sources of learning and considers the mind to be a distributed entity extending beyond the bounds of the human body into the social environment.

Spatial intelligence (Gardner, 1999b): The biopsychological capacity to recognize and manipulate patterns in both wide spaces and confined areas.

Stereotype user model (Kobsa, 1993): A model used to represent the user's knowledge offering a quick assessment of the user's background knowledge. Stereotype user models can be used to classify a new user and initialize the state.

Structural linguistics (Wilson, 1997): A model of language developed by Ferdinand de Saussure (1857–1913), based on the belief that meaning comes not from analyzing individual words but from considering the structure of a whole language.

Structuralism (Wilson, 1997): A term credited to anthropologist Claude Levi-Strauss (1908–2009), who applied models of linguistic structure to the study of the customs and myths of society as a whole. Believing that individuals do not control the linguistic, sociological, and psychological structures that shape them and that can be uncovered through systematic investigation, structuralists moved away from the existentialist view that individuals are what they make themselves.

Symbolicism (Eliasmith, 1998): A school of thought in cognitive science that employs what is now referred to as classicism, using symbolic processing to model thought processes.

Synchronous learning environments (Smith et al., 2001): Online learning systems that use audio or video conferencing (or a combination thereof) as their primary delivery modality to support live simultaneous interaction, similar to an in-person instructor-led classroom situation.

Teaching for understanding (TfU) framework (Perkins and Blythe, 1994): Educational methodology designed to assist teachers in course development. The starting point in teaching for understanding is to develop generative topics, topics that are central to a discipline, and understanding goals to provide focus to the instruction.

Theory of multiple intelligences (Gardner, 1983/1993): The cognitive theory, developed by Howard Gardner, that each individual possesses multiple intelligences rather than one single intelligence. Based on evidence from psychology, biology, and anthropology, Gardner delineates criteria used to define eight specific human intelligences: linguistic, logical–mathematical, bodily kinesthetic, interpersonal, intrapersonal, musical, spatial, and naturalist. According to Gardner, these intelligences are both biological and learned or developed. Though everyone possesses these intelligences, individuals differ in which intelligences are more developed than others.

Thinking style (Sternberg, 1997): A preferred way of using a person's abilities according to how the individual likes to do something rather than how well he/she can actually carry out a task.

Throughlines (Perkins, 1998): Ideas that are developed across the curriculum.

Understanding goals (Perkins, 1998): What the teacher wants the students to learn; explicit and public goals that are focused on key concepts, methods, purposes, and forms of expression, as well as linked to assessment criteria.

User-adaptive system (Kobsa, 1993): An interactive computer system that adapts itself to current users, employing a user model for adaptation purposes.

User model (Wu et al., 2000): A component of an adaptive hypermedia application that represents such individual characteristics as the user's preferences, knowledge, goals, and navigation history and may include observations of the user's behavior while using the system.

Web-based online learning (Harasim, 1999): Educational technology using computer-mediated communication facilities based on World Wide Web.

Websites

http://bayes.cs.ucla.edu/BOOK-99/book-toc.html.
http://bayesian-intelligence.com/bwb/2012-03/how-to-model-with-bayesian-networks/.
http://ftp.cs.ucla.edu/pub/stat_ser/r350.pdf.
http://spectrum.ieee.org/tech-talk/computing/software/predictive-analytics-and-deciding-who-should-receive-organ-transplants.
http://stanford.edu/~ngoodman/papers/LTBC_psychreview_final.pdf.
http://www.9-11commission.gov/report/.
http://www.bayesserver.com/.
http://www.brainjolt.com/multi-intelligent-e-learning/glossary/.
https://www.cs.cmu.edu/~dmarg/Papers/PhD-Thesis-Margaritis.pdf.
http://www.cs.helsinki.fi/u/myllymak/bnets.pdf.

http://www.cs.ubc.ca/~murphyk/Bayes/bnintro.html.
http://www.gartner.com/it-glossary/predictive-analytics.
http://www.predictiveanalyticstoday.com/top-15-predictive-analytics-software/.
https://www.smartgrid.gov/the_smart_grid.

References

Joshy Joseph, Craig Fellenstein, "Grid Computing", IBM Press series 2004, Prentice Hall, ISBN 0-13-145660-1.

Richard Murk, "Autonomic Computing", IBM Press Series 2004, Prentice Hall, ISBN 0-13-144025-X.

Carl Kesselman, "The Grid: Blueprint for a New Computing Infrastructure", Morgan Kaufmann 1999, ISBN 1-55860-475-8.

6

CEWPS KNOWLEDGE AND INTELLIGENCE

CEWPS Is the Beginning of Singularity

One of the most inspirational terms in our technology millennium is *singularity*. The term was originally coined by mathematician John von Neumann in 1958. Then, Ray Kurzweil picked it up and made it famous. So, technological singularity is synonymous to human intelligence explosion. Although technological progress has been accelerating, it has been limited by the basic intelligence of the human brain, which has not, according to Paul R. Ehrlich, changed significantly for millennia. However, with the increasing power of computers and other technologies, it might eventually be possible to build a machine that is *more intelligent than humans*. The movie *Terminator* gives us a quasi-realistic scenario how a cyborg (short for *cybernetic organism*) assassin with his runaway bionic mind was programmed to create havoc and massive destruction. Well, the symmetric warfare between good and evil will resume.

Singularity is something new but it has already a value in the scientific community. To say that the accelerating progress in technologies will cause a runaway effect wherein artificial intelligence will exceed human intellectual capacity and control. Simplistically, we can say that if we add artificial intelligence, which is the work of man, to human intelligence, we can benefit and improve the quality of life, but at the same time, it will benefit the evil mind. CEWPS is designed with AI technologies with a new approach to defeat the evil mind.

We would like to define some key terms that CEWPS uses extensively throughout the book:

Experience: Is the biological process created by external sensation and/or internal reflection. We can say that an episode is an experience event that took place of the past, and it may be repeated in the future. *For example, I have the experience of driving a car.*

Knowledge: A neurological (related to the nervous system) description of experience, stored in the brain. We could refer to it as the derivative of experience. We can say that knowledge is experience stored as a neurological data in the brain. Without experience, there is no knowledge. *For example, I gained knowledge to avoid accidents.*

Episode: CEWPS considers it an event of attack on a critical system, with defined purpose and objective, duration, start and stop times.

Ontology: The collection of related objects that constitute a knowledge model. Ontology is built with a special XML language called Web Ontology Language (OWL), which is a knowledge representation language.

Semantics: The science that takes a word with different meanings and builds a relationship among them. A word can have many meanings. Semantics builds a relationship tree for them. Here is an example of how semantics work:

Crash can mean auto accident, a drop in the stock market, to attend a party without being invited, ocean waves hitting the shore, or the sound of a cymbal being struck together.

The unique thing about CEWPS is that it stores human intelligence in the form of knowledge and experience. In this respect, CEWPS achieves the judgmental capacity of the human mind.

Quantitatively, we can represent CEWPS in the following polynomial:

$$CEWPS = Early\,Warning + Digital\,Immunity + Predictive\,Causality$$

$$+ Human\,Knowledge + Cyber\,Terrorism\,Knowledge$$

When we talk about knowledge representation (KR) in CEWPS, we are referring to cybercrime (we use cybercrime and cyberterrorism interchangeably) episodes. CEWPS represents cybercrime episodes as a knowledge model as shown in Figure 6.1. In semantic network modeling, we know the objects (in the circle) of the episode and the causal relation among the objects (arrows, not necessarily one-on one). Here is a sample of a cybercrime episode represented as a semantic directed acyclic graph (DAG).

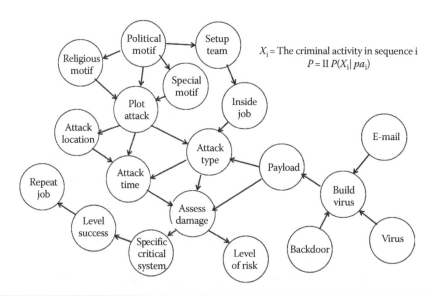

Figure 6.1   This directed acyclic graph represents a knowledge model of a cyberattack. It is also called the Bayesian network model. All cyberattacks can be transformed into this model. Ontology is the technique that is used to convert a cyberattack into a knowledge model. Web Ontology Language (OWL) does the conversion. The Semantic Resource Description Framework (RDF) stores it in the Attack Knowledge Base. The vertices (circles) represent the variables (criminal activity), and the arcs (arrows) represent the causal relationship between the activities.

Structure of the CEWPS Knowledge Center

One of the most original and vital components of CEWPS is its Knowledge Center, which comprises the Reasoning Engine and the Virus Knowledge Base and the Vaccine Knowledge Base. The diagram in Figure 6.2 describes how the incoming attack is detected by the Early Warning Center (EWC), which in turn instantiates a series of command requests to the Smart Vaccine Commander (SVC) to be ready for a vaccination mission. SVC issues a mobilization request to its army. These activities constitute the Digital Immunity process.

The Knowledge Center is where all the reasoning and causality analyses take place. It is the cognition center where all the intelligent thinking processes take place. The KC decides based on the outcome of its Reasoning Engine what the next decision will be. The KC establishes the causality rules and the reasoning metrics for all vaccination services.

Ontology creates knowledge model from similar concepts (objects). In other words, it takes several objects that are related to one another and creates a model. Let's give an example: we take the human parts, the nervous system, the skeletal system, and the digestive system and link them all together through relations. In the end, we have a human ontology. In CEWPS, a cyberattack *episode* is represented as an ontology model. The model is structured as a schema with related attributes (classes). Figure 6.3 is an ontological representation of a cyberattack that is stored in the Attack Knowledge Base (AKB). Any user could retrieve any specific attack by searching on any attribute.

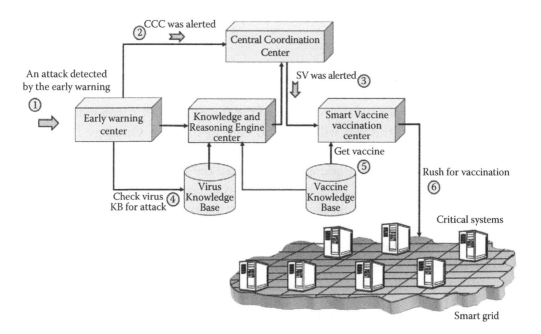

Figure 6.2   CEWPS with its major components represents the nuclear reactor of Digital Immunity. We can consider each center as a factory or an assembly line of many information pieces, all work together to provide services for the center. This comprises many subcomponents that perform specific cognitive duties to provide complete protection to the critical systems.

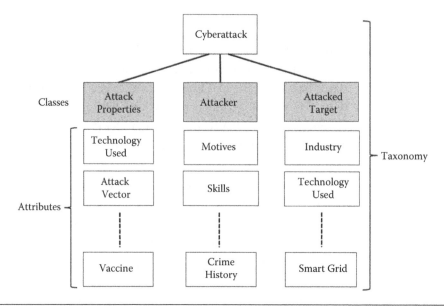

Figure 6.3   The ontological structure of a cyberattack. Ontology is the glue that we use to put together a structure that we call the knowledge model. The cyberattack has three basic classes that describe completely the nature of the attack, the cyberterrorist, and the destination of the attack.

The Cybercrime Knowledge Model

The ontological structure of the smart grid cyberattack is a hierarchical representation of the classes, and they are related to each other, as shown in the layout that follows:

1. Subschema 1 describes the *attack*.
2. Subschema 2 qualifies the *attacking organization*.
3. Subschema 3 describes the *attacked infrastructure*.

Here are the descriptions of the attributes of the three classes that represent a cyber-attack on the smart grid and will be coded later in the Web Ontology Language (OWL). Actually, OWL is not a real acronym. The language started out as the Web Ontology Language but the working group disliked the acronym WOL. We decided to call it OWL. The working group became more comfortable with this decision when one of the members pointed out the following justification for this decision from the noted ontologist A.A. Milne who, in his influential book *Winnie the Pooh*, stated of the wise character OWL: "He could spell his own name WOL, and he could spell Tuesday so that you knew it was not Wednesday…" a quote from *Jim Hendler, co-chair of the W3C Web Ontology Working Group, and the W3C Communications Team.*

> *Index*: Is the key of the schema for faster search and retrieval.
> *Attack type*: Describe the type of attack: Trojan, virus, DOS … and if the attack was sent as an e-mail, picture, or website, also if it was physically stored on a USB, CD, or sent via a mobile device.

Subschema 1   Subschema 2   Subschema 3

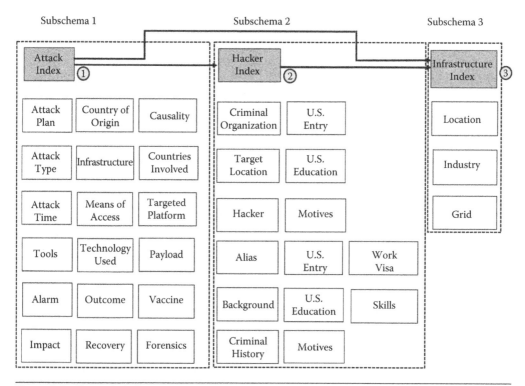

Figure 6.4 The ontological representation of a cyberattack with its three interrelated subschemas will be stored in the Attack Knowledge Base under the cybercrime ontology domain.

Causality: This attribute is so critical and mathematically true. David Hume (1711–1776), the British Empiricist of the Early Modern period, is one of the most famous contributors to the philosophy of causation (Figure 6.4). In his *A Treatise of Human Nature*, he states the following rules:

An object precedent and contiguous to another, and where all the objects resembling the former are placed in like relations of precedency and contiguity to those objects that resemble the latter. An object precedent and contiguous to another, and so united with it, that the idea of the one determined the mind to form the idea of the other, and the impression of the one to form a more lively idea of the other.

So, causation is the relation between two interrelated events where the second event is caused by the first one. It can be political, religious, or social. Attacking critical infrastructures is a serious crime triggered by a major event. CEWPS examines a multitude of factors and adds them to the causality of the attack. When there is a war between two countries, it is very likely that one country will resort to attacking critical infrastructure of the other country. Although the attacking country will deny it, crime will always leave a trail.

Outcome: The result of the attack, which could be physical or digital. CEWPS examines the impact and the damages of the attack and computes the threat coefficient, which is critical for the future attacks.

Attack time: The time of the attack. CEWPS computes the preattack planning and rehearsal times. This information becomes very valuable for the alert broadcasting and informs the Smart Vaccine for its preattack vaccination services.

Technology used: The type of hacking technique and tools used for the attack. CEWPS will determine the spying technique, the nature of the malware, and its currency.

People: the qualifications of the attackers, where the attack was launched from and the terrorist organization they belong to. CEWPS has the skills to assemble all the pieces on the identity of the attackers, their skills, and their motivation for the attack.

Vaccine used: The vaccine that was used to abort the attack. Often, the attack infects some of the servers on the smart grid, and the Smart Vaccine has to rush and vaccinate the healthy servers before the attack. If the attack took place and there was no time to perform any vaccination, then the attack will be reverse engineered and a new vaccine will be developed for future attacks.

Target: The critical infrastructure that was targeted during the attack. There is a correlation between the nature of the infrastructure and the type of attacks. CEWPS will study the evidence, and with the help of the inference engine, it will be easier to determine how to learn more about the anatomy of the attack.

Location: The geographical location where the attack took place. The attack may have been launched from another continent or from a vessel in the ocean, or from several simultaneous locations. CEWPS will study the evidence and store it in the Attack Knowledge Base (Figure 6.5).

How Does CEWPS Predict Cyberattacks on the Smart City?

Predicting a cybercrime does not rely on prayers. It is based on scientific foundation, human intelligence, and computing power. Computer scientists and AI specialists have developed sophisticated mathematical models that use complex algorithms and previous cybercrime episodes to predict when the second shoe will drop. Academia researchers have claimed that major international cyberattacks follow predictable patterns. It is a *qualified* truth.

It is true that all infrastructures share several common denominators, but they differ in technical structure, the type of service rendered, and the skill set of people to support them. Table 6.1 shows how attacks differ from one infrastructure to another.

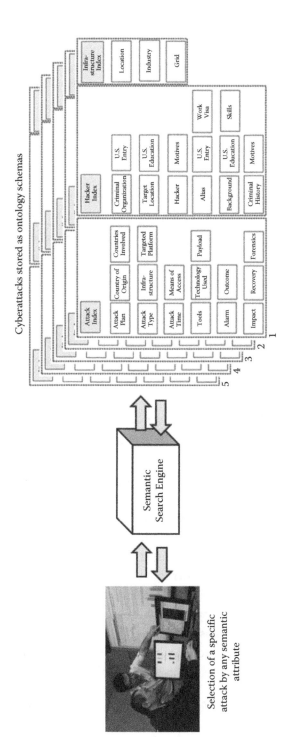

Figure 6.5   Law enforcement agents from their remote station can zoom in with a magnifying glass on the details of crime. They can run an ad-hoc queries from to the Attack Knowledge Base by using the semantic search engine. They retrieve five cyberattack cases for review. By running several iterations, they will be able to get more information on the crime. If none of the cases apply to the crime, CEWPS has an interface adapter to other crime repositories. The schema is open ended and new attributes can be added to the Attack Knowledge Base.

Table 6.1   Infrastructure Attacks and Their Related Impact and Physical Damage

INFRASTRUCTURE	THREAT/IMPACT	CONTROL SYSTEM	DATA ASSETS	PHYSICAL DAMAGE
Power plants/substations	Very high/panic	Cascade failure	Sabotage	Partial
Airports/roads/bridges	Very high/panic	Hard failure	Sabotage/compromise	Partial
Water systems	Very high/panic	Soft failure	Sabotage/compromise	Partial
Public health	Moderate	Partial	Sabotage/compromise	Partial
Telecom	Very high/panic	Hard failure	Sabotage	Sabotage
Banking and finance/retail	Very high	Hard failure	Sabotage	Sabotage
Food and agriculture	Very high	Partial	Sabotage	Partial
Defense/military/law enforcement	Very high	Soft failure	Sabotage	Partial
Chemical plants	Very high	Hard failure	Sabotage	Sabotage
Postal and shipping	Very high	Soft failure	Sabotage	Partial
Academia	High	Partial	Sabotage/compromise	Partial

Note: Cascade failure: Breakdown in workload, causing one system to collapse after another
Hard failure: System abruptly goes down
Soft failure: System quickly goes down
Sabotage: Data damage, theft, or deletion
Compromise: Data theft

Now that we have shown how deep the Internet is, predicting smart city cyberattacks is a fairly complicated task. At the same time, cybercriminals are increasingly using sophisticated social engineering techniques leading to disruptions in the societal fabric of the Smart City.

CEWPS utilizes sophisticated modeling tools including a stochastic model and a Bayesian network model to analyze and predict an incoming surprise attack on the smart grid.

In modeling an attack, we have to consider so many quantitative assumptions derived from past attacks on the grid, attacks extracted from Big Data, the Deep Web, and the knowledge security domain experts. Here are some of the variables that will play a big role in the outcome of the predictive model:

The target of the attack should be defined first by location, nature, and impact. There are two important security *metrics* that need to be included in the model: vulnerability and exploitability. The Common Vulnerability Scoring System (CVSS) is an open standard for scoring IT security vulnerabilities. It was developed to provide organizations with a mechanism to measure vulnerabilities and prioritize their mitigation. There are six metrics that are used to calculate the exploitability and impact subscores of the vulnerability. These subscores are used to calculate the overall base score.

$$\text{Exploitability} = 20 \times \text{AccessVector} \times \text{AccessComplexity} \times \text{Authentication}$$

$$\text{Impact} = 10.41 \times (1 - (1 - \text{ConfImpact}) \times (1 - \text{IntegImpact}) \times (1 - \text{Avail Impact})$$

$$\text{BaseScore} = \text{roundTo1Decimal} \ (0.6 \times \text{Impact}) + (0.4 \times \text{Exploitability}) - 1.5 \times f(\text{Impact})$$

The U.S. federal government uses the CVSS standard as the scoring engine for its National Vulnerability Database (NVD), which has a repository of over 45,000 known vulnerabilities and is updated on an ongoing basis.

Prediction requires the knowledge of trained *people* with previous experience in cyberattacks, which includes a repertoire of advanced prediction *tools* to model the attack.

The vaccination process is a follow-up to the attack (whether it succeeds or not).

The diagram in Figure 6.6 sheds more light on the stages of the attack and the Smart Vaccine.

Explanation of the prediction screen: The early warning predictive system (EWS) will broadcast prediction at regular intervals. If the incoming attack is caught by the second prediction, a series of alerts will be broadcast throughout the grid. In the meantime, the CEWPS Central Coordination Center will order the vaccination center to dispatch Smart Vaccine agents throughout the grid for protective (unscheduled) vaccination. The attack was caught, quarantined, and decomposed, and a new vaccine was assembled before it was stored in the Vaccine Knowledge Base (VaKB).

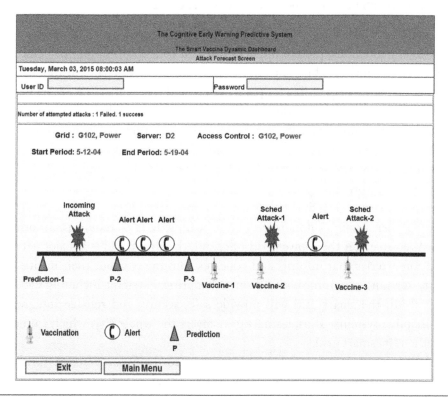

Figure 6.6   Here is explanation of how CEWPS is fighting and defusing the attack. Prediction-1 (P-1) sent an alert that there is an attack coming soon. Another prediction-2 (P-2) followed with three alerts to the Central Coordination Center (CCC). A third prediction (P-3) predicted that the attack is scheduled to hit the grid at T_0. An urgent vaccination mission arrived at T_{v2} and vaccinated the target system. The first attack never happened. The second attack was going to hit at T_3 that did not materialize either. Vaccination mission 3 vaccinated the system and Attack-2 never occurred.

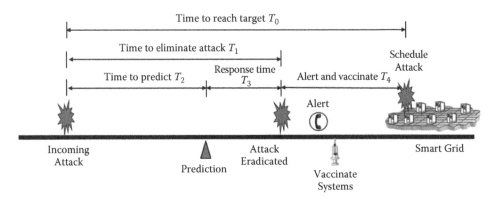

Figure 6.7 The same attack scenario in terms of timing: The prediction time is crucial and it should be a minimum: $T_2 < T_0$. Response time + vaccinate should be done before the attack reaches the grid: $T_3 + T_4 < T_0$.

The attack will never reach the targeted critical system on the Smart Vaccine Grid (SVG). Figure 6.7 shows the sequence of events before and during the attack.

How Does CEWPS Prevent Cyberattacks on Smart Cities?

Smart cities depend on a smart grid to ensure resilient delivery of energy to supply their many functions, present opportunities for conservation, improve efficiencies, and, most importantly, enable coordination between urban officialdom and infrastructure operators, those responsible for public safety and the public. The Smart City is all about how the city *organism* works together as an integrated whole and survives when put under extreme conditions. Energy, water, transportation, public health and safety, and other aspects of a smart city are managed in concert to support smooth operation of critical infrastructure while providing for a clean, economic and safe environment in which to live, work, and play.

The city's smart grid (CSG) has three functionalities. First, it connects all power systems together through autonomic and self-healing designs, remote monitoring, and control. We can call it the "power grid." Second, the smart grid is a major network of information arteries that informs and educates consumers about their utilities usage and cost, in addition to information from other critical systems including cybercrime attacks. Third, the smart grid will provide safe, secure, and reliable integration of cross-discipline systems. Thus, a smart grid covers the whole city, which cannot fully exist without its smart grid.

CEWPS uses its own smart grid which is called the Smart Vaccine Grid (SVG) to connect all critical systems to the Central Coordination Center in real time mode. The SVG is tightly coupled with the City Smart Grid (CSG), and its main objective is to protect the systems that operate the critical infrastructures. CEWPS provides early warning attack forecasts, and the Smart Vaccine provides scheduled and unscheduled vaccination services. If any of the critical systems gets accidentally or intentionally a viral attack, the CEWPS Central Coordination Center (CCC) will know immediately and will dispatch an army of the Smart Vaccine to inoculate all the healthy and compromised systems on the grid. Inoculation is a routine preventive measure that takes place all year around, and not necessarily after an attack.

Causality Rules

We define causality (also referred to as causation) as the relation between a cyberattack (*the cause event*) and its outcome on a system (*the effect event*), where the outcome is understood as a physical consequence of the attack. As is known, "correlation does not mean causation." More generally, observing a statistical dependency between a cyberattack and a circuit breaker failure or that a circuit breaker failure causes a cyberattack.

Causality is likened to *conditional probabilities* as in P(cancer | smoking) reads "the probability of finding cancer in a person known to smoke," or P(power failure | cyberattack), which reads "the probability of having a power failure must be because of a cyberattack on the grid."

Hills Criteria of Causation outlines the minimal conditions needed to establish a causal relationship between two items:

Temporal relationship: Exposure always precedes the outcome. If attack "A" is believed to cause a damaging outcome, then it is clear that attack "A" must necessarily always precede the occurrence of the outcome.

Strength: This is defined by the size of the association as measured by appropriate statistical tests. The stronger the association, the more likely it is that the relation of the attack "A" to the outcome "B" is causal.

Dose–response relationship: An increasing amount of exposure increases the risk. If a dose–response relationship is present, it is a strong evidence for a causal relationship.

Consistency: The association is consistent when results are replicated. This is true with most cyberattacks. They follow pretty much the same attack pattern: plan, rehearse, set a time, attack, watch outcome, repeat.

Plausibility: There needs to be some theoretical basis for positing an association between the attack vector and the outcome of the attack. One may, by chance, discover a correlation between Siemens SCADA and the attack of Stuxnet, but there is not likely to be any logical connection between the two agents.

Specificity: When specificity of an association is found, it provides additional support for a causal relationship. Causality is most often multiple. Therefore, absence of specificity in no way negates a causal relationship. For example, Siemens SCADA collects and monitors the smart grid, but it is not the only SCADA system. There are other SCADAs that will do the job just as well.

Coherence: Another important criterion in predicting reasoning. The association should be compatible with existing theory and knowledge. For example, Microsoft (IE) browser, in theory, is an excellent browser, but it picked up bad reputation with its zero-day bug. However, as with the issue of plausibility, research that disagrees with established theory and knowledge is not automatically false. So, there still could be a relationship between an IE tarnished credibility and cyberattacks.

Cybercrime Predictive Analytics for Smart Cities

Predictive Analytics (PA) is one of the most versatile sciences of mathematics, statistics, and even operations research. People like its fancy term and it was stretched in every direction. We can define *Predictive Analytics* as the science of predicting the future by extracting and analyzing data from the past.

The worldwide explosion of user-generated digital information has created a tsunami of information about individuals' and organizations' past, present, and planned actions and intentions.

Criminal interests also find this digitized information to be multibillion dollar businesses. A June 2014 report from cybersecurity firm McAfee places the annual global cost of cybercrime to be between $400 and $575 billion, exceeding the national income of most countries. Also, a new report from the Center for Strategic and International Studies (CSIS) estimates that cybercrime costs businesses some $400 billion a year worldwide. These figures will be on the rise, and cybercrime will continue to win the battle and the war. Why? Because there are so many bad cats out of the bag already, which makes the situation hard to control. But at least, we believe some of the influencing factors could identified, which in turn are contributing to the "accelerating returns" of cybercrime.

Universities in the United States and Canada report that international student enrollments at colleges and universities in the United States increased by 3% since last year, according to the annual Open Doors report. China is the leading country of origin of international students, overtaking India. The number of students from China is up 30% from 2008 to 2009. The most popular host state is California; while the most popular city is New York. Most of the Chinese students major in Business and Management and Engineering. Forty-five percent of the Chinese graduates go back to China enriched with the latest technologies in information and communication technologies (ICT).

According to a report sponsored by Intel's McAfee security division, "Allegations of economic espionage in cyberspace have been one of the main issues between the United States and China for several years. Recently, it came to a head when the United States indicted members of the Chinese military for hacking U.S. companies. Though China denied the charges, FBI Director James B. Comey accused the Chinese government of using cyber-espionage as a means to give an advantage to industries it controls."

Antivirus Technology (AVT) vendors realize that cyber vandalism is still on the loose and that it has surpassed AVT by a big shot. Cybercrime statistics are still inconsistent, and forecasts seem often unreliable. But all the major AVT vendors agree on one thing and that the total damage done to the world economy by the activity of virus writers, hackers, and spammers has long since exceeded tens of billions of dollars annually. The amount continues to grow. According to research carried out by Computer Economics, total losses in 2004 were close to $18 billion, with a trend toward a 30%–40% annual growth rate. Although the total market for the AVT industry was estimated as being $2.7 billion in 2003 and $3.3 billion in 2004, with $3.8 billion being the predicted figure for 2005, this figure escalated according to IDC to $14.3 billion for 2014. According to InfoSec Institute, the global price tag of consumer cybercrime is $113 billion for 2012.

General Brian Alexander, who served as the Director of the National Security Agency, told U.S. Congress that cyberattacks are causing "the greatest transfer of wealth in history," and he cited statistics from, among other sources, Symantec Corp. and McAfee Inc., which both sell software to protect computers from hackers. Crediting Symantec, he said the theft of intellectual property costs American companies $250 billion a year. He also mentioned McAfee estimates that the global cost of cybercrime is $1 trillion. "That's our future disappearing in front of us," he said, urging the Congress to enact legislation to improve America's cyber defenses.

Now, how could technology offer a true solution to this malignant suffering? It seems there is a perplexing duality between technology advancement and cybercrime sophistication. As we advance from the first generation of the Internet (client/server) into the second (e-Commerce) and the third (the Cloud), cybercrime has become a very prosperous business growing 31% per year and ballooning into $67 billion in revenues in 2012. While looking at the AVT industry, we see much lower numbers, $14 billion in 2012.

If we analyze the medical progress of the medical field of immunology, we see that as technology has fully permeated into this complex medical field and as a result, we benefited and our immune system became more robust and more predictive. The focus was solely to improve human immunity and predict new diseases and viruses. We need to think a little harder and learn from our immune system. Our ability to analyze and predict new diseases got better, thanks to nanotechnology and artificial intelligence research. We need to tackle cybercrime with the same approach.

Professor Vasant Dhar, Stern School of Business, New York University said, "The powerhouse organizations of the Internet era, which include Google and Amazon, have business models that hinge on predictive models based on Artificial Intelligence and machine learning."

Here is an interesting phenomenon that we can learn from our immune system: When we become infected with a pathogen, for example, a virus, bacteria, fungus, or parasite, there are rapid changes in gene activity in the cells of our immune system at the site of infection. The genes help to produce a large number of a chemical called *cytokines*, which plays the role of cell signaling and alert (i.e., communication), which starts the mobilization for the defense. During infection, the B cells identify the attacking agents and draw a plan of attack. The memory cells and killer cells remember the attack and collectively all the activities resulting from infection is referred to as the *immune signature* of the infection. Immune signatures are generated by an infection with pathogens (we call them the *culprits*).

A close analogy to the immune signature would be the *mug shot* and the criminal record of a criminal. Analyzing immune signatures can give us a composite picture of how the host is responding during disease, how this response will change with drug therapy, and about the processes contributing to disease. In the future, the analysis of immune signatures should play a key role in supporting the detection and identification of more complex inflammatory and infectious diseases and their monitoring and treatment.

CEWPS is a throbbing cognitive system, with capabilities to watch the outside, monitor the inside, collect data, and make decisions. CEWPS is actually a replica of the human intelligence with its *assistive* services to compensate for any missing information during its decision-making process.

Smart cities will rely heavily on CEWPS as its immune system. It offers similar services as the Human Immune System. In addition to protecting the critical systems with vaccination services, CEWPS offers a reliable predictive windows about the future with data mining engines. Enriched by a priori cybercrime knowledge, smart city social, environmental data, and Big Data, CEWPS is truly the "Holy Grail" of the smart city. Offering Digital Immunity to smart cities is a grand endeavor, but who said climbing the Himalayas is a picnic (Figure 6.8).

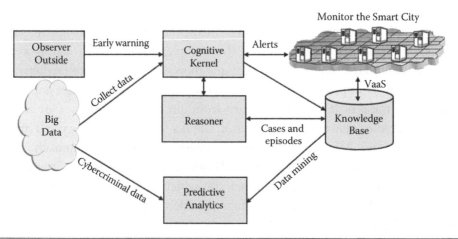

Figure 6.8   CEWPS is an intelligent and fast learning system. Its cognitive ability to transform data from the different components, into decision making knowledge and predictive analytics on potential cyberattacks in Smart City.

Why Do We Need a Predictive Analytics Model for Smart Cities?

Data are static energy; predictive analytics turns it into kinetic energy!

CEWPS is a great architecture that ushers the start of the new paradigm of Digital Immunity. It is a new territory but it will be adopted as the best security layer for the Smart City. Modeling the Smart City is a delightful project, but there are so many loose ends to tie. It is delightful because it gives an aerial view of how the city has transformed from a small town to the present metropolis and how it will become a smart city in the future.

Predictive analytics is blueprinting of the future, it is the map that smart city owners will implement to combat the risk of failure. Cities have many miseries starting with crime, electricity, availability of primary care facilities, traffic, and disconnection everywhere. PA is a fitness program to bounce back and put things in order. Or better than that, PA is bringing back the vision to see ahead! Figure 6.9 shows the mechanism of PA with its basic steps.

Understanding Cybercrime Data in Smart Cities

The project starts with using well-defined security objectives for the Smart City. Setting up the grid is one of the vital elements of the city. A smart grid also has highly critical security

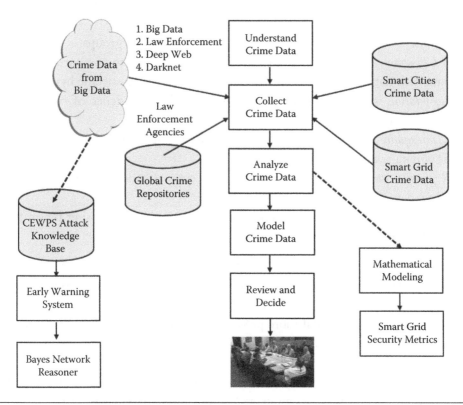

Figure 6.9   The process of building Predictive Analytics for a Smart City with a focus on combating the whole continuum of cybercrime.

requirements and predicting its performance and shortcomings must be entrenched in the plan (Figure 6.9). In short, there are two vital objectives to Predictive Analytics:

1. Persistent and pervasive smart security for the smart grid
2. Early warning of cyberattacks

Collection of Cybercrime Data

There are actually four main feeders of essence data for our smart city's PA. We need to extract every piece of data related to cybercrime and/or cybersecurity. These are the most utilized gold mines of cybercrime:

1. Big Data
2. Law Enforcement
3. Deep Web
4. Darknet

There are not many cyber city–cyber grid predictive analytics sources. CEWPS is unique and going to show the world how Digital Immunity works. But we can use *similar* data, reformat it, and retrofit it for our analysis. Some of the statistical tests and procedures used in our PA process are as follows:

- *Analysis of variance* to compare the variation of two data groups.
- *A Chi-squared test* is the statistical test commonly used to compare observed data with data we would expect to obtain according to a specific hypothesis.
- *Correlation* is an important test to compare the dependence of two sets of crime data.
- *Mean square weighted deviation* (MSWD) is used to measure the goodness of fit of data relative to a criterion.
- *Regression analysis* is an important test to estimate the relationship among crime data.
- *The naïve Bayes classifier* is the probabilistic classier based on using Bayes' formulas to analyze crime data and recognize patterns.

Cybercrime data from other established smart grids would be very useful to enrich our PA. Big Data is a deep universe by itself that is expanding at an astronomical rate. Pumping relative data and cleansing it takes time, but Big Data is an effective course to train our model and make it more predictive. Overall, the quality of the final data indicates the quality of our model.

Let's not forget that cybercrime data from Big Data and global crime repositories are also potential data feeders to CEWPS Virus Knowledge Base to receive cybercrime episodes that get reverse engineered and stored with its attack vectors and signature. This is shown in Figure 6.9.

Building the Cybercrime Data Model

There is a big menu of predictive analytics software packages on the market that can be used. You cannot believe the sales people, so you need to resort other smart way to select the most suitable product. Academia is another source, where most of the statistical packages are available for their students. These geeks will tell you the best program. Or, we can try to run several of them on the same data and choose the final model by scoring them and select the highest.

Deployment of the Cybercrime Data Model

Predictive modeling leverages statistics to have better understanding of the outcomes. In predictive modeling, we have two important variables that need to be available. By definition, a *predictor* variable is an independent variable used in predictive modeling to predict another variable, which is called response. The *response* variable is the variable whose value is dependent upon the value of the predictor variable. So, if we change the value of the predictor variables, it will change the value of the response variable. Think of a predictor variable as a *changing factor* and response variable as *influenced factor*.

What we want to predict is how well CEWPS and the Smart Vaccine will protect the smart grid from malicious and stealth attacks. We believe there is a reputable product using Bayesian network modeling called *Bayesialab* that CEWPS uses for cyberattack knowledge representation and prediction. http://www.bayesia.com/en/products/bayesialab.php.

A list of classified data by subject that were extracted from data feeders is as follows:

- Growth of the critical systems on the smart grid
- Distribution of the type of the critical systems on the smart grid
- Future logistics of the Smart Vaccine during vaccination services
- Growth pattern of the attacks on the smart grid
- Time to predict an incoming attack
- Response time to eliminate an attack on a critical system
- Time improvement to vaccinate a critical system
- Pattern to dispatch an alert to the critical systems on the smart grid
- Distribution of the type of attacks on the smart grid
- Estimated number of attacks on the smart grid
- Time to catch an attack with a honey net
- Time to reverse engineer an attack vector
- Time to manufacture a vaccine

Mathematical modeling is another viable tool that aims to describe the different aspects of the real world, their interaction, and their dynamics through mathematics. Our mathematical model uses mathematical equations to forecast their future behavior. Queuing theory will be used as the science to create and evaluate the behavior of our CEWPS attack model relative to protecting the smart grid. A detailed mathematical model is beyond the scope of this book.

Processes and Variables of the Data Model

The Attacker

- Planning an attack
- The attacker
- The attacking machine
- The virus used
- The attacker escapes or is caught

The Immune System

- The vaccine smart grid
- The alert response system
- The target systems
- The systems in the grid
- The vaccine commander
- Mobilize vaccinators and paramedics

The Engagement

- Vaccinators have recognized the virus
- The killer vaccinators have quarantined the virus
- Paramedics service time and utilization
- Total time of the attack

The Recovery

- Recovery time
- Mean time between failures

Storing the Experience

- The attack vector is decomposed and the strategy of the attack has been deciphered. The whole attack episode is saved and stored in the Document Knowledge Base for future referral (Figure 6.10).

The general model evaluates the response time of the attack. We can manipulate the arrival rate of the attacker and change the time to select the virus to get a family of curves for different input assumptions.

The Smart Vaccine inoculation (vaccination) service is unique. The Smart Vaccine has to work with three types of systems: healthy, infected (sick), dead (the operating system was crippled by the attack). Priority number one is to capture the virus (culprit) and save the healthy system. The captured system will be sent for pathology and forensic analysis.

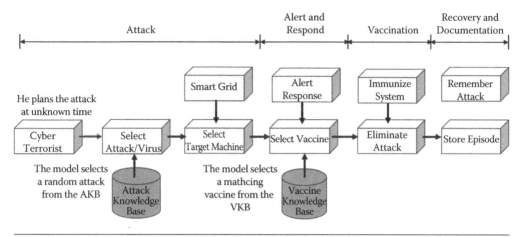

Figure 6.10 The model replicates (with 10 stages) how the Smart Vaccine uses the strategy of defense by offense to nullify the attack.

Figure 6.10 shows a simple model of an attack using 10 activities.

It is not surprising that the behavior of the vaccination service is asymptotic. The more critical systems are attacked, the more they need help, the longer the time to response. This is true in the emergency department with many patients and minimum nurses and care providers. A queuing model, as shown in Figure 6.11, is an operating necessity to describe the basic steps of attacks (with different parameters),

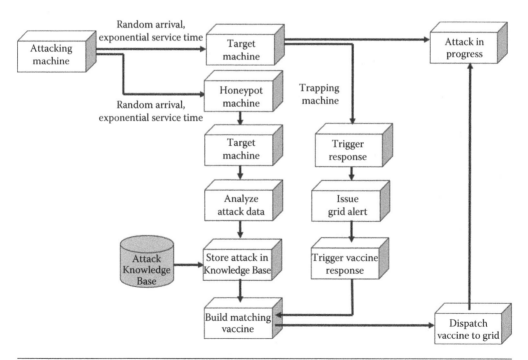

Figure 6.11 This is the process flow of the queuing model to replicate a typical attack scenario on a critical system on the grid.

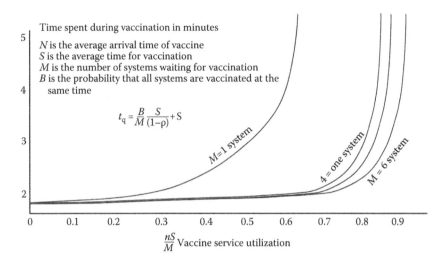

Figure 6.12 Modeling the performance of the Smart Vaccine service is nonlinear and is a function of the number of critical systems on the Smart Grid. The behavior is asymptotic and is normal and fully understood. The Smart Vaccine server could be upgraded whenever necessary to meet the service level agreement.

which helps in sizing CEWPS and planning its capacity for the city's smart grid (CSG). The results of the model after several *what ifs* trials will determine the behavior of CEWPS and the Smart Vaccine on the city's smart grid. Figure 6.12 shows the behavior of the system with different trials.

CEWPS Abbreviations

AKB	Attack Knowledge Base
CCC	Central Coordination Center
CSG	City Smart Grid
DI	Digital Immunity
DKB	Document Knowledge Base
KC	Knowledge Center
RE	Reasoning Engine
SG	Smart Grid
SVG	Smart Vaccine Grid
VaKB	Vaccine Knowledge Base
ViKB	Virus Knowledge Base

References

Kleinrock, L., *Queueing Systems. Vol. 1: Theory*, Wiley, January 2, 1975.
Kleinrock, L., *Queueing Systems. Vol. 2: Theory*, Wiley, April 22, 1976.

Websites

http://en.wikipedia.org/wiki/CVSS.

http://en.wikiquote.org/wiki/James_Martin_%28author%29.

http://securelist.com/analysis/36063/the-contemporary-antivirus-industry-and-its-problems/.

http://www.businessdictionary.com/definition/mathematical-model.html#ixzz3TWlzOyzv.

http://www.nimr.mrc.ac.uk/mill-hill-essays/immune-signatures-in-disease-and-visions-for-their-future-use.

http://www.paecon.net/PAEReview/issue65/ChenPearl65.pdf.

http://www.predictiveanalyticstoday.com/top-15-predictive-analytics-software/.

http://www.securityaffairs.org/about.

http://www.securityweek.com/cybercrime-costs-businesses-more-400-billion-globally-report.

http://www.universitiesintheusa.com/opendoors-2009–10-news.html

7

Big Data of Cybercrime and Terrorism

How to Capture and Manage It

What Is Big Data and What Does It Mean?

To set the right tone for *Big Data*, I would like to tell you about the legend of the chessboard.

About AD 1260, Ibn Khallikan, a Kurdish historian living in the Abbasid Empire (modern Iraq), wrote an encyclopedia with biographies of many famous men (though no women). One of the biographies includes a story about chess and the meaning of *exponential growth*. The story takes place in India, because Ibn Khallikan knew that chess was a game that came from India.

According to this story, King Shihram was a tyrant who oppressed his subjects. One of his subjects, a wise man named Sissa ibn Dahir, invented the game of chess for the king to play and to show him that a king needed all his subjects and should take good care of them. King Shihram was so pleased that he ordered that the game of chess should be preserved in the temples and said that it was the best thing he knew of to train generals in the art of war, a glory to religion and the world, and the foundation of all justice.

Then King Shihram asked Sissa ibn Dahir what reward he wanted. Sissa answered that he did not want any reward, but the king insisted. Finally, Sissa said that he would take this reward: the king should put one grain of wheat on the first square of a chessboard, two grains of wheat on the second square, four grains on the third square, eight grains on the fourth square, and so on, doubling the number of grains of wheat with each square (an exponential rate of growth).

"What a dummy!" thought the king. "That's a tiny reward; I would have given him much more." He ordered his slaves to bring out the chessboard and they started putting on the wheat. Everything went well for a while, but the king was surprised to see that by the time they got halfway through the chessboard the 32nd square required more than 4 billion grains of wheat, or about 100,000 kg of wheat. Now Sissa did not seem so stupid anymore. Even so, King Shihram was willing to pay up.

But as the slaves began on the second half of the chessboard, King Shihram gradually realized that he could not pay that much wheat—in fact, to finish the chessboard you would need as much wheat as six times the weight of all the living things on Earth.

175

How many grains total are placed on a chessboard? Since this is a geometric series, the answer for n squares called a Mersenne Prime number:

$$\sum_{i=0}^{n-1} 2^i = 2^n - 1$$

Plugging in $n = 8 \times 8 = 64$ then it gives $2^{64} - 1 = 18,446,744,073,709,551,615.$*

The term *Big Data* is a very interesting word ... we live among so many big things without realizing. The Internet has made us aware of the term *big*. Everything is relative though, for example, 1 light year is the distance light can travel in vacuum in 1 year's time. This distance is equivalent to roughly 9,461,000,000,000 km or 5,878,000,000,000 miles. This is such a large distance. For comparison, consider the circumference of the Earth when measured at the equator: 40,075 km!

So, the Internet is the culprit which is making us thirstier for information. We all have become information junkies, with excessive affinity for more information digging. We create more information waste than information that we could use to our benefit. My research into Big Data reveals an interesting reality:

$$\frac{\text{Useful extracted information}}{\text{Total searched information}} = 0.0025$$

In other words, we search 10,000 documents before we extract 25 useful *actionable* documents. This is truly overwhelming.

Our Societal Waste Is Big Data

Big Data is similar to a large solid waste dump where almost all of it is recyclable. Every year, the United States generates approximately 230 million tons of *trash*—about 4.6 lb per person per day. Less than one-quarter of it is recycled; the rest is incinerated or buried in landfills. With a little forethought, we could reuse or recycle more than 70% of the landfill waste, which includes valuable materials such as glass, metal, and paper. This would reduce the demand on virgin sources of these materials and eliminate potentially severe environmental, economic, and public health problems.

According to the U.S. Environmental Protection Agency, many of the country's landfills have been closed for one or both of these two reasons:

1. They are full.
2. They are contaminating groundwater. The water that flows beneath these deep holes is our drinking water. Once groundwater is contaminated, it is extremely expensive and difficult, and sometimes even impossible, to clean it up.

---

* London, 1843–1871, *Biographical Dictionary of Ibn Khallikan*, vol. III, p. 71.

The U.S. Environmental Protection Agency, Office of Resource Conservation and Recovery published a report in February 2014 "Municipal Solid Waste Generation, Recycling, and Disposal in the United States," referenced in website http://www.epa.gov/solidwaste/nonhaz/municipal/pubs/2012_msw_dat_tbls.pdf. The report discusses our affinity to paper. We focused specifically on paper (books, magazines, wrapping paper). The pie charts in Figure 7.1 reveals interesting realities about our social habits.

Even though we are totally submerged in the cyber world, we breathe, eat, drink soft data, and we are generating half of the municipal waste from residential, commercial, institutional, and industrial sources. But we are doing great job in recovering a significant amount of paper and paperboard 76%, compared to metal 5.5%. Unfortunately, 24.9% of the paper used gets discarded and buried in the ground.

In the Beginning, There Was a Crashed Message

This is the way the Internet started: On Friday October 29, 1969 at 10:30 PM, the first Internet message was sent from computer science Professor Leonard Kleinrock's laboratory at UCLA, after the second piece of network equipment was installed at Stanford Research Institute (SRI). This connection not only enabled the first transmission to be made but is also considered the first Internet backbone. The first message to be distributed was "LO," which was an attempt at "LOGIN" to log into the SRI computer from UCLA. However, the message was not completed because the SRI system crashed. Shortly after the crash, the issue was resolved, and he was able to log into the computer.

The Internet started with two computers in 1969 with modest fanfare. Today, Mother Internet carries 8.7 billion devices in its belly with no complain. How did this cyber bang take off like this? Leonard Kleinrock, one of the pioneers of the Internet, explains

> "As we talk about some of the technology, you have to understand the key to the success of the Internet wasn't the technology being developed, but the environment," he said. "It was a golden era where creativity and good ideas were flowing all over the place. It's an era not to be repeated, unfortunately."

Today, we take the Internet for granted as it is a part of everyday life, but how often do we think about its true impact on the world today? Let's take cyber waste, for example. We are talking about digital waste. Today, there are 2,802,478,934 users on the Internet, and each user session creates more data, more pictures, more upload files, more download files, more e-mails. It reminds us of air pollution in the 1960s when we became aware that it will be our demise unless we do something about it. Well, we did a lot about it. Now, everything is turning green because we now abide by the rules of ecology and we are reaping tremendous benefits.

My focus in dedicating a chapter to Big Data is cybercrime data. I am going to call it *Cybercrime Big Data*. It is true that Big Data will follow informatics and Internetworking to take its place as the third epoch of the information age. It will definitely change the way corporations and business will evolve.

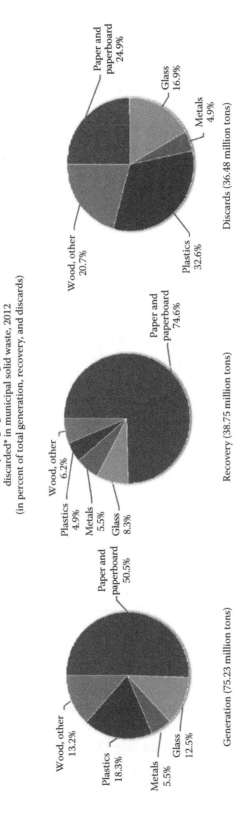

Containers and packaging materials generated, recovered, and discarded* in municipal solid waste, 2012 (in percent of total generation, recovery, and discards)

Paper and paperboard 24.9%

Glass 16.9%

Metals 4.9%

Plastics 32.6%

Wood, other 20.7%

Discards (36.48 million tons)

Paper and paperboard 74.6%

Wood, other 6.2%

Plastics 4.9%

Metals 5.5%

Glass 8.3%

Recovery (38.75 million tons)

Paper and paperboard 50.5%

Wood, other 13.2%

Plastics 18.3%

Metals 5.5%

Glass 12.5%

Generation (75.23 million tons)

Figure 7.1 Municipal Solid Waste Generation, Recycling, and Disposal in the United States. Tables and Figures for 2012. (From the U.S. Environmental Protection Agency; Office of Resource Conservation and Recovery.)

Gordon Moore came up with his golden law that says "The number of transistors incorporated in a chip will approximately double every 24 months." It was the driver behind designing better cost/performance integrated circuit, faster and less heat, given that electrons would consequently travel less distance and processing cycle would be shorter. The big mainframes, which weighed several tons, mutated to few ounces iPads and with Mac Book Air. Ray Kurzweil proposed "The Law of Accelerating Returns," according to which the rate of change in a wide variety of evolutionary systems tends to increase exponentially. He gave further focus to this issue in a 2001 essay entitled "The Law of Accelerating Returns," which described the extension of Moore's law to describe the exponential growth of diverse forms of technological progress. Whenever a technology approaches some kind of a barrier, according to Kurzweil, a new technology will be invented to allow us to cross that barrier. We definitely support Kurzweil's theory when digital computing bit itself in the *derrière* and merged with cyber computing to create a new chapter of the information age. Big Data is the offspring of this new age. We can conservatively say that Big Data is a snowball rolling downhill with exponential acceleration. The snowball is getting bigger picking up more mass and is smashing everything in its way. By the way, The Deep Web and the Dark Web that are the invisible part of the Internet carry a universe of solved and unsolved cases of cybercrime. These two Webs cannot be indexed by search engines, or available to the public.

Attributes of Big Data

Here are the six gracious attributes:

Generated volume—The quantity of data that are generated is very important in this context. It is the size of the data that determines the value and potential of the data under consideration and whether it can actually be considered as Big Data or not.

Variety—The next aspect of Big Data is its variety. This means that the category to which Big Data belongs to.

Generation speed—The term *speed* in the context refers to how fast the data are generated and processed.

Variability—This refers to the inconsistency and nonuniformity.

Veracity—The quality of the data being so close to representing truth and reality.

Multisegment complexity—Data management can become a very complex process, especially when large volumes of data come from multiple sources. These data need to be linked, connected, and correlated in order to be able to grasp the information that is supposed to be conveyed by these data.

The New Cybercrime Big Data

Mind-boggling statistics: BusinessWire site in its issue of January 8, 2013 mentioned that a newly released forecast, from International Data Corporation (IDC), projects that the worldwide Big Data technology and services market will grow at a 31.7% Compound Annual Growth Rate (CAGR) about seven times the rate of the overall information and communication technology (ICT) market with revenues reaching $23.8 billion in 2016.

Gartner estimates that "Big data will drive $28 billion of worldwide IT spending in 2012, according to Gartner, Inc. In 2013, Big Data is forecast to drive $34 billion of IT spending." The truth is that Big Data is not exact science. No one can count its beans and give an exact figure.

As we said earlier, our main focus is to collect Big Data for cybercrime and cybersecurity. Big Data promises an enormous revolution in fighting global terrorism and cybercrime. Right now, the attention of Big Data has been on business profitability, productivity, budget planning, and supply chain. Big Data has been the buzzword making headlines from improving medical diagnosis and treatment to energy conservation. Businesses around the world are using Big Data analytics to transform the data they stored into actionable information.

Open Sesame Big Data

Big Data is a goldmine when it comes to fighting cyberterrorism and cybercrime. It is unfortunate that Big Data has been applied to most of the business sectors, and fighting cybercrime was left on the back burner. Big Data has the potential to offer intelligent-driven model to support reliable early warning cyberattack prediction. Big Data analytics must enter the combat of cybercrime combat from the front gate. Figure 7.2 gives an idea about the Big Cybercrime Data traffic in the world. The big

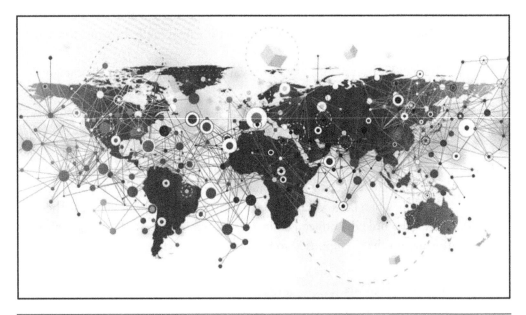

Figure 7.2   This is not the telecommunications network in the world, it is Big Data crime activities. No country is immune from it. The term *Big Data* will soon be replaced with *Bigger Data*. (From http://binarybiryani.com/2013/12/big-data-in-india/.)

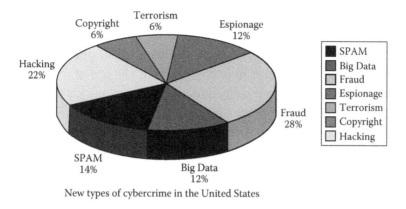

New types of cybercrime in the United States

Figure 7.3 Cybercriminals are becoming smarter by harnessing Big Data to their advantage, since Big Data has become a dynamic source of information assets for big corporations, global banks, retail chains, and insurance companies. (From International Crime Data, 2013.)

challenge in Big Data is usability. The interesting thing about the crime pie in Figure 7.3 is how the U.S. government can store the tsunami of crime records since the creation of the computing age.

Cybercriminals have been clever by harnessing Big Data to their advantage. They have been using Big Data engineering to learn more about actionable intelligence to improve their own efficiency. They have developed a variety of tools to better sort, analyze, and monetize the volumes of data they collect. For cybercriminals, the information collected in drop zones through Trojans on infected PCs (some of which have over a million infected PCs) is clogging their infrastructure. As a result, malware authors have developed different parsing solutions and implemented the use of separate databases in their command and control administration panels in order to distill only the most pertinent data.

Several security companies have diligently got on the bandwagon to learn more about these malware professionals and the way they are robbing banks, stealing trade, and compromising government secret records. One of these security companies is Rivest, Shamir, and Adelman company known as (RSA). It was using sophisticated forensics tools to trace and reverse engineer the ways that cybercriminals are using Big Data methodologies within their illicit operations. We can name the two tools *IntelegentBot* log-parser plug-in and the Citadel Trojan's *Money Panel* plug-in, used for their clever evil work.

IntelegentBot plug-in for log parsing allows botmasters to connect to their Trojan databases and search for specific words such as bank URLs or names. It also allows botmasters to search for only credit card data. Through the use of this plug-in, botmasters are able to quickly and easily mine and monetize credit card data.

Money Panel plug-in is designed to steal only credit card data. It uses a special set of Web injections specifically targeting credit card data, 16 numerical characters. The Web injection displays when a victim accesses a specific site, such as a bank site or Facebook. As soon as a victim enters their card information into the injected field, the data are collected.

In addition, cybercriminals use Big Data analytics to enhance their cracking techniques and to acquire more cybercrime experience for more complex attacks. The sophistication, agility, and speed at which a cybercriminal operates and monetizes their fraudulent information have improved through the use of Big Data analytics. Cybercriminals can now sort their collections of data more quickly to extract financial details and view performance metrics for current malware applications. This is certainly a trend to keep an eye on. As cybercriminals continue to master the concepts of Big Data and apply it to their operations, their cyberattacks stand to become more effective. To combat these attacks, businesses will need to use *intelligence-driven* solutions that also leverage Big Data to deliver timely, actionable security decisions.

CEWPS and Big Data Synergism

There will be great synergism between CEWPS and Big Data. CEWPS is a very smart system that runs on cybercrime data. CEWPS is a power plant that delivers Digital Immunity and vaccination services to Smart City's critical infrastructures. Big Data is a gargantuan *dump* of unstructured data that were discarded by 2.802 billion information consumers while using 8.7 billion devices. A snapshot in October 2014 registered, in 1 day, 2.5 exabytes (2.5×10^{18}) of data that were processed and consumed over the Internet.

The technology of Big Data and CEWPS is compatible. Hadoop, which is a cluster of distributed file system (HDFS) running on commodity server, can definitely be the *big brother* of CEWPS. MapReduce processor can feed CEWPS with significant data about cybercrime for its early warning analytics (Figure 7.4).

CEWPS Cybercrime Analytics

Let's start first with the definition of analytics. It is an attractive and rich term that is much fancier than its cousin *analysis*. It also implies deep intelligent thinking.

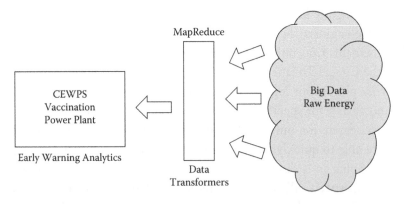

Figure 7.4 Conservation of data energy from static data into kinetic data. We may be impressed to know that Big Data contains mega heaps of cybercrime data that CEWPS can use to develop effective vaccines. It maybe tedious but it pays off. We would also be impressed to know that one ton of ore contains only a quarter of an ounce of gold.

But in simple terms, it is the discovery of meaningful patterns in data. It relies on statistics, computer programming, and operations research to quantify performance. It also favors data visualization (bar charts and pies) to be more expressive and communicative insight.

What Kind of Data Do Smart Cities Need?

CEWPS will be the vehicle to extract some of the significant data for the Smart City and its smart grid. Once we tap into Big Data, we need ample data for the Smart City. There are over 30 smart cities in the world that are considered models and met the newest smart city standard (*ISO 37120:2014*). ISO 37120 defines 100 city performance indicators that could or should be measured, and how. Specifically, ISO 37120 defines 46 core and 54 supporting indicators that cities either *shall* (core) or *should* (supporting) track and report. ISO 37120 also provides for a set of profile indicators, such as population and GDP, to help cities determine which cities are most relevant for comparisons. Table 7.1 shows the 17 subjects for city services and quality of life. Strangely enough, a security indicator is not included.

Security unfortunately is not included in the standards, but we are sure crime will be a vital issue for law enforcement. However, Big Data has lots of raw data about cybercrime in smart cities. Here are some of the cybersecurity data that we got from Big Data shown in Figure 7.5:

Marketing analytics has been used successfully in the business world for years. For example, cell phone providers use *churn* models that predict the likelihood that certain customers will switch service providers, online retailers model buying habits in an effort to identify and suggest additional purchases, and grocery stores display ready-to-eat mashed potatoes in the meat section to remind you to buy side dishes to go with your pot roast. The same approach that lenders use to prequalify potential loan applicants can be used to assess the risk for escalation in a series of burglaries, while the models used to classify shopping patterns and purchasing decisions can be used to identify the motive in a homicide or predict the next incident in a crime series.

Table 7.1　ISO 37120 Indicators for City Services and Life Quality

Economy	Safety
Education	Shelter
Energy	Solid waste
Environment	Telecom
Fire and emergency	Transportation
Finance	Urban planning
Governance	Wastewater
Health	Water and sanitation
Recreation	Economy

Note that the security of the city is not included.

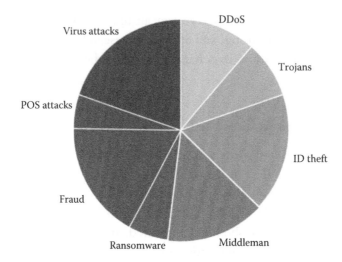

Figure 7.5 Methods of attack derived from Big Data raw files. Each cybercrime research study focuses on specific subjects of interest, as shown in this pie chart. Antivirus Technology providers have the most reliable data. It can be seen that the big bang of Big Data is expanding and carrying with it cybercrime and cyberterrorism. (Courtesy of Kaspersky Lab, June 3, 2013).

Data analytics covers the process of examining hidden *cybercrime* patterns and relationships in large amounts of information. This also allows us to make accurate and reliable predictions of future events, based on the characterization of these patterns and trends in historical data. The data analytics approach helps us solve the revolving door problem: the more information, the more difficult and time-consuming it is to effectively extract meaning from the data. By using a clear process and powerful analytic technologies, data mining quickly and thoroughly explores mountains of data, helping us identify the valuable or actionable nuggets of information.

Data analytics uses extensively data mining engines in law enforcement investigations to discover hidden crime patterns that become visible and complete the crime puzzle. Dark Reading Web magazine published on January 12, 2012 the article "FBI Seeks Data-Mining App for Social Media." Crime analytics has been tremendously successful in capturing serial killers, human traffickers, drug dealers, and credit card fraudsters.

Perhaps the most important required skill in cybercrime analytics is to be immersed in the knowledge reasoning domain. For example, we could find a strong relationship between firing a data center analyst and hacking the payroll system a week after. On the other hand, identifying a relationship between exit interview procedures, employee's last performance review, his social behavior, and his access authorization level could certainly connect the dots and make necessary security precautionary measure before dismissing disgruntled employees.

Now, if we examined say, 100 cases of corporate data breaches, we could develop a knowledge model that would help us learn more about the human character to commit crime. If we had 1000 cases of corporate data breaches, we could learn more about the demographic profile of the hackers, their motif, their civility at work, and their IT skills. But most importantly, infer the causality of the attack, and the tools that were used in the attack. Once we build the Knowledge Base, we could use the data to generate some interesting predictive analyses and probabilistic projections, for attack profiling on the smart grid, in the future based on historical evidence. Some of the gold nuggets that we can use:

- Data center downtime due to a cyberattack
- Breakdown of the infrastructure systems by attack
- What frequency of attacks each type of infrastructure gets (per day, per month)
- Methods of penetration into the critical system
- Antivirus performance
- Role of the Chief Security Officer, his employees, and their security level

Data Extracted from Law Enforcement Crime Repositories

Criminal data are abundant in Big Data, but obtaining them is a great challenge. We can turn to law enforcement agencies around the world to get crime data in smart cities. Each country has a cluster of computer crime-related data. Here in the United States, we have federal data, state data, and city data. The U.S. National Crime Information Center (NCIC) (https://www.fbi.gov/about-us/cjis/ncic) stores all the crime data for the FBI. In the United Kingdom, all law enforcement agencies can enter information into the Police National Computer. In Poland, they have the National Criminal Register (KRK). Germany has the Federal Central Criminal Register. The Swedish Criminal Records Registry is administered by the Swedish National Police Board. All European Countries has a centralized data register. The Integrated Automated Fingerprint Identification System (IAFIS) (https://www.fbi.gov/about-us/cjis/fingerprints_biometrics/iafis/iafis) is the national fingerprint and criminal history system that responds to requests 24/7/365. And the list goes on.

Big Data Support for the Critical Infrastructures

The devil advocates are targeting now juicier critical application domains such as e-commerce, corporate networks, data centers, and selected critical infrastructures. On July 2010, the well-known *Stuxnet* cyber missile was launched to damage gas centrifuges located at the Natanz fuel enrichment plant in Iran by accelerating their speed very quickly and sharply. On August 2012, the Saudi oil giant Aramco was subjected to a large cyberattack that affected about 30,000 workstations. On April 2012, the big payment processing provider Global Payments (www.globalpaymentsinc.com) confirmed a massive breach that compromised about 1.5 million cards. On January 2013, the U.S. Department of Energy underwent an intrusion to 14 of its servers with many workstations located at the Department's headquarters, aimed at stealing employees' personal information.

So, cyberspace has become the *Mecca* for technological malware innovation. It is the new Olympiad of crime with a new type of event: Terror as a Service. The race is open for everyone. The event is called a *Paralysis of Critical Infrastructures* (PCI).

The malware spectrum covers attractive items such as smart power grids, transport systems, and financial infrastructures.

There is one scary tag attached to these holy systems and that is *no resilience* tag. These critical systems were erected some time ago with commodity computing facilities some two generations ago, with little planning on cyberterror and cyber threats. Despite the use of monitoring tools, recent attacks have proven that current defensive mechanisms for these critical infrastructures are not effective enough against most advanced threats. The accelerating pace of the Internet has also accelerated the technological advancement and proliferation of industrial sabotage and brought to the surface an advance face of malware continuum.

Amazingly, Big Data analytics showed some pretty interesting surprises in the domain of cybercrime. While technology has advanced at a logarithmic pace, Internet has become our Aladdin lamp, we can rub it and request anything, et voilà! And with this Amazonian explosion, cybersecurity collapsed under the pressure. Our present Antivirus Technologies (AVT) have been humiliated and got overrun by a tsunami of malicious cyberattacks managed like a business by organized mafias. Big Data has the unstructured evidence and documentation to all these attacks that no country was immune of, nor is capable to overcome and win the malware battle. CEWPS is capable with its early warning immunity mechanism to immobilize cyberattacks and win the battle against malware.

When the term *ecology* was born some short time ago, we started to pay attention to protecting the environment and to waste recycling. Then Big Data was born and we became conscious of the fact that our digital dump contains priceless nuggets that can help us acquire more visibility for a better future. At the same time, Big Data has, in its ore, significant amount of residual knowledge on cybercrime. We can extract this crime organism from the big heap and recycle it and learn the atomic structure of malware, but more importantly, the psychological motives for cyber sabotage. Extracting cybercrime data from Big Data warehouses is a great resource for CEWPS Attack Knowledge Base.

Interfacing CEWPS with Big Data

Right now, Web attackers are amassing a global arsenal of knowledge and resources, which is allowing them to expand their reach well beyond financial services to virtually every industry, everywhere. Smart city infrastructures are the most attractive *low hanging fruits* for these modern information terrorists. They have the knowledge, the tools, and the time.

Let's go back to extracting data from Big Data. We use Hadoop to do its magic… this is how:

Hadoop is an open-source software framework for storing and processing Big Data in a distributed fashion in large clusters of commodity hardware. Essentially, it accomplishes two tasks: massive data storage and faster processing. Open-source software differs from commercial software due to the broad and open network of

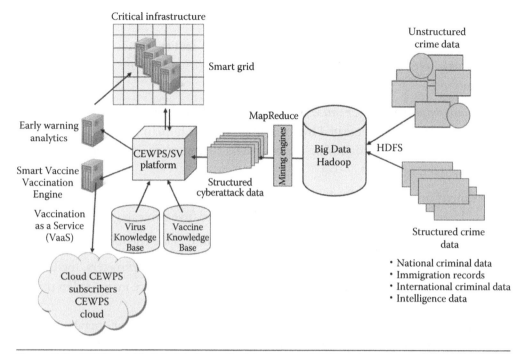

Figure 7.6 CEWPS and Big Data interfaces. Big Data leverages CEWPS early warning prediction and analytics. Vaccinations can also be offered as a service in the cloud.

developers that create and manage the programs. Traditionally, Open-source has been free to download, use, and contribute, although more and more commercial versions of Hadoop are becoming available.

Big Data is an incredible value-added resource to CEWPS. Big Data has two large data feeders into CEWPS: structured and unstructured. Figure 7.6 shows the interconnectivity of Big Data (BD) with CEWPS.

Hadoop consists of a storage part *Hadoop Distributed File System (HDFS)* and a processing part *MapReduce*. Hadoop splits files into large blocks (default 64 MB or 128 MB) and distributes the blocks among the nodes in the cluster. Hadoop's MapReduce and HDFS components were inspired by Google papers on their MapReduce and Google File System.

Facebook and Yahoo are users of Hadoop which is used in regular data centers as well as via the cloud. It is available on Microsoft Azure, Amazon Elastic Compute Cloud (EC2). CEWPS will be using Hadoop to extract and process Big Data's cybercrime data (Figure 7.6).

Big Data Cybercrime Data

Intelligent data mining engines will extract significant amount of infrastructure malware data from Big Data clusters. We're going to extract from Big Data the two categories of data as shown in Figure 7.6.

Category 1: Structured Data

Although this might seem like business as usual, in reality, structured data is taking on a new role in the world of Big Data. The sources of data are divided into two classifications:

1. *Computer or machine generated classification*: Machine-generated data generally refer to data that are created by a machine without human intervention.
2. *Human generated classification*: These are data that humans, in interaction with computers, supply.

Some experts argue that a third category exists that is a hybrid between machine and human. Here though, we are only concerned with the first two categories.

Classifcation 1 Machine-generated structured data can include the following:

- *Sensor data*: Examples include radio frequency ID tags, smart meters, medical devices, and Global Positioning System data. Companies are interested in this for supply chain management and inventory control.
- *Web log data*: When servers, applications, networks, and so on operate, they capture all kinds of data about their activity. This can amount to huge volumes of data that can be useful, for example, to deal with service-level agreements or to predict security breaches.
- *Point-of-sale data*: When the cashier swipes the bar code of any product that you are purchasing, all the data associated with the product are generated.
- *Financial data*: Lots of financial systems are now programmatic; they are operated based on predefined rules that automate processes. Stock-trading data is a good example of this. It contains structured data such as the company symbol and dollar value. Some of these data are machine generated, and some are human generated.

Classifcation 2 Examples of structured human-generated data might include the following:

- *Input data*: This is any piece of data that a human might input into a computer, such as name, age, income, non-free-form survey responses, and so on. These data can be useful to understand basic customer behavior.
- *Click-stream data*: Data are generated every time you click a link on a website. These data can be analyzed to determine customer behavior and buying patterns.
- *Gaming-related data*: Every move you make in a game can be recorded. This can be useful in understanding how end users move through a gaming portfolio.

When both classes are used by millions of other users submitting the same information, the size is astronomical. Additionally, much of these data have a real-time component to them that can be useful for understanding patterns that have the potential of predicting outcomes.

Category 2: Unstructured Data

Unstructured data are data that do not follow a specified format for Big Data. If 20% of the data available to enterprises is structured data, the other 80% is unstructured. Unstructured data are really most of the data that you will encounter. Until recently, however, the technology did not really support doing much with them except storing them or analyzing them manually.

Unstructured data are everywhere. In fact, most individuals and organizations conduct their lives around unstructured data. As with structured data, unstructured data are either machine generated or human generated.

Here are some examples of machine-generated unstructured data:

- *Satellite images*: This includes weather data or the data that the government captures in its satellite surveillance imagery. Just think about Google Earth, and you get the picture.
- *Scientific data*: This includes seismic imagery, atmospheric data, and high-energy physics.
- *Photographs and video*: This includes security, surveillance, and traffic video.
- *Radar or sonar data*: This includes vehicular, meteorological, and oceanographic seismic profiles.

The following list shows a few examples of human-generated unstructured data:

- *Text internal to your company*: Think of all the text within documents, logs, survey results, and e-mails. Enterprise information actually represents a large percent of the text information in the world today.
- *Social media data*: These data are generated from the social media platforms such as YouTube, Facebook, Twitter, LinkedIn, and Flickr.
- *Mobile data*: These include data such as text messages and location information.
- *Website content*: This comes from any site delivering unstructured content, like YouTube, Flickr, or Instagram.

Where to Get Cyberterrorism Data?

Our addiction to information has created golden opportunities for terrorism and its sibling cyberterrorism. The FBI website www.fbi.gov posted on September 10, 2014, the testimony of Robert Anderson, Jr. Executive Assistant Director of FBI, before the Senate Committee on Homeland Security and Governmental Affairs that "The US government estimates 3 million anti-American cyberterrorists in the United States and abroad." They are highly educated, professionals, and veterans who accumulated considerable amount of knowledge about critical infrastructures. They are highly paid intelligence gurus and spies, spending their full time to collect engineering data on *target* critical infrastructures and to build plans of attacks. It is easy to find information about drug trafficking, human trafficking, money laundering, but cyberterrorism is one of the most secretive networks that involve affluent intelligence operatives, industry spies, politicians, and large number of computer scientists who use sophisticated computers to extract infrastructure data from Big Data warehouses.

Some of the most crucial data that we get from Hadoop are the following:

Unsolved Cybercrime Cases: From smart cities as well as from law enforcement databases.

Cyberattacks from Foreign Countries: The attacks will continue on smart grids and the CEWPS needs to learn the attacker's profile and the attack vectors.

Attacks to Damage Infrastructures: The attack starts online from somewhere and it affects the computers in substations, metros, bridges, and so on.

Industrial Espionage: Crime cases.

Organized Crime Organizations: In foreign countries and in adversary countries.

Intelligence Information: Data caught between terrorist organizations over the Internet to plot attacks on U.S. soil.

Websites: Those which are used by terrorists to plot attacks on U.S. soil.

Immigration Records and Cases: About suspects who legitimately entered the United States.

Technology Standards Organizations

We found lots of resources that can help us start making sense of the Big Data world. Standard organizations are tackling some of the key emerging issues with getting data resources to work together effectively. Open-source offerings can help you experiment easily so that you can better understand what is possible with Big Data. Lots of Big Data conferences and research groups are out there. Of course, all the vendors in the market have research, white papers, and best practices that they are happy to share. In this chapter, we offer you some ideas of the resources that are out there to help you.

For Big Data to mature and be able to fully help smart city, standards are required. A number of organizations are working hard to bring vendors together to help move the process forward. The following sections describe some of these organizations. Here is the list of standard organizations that will help establish a great bond between Big Data, CEWPS, and the smart grid.

The *Open Data Foundation*: The Open Data Foundation (ODaF) is a nonprofit organization that is organized to help promote the adoption of global metadata standards as well as the development of open source for the use of statistical data. The organization focuses on improving metadata in the fields of economics, finance, health care, education, labor, social science, technology, agriculture, development, and the environment. Its website is: www.opendatafoundation.org.

The *Cloud Security Alliance*: The Cloud Security Alliance (CSA) was established to promote the use of best practices for providing and ensuring security within cloud computing and to educate people about the uses of cloud computing to help secure all other forms of computing. The organization has established the Big Data Working Group (BDWG) to help identify the scalable techniques for data-centric security and privacy problems in Big Data (https://cloudsecurityalliance.org/research/big-data).

The *National Institute of Standards and Technology*: The National Institute of Standards and Technology (NIST) is a U.S. government agency that focuses on emerging standards efforts. This organization has done a considerable amount of work defining and providing good information on everything from cloud computing to Big Data. In March 2012, NIST started a Big Data initiative. The focus of the new initiative is to help transform the capability of organizations to use Big Data for scientific discovery, environmental and biomedical research, education, and national security. It will collaborate with the National Science Foundation (NSF) Center for Hybrid Multicore Productivity Research (CHMPR) in setting up a Big Data workshop. The issues to be addressed include the following:

- State-of-the-art core technologies needed to collect, store, preserve, manage, analyze, and share Big Data that could benefit from standardization
- Potential measurements to ensure the accuracy and robustness of methods that harness these technologies (www.nist.gov/itl/ssd/is/big-data.cfm)

The *International Organization for Standardization*: ISO 37120 is important in that it is the first ISO standard for smart city indicators. ISO 37120 defines 100 city performance indicators that could or should be measured and how. Specifically, ISO 37120 defines 46 core and 54 supporting indicators that cities either *shall* (core) or *should* (supporting) track and report. Note that ISO 37120 conformance will require third-party verification of data, and the organization is in the process of defining an audit process with pilot cities. ISO 37120 also provides for a set of profile indicators, such as population and GDP, to help cities determine which cities are most relevant for comparisons (www.iso.org/iso/catalogue).

The *Apache Software Foundation*: The Apache Software Foundation provides organizational, legal, and financial support for a broad range of open-source software projects. It was founded in 1999 as a membership-based, not-for-profit corporation to ensure that the Apache projects continue to exist beyond the participation of individual volunteers. One of the organization's key projects is its management of Hadoop. It offers an open-source software library that is a standards-based framework for processing large data sets across clusters of computers (http://hadoop.apache.org).

The *Open Access Same-Time Information System*: One of the most important standards organizations is Open Access Same-Time Information System (OASIS), the Organization for the Advancement of Structured Information Standards. It is a nonprofit organization that has started to focus on Big Data standards. This process is at an early stage, but we expect that the organization will begin to focus on creating Big Data standards.

Glossary: Big Data

We wanted to enrich the knowledge of the reader and provide additional information about the terms that joined the technical lingo. This glossary is related specifically to

Big Data and Predictive Analytics. There may be some additional terms that are outside the context of this chapter.

Aggregation: A process of searching, gathering, and presenting data.

Algorithm: A mathematical formula placed in software that performs an analysis on a set of data.

Anonymization: The severing of links between people in a database and their records to prevent the discovery of the source of the records.

Artificial intelligence: Developing intelligence machines and software that are capable of perceiving the environment and take corresponding action when required and even learn from those actions.

Automatic identification and capture (AIDIC): Any method of automatically identifying and collecting data on items, and then storing the data in a computer system. For example, a scanner might collect data about a product being shipped via a radio frequency identification chip (RFID).

Avro: Avro is a data serialization system that allows for encoding the schema of Hadoop files. It is adept at parsing data and performing remote procedure calls.

Behavioral analytics: Using data about people's behavior to understand intent and predict future actions.

Big Data scientist: Someone who is able to develop the algorithms to make sense out of Big Data.

Business intelligence (BI): The general term used for the identification, extraction, and analysis of data.

Cascading: Cascading provides a higher level of abstraction for Hadoop, allowing developers to create complex jobs quickly, easily, and in several different languages that run in the JVM, including Ruby, Scala, and more. In effect, this has shattered the skills barrier, enabling Twitter to use Hadoop more broadly.

Cassandra: Cassandra is a distributed and open-source database designed to handle large amounts of distributed data across commodity servers while providing a highly available service. It is a NoSQL solution that was initially developed by Facebook. It is structured in the form of key value.

Cell phone data: Cell phones generate a tremendous amount of data, and much of it is available for use with analytical applications.

Classification analysis: A systematic process for obtaining important and relevant information about data, also called metadata; data about data.

Cloud computing: A distributed computing system over a network used for storing data off-premises.

Clustering analysis: The process of identifying objects that are similar to each other and cluster them in order to understand the differences as well as the similarities within the data.

Cold data storage: Storing old data that are hardly used on low-power servers. Retrieving the data will take longer.

Comparative analysis: It ensures a step-by-step procedure of comparisons and calculations to detect patterns within very large data sets.

Chukwa: Chukwa is a Hadoop subproject devoted to large-scale log collection and analysis. Chukwa is built on top of the Hadoop distributed file system (HDFS) and MapReduce framework and inherits Hadoop's scalability and robustness. Chukwa also includes a flexible and powerful toolkit for displaying monitoring and analyzing results, in order to make the best use of this collected data.

Clojure: Clojure is a dynamic programming language based on LISP that uses the Java virtual machine (JVM). It is well suited for parallel data processing.

Cloud: A broad term that refers to any Internet-based application or service that is hosted remotely.

Columnar database or column-oriented database: A database that stores data by column rather than by row. In a row-based database, a row might contain a name, address, and phone number. In a column-oriented database, all names are in one column, addresses in another, and so on. A key advantage of a columnar database has faster hard disk access.

Comparators: Two ways you may compare your keys is by implementing the interface or by implementing the Raw Comparator interface. In the former approach, you will compare (deserialized) objects, but in the latter approach, you will compare the keys using their corresponding raw bytes.

Confabulation: The act of making an intuition-based decision appears to be data based.

Cross-channel analytics: Analysis that can attribute sales, show average order value, or the lifetime value.

Data aggregation: The act of collecting data from multiple sources for the purpose of reporting or analysis.

Data architecture and design: How enterprise data are structured. The actual structure or design varies depending on the eventual end result required. Data architecture has three stages or processes: conceptual representation of business entities, the logical representation of the relationships among those entities, and the physical construction of the system to support the functionality.

Database as a Service (DaaS): A database hosted in the cloud and sold on a metered basis. Examples include Heroku Postgres and Amazon Relational Database Service.

Data cleansing: The act of reviewing and revising data to remove duplicate entries, correct misspellings, add missing data, and provide more consistency.

Data-directed decision making: Using data to support making crucial decisions.

Data exhaust: The data that a person creates as a by-product of a common activity, for example, a cell call log or Web search history.

Data feed: A means for a person to receive a stream of data. Examples of data feed mechanisms include RSS or Twitter.

Data governance: A set of processes or rules that ensure the integrity of the data and data management best practices are met.

Data integrity: The measure of trust an organization has in the accuracy, completeness, timeliness, and validity of the data.

Data mart: The access layer of a data warehouse used to provide data to users.

Data mining: The process of deriving patterns or knowledge from large data sets.

Data model, data modeling: A data model defines the structure of the data for the purpose of communicating between functional and technical people to show data needed for business processes, or for communicating a plan to develop how data are stored and accessed among application development team members.

Data point: An individual item on a graph or a chart.

Data profiling: The process of collecting statistics and information about data in an existing source.

Data quality: The measure of data to determine its worthiness for decision making, planning, or operations.

Data replication: The process of sharing information to ensure consistency between redundant sources.

Data repository: The location of permanently stored data.

Data science: A recent term that has multiple definitions, but generally accepted as a discipline that incorporates statistics, data visualization, computer programming, data mining, machine learning, and database engineering to solve complex problems.

Data scientist: A practitioner of data science.

Data security: The practice of protecting data from destruction or unauthorized access.

Data set: A collection of data, typically in tabular form.

Data source: Any provider of data, for example, a database or a data stream.

Data steward: A person responsible for data stored in a data field.

Data structure: A specific way of storing and organizing data.

Data visualization: A visual abstraction of data designed for the purpose of deriving meaning or communicating information more effectively.

Data warehouse: A place to store data for the purpose of reporting and analysis.

Deidentification: The act of removing all data that link a person to a particular piece of information.

Demographic data: Data relating to the characteristics of a human population.

Deep Thunder: IBM's weather prediction service that provides weather data to organizations such as utilities, which use the data to optimize energy distribution.

Distributed cache: A data cache that is spread across multiple systems but works as one. It is used to improve performance.

Distributed object: A software module designed to work with other distributed objects stored on other computers.

Distributed processing: The execution of a process across multiple computers connected by a computer network.

Distributed file system: Systems that offer simplified, highly available access to storing, analyzing, and processing data.

Document store databases: A document-oriented database that is especially designed to store, manage, and retrieve documents, also known as semistructured data.

Document management: The practice of tracking and storing electronic documents and scanned images of paper documents.

Drill: An open-source distributed system for performing interactive analysis on large-scale data sets. It is similar to Google's Dremel and is managed by Apache.

Elastic search: An open-source search engine built on Apache Lucene.

Event analytics: Shows the series of steps that led to an action.

Exabyte: 1 million terabytes or 1 billion gigabytes of information.

Exploratory analysis: Finding patterns within data without standard procedures or methods. It is a means of discovering the data and to find the data sets main characteristics.

External data: Data that exist outside of a system.

Extract, transform, and load (ETL): A process used in data warehousing to prepare data for use in reporting or analytics.

Failover: The automatic switching to another computer or node should one fail.

Flume: Flume is a framework for populating Hadoop with data. Agents are populated throughout ones IT infrastructure—inside Web servers, application servers, and mobile devices, for example—to collect data and integrate it into Hadoop.

Grid computing: The performing of computing functions using resources from multiple distributed systems. Grid computing typically involves large files and is most often used for multiple applications. The systems that comprise a grid computing network do not have to be similar in design or in the same geographic location.

Graph Databases: They use graph structures (a finite set of ordered pairs or certain entities), with edges, properties, and nodes for data storage. It provides index-free adjacency, meaning that every element is directly linked to its neighbor element.

Hadoop: An open-source software library project administered by the Apache Software Foundation. Apache defines Hadoop as "a framework that allows for the distributed processing of large data sets across clusters of computers using a simple programming model."

Hama: Hama is a distributed computing framework based on Bulk Synchronous Parallel computing techniques for massive scientific computations, for example, matrix, graph, and network algorithms. It is a top-level project under the Apache Software Foundation.

HANA: A software/hardware in-memory computing platform from SAP designed for high-volume transactions and real-time analytics.

HBase: HBase is a nonrelational database that allows for low-latency, quick lookups in Hadoop. It adds transactional capabilities to Hadoop, allowing users to conduct updates, inserts, and deletes. EBay and Facebook use HBase heavily.

HCatalog: HCatalog is a centralized metadata management and sharing service for Apache Hadoop. It allows for a unified view of all data in Hadoop clusters and allows diverse tools, including Pig and Hive, to process any data elements without needing to know physically where in the cluster the data are stored.

Hadoop distributed file system: Hadoop distributed file system (HDFS), the storage layer of Hadoop, is a distributed, scalable, Java-based file system adept at storing large volumes of unstructured.

Hadoop User Experience (HUE): HUE is an open-source Web-based interface for making it easier to use Apache Hadoop. It features a file browser for HDFS, an Oozie Application for creating workflows and coordinators, a job designer/browser for MapReduce, a Hive and Impala UI, a Shell, a collection of Hadoop API, and more.

Hive: Hive is a Hadoop-based data warehousing-like framework originally developed by Facebook. It allows users to write queries in a SQL-like language called HiveQL, which are then converted to MapReduce. This allows SQL programmers with no MapReduce experience to use the warehouse and makes it easier to integrate with business intelligence and visualization tools such as Microstrategy, Tableau, and Revolutions Analytics.

Impala: Impala (by Cloudera) provides fast, interactive SQL queries directly on your Apache Hadoop data stored in HDFS or HBase using the same metadata, SQL syntax (Hive SQL), ODBC driver and user interface (Hue Beeswax) as Apache Hive. This provides a familiar and unified platform for batch-oriented or real-time queries.

In-database analytics: The integration of data analytics into the data warehouse.

In-memory database: Any database system that relies on memory for data storage.

In-memory data grid (IMDG): The storage of data in memory across multiple servers for the purpose of greater scalability and faster access or analytics.

Kafka: Kafka (developed by LinkedIn) is a distributed publish–subscribe messaging system that offers a solution capable of handling all data flow activity and processing these data on a consumer website. This type of data (page views, searches, and other user actions) is a key ingredient in the current social Web.

Key value stores: Key value stores allow the application to store its data in a schemaless way. The data could be stored in a data type of a programming language or an object. Because of this, there is no need for a fixed data model.

KeyValue databases: They store data with a primary key, a uniquely identifiable record, which makes easy and fast to look up. The data stored in a KeyValue are normally some kind of primitive of the programming language.

Latency: Any delay in a response or delivery of data from one point to another.

Linked data: As described by World Wide Web inventor Time Berners-Lee, "Cherry-picking common attributes or languages to identify connections or relationships between disparate sources of data."

Load balancing: The process of distributing workload across a computer network or computer cluster to optimize performance.

Location analytics: Location analytics brings mapping and map-driven analytics to enterprise business systems and data warehouses. It allows you to associate geospatial information with data sets.

Location data: Data that describe a geographic location.

Log file: A file that a computer, network, or application creates automatically to record events that occur during operation, for example, the time a file is accessed.

Machine-generated data: Any data that are automatically created from a computer process, application, or other nonhuman source.

Machine2Machine data: Two or more machines that are communicating with each other.

Machine learning: The use of algorithms allows a computer to analyze data for the purpose of *learning* what action to take when a specific pattern or event occurs.

Mahout: Mahout is a data mining library. It takes the most popular data mining algorithms for performing clustering, regression testing, and statistical modeling and implements them using the MapReduce model.

MapReduce: MapReduce is a software framework that serves as the compute layer of Hadoop. MapReduce jobs are divided into two (obviously named) parts. The "Map" function divides a query into multiple parts and processes data at the node level. The "Reduce" function aggregates the results of the "Map" function to determine the "answer" to the query.

Mashup: The process of combining different data sets within a single application to enhance output, for example, combining demographic data with real estate listings.

Metadata: Data about data; gives information about what the data are about.

MongoDB: MongoDB is a NoSQL database oriented to documents, developed under the open-source concept. It saves data structures in JSON documents with a dynamic scheme (called MongoDB BSON format), making the integration of the data in certain applications more easily and quickly.

MPP database: A database optimized to work in a massively parallel processing environment.

Multidimensional databases: A database optimized for data online analytical processing (OLAP) applications and for data warehousing.

MultiValue databases: They are a type of NoSQL and multidimensional databases that understand 3D data directly. They are primarily giant strings that are perfect for manipulating HTML and XML strings directly.

Network analysis: Viewing relationships among the nodes in terms of the network or graph theory, meaning analyzing connections between nodes in a network and the strength of the ties.

NewSQL: An elegant, well-defined database system that is easier to learn and better than SQL. It is even newer than NoSQL.

NoSQL: NoSQL (commonly interpreted as "not only SQL") is a broad class of database management systems identified by nonadherence to the widely used relational database management system model. NoSQL databases are not built primarily on tables and generally do not use SQL for data manipulation.

Object databases: They store data in the form of objects, as used by object-oriented programming. They are different from relational or graph databases and most of them offer a query language that allows object to be found with a declarative programming approach.

Object-based image analysis: Analyzing digital images can be performed with data from individual pixels, whereas object-based image analysis uses data from a selection of related pixels, called objects or image objects.

Online analytical processing (OLAP): The process of analyzing multidimensional data using three operations: consolidation (the aggregation of available), drill-down (the ability for users to see the underlying details), and slice and dice (the ability for users to select subsets and view them from different perspectives).

Online transactional processing (OLTP): The process of providing users with access to large amounts of transactional data in a way that they can derive meaning from it.

Open Data Center Alliance (ODCA): A consortium of global IT organizations whose goal is to speed the migration of cloud computing.

OpenDremel: The open-source version of Google's Big Query java code. It is being integrated with Apache Drill.

Operational data store (ODS): A location to gather and store data from multiple sources so that more operations can be performed on it before sending to the data warehouse for reporting.

Oozie: Oozie is a workflow processing system that lets users define a series of jobs written in multiple languages—such as MapReduce, Pig, and Hive—then intelligently link them to one another. Oozie allows users to specify, for example, that a particular query is only to be initiated after specified previous jobs on which it relies for data are completed.

Parallel data analysis: Breaking up an analytical problem into smaller components and running algorithms on each of those components at the same time. Parallel data analysis can occur within the same system or across multiple systems.

Parallel method invocation (PMI): Allows programming code to call multiple functions in parallel.

Parallel processing: The ability to execute multiple tasks at the same time.

Parallel query: A query that is executed over multiple system threads for faster performance.

Pattern recognition: The classification or labeling of an identified pattern in the machine learning process.

Pentaho: Pentaho offers a suite of open-source business intelligence (BI) products called Pentaho business analytics providing data integration, OLAP services, reporting, dashboarding, data mining, and ETL capabilities

Petabyte: 1 million GB or 1024 TB.

Pig: Pig Latin is a Hadoop-based language developed by Yahoo. It is relatively easy to learn and is adept at very deep, very long data pipelines (a limitation of SQL).

Predictive analytics: Using statistical functions on one or more data sets to predict trends or future events.

Predictive modeling: The process of developing a model that will most likely predict a trend or outcome.

Public data: Public information or data sets that were created with public funding.

Query: Asking for information to answer a certain question.

Query analysis: The process of analyzing a search query for the purpose of optimizing it for the best possible result.

R: R is a language and environment for statistical computing and graphics. It is a GNU project, which is similar to the S language. R provides a wide variety of statistical (linear and nonlinear modeling, classical statistical tests, time-series analysis, classification, clustering,...) and graphical techniques and is highly extensible.

Real-time data: Data that are created, processed, stored, analyzed, and visualized within milliseconds.

Recommendation engine: An algorithm that analyzes a customer's purchases and actions on an e-commerce site and then uses that data to recommend complementary products.

Reference data: Data that describe an object and its properties. The object may be physical or virtual.

Reidentification: Combining several data sets to find a certain person within anonymized data.

Risk analysis: The application of statistical methods on one or more data sets to determine the likely risk of a project, action, or decision.

Root cause analysis: The process of determining the main cause of an event or problem.

Routing analysis: Finding the optimized routing using many different variables for a certain means of transport in order to decrease fuel costs and increase efficiency.

Scalability: The ability of a system or process to maintain acceptable performance levels as workload or scope increases.

Schema: The structure that defines the organization of data in a database system.

Search data: Aggregated data about search terms used over time.

Semistructured data: Data that are not structured by a formal data model but provide other means of describing the data and hierarchies.

Sentiment analysis: The application of statistical functions on comments people make on the Web and through social networks to determine how they feel about a product or company.

Server: A physical or virtual computer that serves requests for a software application and delivers those requests over a network.

Software as a Service (SaaS): Application software that is used over the Web by a thin client or Web browser. Salesforce is a well-known example of SaaS.

Spatial analysis: It refers to analyzing spatial data such as geographic data or topological data to identify and understand patterns and regularities within data distributed in geographic space.

SQL: A programming language for retrieving data from a relational database.

Sqoop: Sqoop is a connectivity tool for moving data from non-Hadoop data stores—such as relational databases and data warehouses—into Hadoop. It allows users to specify the target location inside of Hadoop and instruct Sqoop to move data from Oracle, Teradata, or other relational databases to the target.

Storage: Any means of storing data persistently.

Storm: (1) Storm is a system of real-time distributed computing, open source and free, born into Twitter. Storm makes it easy to reliably process unstructured data flows in the field of real-time processing, which made Hadoop for batch processing. (2) An open-source distributed computation system designed for processing multiple data streams in real time.

Structured data: Data that are organized by a predetermined structure.

Structured Query Language (SQL): A programming language designed specifically to manage and retrieve data from a relational database system.

Text analytics: The application of statistical, linguistic, and machine learning techniques on text-based sources to derive meaning or insight.

Transactional data: Data that change unpredictably. Examples include accounts payable and receivable data, or data about product shipments.

The Internet of Things: Ordinary devices that are connected to the Internet at any time anywhere via sensors.

Thrift: "Thrift is a software framework for scalable cross-language services development. It combines a software stack with a code generation engine to build services that work efficiently and seamlessly between C++, Java, Python, PHP, Ruby, Erlang, Perl, Haskell, C#, Cocoa, Smalltalk, and OCaml."

Unstructured data: Data that have no identifiable structure, for example, the text of e-mail messages.

Value: All the available data will create a lot of value for organizations, societies, and consumers. Big Data means big business and every industry will reap the benefits from Big Data.

Volume: The amount of data, ranging from megabytes to brontobytes.

Visualization: A visual abstraction of data designed for the purpose of deriving meaning or communicating information more effectively.

Weather data: Real-time weather data are now widely available for organizations to use in a variety of ways. For example, a logistics company can monitor local weather conditions to optimize the transport of goods. A utility company can adjust energy distribution in real time.

WebHDFS Apache Hadoop: WebHDFS Apache Hadoop provides native libraries for accessing HDFS. However, users prefer to use HDFS remotely over the heavy client side native libraries. For example, some applications need to load data in and out of the cluster or to externally interact with the HDFS data. WebHDFS addresses these issues by providing a fully functional HTTP REST API to access HDFS.

XML databases: XML databases allow data to be stored in XML format. XML databases are often linked to document-oriented databases. The data stored in an XML database can be queried, exported, and serialized into any format needed.

ZooKeeper: ZooKeeper is a software project of the Apache Software Foundation, a service that provides centralized configuration and open code name registration for large distributed systems. ZooKeeper is a subproject of Hadoop.

Websites

http://aws.amazon.com/big-data/.
http://bigdatauniversity.com/.
http://csis.org/.
http://hackmageddon.com/.
http://research.google.com/.
http://research.microsoft.com/en-us/projects/bigdata/.
http://wikibon.org/wiki/v/2012_Big_Data_Revenue_by_Vendor.
http://www-01.ibm.com/software/data/bigdata/.
http://www.cloudera.com/content/cloudera/en/why-cloudera/hadoop-and-big-data.html.
http://www.csl.sri.com/projects/cyber-ta/.
http://www.dummies.com/how-to/computers-software/Big-Data.html.
http://www.oracle.com/us/technologies/big-data/index.html.
http://www.sas.com/.
http://www.teradata.com/business-needs/BigData-Analytics/.
https://downloads.cloudsecurityalliance.org/initiatives/bdwg/Big_Data_Analytics_for_Security_Intelligence.pdf.
https://hbr.org/2012/10/big-data-the-management-revolution/ar.
www.oasis-open.org.

PART II

8

CEWPS ANATOMY, THE SMART VACCINE, AND THE MAN-MADE B CELL

A Word on Virus Anatomy

Humans have a skewed view of viruses because we only notice them if they cause disease. In reality, however, viruses are much more than just pathogens. In fact, they play a crucial role in the evolution of life. Viruses were not only the probable precursors of the first cells, but they have helped shape and build the genomes of all species, including humans. Viruses are present in every species and every ecological niche and affect every organism. They even influence the global climate by regulating the population densities of microorganisms—and thereby nutrient availability—in the oceans. We are the invaders of the viral world, not vice versa. Viruses have also been a major factor for the evolution of all life. They helped build the genomes (A genome contains the complete set of genetic instructions, needed to build an organism). Almost 50% of our genome is comprised of retro elements. If the shortest retro elements, 500,000 long terminal repeat promoters, were once full-length retroviruses, they would add up to the size of our genome. Are we therefore the descendants of viruses? This is impossible to prove, because viral footprints disappeared with time.

Tracing the origins of viruses is difficult because they do not leave fossils and because of the tricks they use to make copies of themselves within the cells they have invaded. Some viruses even have the ability to stitch their own genes (A gene is a small piece of the genome that contains information about the basic characteristics of the organism, like eye and hair color) into those of the cells they infect, which means studying their ancestry requires untangling it from the history of their hosts and other organisms. What makes the process even more complicated is that viruses do not just infect humans, they can infect basically any organism—from bacteria to horses, seaweed to people.

A virus has either a DNA or an RNA genome and is called a DNA virus (A DNA is the building block of an organism that contains the genetic code) or an RNA virus (An RNA is another type of building block similar to DNA), respectively. Viruses are by far the most abundant biological entities on Earth, and they outnumber all the others put together. They infect all types of cellular life including animals, plants, bacteria, and fungi. Interestingly enough, viruses that infect plants are harmless to animals, and most viruses that infect other animals are harmless to humans. The main purpose of a virus is to deliver its genome into the host cell to allow its expression (transcription and translation) by the host cell.

The Digital Immune System

Innovation in medicine is galloping in gigantic strides to catch up with infectious diseases and antibody synthesis. One of the great contributions to humanity was the discovery of the vaccine. Without adaptive immunity, one-fourth of the human race would have been terminally ill. Dr. Edward Jenner and Louis Pasteur share this honorable credit. Interestingly enough, with vaccination, man was able to conquer disease. It was unimaginable that immunity can be acquired and stored in the human body for the next attack.

On December 17, 1903, the Wright Brothers successfully replicated bird flying with their three-axis control invention. Human immunity was added to the annals of human wonders as super physicians and chemists raced to learn more about its mystery. It took 300 years of sweat and frustration before immunology produced a mature immune system based on molecular recognition of the attack. Fortunately, for most of us, our immune systems kept steadfastly vigilant in monitoring themselves to ensure that each cellular component behaves and interacts symbiotically to generate protective immune responses. Amazingly, the concept of human immunity can also be replicated and applied to the digital world. It is a revolutionary leap forward in the future of cybersecurity.

Computers can also be immunized with the help of an artificially intelligent agent called the Smart Vaccine™. Digital Immunity is a new concept that was never thought of before. After thoroughly studying immunology and the way it works, it was possible to replicate the human model and blueprint an architecture for the digital world. We called it Digital Immunity (DI).

Ever since Antivirus Technology (AVT) came into existence, AVT vendors have been paying homage to Microsoft and wouldn't dare to outpace it. They have been marching to Microsoft's drum beat and cautiously trying not to step on the turf of the software giant. The saying "what's good for Microsoft is good for AVT" was true in the nineties but not in the post-9/11 years. Internet Explorer (IE) proved to be Microsoft's Achilles' heel. ... Cybercrime lords and terrorists got away with day-zero and the business world suffered from a global viral epidemic. Now, cyberterrorists have jumped on the Cloud bandwagon to market its novelty of *Attack-as-a-service*. AVT has not been able to match the sophistication of malware. Meanwhile, a silent worm called Stuxnet was able with its ingenious camouflage to penetrate Natanz nuclear enrichment plant and create havoc. Thus, cyberterrorism has become a real strategic weapon launched from anywhere in the world. There are over 3000 terror schools and institutes that have graduated professional terrorists with formal degrees in modern terrorism. Viral attacks have become self-mutating, self-healing, self-navigating and could outsmart the best firewalls, the Forbidden city moat, and the Great Wall of China. Terrorism has actually become the mother of invention.

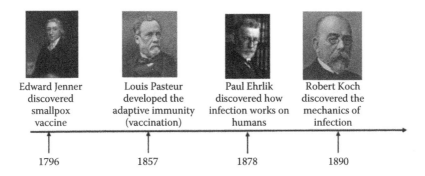

Edward Jenner discovered smallpox vaccine	Louis Pasteur developed the adaptive immunity (vaccination)	Paul Ehrlik discovered how infection works on humans	Robert Koch discovered the mechanics of infection
1796	1857	1878	1890

Figure 8.1 The famous timeline of the pioneers of the Human Immune System. Not only were they life savers, but humanity savers. No reward could be enough for these crusaders who defied the reaper.

Throughout history, we are finding out that man's most worrisome fear was sickness. Once a virus attacks the body, then it is a fight between God and the Devil. Longevity was a mysterious and unexplainable quandary. Immunity was unknown and like a touch of luck. During the plague of Athens in 430 BC, the historian Thucydides noted that people who had recovered from a previous bout of the disease could nurse the sick without contracting the illness a second time. Louis Pasteur in 1857 developed the *acquired immunity* through vaccination. It was not until Robert Koch's 1891 proofs, for which he was awarded a Nobel Prize in 1905. The timeline shows the contribution of the four immunology pioneers, who without them, the human race would have drastically fallen in jeopardy (Figure 8.1).

Today, the world is healthier with longer human life span because we now have the adaptive vaccine that helps the human body defeat the attacking virus. The human body also has become smarter with preventive vaccination ahead of the danger. It really makes the body invincible.

The secret sauce is to replicate the way vaccine helps the infected body. Let's review how the vaccine works.

Vaccinations protect you from specific diseases that can make you very sick, disable, or even kill you. They boost your body's own defense system, which is also called the immune system. Vaccines create immunity to protects us from an infection. Here is a list of how vaccines work:

- Most vaccines contain a little bit of a disease germ that is weak or dead. Vaccines do not contain the type of germ that makes you sick. Some vaccines do not contain any germs.
- Having this little bit of the germ inside your body makes your body's defense system produce *antibodies* to fight off this kind of germ. Antibodies help trap and kill germs that could lead to disease.
- Your body can make antibodies in two ways: by getting the disease or by getting the vaccine. Getting the vaccine is a much safer way to make antibodies without having the suffering of the disease itself and the risk of becoming disabled, or even dying.

- Antibodies stay with you for a long time. They remember how to fight off the germ. If the real germ that causes this disease (not the vaccine) enters your body in the future, your defense system knows how to fight it off.
- Often, your defense system will remember how to fight a germ for the rest of your life. Sometimes, your defense system needs a booster shot to remind it how to fight off this germ.

Analogy between the Human Immune and the Digital Immune Systems

The immune system protects the body against disease or other potentially damaging foreign bodies. When functioning properly, the immune system identifies and attacks a variety of threats, including viruses, bacteria, and parasites while distinguishing them from the body's own healthy tissue. The most important components of the Human Immune System (HIS) are:

- *The lymphatic system (white cells generator)* consists of bone marrow, spleen, thymus, and lymph nodes. It is considered the smart grid for the Human Immune System.
- *The spleen* is the largest lymphatic organ in the body that contains white blood cells that fight infection or disease.
- *The thymus (T cells generator)* a specialized organ of the immune system where T cells mature. T cells help destroy infected or cancerous cells.
- *Lymph nodes* are nodes from the lymphatic grid, distributed widely throughout the body including the armpit and stomach. A distributes generating plant of B and T cells ready to fight infection and disease.
- *Lymphocytes (B cells—white blood cells)* are the generals of the infection war. They give orders to the natural killer cells (NK cells), mobilize the T cells (the communication cells), and alert the lower rank of B cells to be ready for fighting.
- *Leukocytes (B cells—white blood cells)* to observe enemy lines.

Vaccines like a catalyst to expedite the deployment of body immunity, by mimicking an infection. It is a drill to familiarize the defense system about the enemy. The immune system gets empowered by the vaccine and the morale gets high. By the way, fever is an attack alert and it supplies ammunition to the fighting B cells.

Once the infection drill goes away, the body is left with a supply of *memory cells*, another department of the T cells (T lymphocytes) that will remember how to fight that disease in the future. So, the invention of the vaccine is one of the most remarkable inventions that saves mankind, because it allows memory cells to remember the disease in future attacks. We all are grateful to Pasteur for giving us a life extender. So do not forget to get flu shots on time.

Replicating the Human Immune System is an amazing idea. The Smart Vaccine (SV) replicates what the B cells and T cells are doing. It creates a miniature attack through a vaccination service, then have the system eliminate the attack and learn

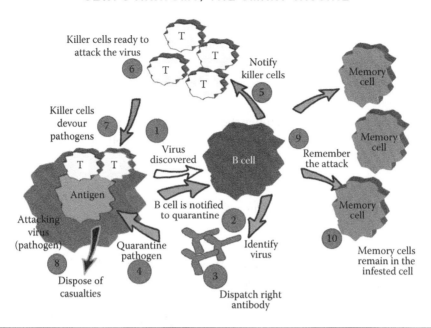

Figure 8.2 The Human Immune System implements the defense-by-offense mechanism to eradicate the virus. This is an atrocious battle that B cells and T cells fight to the death. Our amazing immune system is highly autonomic and self-learning. The memory cells retain the dead infested cells to learn everything about the virus. The B cells would get the training for the next attack.

from it how to combat similar attacks. Thus, the system acquires immunity and the attack is saved as *episode* in the Attack Knowledge Base (AKB). The Smart Vaccine (SV) and the system antivirus share virus *signature* data for future attacks.

We will provide several examples of how the Smart Vaccine commands the battle.

Figure 8.2 shows how the Human Immune System fights the attacking virus (called pathogen). In actuality, it is a battle to the death between the attacking pathogens (biological virus) and between the B cells army. There will be many casualties for sure. If the body wins the battle, then it will be more immune against this particular attack. If the body loses the battle, then additional "specific" vaccine will be supplemented or the body will suffer (this means that the body is not producing enough B cell fighters) and eventually it will be a life-and-death situation.

Let's describe how the body fights a viral attack step by step:

1. The virus is discovered after penetrating the skin.
2. The B cells try to identify the virus by coupling with it.
3. As soon as it recognizes the nature of the virus, antibody generators (antigen) will induce an immune response in the body.
4. Antibody will rush to capture the virus (pathogen) and quarantine it before it starts to reproduce.
5. At the same time, the B cells will notify the T cells (killer cells) to be ready for the attack.

6. The T cells are getting ready for the attack.
7. The T cells capture the virus and devour a portion of it for future recognition and to quickly produce antibody.
8. The remains of the virus are disposed of either through the blood or through the skin.
9. The memory cells will remember the nature of the virus and keep it.
10. They will remain in the infested cells and nurse the cells with antibody until they heal or die.

Anatomy of the Present Computer Virus

A Word about the Black Hat Community

We confess that the Black Hat Community, which started in 1997, is one of the most reputable organizations in global information security in the world. We do not know much about the foreign hack virtuosos. Black Hat has offered great knowledge to the security community around the world. Black Hat inspires professionals at all career levels, encouraging growth and collaboration among academia, world-class researchers, and leaders in the public and private sectors. They have great educational videos on youtube.com. You can visit their great website (https://www.blackhat.com/) and register to become a member.

A Word on Hackers

Hackers are gifted programmers who can build cyber bombs, traps, backdoor Trojans and be anywhere and can compromise any system. Virus designers are super software engineers with an arsenal of prefab rootkits. Most hackers are Internet junkies who live in the wild. Every company should hire ethical hackers and ask them to invade into their own critical systems, their clouds, and their networks.

Hackers are easily solicited to join anti-establishment or even terrorist electronic armies. Today, the world is plagued with cyber banditos and Jesse James who can rob any data vault. Oh, they are incredible spies who could snatch any design blueprint or top secret or and uncover any scandal. The FBI siphons their brain for lesser jail sentences. Their menu includes Robo-Stuxnet, Cloud Virus Rain, Ransomware, ID Theft, Grid-Lockers, Critical Infrastructure Bombs, Industrial Intelligence, Darth Vaders, Cyber Heart Attacks, Espionage, and Zombie Salvation Army.

We assume that an attack will have a smart payload and sophisticated attack vector. Most destructive attacks seem to be politically motivated to spy on global corporations, governments, and large cloud centers.

The virus is a master piece of ingenuity engineering and malice. It is a software booby trap to create havoc and most of the time some substantial destruction to vulnerable infrastructures.

The anatomy of the virus

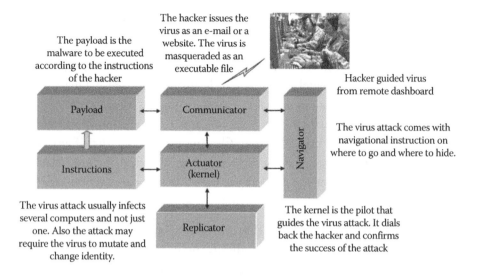

Figure 8.3 A virus is a Swiss Army software robot (called a *bot*) that carries instructions (the payload to be executed once the target is reached). It travels in a stealth mode on the Internet (TCP/IP) and navigates its way until it reaches its destination. It can be a Backdoor Trojan, an e-mail, transfered file, or distributed through social media.

Figure 8.3 shows the ingenious architecture of a smart virus:

1. *The Remote Dashboard*: This is where the terrorist is hiding. He knows where his guided missile is going. There could be more than one terrorist to conduct a massive attack. They could be using IRC or spoofed IP to guide the Trojan.
2. *Instructions*: These are instructions that are wired inside the kernel. They cover all possible situations that the attack could encounter. Some advanced attacks are autonomic and very lethal.
3. *Payload*: A block of code designed to override the normal operation of a critical system, and hijack it, and change the software that control the infrastructure. Sometimes, the payload remains hiding until the right moment.
4. *Communicator*: It is the dispatch center where communications from the terrorists are relayed to the kernel and reports to them the attack progress.
5. *Actuator (Kernel)*: It is the Commander in charge. Its main mission is to launch the planned attack without any glitches.
6. *Replicator*: It is part of the attack to create clones with different payload and identity and to slow down and delay the vaccination process with different hostile codes.
7. *The Navigator*: Smart attacks need a good navigator that knows its way through firewalls and intrusion and detection systems.

How Does the Classic Antivirus Work?

Generally, there are two ways that an *off-the-shelf* antivirus program can detect and identify a virus:

1. *The signature dictionary*: Scans/monitors the programs by their code; if it finds a program code that match the virus code in its signature database, it will consider that program a virus.
2. *Behavior analysis*: Scans/monitors the programs by analyzing their behavior, such as modification of critical system files/important data files; if any behavior seems suspicious, then the antivirus program will alert the user that there is suspicious behavior, or it may alert the user that malicious actions are about to be performed and block that behavior.

These are the two most common ways that antivirus programs identify viruses.

Both of them have advantages and disadvantages. Signature-based detection can correctly detect a virus but cannot detect viruses that are not in the signature database.

Behavior-based detections (or heuristic detections) can detect viruses that are not in the signature database but can produce false positives, which means that a legitimate file might be identified as a virus.

Anatomy of the Smart Vaccine

If Stuxnet, Flame, Duqu, and Aurora are the most destructive cyber missiles for any country's infrastructures, then the Smart Vaccine is David who beat Goliath. We can also claim that the Smart Vaccine is the holy grail of Digital Immunity. The secret is that the Smart Vaccine is designed with a quantum leap into a far more superior technology than malware technologies. I believe the future generations of the Smart Vaccine will be even smarter and will be programmed with the formidable reasoning repertoire of a chess grandmaster.

A Word on Artificial Intelligence

Before describing the different components of the Smart Vaccine, let us review some thoughts about artificial intelligence (AI) to accelerate the understanding of the reader.

Our intention was to build an intelligent *cyborg* (short for *cybernetic organism*) program it with indestructible bionic power, pretty much like the terminator in the movie *Terminator 2*. We have injected so much intelligence and cognitive skills into its structure, including the ability to defend itself, and interactively reason and decide to take the optimum solution. The Smart Vaccine (SV) is like the *robo-cop* of the Smart City Grid, roaming around looking for cyber villains. The Smart Vaccine is designed to reason and solve difficult situations and to manage its resources to

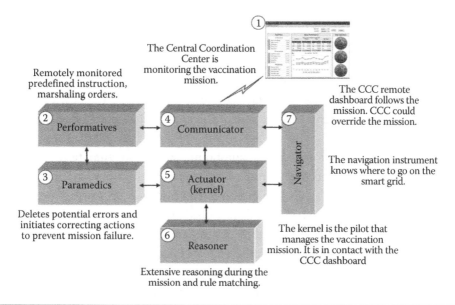

The Central Coordination Center is monitoring the vaccination mission.

Remotely monitored predefined instruction, marshaling orders.

The CCC remote dashboard follows the mission. CCC could override the mission.

② Performatives

④ Communicator

⑦ Navigator

③ Paramedics

⑤ Actuator (kernel)

The navigation instrument knows where to go on the smart grid.

Deletes potential errors and initiates correcting actions to prevent mission failure.

⑥ Reasoner

The kernel is the pilot that manages the vaccination mission. It is in contact with the CCC dashboard

Extensive reasoning during the mission and rule matching.

Figure 8.4 The Smart Vaccine is more than the sum of its parts—It is a live robot programmed with artificial intelligence, and equipped with an autonomic brain, vaccination management, self-healing, and even self-resurrecting skills. An avid learner from previous viral attacks.

nullify attacks, but most importantly, the Smart Vaccine amplifies its commanding knowledge from the experience of previous battles. Its additive experience makes the Smart Vaccine computationally intelligent to resolve complex battle situations. Its autonomic strength makes the Smart Vaccine persistent and self-protecting against surprise attacks. If you have not seen the movie *Terminator 2*, then go and see it, it will remind you of the Smart Vaccine (Figure 8.4).

Now let's raise the hood and take a look at the engine of the Smart Vaccine:

1. *The Central Coordination Center (CCC)*: In the object programming world, objects communicate with one another, exchange information, and can couple with one another, start a service, and terminate it. It is a dynamic world by itself. This is what happens inside CEWPS™. CCC serves as the center of the constellation. It is the control tower of CEWPS, which is equipped with information dashboards collecting real-time data from the smart grid and all the systems attached to it. The main responsibility of CCC, as an information hub, is to make sure that the smart grid is secure. When CCC gets alert messages from the Early Warning Center about an attack, it will broadcast the alert to all the systems on the city grid and dispatch an emergency response request to the Smart Vaccine Commander (SVC).

2. *Performatives*: A collection of instructions to make sure the kernel execute them in a predefined order. These instructions are usually persistent (survive under any circumstance), serialized, and marshaled from one state into another.

3. *Paramedics*: This is a very vital component in the design of the Smart Vaccine. Each agent carries its own paramedic in case it gets clobbered by the attacking virus. Rules of self-healing are carefully defined and embedded in the paramedic component. Each Smart Vaccine agent will learn quickly from its own mistakes, and these incidents will be stored in the SV Knowledge Base to train other SV agents. This is one of the crucial characteristics of being an autonomic engine.

4. *The Communicator*: It is another autonomic with two vital tasks: First, it allows the Smart Vaccine Commander to communicate with the Central Coordination Center (CCC) to get directives and pass on progress report on the status of attacks on the City's Smart Grid and the outcome of the vaccination service. Second, it helps the SV Commander conduct the battle with its SV army and communicate with the SV vaccinators and the SV Paramedics.

5. *The Actuator (Kernel)*: It helps pass the commands of the battle to the rest of the Army. It checks the outcome of the vaccination services and dispatches progress data to CCC.

6. *The Reasoner*: It has an important role to advise the SV Commander with its probabilistic reasoning on the success of the vaccination mission and outcome of the battle.

7. *The Navigator*: The logistics of vaccinating several critical systems requires good navigation. Locating the right critical systems on the complex grid is challenging and requires real-time response. A good navigator is like the driver of a caring car, minimizing the risk when the situation gets messy.

Like any response mission, time and location to reach the compromised system are critical. The SV Commander gets all the attack information before it initiates its vaccination mission. The Commander also checks the Attack and the Vaccine Knowledge Bases for additional reference data.

The Smart Vaccine in the Battlefield

Figure 8.5 is the 3D panoramic view of how CEWPS is designed to defend the city's smart grid (CSG). The Central Coordination Center (CCC) is the control tower where the total operations of CEWPS are displayed on dashboards in real time mode.

CEWPS has control over three major grids:

1. *The Top Grid*: It is where the Central Coordination Center (CCC) is located, with the early warning predictor and malware collector. This grid has all the intelligence to predict an attack, capture the attack, and get to know its internals, and save it in the Attack Knowledge Base (AKB). The Attack Reasoning Engine (ARE) calculates the probability of causation and other discovery data about the origin of the attack. CCC gives orders to the Smart Vaccine Commander.

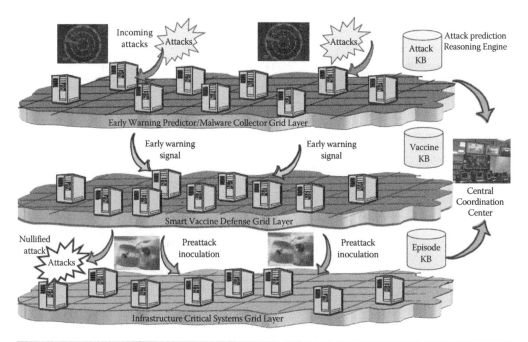

Figure 8.5 The three layers of CEWPS showing (the top layer) how the early warning attack alerts trickle down to the Smart Vaccine (the center layer) with the vaccination response to the critical systems (the bottom layer).

2. *The Middle Grid*: It is the Smart Vaccine Grid (SVG) where the Smart Vaccine Commander (SVC) receives the early warning alert and mobilizes an army of Smart Vaccine agents (warriors) for the incoming battle. The Smart Vaccine Commander gets instructions from CCC and instantiates the vaccination process also called Vaccination-as-a-Service. The commander fires two service requests. The first request is to vaccinate prior to the attack all healthy critical systems of the grid. The second request is to repair the attacked system and quarantine the attack and send it to the Attack Knowledge Base.

3. *The Bottom Grid*: It is the city's smart grid (CSG) where all the infrastructure critical systems reside on. Each critical system will be immunized with the proper vaccine. The CCC gets fresh information from the battle activities. The attack episode is recorded in the Attack Knowledge Base (AKB) to help the Smart Vaccine to outsmart all the incoming attacks in future.

The Digital Immuny Battlefield

The similarity between a computer attack and a biological viral attack are amazingly close. Like infectious agents (pathogens), digital attacks are open-ended and are becoming smarter and more vicious. We will describe the power grid attack later on, but for now, let's explain a sample attack step by step. (Figure 8.6) shows in details the

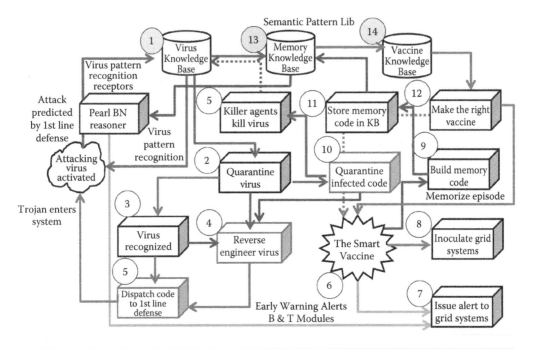

Figure 8.6   The amazing similarity between the Human Immunity and Digital Immunity. CEWPS is the replication system in the digital world. The Smart Vaccine which is like the B cells uses the same approach used in human immunity: defense by offense.

magnificent fight between the Smart Vaccine and the attacking virus. Let's go over each step:

1. The attacking virus is activated after it used a backdoor as a dormant worm. Instantly, the early warning system informed the Virus Knowledge Base about its behavior and it needs to be quarantined. Again, it is possible that CEWPS honeypot system caught it, and it means there will not be an attack. We rely on Hadoop data analytics, which come very handy.

2. The attacking foreign virus was captured, and it is time to know everything about it, and the Smart Vaccine Commander was informed.

3. The attacking foreign virus was quarantined ready for formal forensics to know its attack vector and its signature.

4. The Smart Vaccine inquired from CCC to reverse engineer in order to know what was going to be damaged. The first line of defense (the Smart Vaccine intelligence) was sent for more information about the attack, in case there are other copies of the virus. Mutation could be possible.

5. The Smart Vaccine Commander ordered to kill the attacking virus. Like in the human body, the B cells dismember the virus and retain the part as a memory taken for the next similar attack. The attack vector and payload will be documented and packaged ready to send to the Attack Knowledge Base. By now, the Smart Vaccine knows the strategy of the attack and its impact.

6. The Smart Vaccine Commander issued an alert to the army of vaccinators to inoculate all critical systems with the created vaccine, just in case the worm might spread to the other systems.

7. The Smart Vaccine Commander issues an alert to all the administrators of the critical system. CEWPS is an extremely intelligent and cognitive system with several autonomous subsystems as specific service providers. During the attack, the Smart Vaccine Commander orders vaccination service instances and each service instance has a destination, start, and finish.

8. The inoculation services are taking place on the grid. Vaccine paramedics are also available to fix any damage caused by the attack.

9. Once the anatomy of the virus has been known and the attack vector code has been reverse engineered, it will be packaged and ready to be stored in the Vaccine Knowledge Base.

10. The proper vaccine code has already been coded and been ready for vaccination by the Smart Vaccine.

11. The Attack Knowledge Base is the repository that stores all the attack vectors as documentation and reference for future attacks.

12. The Vaccine Knowledge Base is the repository that stores all the prepared vaccines for the attack.

13. As we can see, a viral attack is a complex operation and needs to be matched to a very intelligent commanding agent with lots of hands-on experience. This is why we call it the Smart Vaccine. The AVT is different from the autonomic intelligence of the Smart Vaccine. While viral attacks are becoming intelligent and more potent, only the Smart Vaccine with his highly scalar intelligence will take down the virus and nullify the attack.

14. The Virus Knowledge Base (ViKB) stores the virus signature, structure and its ontology model for future battles.

The Appeal of Cyberterrorism

Cyberterrorism is an attractive alternative for modern terrorism for the following:

- *First*, it is more straightforward and easier than traditional terrorist methods. The young generation is highly hands-on in computer hacking learned in school and social media. They do not even need to learn using arms. They can build cyber missiles and launch then through a telephone line, a cable, or a wireless connection.

- *Second*, cyberterrorism could be stealth and committed from anywhere in the world as long as there is the Internet. They learned how to circumvent firewall, DMZ, and other intrusion tools.

- *Third*, cyberterrorists are aiming now at the critical infrastructures in large metropolitan cities, which are still vulnerable with high risk of attacks.

- *Fourth*, there are over 20 organized cybercrime companies that provide *crime-as-a-service* to wealthy and influential terrorists. There are over 150 schools that offer an advance certificate in cyberterrorism.
- *Fifth*, the well-organized terrorists groups such as ISIS are recruiting young people from the United States and Europe to form their *electronic army*. They are luring the young with money and status.

Here is the list of the most notorious and destructive cyberattack types blessed by cyberterrorists:

Terrorism Levels

Terrorism Level 1: *Information Theft*—Cybercriminals are professional thieves. No, they do not snatch the purse of an old lady in the mall. They are smarter than that. Digitally, they tiptoe into the data banks of large corporations and, in particular, the government and grab copies of confidential records, money certificates, secret documents, and even classified military documents on foreign plots.

Terrorism Level 2: *Espionage*—It is considered an *honest* act for spies. The ends justify the means. Technology spies are back stabbers and cat burglars. An article from INFOSEC Institute describes in detailed granularity that "Cyber espionage is the greatest transfer of wealth in history…. The Chinese government is considered the biggest aggressor in cyber-espionage, while US networks are the privileged targets of cyberattacks that hit every sector, from media to military." We can write an encyclopedia on this subject.

Terrorism Level 3: *Crime Service Provider*—Equally alarming is the prospect of terrorists themselves designing computer software for government agencies. Remarkably, as Denning describes in "Is Cyber Terror Next?" at least one instance of such a situation is known to have occurred.

Terrorism Level 4: *Organized Crime*—This is the Mafia revisited. The Russian Business Network (RBN) and the Chinese Triads are very active in orchestrating cyberattacks in the United States and Europe. Zeus Trojan is a malware designed as an open project that can be customized with new features to meet customer demands. Zeus Trojan is an agent able to steal banking information by logging keystrokes and form grabbing; it is spread mainly through phishing and drive-by downloads schemes.

CEWPS uses the famous *ZeuS Tracker*, which is a crimeware kit that steals credentials private data from online services like social networks, online banking accounts, ftp accounts, e-mail accounts, phishing tricks. It also tracks ZeuS Command & Control (C&C) host servers, which control a huge network of remote botnets and malicious hosts that store files associated configuration files, binaries and drop zones. CEWPS provides special alerts to the administrators of the critical systems on the smart grid with ZeuS Tracker to block the spying from well-known ZeuS hosts and any potential infections on their internal networks. CEWPS main Central Coordination Center dashboard uses ZeuS Tracker (and other tracking tools) to alert smart grid subscribers. Interestingly enough, Web admins can purchase access to ZeuS for $700 (*source*: RSA Security 4/21/2008) or purchase the exe builder for $4000. The ZeuS Tracker shows the topology of botnets and the millions of compromised computers (around 3.6 million in the United States). As of October 28, 2009, over 1.5 million phishing, messages carrying Zeus Trojan were sent through Facebook. The website https://zeustracker.abuse.ch/ provides updated statistics on the place of the Command & Control servers of the botnet network.

Terrorism Level 5: *Nation-State Cyber Digital Attacks*—These attacks are just as bad as level 5, except the targets are data centers and control houses that manage the physical infrastructures. If these critical systems are compromised and fail, then backup systems have to be activated until the primary systems are fully operational. CEWPS smart grid is the effective savior.

Terrorism Level 6: Nation-State Cyber-Enabled Infrastructure Attacks—They are true curses from hell. Wealthy nations sponsor such attacks with the help of stealth backdoor Trojans such as Stuxnet, Flame, and Duqu. These attacks are hard to trace their exact origin. Also they sneak inside in stealth mode and find the right time to get out of the closet. And when they are discovered, they already dumped their payload and went back into the closet.

These cyber missiles are aimed at physical infrastructures with high vulnerability. For example, mass transit systems, electrical power network, including generation plants, electrical grid, substations, and local distribution are very attractive target. CEWPS/SV has enough intelligence to immobilize backdoor Trojans and reverse engineer them. We will provide scenarios of how the Smart Vaccine catches them before they unleash their payloads (Scenario-Power Grid later).

The Most Challenging Attacks for the Smart Vaccine

Since CEWPS is a replication of the human immune system (HIS), its success comes not only from its reasoning clout and the intelligence of its smart vaccine (SV), also its autonomic and cognitive smart grid. The grid covers the whole city and is connected pathologically (closely couples) to the City's mart Grid (CSG) and all the critical systems. We can compare the grid to neural network where Smart Vaccine messages propagate bidirectionally to reach the compromised system. Simplistically, we can say the grid is a mesh of smart information buses with busy brokers routing and marshaling SV massages. Then we have the knowledge engines that work overtime to provide heuristic evaluations and prediction scenarios to CEWPS Central Coordination Center (CCC). It should be known that the Smart Vaccine Grid (SVG) is tightly coupled with the City's Smart Grid (CSG). Service-Oriented Architecture (SOA) was implemented to facilitate the management of the messages. This is the most expedient way to immunize and guard the critical system.

It is remarkable to know that the nervous system works hand in hand with the immune system. Evidence is clear that the immune system and the nervous system are linked in several ways. For example, the hormones and other chemicals that convey messages among nerve cells also *speak* to cells of the immune system. Indeed, some immune cells are able to manufacture typical nerve cell products and use T cells to help transmit information to the nervous system. Wow… that is what we replicated with CEWPS/Smart Vaccine to protect the city's smart grid.

Analysis of Cyberterrorism

One of the advanced features of the Smart Vaccine is its ability to learn from its vaccination services. Cybercrime is actually the cross section between the creative mind and technology, but unfortunately, it has expanded into cyberterrorism driven by religious jihadism and political radicalism. As Jeremy Hammond described in the *Guardian* "Their blatant hypocrisy, threat inflation and militaristic rhetoric must be challenged if we are to have a free and equal internet." We all know that no one owns cyberspace and cyberterrorists know it very well. Cyberspace does not have stop signs, red lights, lanes or tolls, or even cops. Cybertechnology has given us the good, the bad and ugly produced wonderful. We need to holistically address the ugly side of cyberspace.

We need a new holistic "defense-by-offence" approach to give us the upper hand in cyberwarfare. To win the battle, we need to know the enemy and the time of attack.

Cyberterrorism is an indispensable lethal weapon in political or religious conflicts. Cyberterrorism is the convergence of cyberspace and terrorism. Cyber vengeance (*as I coin it*) seems very rewarding to any terrorist group who could launch massive attack and knock down cyber defenses of the Smart City and cause substantial devastation or ransack financial data from any financial institution. The continuum of evil includes crippling control communications of the city and creating public hysteria. They could launch botnet-driven distributed-denial-of-service (DDoS) attacks to blind security forces at a border crossing point as a means of facilitating an infiltration operation, or a cyberattack in one area of a country could act as a diversion, while a plain terrorist attack can occur elsewhere. They could conduct Siemens Supervisory Control and Data Acquisition SCADA attacks on specific sites and the system is showing *normal* operation. A good example would be to open the valves at a chemical plant near a population center, creating a Bhopal-like event. The sophistication of malware got to the point terrorists could commandeer a civilian airplane. If we're going to build smart cities, we'd better have good cyber fences to block any poisonous attack vectors.

Figure 8.7 is an interesting aerial view of a modern smart city. The city is fenced with two intelligent superimposed grids. The first one is the city's smart grid (CSG), and the second one is the Smart Vaccine Grid (SVG). Both grids shown as dotted lines are linked to all infrastructure critical systems (not to confuse the dotted lines with cloud bubbles).

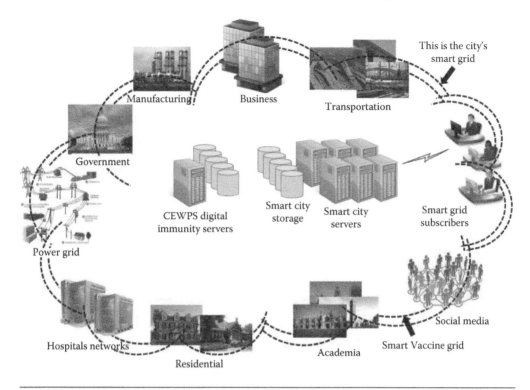

Figure 8.7 The City's Smart Grid (CSG) ties all the critical systems together. The Smart Vaccine Grid (inside the City's Smart Grid) is also tied to the critical systems through the City Smart Grid. The city's servers preserve the key performance and contract data collected from the critical systems. The Smart Vaccine Grid (SVG) guards and maintains the immunity of city's critical systems. Vaccination-as-a-Service is one of the unique services that the city cannot ignore.

The Miraculous Fight of the Smart Vaccine

The Attack on the Power Grid

Figure 8.8 is the topology of a large metropolitan smart city. Cyberattacks are actually premeditated and well planned. Random attacks simply do not exist. All attack vectors are carefully calculated and directed at a target. Cyberattacks on smart cities are a reality that should not be ignored. Power grids have become "the happy hour" of cyberterror, simply because the power grid is the most critical and vulnerable infrastructure in any smart metropolis. The Darth Vaders know that a cascaded blackout could paralyze the city and create an apocalyptic panic and disorder.

The city's smart grid (CSG) is the nervous system of the Smart City (the outer perimeter in the diagram). The power grid are protected by the city's smart grid (CSG), and of course, by the Smart Vaccine Grid (SVG) (the inner perimeter). The three SCADA systems balance the electricity load and collect data over the whole city.

The city purchased three Siemens SCADA top-of-the line control systems to manage the power grid. The three substations are interconnected to maintain load balancing.

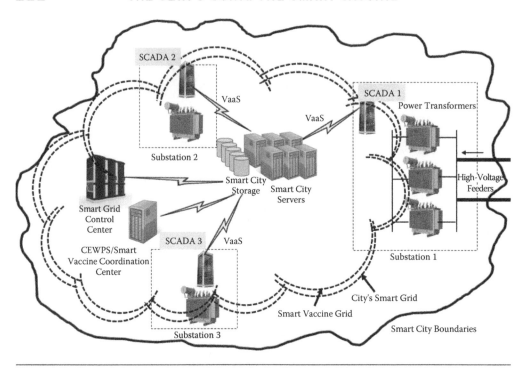

Figure 8.8 The topological view of the smart city showing the City Smart Grid (outside dotted circle) which watches the power grid, while SCADA and the Smart Vaccine Grid (inside circle) are tightly coupled to protect the three critical substation systems. If the Smart City decides to have a Smart Cloud, then the SCADA systems will be securely connected to the cloud.

The three SCADA systems have their own secure private network that connects them with their remote terminal units (RTU) located in the substations. CEWPS Central Coordination Center is also connected to the Smart Vaccine Grid and the City's Smart Grid. If the Smart City decides to have a Smart Cloud, then SCADA systems will be securely connected to the cloud (which will be discussed in Chapter 9).

The attack aims at the major metropolitan city of 5 million people. The city is ramping up its technologies to become a smart city. There is one major power-generating plant (not included in the diagram) that feeds power to the city through five distribution substations. Three substations are shown in the diagram shown in Figure 8.8 as follows: *Substation-1* is the primary power substations that receive two high-voltage feeders (three-phase 500 KV). *Substation-2* is located in the downtown area, which offers power to thousands of businesses, plus two hospitals. *Substation-3* is located in the southside residential area of the city and serves 1500 homes plus 2 elementary, 1 intermediate, and 1 high school.

The vulnerability arises from the fact that if the power substation goes down, it will affect substations 2 and 3 and eventually trigger a cascaded blackout. The diagnostics and repair will take at least 3 days. This will impact the credibility of the Smart City government, loss of revenues, loss of life, and the city life turns into havoc. The blackout incident will go viral.

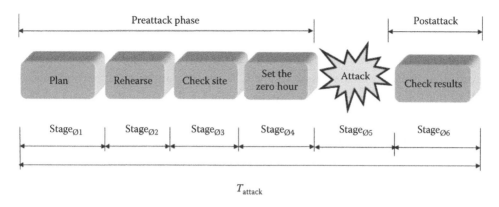

Figure 8.9 There are six stages to a cyberattack. The attack is just as good as its plan. One successful attack will breed more wicked terror with more intelligent and highly technological missiles, to attack brittle or even life-threatening systems without notice and mistakes. Most attacks follow the same pattern.

The Six Phases of the Attack

The terrorists were trained and paid by adversary government and were instructed to create a blackout in the Smart City. The selected attack time would be before a major holiday where roadways, bridges, and airports are into an almost a gridlock. The attack had six phases that were carefully planned and rehearsed to perfection, before the *green light to launch* was given for the three attacks. Figure 8.9 shows the systematic sequence of the attack plan. They spent more time planning because they are taking a big risk. The plan has to be executed with 100% success, otherwise there will not be a blackout. They do not know that the Smart Vaccine Grid is the juggernaut that will quash the attack.

The Purpose of the SCADA System

This is a short explanation of the Siemens Supervisory Control and Data Acquisition (SCADA) System, which is the de facto system for process visualization and data collection in the control engineering industry. SCADA is designed with three tiers: First, the master control system (MCS) is on the top of the hierarchy; second, the master communication server is the intermediary layer; and third, the physical process is the third layer, which has the field data collection devices and programmable logic controllers (PLC). SCADA's master control system is Windows based, which is considered *first vulnerability*. The hardware is acquired from HP, Sun Microsystems, and from Fujitsu. Siemens main integrated software is SIMATIC, which is compliant with ISO 9000, IEEE, and NIST standards. SCADA is an open system that can run JAVA, C++, PERL, and PHP applications. SIMATIC uses Microsoft SQL server (*second vulnerability*) for real-time data logging, ad hoc reporting, and business intelligence. SCADA programmable logic controller (PLC) runs on proprietary software called SIMATIC WinCC/Step 7.

As we said earlier, the purpose of the attack is twofold: First, to drill a hole in the power grid that connects all the five substations then get to substation 1 and raise the temperature of the oil circuit breakers (OCBs) beyond the specified threshold, which will cause an *explosion* that will put the OCBs out of commission. Second, damage the PLC that controls the oil circuit breakers, which will eventually trip and bring the power station to a halt.

Oil circuit breakers rely upon vaporization of some of the oil to blast a jet of oil along the path of the arc. The vapor released by the arcing consists of hydrogen gas. Arc flash temperatures can reach or exceed 35,000°F (19,400°C) at the arc terminals. The massive energy released in the fault rapidly vaporizes the metal conductors involved, blasting molten metal and expanding plasma outward with extraordinary force.

Switchgears are the control boxes that control the oil circuit breakers (located outside the yard of the substation). A switchgear is physically connected to a remote terminal unit (RTU), which is on the SCADA network. The switchgear is controlled and monitored by the substation control terminal. Operators watch the operation through the substation control terminal. The substation control terminal is connected to SCADA via radio, microwave, and secure Virtual Private Network (VPN).

The team wants to replicate Stuxnet attack (corrupted the power plant in Iran), which is designed to programmatically alter programmable logic controllers (PLCs) used in those facilities. In an industrial control system environment, the PLCs automate industrial type tasks such as regulating flow rate to maintain pressure and temperature controls.

The Terrorist Team

Any terrorism group that attempts to damage a metropolitan substation must satisfy four success factors: First, knowledge in power generation and distribution, substation engineering and operations. The second factor is hands-on in networking and communications. Third, extensive knowledge in hacking and malware programming. The fourth, extensive system administration of SCADA system.

The suggested terrorist group is made of six people covering the whole spectrum of cyberterrorism: two system engineers with experience in Siemens SCADA power and distribution system; two computer specialists with experience on hardware and software; and two specialists in hacking with experience in DDoS, SQL injection, SCADA SIMATIC WinCC Step-7 Zero-Day hacking.

The Smart City Attack

The group is solicited by a well-known Crime Service Provider from Eastern Europe to create a blackout in the Smart City. From a unknown remote server connected to the city, the terrorists would slip a backdoor Trojan into SCADA systems, so the group could roam around the systems and secretly distort the collected data from the remote terminal units (RTU) that monitor the substation transformers.

The first thing the terrorist group had to do is to develop a blueprint for the awesome attack, a back-up plan, and an exit plan.

The group got a small-scale SCADA for practice and configured it to connect with the ones in the city. The remote SCADA server of the terrorist group was invisibly connected to the city SCADA network as well as to the outside Internet.

The terrorist group have already programmed a malicious two backdoor Trojans. They ran a port scan first and selected on open port for *Backdoor Trojan-1* to slip into SCADA-1. *Backdoor Trojan-1* loads a keylogger and one rootkit to steal admin passwords. *Backdoor Trojan-2* uploads a program to override the present configuration and *softly* change the operational parameters that control the temperature in the transformers and oil-circuit breakers, controlled by SCADA-1 RTU.

The group knows from a partner group about the two security flaws that are still perking in Windows. Two Zero-Day Trojans are set to do the devilish task. A war dialer (telephone hacker) was also available to get entry access through dial-up communication.

The critical part of the mission is to remain stealth as long as possible while removing any evidence behind them. Backdoors were to carefully slip into the substation master computer to gain administrative access and change disk access permissions.

Here Is What the Smart Vaccine Did

Let's not forget that the Smart Vaccine will demonstrate how artificial intelligence and autonomic computing work together. The Smart Vaccine is the culmination of the merger of our biological thinking and computing technology, resulting into a fully cognitive system fueled by computational intelligence. The Smart Vaccine grid is like a complex arteries with a mesh of autonomic nodes that control the exchange of (request/VaaS) messages between the CEWPS Central Coordination Center and the Smart Vaccine commander. Figure 8.10 is a cross section of a wide-band artery of the Smart Vaccine Grid (SVG), which carries all the intelligent communication commands with the SCADAs and the three substations.

As already shown in Figure 8.5, the top grid is the *Early Warning Predictor and CCC*. The middle grid is the *Smart Vaccine Defense grid* (SVG) that includes the Smart Vaccine army and the knowledge engines. The bottom grid is the *City's Smart Grid* of the Smart City where all the other critical systems are connected to.

In reality, the city's smart grid is the backbone information highway network of the city. The smart vaccine grid (SVG) is the immunity grid (call it the mobile Vaccination network) of the city. All grids are connected together, like in the human body all pipelines work together. SCADA systems collect data from the critical systems. Let's not forget that all city's critical systems, including SCADA systems, have their own antivirus software. The Smart Vaccine will immunize all the systems and leave the antivirus neutral shift.

In the Human Immune System, the vaccine imitates an infection by injecting a *watered-down* version of the pathogen (attacking disease), which will trigger the

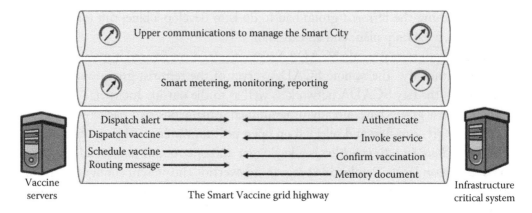

Figure 8.10 The canonical rule states: Without a Smart Grid, there is no smart city. The Smart Vaccine Grid (SVG) is the immune and nervous system of the smart city. The SVG is tightly coupled with the Smart City Grid. The ultrafast wide bandwidth carries attack alert messages from the critical systems directly to the SVG. The bottom pipeline is used by the Smart Vaccine team to save the attacked system. You can see that a Smart Grid is like an information bus where the Smart Vaccine takes the role of a dynamic cognitive broker.

mobilization of the B cells armies and their arsenal of antibodies to fight the attacking microbe. Having this little bit of the germ inside the body will create a a mock attack for the B cells. So, vaccination makes the body more immune with better defense system against germs. The B cells will remember the mock drill and be ready for the real attack.

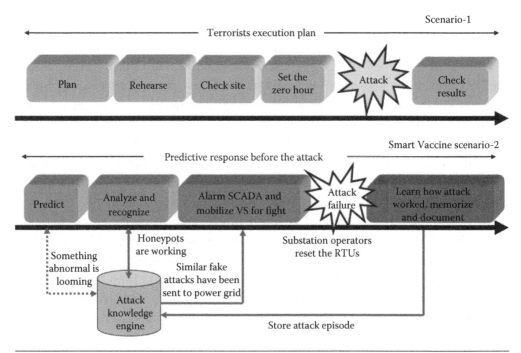

Figure 8.11 Comparison of Scenario-1 and Scenario-2: the Early Warning Predictor acted like a RADAR. This is where the versatility of CEWPS...Then the defense by offense strategy executed by the Smart Vaccine before the attack.

Figure 8.11 shows how CEWPS eradicates the attack. In *scenario-1*, the terrorist group will launch a surprise attack. The group drafted a blueprint of the attack. The group studied the plan and and each got an assignment indicating the time and the place. The group had all the tools to attack backdoor Trojan, password cracker, and the malignant code.

In Scenario-2, the CEWPS/SV system was implemented. The predictor works full time to give the Central Coordination Center reliable forecasts. The Reasoning Engine uses heuristic and Bayesian modeling techniques to generate optimal prediction models of future attacks. Since most attacks follow a similar pattern, CEWPS stays ahead of the attack. The regular vaccination keeps the systems immunized.

The Making of an Antidote with Honeypots

A honeypot farm is configured to detect intruders by mirroring a real production system. It appears as an ordinary server doing work, but all the data and transactions are phony. Located inside and outside the firewall, the honeypot is used to learn about an intruder's techniques as well as determine vulnerabilities in the real system.

CEWPS/SV for the Smart City is equipped with a distributed network of honeypots to protect SCADA and substation computers. The trapped attack will be forwarded to the CEWPS Reverse Engineering Center (REC) for autopsy and learn more about its code. CEWPS Reverse Engineering analyzes the attack vectors, viruses, Trojans, and backdoors and creates replica of the program logic and works backward to understand the impact of the program (the poison). Then the Reverse Engineering Center writes the antidote (the vaccine code) and gives it to the Vaccine Knowledge Base (VaKB) and to the vaccinators for immediate vaccination. This completes one mission of one vaccination.

The vaccine code (digital antidote) is actually a mock attack very similar to a real human one. The Smart Vaccine executes the mock attack and fights it as though it is the real one. The critical system will acquire adaptive immunity against this type of malware, and more importantly, the VaKB will save the mock attack file and remember how to fight it in the next real attack.

Additional Reading for Electrical Engineers

Learning more about the operation of the oil circuit breaker (OCB), this high-voltage gradient between the contacts ionized the oil and consequently initiates arcing between the contacts. This arc will produce a large amount of heat in surrounding oil and vaporizes the oil and decomposes the oil in mostly hydrogen and a small amount of methane, ethylene, and acetylene. The hydrogen gas cannot remain in molecular form, and it is broken into its atomic form releasing lot of heat. The arc temperature may reach up to 5000 K. Due to this high temperature, the gas is liberated, surrounds the arc very rapidly, and forms an excessively fast-growing gas bubble around the arc. It is found that the mixture of gases occupies a volume of about one thousand times that of the oil decomposed. From this figure, we can assume how fast the gas bubble around the arc will grow in size. If this growing gas bubble around the arc is compressed by any means, then the rate of deionization process of ionized gaseous media in between the contacts will accelerate, which rapidly increase the dielectric strength between the contacts, and consequently, the arc will be quenched at zero crossing of the current cycle. This is the basic operation of an oil circuit breaker. In addition to the cooling effect of hydrogen gas, surrounding the arc path also helps the quick arc quenching in oil circuit breaker.

Websites

http://resources.infosecinstitute.com/cyber-espionage-the-greatest-transfer-of-wealth-in-history/.
http://www.cleanenergyresourceteams.org/glossary.
http://www.siemens.com/.
http://www.theguardian.com/commentisfree/2015/feb/04/government-cyberterrorism-concerns-pretext-their-own-hacking.
http://www.usip.org/sites/default/files/sr119.pdf.
www.thesmartvaccine.com.
http:/ /www.iso.org/iso/smart_cities_report-jtc1.pdf; Smart Cities Preliminary Report 2014.

References

Joseph Weiss; Protecting Industrial Control Systems From Electronic Threats; Momentum Press 2010; ISBN-10 1-60650-197-6.
Frank J. Cilluffo & Richard Knop, The Journal of International Security Affairs -winter 2012; Getting Serious About Cyberwarfare.
Edward G. Amoroso; Cyber Attacks -Protecting National Infrastructure; Butterworth-Heinemann 2013; ISBN:978-0-12-391855.

9

The Smart Cloud Is Here: Vaccination as a Service

Introduction of Digital Immunity

In this chapter, we are elevating Digital Immunity to the cloud. The CEWPS/ Smart Vaccine will bring a new dimension in cloud computing: A unique service that will bring a new paradigm in cybersecurity that we call *Vaccination as a Service* (VaaS).

Gartner's 2014 Hype Cycle Special Report provides strategists and planners with an assessment of the maturity, business benefit, and future direction of more than 2000 technologies, grouped into 119 areas. We took a few excerpts from this magnificent report for knowledge enlightenment.

Here is what the report said about the Hype Cycle and Emerging Technologies:

Since the Hype Cycle for Emerging Technologies is purposely focused on more emerging technologies, it mostly supports the last three of these stages: digital marketing, digital business, and autonomous.

The following technologies on the Hype Cycle represent the Digital Marketing stage: *Software-Defined Anything; Volumetric and Holographic Displays; Neurobusiness; Data Science; Prescriptive Analytics; Complex Event Processing; Big Data; In-Memory DBMS; Content Analytics; Hybrid Cloud Computing; Gamification; Augmented Reality; Cloud Computing; NFC; Virtual Reality; Gesture Control; In-Memory Analytics;*

It is ironic that research companies like Forrester and Gartner in their yearly predictions could not foresee the concept of *Digital Immunity* (DI) as the viable paradigm shift in cyber secularity for the next decade. We challenge Gartner that Digital Immunity will prevail and it will chart a different course from the hype cycle of 2015. We believe that Smart Cities and Cloud Computing Providers will eventually adopt it. Figure 9.1 shows the trajectory of the Smart Vaccine as it matures and acquires experience for the next five years.

The focus in this chapter is twofold. First, it is necessary to explain the anatomy of Vaccination as a Service (VaaS) as one of the services of the cloud. A clear understanding of the anatomy of the cloud would set the right tempo for the second item. Second, it is necessary to show how the Smart Vaccine immunizes the critical infrastructures of the Smart City with VaaS.

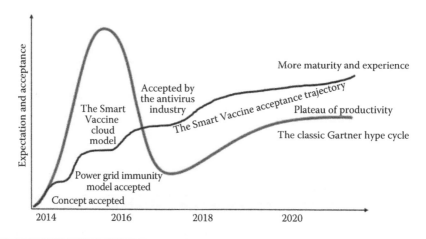

Figure 9.1 The Smart Vaccine is taking a more realistic course than Gartner's hype cycle. It will bypass the inflated expectation hump. Its rapid acceptance will be overwhelming, even though it is considered a disruptive technology.

Cloud 101 Primer

In 2006, Amazon's chief Jeff Bezos took the stage at MIT's Emerging Technologies conference to talk about two cloud computing products the company had announced and the ambitions the company had for them. Three years earlier, one of these products—EC2—was only an idea. EC2 stands for *Elastic Compute Cloud* and was developed first and foremost for Amazon's internal infrastructure. It started out as an idea in the head of Chris Pinkham, who worked as an engineer in charge of Amazon's global infrastructure in the early 2000s. Since its official launch in 2006, EC2's value has grown and it has become the cornerstone of Amazon's ecosystem of cloud services.

On March 1, 2011, IBM announced the IBM smart_cloud framework to support Smarter Planet. Among the various components of the Smarter Computing foundation, cloud computing is a critical piece. On June 7, 2012, Oracle announced the Oracle Cloud. While aspects of the Oracle Cloud are still in development, this cloud offering is posed to be the first to provide users with access to an integrated set of IT solutions, including the applications (SaaS), platform (PaaS), and infrastructure (IaaS) layers.

The name *cloud* is very interesting. We have the terms like *the Web*, crawler, metacrawler, cyber everything, and smart everything from smart chip to smart city, and now we have the cloud! No wonder, everybody is jumping on the cloud bandwagon. It is like a flock of geese following the leader. Amazon's chief, Jeff Bezos, has already started setting up the rules for cloud computing.

The cloud is just a metaphor for the Internet. We are used to represent the Internet as a puffy, white cumulonimbus cloud, accepting connections and doling out information as it floats. The big story is not about cloud technology but how it transforms organizations. CEWPS is about protecting systems from malware attack. We believe cloud computing is a value-added that should be included in the technology of the Smart Vaccine.

The cloud is simply a collection of distributed data centers that are tied as a secure meganetwork that holds thousands of interconnected servers for applications and data repositories. The cloud is often referenced by its glamorous name *Cloud Ecosystem*. It is much more than the sum of these components. It is a formidable elastic multifaceted infrastructure. It is the trend in future. The cloud promotes the theme "it's better to rent than to purchase." A basic analogy is opening a checking/saving account at your friendly bank. We would feel better because the bank will save our money better than a safe at home. But we have to abide by the rules and regulations of the bank. The same applies to cloud computing subscription. We have to accept the rules of the Cloud Service Providers (CSP) and accept our dependence on their services. Utility companies are another similar model to the cloud. We connect to the utility network and do not worry about the way power is generated and distributed to our house. As long as we pay for the service, we would accept the heavy dependence on the service and take it for granted.

Almost all companies are moving, slowly but surely, to the cloud and cutting down their IT expenses. Technology companies realized the importance of the cloud and decided to revise their business plans and invest in the cloud. Google invested $850 million in its data center infrastructure in the first quarter of 2011. Microsoft invested $500 million in Dublin-based data center. Apple invested $1 billion in North Carolina data center. All of the major technology-providing companies are all of a sudden committed to cloud computing. This is another new world that we have to pay attention to.

Three Technologies into One: Cloud Computing, Web Services, and Service-Oriented Architecture

There is a strong coexisting relationship between Web services, SOA, and cloud computing. Web services encapsulate cloud computing because cloud computing uses Web services for connectivity and messaging. It is also possible to use Web services as part of SOA for connection. Service Oriented Architecture (SOA) ushers a new chapter in building platform-agnostic systems. SOA is the true software engineering bible that should be used in every critical project. We will be covering the three technologies and illustrate how they work together relative to CEWPS and Smart Vaccine as shown in Figure 9.2.

First Technology: Cloud Computing

Amazon is the leader in cloud computing with its formidable platforms called Amazon Web Services (AWS), which make up the Amazon cloud since 2006. The most central and well known of these services are Amazon Elastic Compute Cloud (EC2) and Amazon Simple Storage Service (S3). Let us not confuse AWS with the Web services.

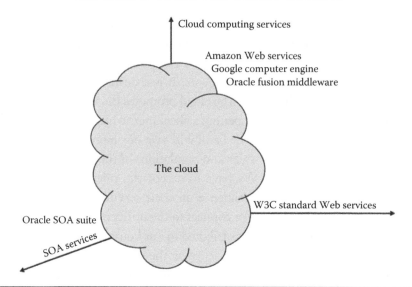

Figure 9.2 Cloud computing still does not appear in the *Oxford English Dictionary*, but like the Trinitarian formula, everyone believes in it. It does not matter who started the word, it is on the tip of every tongue. But for one thing, cyberterrorists use the cloud as their crime incubator: the three technologies symbiotically work together but compete against each other!

The National Institute of Standards and Technology (NIST) has a comprehensive definition of cloud computing. We would like to share it with you.

"Cloud computing is a model for enabling ubiquitous, convenient, on-demand network access to a shared pool of configurable computing resources (e.g., networks, servers, storage, applications, and services) that can be rapidly provisioned and released with minimal management effort or service provider interaction."

This cloud model is composed of five essential characteristics, three service models, and four deployment models.

Essential Characteristics

On-Demand Self-Service: A consumer can unilaterally provide computing capabilities, such as server time and network storage, as needed automatically without requiring human interaction with each service provider.

Broad Network Access: Capabilities are available over the network and accessed through standard mechanisms that promote use by heterogeneous thin or thick client platforms (e.g., mobile phones, tablets, laptops, and workstations).

Resource Pooling: The provider's computing resources are pooled to serve multiple consumers using a multitenant model, with different physical and virtual resources dynamically assigned and reassigned according to consumer demand. There is a sense of location independence in that the customer generally has no control or knowledge over the exact location of the provided resources but may be able to specify location at a higher level of abstraction (e.g., country, state, or data center). Examples of resources include storage, processing, memory, and network bandwidth.

Rapid Elasticity: Capabilities can be elastically provisioned and released, in some cases automatically, to scale rapidly upward and downward commensurate with demand. To the consumer, the capabilities available for provisioning often appear to be unlimited and can be appropriated in any quantity at any time.

Measured Service: Cloud systems automatically control and optimize resource use by leveraging a metering capability 1 at some level of abstraction appropriate to the type of service (e.g., storage, processing, bandwidth, and active user accounts). Resource usage can be monitored, controlled, and reported, providing transparency for both the provider and consumer of the utilized service.

The dynamics to get into cloud computing is mind-bending. Take for example Amazon, which has now more than a million people using its cloud services. Amazon has 11 cloud regions across the world, with each region having multiple sets of data centers, and there are 28 total sets across the world. Each set has one or more data centers, with a typical facility containing 50,000–80,000 servers. A conservative estimate puts Amazon over 1.5 million servers globally. Gartner puts it at 2 million or more.

The Three Cloud Service Delivery Models, and the Fourth One Is Coming Soon

The three predominant cloud service delivery models are Infrastructure as a Service (IaaS), Platform as a Service (PaaS), and Software as a Service (SaaS). Here is a short description of each model:

Software as a Service (SaaS): Required software, the operating system, and network are provided. Defined as service-on-demand, where a provider will license software tailored. In the SaaS model, cloud providers install and operate application software in the cloud, and cloud users access the software from cloud clients. Cloud users do not manage the cloud infrastructure and platform where the application runs. This eliminates the need to install and run the application on the cloud user's own computers, which simplifies maintenance and support.

Examples of SaaS include Google Apps, Microsoft Office 365, Onlive, GT Nexus, Marketo, and TradeCard.

Platform as a Service (PaaS): The operating system and network are provided. In the PaaS model, cloud providers deliver a computing platform typically including operating system, programming language execution environment, database, and Web server. Application developers can develop and run their software solutions on a cloud platform without the cost and complexity of buying and managing the underlying hardware and software layers.

Examples of PaaS include AWS Elastic Beanstalk, Cloud Foundry, Heroku, Force. com, EngineYard, Mendix, OpenShift, Google App Engine, Windows Azure Cloud Services, and OrangeScape.

Infrastructure as a Service (IaaS): Just the network is provided. In the most basic cloud service model, providers of IaaS offer computers physical or (more often) virtual machines and other resources. IaaS clouds often offer additional resources such as a virtual-machine disk image library, raw (block) and file-based storage, firewalls, load balancers, IP addresses, virtual local area networks (VLANs), and software bundles. IaaS cloud providers supply these resources on demand from their large pools installed in data centers.

Examples of IaaS providers include Amazon EC2, Azure Services Platform, Google Compute Engine, HP Cloud, Oracle Infrastructure as a Service, Rackspace Cloud, and ReadySpace Cloud Services.

Big Data as a Service: Google started this by offering connectivity between its cloud and Big Data to the customer. Google has realized that the Internet is polluted with garbage data that can be captured and reincarnated into a valuable source of Predictive Analytics. No one really knows the tonnage of Big Data, and no one tried diligently to measure exactly because it seems irrelevant.

VaaS (Vaccination as a Service): This is the new service on the block, offered by the cloud to companies that have critical operations managed by specialized SCADA systems. CEWPS would reside in the application layer of the cloud and would offer its vaccination services through the Smart Vaccine. VaaS will be running on the Smart Vaccine grid (SVG), or on the Smart Vaccine Cloud (SVC), which connects all city's critical systems on the City's Smart Grid (CSG) or City's Smart Cloud (CSC). Computer systems would like to minimize the risk of being attacked by malicious cyberterrorist acts. We will cover VaaS, in more detail, later in this chapter.

The Five Types of Cloud Models

The morphology of the Cloud can be broken down into five distinct types.

- *Private cloud*: This deployment mode is appropriate for the CEWPS. The cloud infrastructure is provisioned for exclusive use by a single organization comprising multiple consumers (e.g., business units). It may be owned, managed, and operated by the organization, a third party, or some combination of them, and it may exist on or off premises.
- *Community cloud*: This deployment mode is provisioned for exclusive use by a specific community of consumers from organizations that have shared concerns (e.g., mission, security requirements, policy, and compliance considerations). It may be owned, managed, and operated by one or more of the organizations in the community, a third party, or some combination of them, and it may exist on or off premises.
- *Public cloud*: This deployment mode is appropriate for the Smart City. The cloud infrastructure is provisioned for open use by the general public. It may be owned, managed, and operated by a business, academic, or government organization, or some combination of them. It exists on the premises of the cloud provider.
- *Hybrid cloud*: This deployment mode is a composition of two or more distinct cloud infrastructures (private, community, or public) that remain unique

entities but are bound together by standardized or proprietary technology that enables data and application portability (e.g., cloud bursting for load balancing between clouds).

Cloud Storage: This deployment mode is offered by Cloud Service Providers (CSP). Cloud storage means "the storage of data online in the cloud," wherein a company's data are stored in and accessible from multiple distributed and connected resources that comprise a cloud. Cloud storage can provide the benefits of greater accessibility and reliability, rapid deployment, for data backup, archival and disaster recovery purposes, and lower overall storage costs as a result of not having to purchase, manage, and maintain expensive hardware. However, cloud storage does have the potential for security and compliance concerns.

How Does the Digital Vaccination Work as a Service?

Any business that has critical computer systems in a smart city could get the ultimate digitial immunity by subscribing to the Smart Vaccine (VaaS) services. The prospective cloud user should connect first to the City Smart Grid (CSG), then to City Smart Cloud (CSC), and finally connect to the Smart Vaccine Grid (SVG) in this order.

The customer vaccination subscription sequence is shown with circles in Figure 9.3.

1. The customer subscribes directly to the cloud vaccination services; he also may do so through the Smart City smart cloud, if the customer is already on the city grid.

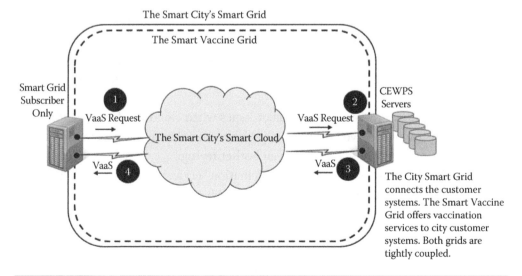

Figure 9.3 For simple illustration purposes only, we separated all the components of the City Cloud. If the cloud customer would like to subscribe to the vaccination services, he may do so through the smart city's smart cloud, which is the big umbrella that contains CEWPS and the Smart Vaccine Grid. If the customer is already on the city grid, he could go directly to CEWPS, through the city's cloud, and get perpetual vaccination membership and eliminate city taxes and service fees.

2. The customer sends a request directly to the CEWPS for regular vaccination, which will immunize his computers from all the attack.
3. The vaccination service will be regularly scheduled for the customer. The customer may keep his antivirus software.
4. The customer will be connected to CEWPS and receives the vaccination service on time, or whenever there is an accidental attack.

Cloud Standards and Practices for the Smart Cloud

There are four standards and best practice areas that we need to examine when we're shopping for a cloud:

Interoperability: It refers to cloud users being able to take their tools, applications, virtual images, and so on and use them in another cloud environment without having to do any rework. Say one application runs in one environment and you need that application to operate with a partner's application in another cloud environment. If the right interoperability standards are in place, you can do this without needing multiple versions of this application.

Simple Object Access Protocol (SOAP), Representational State Transfer (REST), and Atom Syndication Format and Atom Publishing Protocol (both standards referred to as Atom) are all examples of widely used as interoperability standards and protocols.

Portability: It refers to taking one application or instance running on one vendor's implementation and deploy it on another vendor's implementation. For example, you might want to move your database or application from one cloud environment to another.

Integration: It refers to combining various hardware and software components together to create something. The same idea applies in the cloud. One example of integration is: easily integrating your data with a Software as a Service application. This is an example of taking some of your internal IT capability and integrating it into the cloud environment.

Portability and integration become major issues when cloud vendors have different platforms. This can lead to vendor lock-in, which means that moving to another cloud provider is so difficult that you do not even bother trying.

Security: It refers to subscribing to the vaccination services. CEWPS/SV is guaranteed to protect the information assets of the subscriber.

Connectivity Requirements for Cloud-Based Digital Immunity

Vaccination as a Service is the most innovative service on the cloud. It will revolutionize Antivirus Technology with a quantum leap. Traditionally, all that the Antivirus Technology vendors care about is to carve out a larger market share. Over the last

20 years, they have done very well, but the approach to fighting malware has pla-teaued, while other sectors of technology have been galloping with leaps and bounds. The world is still plagued with the second generation of malware and the Smart Vaccine is going to prevail as the new savior.

To vaccinate any critical system, the following connectivity requirements should be performed:

Hardware and software configurations: The customer should have a complete and detailed list of hardware systems and software applications. Also he should know the workload on each system and user acceptance criteria.

Subscriber's Antivirus Role: The subscriber should recognize that the Smart Vaccine is the primary defense system. The Antivirus software becomes sec-ondary, but it will collaborate with the Smart Vaccine Commander.

Connection with the Internet: A high-speed Internet ramp is a must, otherwise no VaaS vaccination will take place.

Registration with CEWPS: The Central Coordination Center (CCC) manages the registrations of all the cloud-based subscribers and critical infrastructure systems. CCC needs to know the presence of all the registrants in order to scale its system. CEWPS is elastic and highly scalable, but a workload man-agement is a part of its fast response service.

Connection to the smart cloud: Companies that would like to be part of the smart cloud need to acquire a cloud Application Programming Interface (API). API is the necessary software interface that lets company's applications plug in to the smart cloud. This is perhaps the most important place for standardization.

Connection with the smart grid: If the cloud subscriber would like his systems to acquire maximum digital immunity, then he should subscribe to the Smart City.

Connection with the grid vaccine grid: if the cloud subscriber would like to get maximum DI, then he should subscribe with the Smart Vaccine Grid, as shown in the diagram presented earlier.

The Smart Vaccine Cloud-Based Reference Architecture

The term *reference architecture* is a highly visible term and it implies systematic design and implementation. No engineer would touch a project without examin-ing a blueprint and feeling comfortable about it. We call it the engineering culture of *measuring twice and cutting it once*. Looking at the following 3D diagram, it gives the reader the level of sophistication of CEWPS/Smart Vaccine ecosystem. Making this reference architecture a reality requires a well-established approach. Service-oriented architecture (SOA) is the roadmap that we will use to build the cloud-centric Smart Vaccine ecosystem (Figure 9.4).

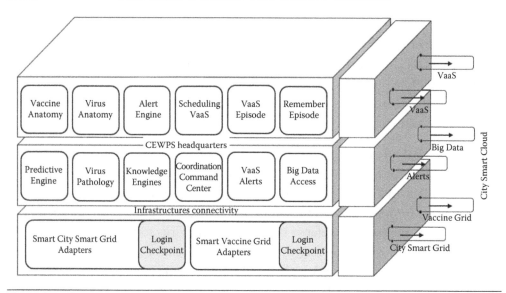

Figure 9.4   The three-story Reference Architecture of CEWPS/Smart Vaccine shows all the operating components and how subscribers connect to the city cloud for vaccination services. It shows the components of each tier. The two advantages of the Reference Architecture (RA) are the use of common vocabulary, which is very useful in the design of the system and the adherence to unified interoperability standards.

Second Technology: Service-Oriented Architecture (SOA)

Before we introduce the SOA approach, I wanted to bring up a philosophical note as a reminder to the folks who do not believe in orderly chaos. In the early days of computing, flowcharting was the only compass systems analysts had to get visibility on the scope of the system to be built. It was a diagrammatic representation and a workflow of the logic that will be coded by programmers. Keep in mind, system analysts were a notch higher than programmers and were responsible for flowcharting. The Data Processing Department was responsible for the delivery of the system, whether the *user* liked it or not. The user's involvement was to explain the business process and the system analyst will convert the process into logic flowchart. The result of the arrogance of Data Processing Department, and the "*no entry*" for the user, the majority of the systems of the 1960s and 1970s were overbudget, brittle, and had no capability for refactoring or scaling for this matter. I remember the Dutch SDM/70 methodology was shoved down everyone's throat. It was a horrible La Brea tar pit. EDP programmers either quit their job, or had a severe meltdown. It was cumbersome with its plethora of forms to fill out. It was a productivity muzzler. The success rate of projects in those years did not exceed 40%, until the Internet became public in 1992 and users took the lead in their projects. Then SOA was born as a true software engineering discipline. With the gracious leadership of Erik Townsend Wells Fargo who implemented SOA in his Internet banking project, success arrived. It was a great success story. The year 1996 was a good year. Today, there are hundreds of books and textbooks written on SOA and its contribution to the success of any IT project. Thank you Thomas Erl.

I can say, having worked with SOA, it is the best disciplinary set of tools for truly professional system designers much more than a technological approach and methodology for creating IT systems. It is also a business approach and methodology. Companies have used the principles of SOA to deepen their understanding of how IT could galvanize business to be more future ready and profitable. One of the key benefits of a service-oriented approach is that software is designed to reflect best practices and business processes instead of making the business operate according to the rigid structure of a technical environment. I rest my case.

Third Technology: Web Services

The number of disparate definitions for the term *Web services* is overwhelming. I decided to give my own simplistic definition. If you go to a petroleum refinery, all what you see is tanks, pumps, valves, and pipelines and lots of noise. On the average, a large-scale refinery has over 50,000 miles of pipes of different nature, such as steel pipes, cast iron pipes, plastic pipes, hot, cold, pressurized, and all of them are connected together. One barrel of crude, which is 42 gal/barrel, is fractionated into 1000 different products from gasoline to pharmaceutical products. Through adapters and interface joints, all the refining processes are tied together.

Web services have the catalytic ability to connect disparate systems and applications together in the Web. So, Web services are a set of tools (adapters) for sending and receiving data over the Internet and allowing programmatic access to that data using standard Internet protocols.

The World Wide Web Consortium (W3C) defines the architecture and associated standards of Web services http://www.w3.org/TR/ws-arch/ as follows:

> Web services provide a standard means of interoperating between different software applications, running on a variety of platforms and/or frameworks. The Web Services Architecture (WSA) is intended to provide a common definition of a Web service, and define its place within a larger Web services framework to guide the community. The WSA provides a conceptual model and a context for understanding Web services and the relationships between the components of this model. The architecture does not attempt to specify how Web services are implemented, and imposes no restriction on how Web services might be combined. The Web services architecture is an interoperability architecture: it identifies those global elements of the global Web services network that are required in order to ensure interoperability between Web services.

Let's try to give a simple description of the four standardized tools of Web services:

1. *HTTP—Hypertext Transfer Protocol*: The standard rules of the road where all the transactions will follow.
2. *SOAP—Simple Object Access Protocol*: The standard rules of how messages will be packaged inside an envelope. It uses XML-based format for its messages.

3. *XML—Extensible Markup Language*: is the standard language used between the service provider and the service requester. The Smart Vaccine will use XML-based format to communicate with CCC the city smart grid (CSG).

4. *WSDL—Web Services Description Language*: is the standard of how to format a document in XML and to describe the functionality offered by the service.

In Digital Immunity context, here is a description of how CEWPS messages transact at the semantic level before and during vaccination session:

A critical system on the city grid is attacked by a Trojan. The system administrator instantiates a help request. Here's how CEWPS responds:

- The help request travels using XML-based SOAP protocol.
- The Smart Vaccine Commander and (CCC) acknowledge the help request.
- The Smart Vaccine sends a request the vaccination army.
- The Smart Vaccine Commander (SVC) asks the Virus Knowledge Base (ViKB) if its has a sample of the virus that compromised the system.
- The Virus Knowledge Base replies that there is a match with the attacking virus.
- The reply comes that there is a match with the attacking virus.
- The Smart Vaccine Commander receives the matching virus.
- The Commander sends a request to the Reverse engineering facility to analyze the virus.
- The Smart Vaccine sends the captured vaccine to the Reverse Engineering facility for analysis.
- The Smart Vaccine Commander sends the virus data to the Vaccine Knowledge Base to check if there is a vaccine (antidote) for the virus.
- The Vaccine Knowledge Base (VaKB) confirms that there is a vaccine for that virus, and a copy of the vaccine is sent back to the Smart Vaccine Commander.
- The Smart Vaccine Commander issues a request to the vaccinator to march and help the compromised system.
- The Vaccinator acknowledges the request and marches to the compromised system.
- The Vaccinator performs the vaccination service and sends a confirmation to the Smart Vaccine Commander.
- The Smart Vaccine Commander issues the attack report to the City Smart Grid Commander and the central Coordination Center.
- Throughout the book, we describe the attack in several different ways to help the reader get a comprehensive understanding the Digital Immunity paradigm.

All CEWPS Vaccination services documented in WSDL format will be stored in the Attack Knowledge Base (AKB). All service transactions will have the following elements:

1. *Types*: Define the data types used by the Web service.
2. *Messages*: Describe the messages that are exchanged between a client and a service. Also describes the data elements of an operation such as function parameters.
3. *Port Type*: Defines a Web service, the operations that can be performed, and refers to input and output messages. Four basic operations supported by WSDL: one way, request response, solicit response, and notification.
4. *Bindings*: Define how an operation will actually be transmitted; the message format and protocol details for each operation in the Port Type section. WSDL includes built-in extensions for SOAP.
5. *Services*: Specifies port address of each binding and the location of the service.
6. *UDDI_Universal Description, Discovery, and Integration*: in Digital Immunity context, this UDDI represents all the knowledge bases of CEWPS:

   The Virus Knowledge Base (ViKB) is the universal registry for all the captures virus and all the information relevant to the attack.

   The Vaccine Knowledge Base (VaKB) is the universal registry for the manufactured vaccine.

   The Attack Knowledge Base (AKB) is the universal registry that holds all the historical combat episodes. We also call it the Documentation Knowledge Base.

   The Inference Knowledge Base (IKB) is the universal registry of all the reasoning rules used in the inference engine.

The Knowledge bases will be discussed in Chapter 12 with more detail.

The availability of a Web service for public consumption can be advertised. The Web service interfaces described by WSDL may be put into a directory called Universal Description, Discovery, and Integration (UDDI). The UDDI is a central directory service where businesses can publish, register, and search for Web services. The data stored in the UDDI directory are in XML format. The data captured within UDDI are divided into three main categories: white pages, yellow pages, and green pages. The white pages contain general information like name, description, and address about a company offering the service. The yellow pages contain general classification data on industrial categories based on standard taxonomies for either the company or the service offered. The green pages contain detailed technical information about a Web service allowing someone to write an application to use the Web service. These categories make it easy for users to search for industry-specific Web services and create client applications to access them.

Cloud Vaccination Services

Let us take a look at another view of CEWPS architecture in Figure 9.5. CEWPS has three functional layers that are responsible for specific duties. The top layer belongs

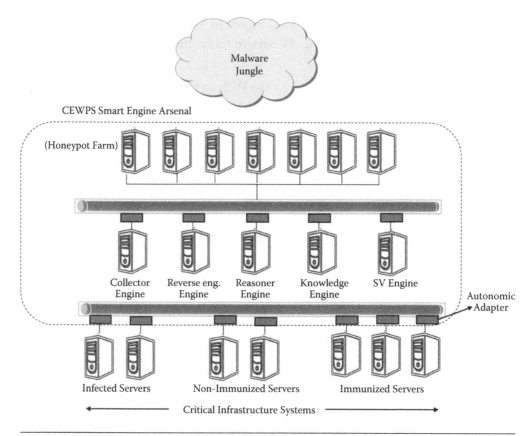

Figure 9.5 A cross section of CEWPS architecture, showing how the message-oriented middleware (bus) is responsible for the delivery of messages to the proper service facility for processing vaccination services on the city grid. SOA and Web services can work together to meet the dynamic response of the Smart Vaccine, before, during, and after the battle.

to the front end of the system, which includes the Early Warning Predictor and the Honeypot farm, and the Central Coordination Center. The second layer contains the heavy duty engines of CEWPS: The Collector engine, the Reverse Engineering, the reasoner, the knowledge libraries, and the Smart Vaccine Command. The third layer contains the critical systems attached to the city smart grid (CSG) and the smart vaccine grid (SVG). All the three grids are tied together and collaborate harmoniously like the human immune system and the nervous system.

The diagram highlights the importance of the information bus in brokering the requests and services of the Vaccination-as-a Service (VaaS) process. Figure 9.6 shows the process cycle of the vaccination service from the start of the attack all the way to the elimination of the attacking villain. Here are the descriptions of each activity of the vaccination service cycle:

Vaccination: The VaaS is the main entity that is served by the Smart Vaccine.
Service provider: The Smart Vaccine is the entity that implements the vaccination specification.
Service requestor: The Subscriber system is the entity that calls for the service provider.

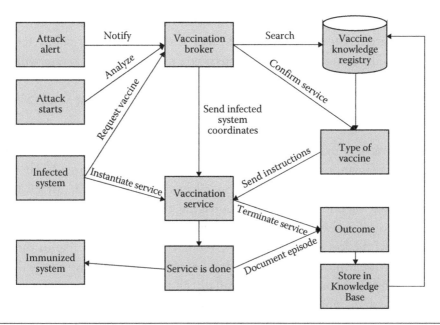

Figure 9.6   Components of the vaccination service model. We see the SOA decomposition of the vaccination service showing the interchange of service units and requested data. Some components provide status, others provide service.

Service locator: The registry that provides important information about where the VaaS will be offered (where is the clinic and what kind of service will be given).

Service broker: The agent that connects the vaccination request to the service provider (i.e., the Smart Vaccine). There may be some queuing issues that will be resolved during the triage. Infected systems get the highest priority. Although, the Smart Vaccine will vaccinate the healthy system to keep them immune.

Alert dispatcher: The central facility that will broadcast the attack alert before the attack.

Alert messenger: The agent that will carry the alert to the subscribing system and notify the Smart Vaccine.

Attack document: The agent that will perform the documentation process right after the attack.

Let's go a little further and show the attributes of each component of the vaccination service model: Each transaction (request or delivery of service) has its pertinent attributes that can be assembled upon request. There are a lot of more information that pass from one service to the other, but SOA uses the Web services for its model.

Process Workflow of the Vaccination Service (VaaS)

The vaccination process is like driving through Europe, you need visa to every country and a reliable and updated Garmin (GPS) navigational tool that will provide you with accurate arrival location. Now that you got the idea, the vaccination process is a pretty complicated mechanism, especially when its service delivery is on the cloud. There are private territories that require entry authorization and public territories that need special permission as well. Preparing a message flow diagram will clarify the process.

We have already characterized the systems on the Smart Vaccine Grid (SVG) and the City Smart Grid (CSG) into three types:

Infected system: is a system that was attacked by an illegitimate entry, either through a Trojan, masqueraded e-mail, or be part of an Internet Relay Chat (IRC), or unwelcome user from a social media network. The attack maliciously and intentionally aims at damaging the system with the help of a small piece of software that we call virus. Infected systems need repair and recovery of the lost data (if possible). We have to remember, like in the real world, a patient has to raise a flag that he needs help, otherwise he will not get any treatment or medication. Similarly, in the CEWPS environment, the infected system, which is on the a grid, sends a "need help" message (*state-1*). The Smart Vaccine Commander instantiates a vaccination service response (*state-2*). Post Vaccination is (*state-3*).

Healthy system: is a system that is on regular vaccination schedule. Also, it gets inoculated whenever there is an attack on the grid. As long as the system is on the Smart Vaccine, it will remain healthy. It is not impossible for a healthy system to be hit by a sophisticated attack. But if the Smart Vaccine has multiple systems, and as soon as one of these systems gets infected, the autonomic grid will alarm the other systems. The alarm will trigger an army of Smart Vaccines (one for each system on the grid). The grid is like the Human Immune System, it will mobilize an army of B cells that fought similar battle and memorized the strategy of the attack! Amazing, is not it?

New system: is a system that joined the Smart Vaccine grid and has no immunization history. It needs to register and be on the schedule of the regular vaccination like the other healthy systems.

Three Scenarios of an SOA-Based Vaccination

The dictionary defines the term *scenario* as a projected sequence of events. We prefer to use this term, because it will be distinguished from the other confusing terms, plus it is easier to remember. In CEWPS context, a vaccination scenario is the artificial induction of immunity by boosting the present immunity of a critical system with a vaccine, which is an artificially intelligent AI software agent that administers the recovery of the critical system from the attacking virus. Artificial induction of immunity is preventive "adaptive" vaccination to specific attacks, which increases the immunity of healthy systems against sneaky attacks before the invasive attack.

The Smart Vaccine in Motion

Figure 9.7 shows an interesting attack-and-response relationship. We assume here the worst-case scenario when the attack reaches the city grid and compromises an infrastructure critical system. The honeypots already identified the attacking virus and its payload is decomposed, and a new vaccine is built. CEWPS Reasoning Engine started to analyze the predictions for similar attacks. The city's smart grid calls for help. The CEWPS Central Coordination Center notifies the City Grid Commander and the Smart Vaccine Commander. The Smart Vaccine Commander mobilizes a SWAT team made of vaccinators and paramedics. The priority of the Smart Vaccine Commander is to keep the healthy systems immunized first, before helping the infected systems.

Scenario-1 Vaccination of infected system: The system is severely damaged. The system was new on the grid and missed its vaccination schedule. The paramedics have to shut down the system and go into disaster recovery mode. The system is totally cleansed and production resumes. The compromised system was the Guinea pig of the grid, but the grid and the agility the Smart Vaccine team helped eliminate a major DDOS attack. Once the immunity war is over, systems will resume normal production. The grid is a survival necessity for the Smart City. The Smart Vaccine is a live organism empowered with human intelligence and experience of expert hackers and forensics expert.

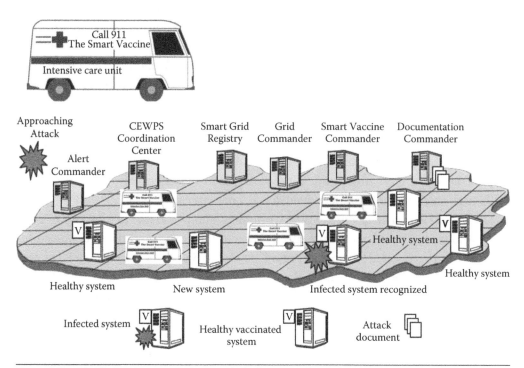

Figure 9.7 All critical systems are physically and logically connected to the Smart Vaccine Grid. When the attack anatomy is recognized and located on the grid, a convoy of SV paramedics rushes to the battlefield and the vaccination process is instantiated. The attacking virus is captured and its attack vector is analyzed, it will then be destroyed before it mutates and multiplies. The SV has two additional services: one to capture the virus and quarantine it. The second is to digest it and keep the remaining virus for the next battle. Once the battle is documented, it will go to the Virus Knowledge Engine.

Let's dig deeper into the vaccination process for the crippled system. Initially, the system administrator notices the abnormal behavior of the system, the screens flicker, and freeze, and strange screen pops up which doesn't belong to the production. The administrator checks the status of the antivirus, which indicates the system is normal. He checks the firewall, and the response comes normal. All of a sudden, the administrator gets an emergency screen instructing him not to shut down or reboot the system. The Trojan, which is now inside the system (in memory), sends the fake pop-up screen to distract the administrator and to give the backdoor virus enough time to sneak into the system. The Trojan activates TCP port 31338 to allow a loaded Back Orifice to scoot into the system. The Back Orifice does not show up in the task list. The asymmetric Back Orifice rootkit is ready to do its evil things: sniff passwords, record keystrokes, access a desktop's file system, while remaining undetected.

The Backdoor bomb arrives in binary executable code (machine-readable only), which is very hard to read. It is sophisticated enough to make changes to the production source code and relocate some DLLs from the operating system while concealing itself. To add more insult to injury, the backdoor subverts the recompilation of the production source code by inserting a copy of itself in the production system. The Operator decides to recompile the compiler to eliminate the backdoor in the production system. But a spare copy of the Backdoor source keeps getting inserted in the compiler. Every time the compiler recompiles, the backdoor gets resurrected.

As it was mentioned earlier, most versatile backdoors are asymmetric. An asymmetric backdoor will only be controlled remotely by the attacker who launches it, which makes it extremely hard to detect its presence or its point of origin. Generally, most backdoors are invisible and designed up to the imagination of the cybercriminal. Persistent attacks could come from compiler backdoor, login backdoor, or boot backdoor.

Scenario-2 Vaccination of healthy system: A normal day for system administrators is when their system dashboards show normal operation. Anytime, the honeypots capture a new attack, the Smart Vaccine Commander (SVC) issues new vaccination alert to all the critical systems on the city's smart grid. City's smart cloud subscribers also get notices from (SVC) that a new vaccine was developed due to a new attack.

Scenario-3 Vaccination of a new system: Customers who would like to subscribe to city's smart grid get registered and all the specification of the system and the level of security and the risk are registered in the smart grid Knowledge Base. Once the system is connect to the city's smart grid or city's smart cloud, they will get routine vaccination and the system administrator will be trained on the emergency services in case of a surprise attack.

Criticality of the Smart Vaccine Response Time

Now, let's analyze the attack graphically in Figure 9.8 for better understanding. Let's assume that the system got attacked and damaged while on the city's smart grid (CSG). Timing is very critical, because like in humans, medication or vaccination may come late and may not be able to save the system. Let us define the timeline variables:

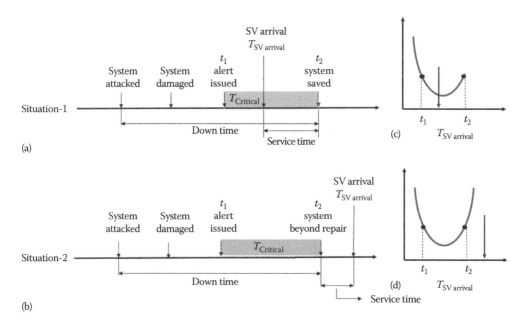

Figure 9.8 The criticality of the response time of the Smart Vaccine. (a) Situation 1, the response of the Smart Vaccine was within the interval (the shaded area), which saves the infected system. (b) Situation 2, the arrival of the Smart Vaccine was outside the critical area (the shaded area), which made the vaccination useless. Graph (c) on the top right shows how criticality of the system (the y axis) is lowest during vaccination. In graph (d), the system waits for the vaccination service, but misses it, and criticality returns back to high level as before.

t_0 is the time when the attack hit the system.

t_1 is the time the alert was issued.

t_{SV} arrival is the time for the Smart Vaccine to vaccinate the attacked system.

$t_{critical}$ is the time between the alert and the arrival of the Smart Vaccine.

t_2 is the time where the system was immunized and saved from the attack.

Therefore, the vaccination time ($T_{critical}$) shown as the gray area, should be between [t_1 and t_2], otherwise the vaccination is not going to help. During the design of the Smart Vaccine Grid, the calculation of the vaccination response time becomes crucial. Capacity planning and queuing theory are fundamental steps that should be applied during the design of the bandwidth of the grid.

Situation 1: The vaccination comes on time, even during the attack. The alert was broadcast to all systems and the Smart Vaccine army was able to vaccinate most of the systems as shown in the first part of the diagram. There may be some situations where confusion takes place and some systems get their help too late. They get attacked and may out of commission for a period of time (Figure 9.8).

Situation 2: The vaccination comes too late, as shown in the second part of the diagram earlier. The Smart Vaccine has to document the attack and learn to improve its response time. The antivirus of the troubled system will get an update on the attacking virus and will add it to the list of the other attacks.

The most important feature that was in the design of the Smart Vaccine is its ability to learn from its vaccination missions and build knowledge models for the next fight. In other words, the Smart Vaccine is equipped with autonomic capability that allows it to make decision on its own. As an expert system, its cognitive reasoning process gets better after every battle. Make no mistake, the Smart Vaccine is not an antivirus. It would not do justice if we compared the two products. The Smart Vaccine was designed to command complex vaccination services and establish persistent immunity throughout the Smart City.

Innate and Adaptive Digital Immunity

The designers of the operating system software such as Windows or Linux have included some basic defense logic against performance abnormalities that we call *exceptions*. These exceptions generate messages indicate something a SNAFU has occurred and the kernel overrode it and took an abrupt default action. These preventive messages are somewhat like what we call *innate immunity* that keeps the system going without crashing. We add to our innate immunity additional immunity with vaccination. Similarly, the Smart Vaccine is the system immunity booster. We call it *adaptive immunity*. We envision the next generation of systems will have more robust immunity against malicious attack vectors, through newer generations of the Smart Vaccine. We also envision all the big league cloud service providers to adopt digital immunity because it will guarantee that their client systems have robust immunity. So how does the Smart Vaccine offer adaptive immunity? The diagram in Figure 9.9 shows how digital immunity is accomplished:

The autonomic Smart Vaccine, once it responds to an alert and rushes toward the infected system, which is already on the grid. The Smart Vaccine will make sure the infected system gets the right vaccine and the right treatment. New systems however need to subscribe to the grid VS. They do not have any attack history in the Knowledge Base, but they will be registered in the regular vaccination program, the same for the healthy systems.

Adaptive immunity is to build system resistance against a specific virus. There is no vaccine that can eliminate all the viral attacks. Like in Human Immune System, each vaccine is for specific disease. This attribute is called *specificity* that should be observed during the vaccination process, otherwise the vaccine will be counterproductive.

We mentioned that vaccination services (VaaS) are provided on the Smart Vaccine grid, which is tightly coupled with the city's smart grid or through the city's smart cloud. SVG is one of the most important factors in the success of the Smart Vaccine. SVG is a real-time network that enables the Smart Vaccine to respond in the most expeditious way. SVG is managed by the Smart Vaccine Commander, and monitored by the Central Coordination Center (CCC) that acts like the air traffic control tower. The control tower gets an alarm signal from the Early Warning quarters where the

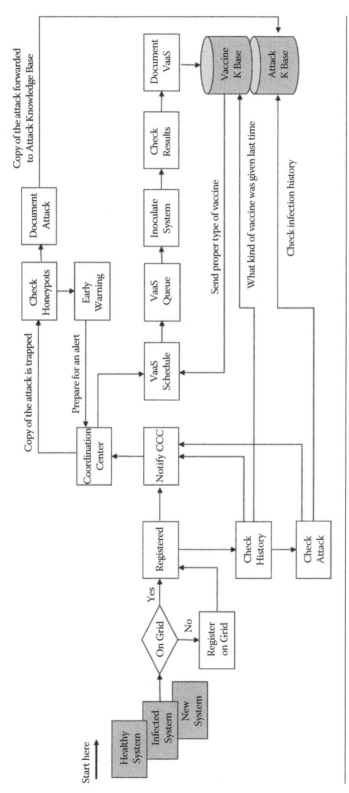

Figure 9.9 The autonomic Smart Vaccine, once it responds to an alert, vaccinators and paramedics arrive to the infected system, they will make sure the infected system gets the right vaccine and the right treatment. New systems on the grid do not have any history, but they will be registered and scheduled on the regular vaccination program, the same for the healthy systems. This is the way Digital Immunity is created for smart grid critical systems.

honeypot traps are located. The alert is dispatched to the Smart Vaccine Commander (SVC). All dispatched information is about the infected server (x, y, time, brand, name, …) At the same, the Smart Vaccine Commander goes to the Attack Knowledge Base (AKB) and the Vaccine Knowledge Base to learn about the attack vectors and the matching vaccine code. (Figure 9.9) tells the whole story.

There are actually two approaches to vaccinating the infected server.

1. *First approach* is when the attack is known and the virus documentation is in the Virus Knowledge Base. The second approach is when the attack was unique, and the virus is new without any history or documentation in the VKB. In fact, the Smart Vaccine will face an uphill battle because it will have to create a brand-new vaccine for the infected server. The Central Coordination Center will get an autonomic notification from the infected server that it needs help. The administrator of the server will be notified by the Central Coordination Center that help is on the way, and that he will need to switch over to the mirror system with complete transparency to the users. The Central Coordination Center will notify the Smart Vaccine for the emergency response. The vaccination process will be performed *off-line* without disrupting the critical production schedule. Again in this approach, previous similar attacks have been disassembled and generates assembly language source code will be generated from machine-executable code. The reverse engineering step follows the capture of the attacker by CEWPS honeypots, and the vaccine code will be assembled and compiled and ready to be used on the infected server. The vaccine code will be loaded into the off-line infected server and gets executed.

2. *Second approach* is where the attack was totally new and its payload has no historical records in the VKB. In fact, the attack was not caught by the honeypot, which indicates that the attack was elusive and well planned by the attackers. In this case, the virus infiltrates into the server through a stealth Trojan that passed from an IRC session. The Smart Vaccine will have to use its past cognitive experience of combating previous attacks to outsmart and defeat the virus. Now that the server is on the operating table, the Smart Vaccine will use its arsenal of tools to perform the necessary forensics to track down the Trojan, extract it from its hiding place, and disassemble its executable code to create its source code, then recompile the source code to analyze the way it detonated its payload and the damages created.

Again, like in the human body, the vaccine will trick the body into thinking it is under assault, and the immune system start making weapons that will provide a defense when a real infection becomes a threat. The Smart Vaccine will enter the *sick* system and will take charge of the cleansing process. The first thing it will do is to check the process monitor for some unusual activities that has nothing with production. One of the ways to understand the threat associated with a malicious software will be to examine its behavior in a controlled environment (off-line) and to watch its actions as it interacts with computer resources and responds to the various stimuli. The B cells do the same while they are getting ready to fire their antibodies. The Smart Vaccine will also examine the download files, because the Trojan may have been its hiding place.

The Smart Vaccine Is a Smart Sherlock Holmes

The Smart Vaccine will use a combination of process, disk, registry, and network monitoring tools to study the Trojan's activity on a sick off-line machine, and watch if the Trojan will attempt to connect to other systems. The Trojan may have created some temporary files that were deliberately deleted by the Trojan. The Smart Vaccine will use undelete utility that will replace the native system Recycle Bin with a Recovery Bin, which is able to capture all deleted files, even those deleted by non-GUI processes.

The Smart Vaccine pulled out its bag of tricks, an intrusion detection system (like SNORT) to analyze the traffic on the sick system, and determine if there was any tracks of payload packets. The Smart Vaccine will run the open port scanner to find out if the Trojan came through the Internet Char Relay (IRC). The Smart Vaccine checks any inbound connection attempts to TCP port 113 from an unknown host on the Internet, as well as unauthorized outbound connection attempts to a remote server on destination TCP port 6667. The Smart Vaccine concludes that the Trojan was connected to an Internet Char Relay network, knowing that 6667 is an often used port for IRC servers. The Smart Vaccine starts up an IRC client with a special IP address and connects to that unknown host. It is indeed an IRC server. A quick check shows several users online are on the IRC.

For those who are not familiar with IRC, let us mention that IRC can be viewed as a network of interlinked servers that allow users to hold real-time online conversations. Participants of a conversation typically join a channel devoted to a particular topic or interest. This is accomplished by having the user's IRC client connect to a server that participates in the desired IRC peering network. When a user types a message meant to be seen by channel participants, it is relayed to the IRC server, and the server resends the message to participating clients, as specified in the Request for Comments (RFC) document 1459.

The Smart Vaccine also examines any open files, and the Domain Name System (DNS) for any translation into an IP address. It also checks the HOST file for any modifications.

Now the Smart Vaccine gets deeper into its vaccination process. Initially, it concentrates on external aspects of the Trojan as it interacts with its environment, but it does not provide sufficient insight into the logic of the virus program. Like in Human Immune System, the B cell will need to identify the virus through its receptor cells. Similarly, the Smart Vaccine needs to decompose the virus and defuse its payload. The Smart Vaccine will use from its repertoire a debugger in conjunction with a disassembler to attempt to reverse engineer the Trojan's executable, since the Smart Vaccine does not have the luxury of looking at its source code of the malware. The Smart Vaccine will rely on its knowledge with previous vaccinations to overcome this challenge. It will rely on a disassembler to understand the basic structure of the Trojan and will proceed by stepping through it with the debugger to study the Trojan's logic and to take a look at its runtime memory contents (smudgy fingerprints while committing the crime). End of the vaccination story.

Harnessing SOA Technology

The following diagram shows the major components of the Smart Vaccine Vaccination Service (VS) molded in the service-oriented architecture.

A system gets an attack and it requests Vaccination Service (VS). The alert service sends a request to the vaccination broker. The broker who acts as a mediator accepts the request that is routed to the Knowledge Registry to get the right vaccine. The right vaccine is selected and it is routed to the vaccination service provider (VSP). The VS is provided to the infected system and the attack is terminated. The outcome of the VS is saved. The diagram in Figure 9.10 shows the sequence of the Vaccination Service and all the attributes of each activity.

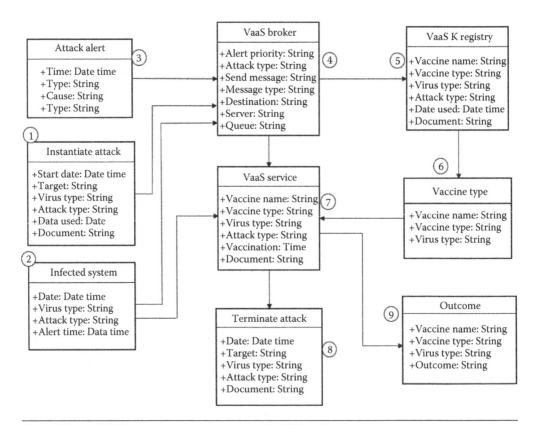

Figure 9.10   CEWPS Digital Immunity process flow using the SOA/service concept.

Glossary: Cloud Computing

Advertising-based pricing model: A pricing model whereby services are offered to customers at low or no cost, with the service provider being compensated by advertisers whose ads are delivered to the consumer along with the service.

Amazon EC2: Amazon's Elastic Compute Cloud Web service, which provides resizable computing capacity in the cloud so developers can enjoy great scalability for building applications.

Amazon S3, Amazon Simple Storage Services: Amazon's cloud storage service.

Billing and service usage metering: You can be billed for resources as you use them. This pay-as-you-go model means usage is metered and you pay only for what you consume.

CDN, content delivery network: A system consisting of multiple computers that contain copies of data, which are located in different places on the network so clients can access the copy closest to them.

Cloud: A metaphor for a global network, first used in reference to the telephone network and now commonly used to represent the Internet.

Cloud application: A software application that is never installed on a local machine—it is always accessed over the Internet. The *top* layer of the Cloud Pyramid where *applications* are run and interacted with via a Web-browser. Cloud Applications are tightly controlled, leaving little room for modification. Examples include Gmail or SalesForce.com.

Cloud arcs: Short for cloud architectures. Designs for software applications that can be accessed and used over the Internet. (Cloud architecture is just too hard to pronounce.)

Cloud as a Service (CaaS): A cloud computing service that has been opened up into a platform that others can build upon.

Cloud bridge: Running an application in such a way that its components are integrated within multiple cloud environments (which could be any combination of internal/private and external/public clouds).

Cloud broker: An entity that creates and maintains relationships with multiple cloud service providers. It acts as a liaison between cloud services customers and cloud service providers, selecting the best provider for each customer and monitoring the services.

Cloudburst: What happens when your cloud has an outage or security breach and your data are unavailable? The term cloudburst is being use in two meanings, negative and positive:

Cloudburst (negative): The failure of a cloud computing environment due to the inability to handle a spike in demand.

Cloudburst (positive): The dynamic deployment of a software application that runs on internal organizational compute resources to a public cloud to address a spike in demand.

Cloud center: A data center in the *cloud* utilizing standard-based virtualized components as a data center–like infrastructure, for example, a large company, such as Amazon, that rents its infrastructure.

Cloud client: Computing device for cloud computing. Updated version of thin client.

Cloud computing: A computing capability that provides an abstraction between the computing resource and its underlying technical architecture (e.g., servers, storage, networks), enabling convenient, on-demand network access to a shared pool of configurable computing resources that can be rapidly provisioned and released with minimal management effort or service provider interaction. This definition states that clouds have five essential characteristics: on-demand self-service, broad network access, resource pooling, rapid elasticity, and measured service. Narrowly speaking, cloud computing is client-server computing that abstract the details of the server away; one requests a service (resource), not a specific server (machine). *Cloud computing* enables Infrastructure as a Service (IaaS), Platform as a Service (PaaS), and Software as a Service (SaaS). Cloud computing means that infrastructure, applications, and business processes can be delivered to you *as a service*, over the Internet (or your own network).

Cloud enabler: A general term that refers to organizations (typically vendors) that are not cloud providers per se but make available technology, such as cloudware, that enables cloud computing. Vendor that provides technology or service that enables a client or other vendor to take advantage of cloud computing.

Cloud envy: Used to describe a vendor who jumps on the cloud computing bandwagon by rebranding existing services.

Cloud governance and compliance: Governance defines who is responsible for what and the policies and procedures that your people or groups need to follow. Cloud governance requires governing your own infrastructure as well as infrastructure that you do not totally control. Cloud governance has two key components: understanding compliance and risk and business performance goals.

Cloud hosting: A type of Internet hosting where the client leases virtualized, dynamically scalable infrastructure on an as-needed basis. Users frequently have the choice of operating system and other infrastructure components. Typically cloud hosting is self-service, billed hourly or monthly, and controlled via a Web interface or API.

Cloud infrastructure: The *bottom* layer, or foundation, of the cloud pyramid is the delivery of computer infrastructure through paravirtualization. This includes servers, networks, and other hardware appliances delivered as either Infrastructure Web Services or *cloud centers*. Full control of the infrastructure is provided at this level. Examples include GoGrid or Amazon Web Services.

Cloud manageability: You need a consistent view across both on-premises and cloud-based environments. This includes managing the assets provisioning as well as the quality of service (QOS) you are receiving from your service provider.

Cloud operating system: A computer operating system that is specially designed to run in a provider's data center and be delivered to the user over the Internet or another network. Windows Azure is an example of a cloud operating system or *cloud layer* that runs on Windows Server 2008. The term is also sometimes used to refer to cloud-based client operating systems such as Google's Chrome OS.

Cloud-oriented architecture (COA): A term coined by Jeff Barr at Amazon Web Services to describe an architecture where applications act as services in the cloud and serve other applications in the cloud environment. An architecture for IT infrastructure and software applications that is optimized for use in cloud computing environments. The term is not yet in wide use, and as is the case for the term *cloud computing* itself, there is no common or generally accepted definition or specific description of a cloud-oriented architecture.

Cloud OS: Also known as Platform as a Service (PaaS). Think Google Chrome.

Cloud platform: The *middle* layer of the cloud pyramid, which provides a computing platform or framework (e.g., NET, Ruby on Rails, or Python) as a service or stack. Control is limited to that of the platform or framework but not at a lower level (server infrastructure). Examples include Google AppEngine or Microsoft Azure.

Cloud portability: The ability to move applications (and often their associated data) across cloud computing environments from different cloud providers, as well as across private or internal cloud and public or external clouds.

Cloud provider: A company that provides cloud-based platform, infrastructure, application, or storage services to other organizations and/or individuals, usually for a fee.

Cloud providers: Computing service providers whose product/platform is based on virtualization of computing resources and a utility-based payment model.

Cloud pyramid: A visual representation of cloud computing layers where differing segments are broken out by functionality. Simplified version includes infrastructure, platform, and application layers.

Cloud security: The same security principles that apply to on-site computing apply to cloud computing security.

Cloud servers: Virtualized servers running Windows or Linux operating systems that are instantiated via a Web interface or API. Cloud servers behave in the same manner as physical ones and can be controlled at an administrator or root level, depending on the server type and cloud hosting provider.

Cloud service architecture: A term coined by Jeff Barr, chief evangelist at Amazon Web Services. The term describes an architecture in which applications and application components act as services on the cloud, which serve other applications within the same cloud environment.

Cloud sourcing: Outsourcing storage or taking advantage of some other type of cloud service.

Cloud standards: A standard is an agreed-upon approach for doing something. Cloud standards ensure interoperability, so you can take tools, applications, virtual images, and more, and use them in another cloud environment without having to do any rework. Portability lets you take one application or instance running on one vendor's implementation and deploy it on another vendor's implementation.

Cloud storage: A service that allows customers to save data by transferring it over the Internet or another network to an offsite storage system maintained by a third party.

Cloud storm: Connecting multiple cloud computing environments. Also called cloud network.

Cloudstorming: The act of connecting multiple cloud computing environments.

Cloudware: A general term referring to a variety of software, typically at the infrastructure level, that enables building, deploying, running or managing applications in a cloud computing environment.

Cloudwashing: Slapping the word *cloud* on products and services you already have.

Cluster: A group of linked computers that work together as if they were a single computer, for high availability and/or load balancing.

Consumption-based pricing model: A pricing model whereby the service provider charges its customers based on the amount of the service the customer consumes, rather than a time-based fee. For example, a cloud storage provider might charge per gigabyte of information stored. See also *Subscription-based pricing model.*

Customer self-service: A feature that allows customers to provision, manage, and terminate services themselves, without involving the service provider, via a Web interface or programmatic calls to service APIs.

Data in the cloud: Managing data in the cloud requires data security and privacy, including controls for moving data from point *A* to point *B*. It also includes managing data storage and the resources for large-scale data processing.

Detection and forensics: Separating legitimate from illegitimate activity.

Disruptive technology: A term used in the business world to describe innovations that improve products or services in unexpected ways and change both the way things are done and the market. Cloud computing is often referred to as a disruptive technology because it has the potential to completely change the way IT services are procured, deployed, and maintained.

Elastic computing: The ability to dynamically provision and de-provision processing, memory, and storage resources to meet demands of peak usage without worrying about capacity planning and engineering for peak usage.

Elasticity and scalability: The cloud is elastic, meaning that resource allocation can get bigger or smaller depending on demand. Elasticity enables scalability, which means that the cloud can scale upward for peak demand and downward for lighter demand. Scalability also means that an application can scale when adding users and when application requirements change.

Encryption: Coding to protect your information assets.

External cloud: Public or private cloud services that are provided by a third party outside the organization. A cloud computing environment that is external to the boundaries of the organization.

Funnel cloud: Discussion about cloud computing that goes round and round but never turns into action (never *touches the ground*).

Google app engine: A service that enables developers to create and run Web applications on Google's infrastructure and share their applications via a pay-as-you-go, consumption-based plan with no setup costs or recurring fees.

Google apps: Google's SaaS offering that includes an office productivity suite, e-mail, and document sharing, as well as Gmail, Google Talk for instant messaging, Google Calendar and Google Docs, spreadsheets, and presentations.

HaaS: Hardware as a Service; see *IaaS.*

Hosted application: An Internet-based or Web-based application software program that runs on a remote server and can be accessed via an Internet-connected PC or thin client. See also *SaaS.*

Hybrid cloud: A networking environment that includes multiple integrated internal and/or external providers. Hybrid clouds combine aspects of both public and private clouds.

IBM smart business: IBM's cloud solutions, which include IBM Smart Business Test Cloud, IBM Smart Analytics Cloud, IBM Smart Business Storage Cloud, IBM Information Archive, IBM Lotus Live, and IBM LotusLive iNotes.

Identity management: Managing personal identity information so that access to computer resources, applications, data, and services is controlled properly.

Infrastructure as a Service (IaaS): Cloud infrastructure services or *Infrastructure as a Service* (IaaS) delivers computer infrastructure, typically a platform virtualization environment, as a service. Rather than purchasing servers, software, data center space or network equipment, clients instead buy those resources as a fully outsourced service. The service is typically billed on a utility computing basis and amount of resources consumed (and therefore the cost) will typically reflect the level of activity. It is an evolution of Web hosting and virtual private server offerings.

Internal cloud: A type of private cloud whose services are provided by an IT department to those in its own organization.

Mashup: A Web-based application that combines data and/or functionality from multiple sources.

Microsoft azure: Microsoft cloud services that provide the Platform as a Service (see PaaS), allowing developers to create cloud applications and services.

Middleware: Software that sits between applications and operating systems, consisting of a set of services that enable interoperability in support of distributed architectures by passing data between applications. So, for example, the data in one database can be accessed through another database.

On-demand service: A model by which a customer can purchase cloud services as needed; for instance, if customers need to utilize additional servers for the duration of a project, they can do so and then drop back to the previous level after the project is completed.

Pay as you go: A cost model for cloud services that encompasses both subscription-based and consumption-based models, in contrast to traditional IT cost model that requires up-front capital expenditures for hardware and software.

Personal cloud: Synonymous with something called MiFi, a personal wireless router. It takes a mobile wireless data signal and translates it to Wi-Fi. It is pronounced ME-fi, as in "the personal cloud belongs to me—but if you're nice I'll let you connect."

Platform as a Service (PaaS): Platform as a Service—Cloud platform services, whereby the computing platform (operating system and associated services) is delivered as a service over the Internet by the provider. The PaaS layer offers black-box services with which developers can build applications on top of the compute infrastructure. This might include developer tools that are offered as a service to build services, or data access and database services, or billing services.

Private clouds: Private cloudvirtualized cloud data centers inside your company's firewall. It may also be a private space dedicated to your company within a cloud provider's data center. An internal cloud behind the organization's firewall. The company's IT department provides Software and Hardware as a Service to its customers—the people who work for the company. Vendors love the words *private cloud*.

Public cloud: Services offered over the public Internet and available to anyone who wants to purchase the service.

Roaming workloads: The backend product of cloud centers.

REST: Representational State Transfer, a stateless architectural approch that runs on HTTP.

Salesforce.com: An online SaaS company that is best known for delivering customer relationship management (CRM) software to companies over the Internet.

Self-service provisioning: Cloud customers can provide cloud services without going through a lengthy process. You request an amount of computing, storage, software, process, or more from the service provider. After you use these resources, they can be automatically deprovisioned.

Service level agreement (SLA): A contractual agreement by which a service provider defines the level of service, responsibilities, priorities, and guarantees regarding availability, performance, and other aspects of the service.

Service migration: The act of moving from one cloud service or vendor to another.

Service provider: The company or organization that provides a public or private cloud service.

Software as a Service (SaaS): Cloud application services, whereby applications are delivered over the Internet by the provider, so that the applications do not have to be purchased, installed, and run on the customer's computers. SaaS providers were previously referred to as ASP (application service providers). In the SaaS layer, the service provider hosts the software so you do not need to install it, manage it, or buy hardware for it. All you have to do is connect and use it. SaaS Examples include customer relationship management as a service.

Standardized interfaces: Cloud services should have standardized APIs, which provide instructions on how two application or data sources can communicate with each other. A standardized interface lets the customer more easily link cloud services together.

Subscription-based pricing model: A pricing model that lets customers pay a fee to use the service for a particular time period, often used for SaaS services. See also *Consumption-based pricing model.*

Utility computing: Online computing or storage sold as a metered commercial service in a way similar to a public utility.

Vendor lock-in: Dependency on the particular cloud vendor and difficulty in moving from one cloud vendor to another due to lack of standardized protocols, APIs, data structures (schema), and service models.

Vertical cloud: A cloud computing environment that is optimized for use in a particular industry, such as health care or financial services.

Virtual private cloud (VPC): A term coined by Reuven Cohen, CEO and founder of Enomaly. The term describes a concept that is similar to, and derived from, the familiar concept of a Virtual Private Network (VPN), but applied to cloud computing. It is the notion of turning a public cloud into a virtual private cloud, particularly in terms of security and the ability to create a VPC across components that are both within the cloud and external to it. For example, the Amazon VPC that allows Amazon EC2 to connect to legacy infrastructure on an IPsec VPN.

Virtual private data center: Resources grouped according to specific business objectives.

Windows live services: Microsoft's cloud-based consumer applications, which include Windows Live Mail, Windows Live Photo Gallery, Windows Live Calendar, Windows Live Events, Windows Live SkyDrive, Windows Live Spaces, Windows Live Messenger, Windows Live Writer, and Windows Live for Mobile.

References

Erl, T., *Principles of Service Design*. Prentice Hall, Upper Saddle River, NJ, 2008.
Erl, T., *Cloud Computing*. Prentice Hall, Upper Saddle River, NJ, 2013.
Kurtz, R. and Vines, R.D., *Cloud Security*. Wiley Publishing, New York, 2010.

Websites

http://aws.amazon.com/.

https://code.google.com/p/soafaces/.

http://www.gartner.com/newsroom/id/2819918.

http://www.networkworld.com/article/2172366/cloud-computing/google-compute-engine-
    vs-amazon-web-services-cloud--the-battle-is-on.html.

http://www.oracle.com/us/products/middleware/soa/overview/index.html.

http://www-01.ibm.com/software/solutions/soa/.

https://www.hex-rays.com/products/ida/support/download.shtml.

http://www.NIST.gov.

http://www.soasystems.com.

10

THE INTERNET OF THINGS, CONVERGENCE OF SCADA AND CEWPS

The Internet of Things (IoT) Is the Internet of Internet

It is a strange term but not a hostile one. It certainly is a new disruptive technology storm around the block. We have developed an excessive affinity toward the Internet that goes beyond computers and phones. As a matter of fact, any black box, either electric or electronic, solar, or wind driven, can subscribe to become a member of the IoT. Gartner claims that by 2020, there will be over 26 billion connected devices. I would say 54 billion devices will connect to the IoT tree. Time will tell who is right.

The Internet of Things is rather a galaxy of interconnected clouds connecting everything to everything. It did not fall down from the sky, but we created it, and now we need to seriously think about it. If you cannot visualize how it looks, think of a massive snowball rolling downhill and growing at geometric pace. Or, just look at the sky on a clear night and imagine all these stars are connected together. Now, you got the picture of our Internet of Things.

Thirty years ago, no one really anticipated that the Internet would grow as such an astronomical pace. It seems that there will not be any limit to it. Now that it morphed into the Internet of Things, it looks like a galaxy drifting in open space at its own pace.

If we examine the Internet of Things at the molecular level under a microscope, we will be amazed by its morphology and its structure. The Internet of Things follows an orderly pattern of chaos, which is a mysterious type of order. We all know that chaos is the science of surprises. The theory was summarized by Edward Lorenz as follows: "Chaos: When the present determines the future, but the approximate present does not approximately determine the future."

Take, for example, the butterfly effect: it grants the power to cause a hurricane in China to a butterfly flapping its wings in New Mexico. It may take a very long time, but the connection is real. If the butterfly had not flapped its wings at just the right point in space/time, the hurricane would not have occurred. In other words, small changes in the initial conditions lead to drastic changes in the results. Our lives are an ongoing demonstration of this principle as shown in Figure 10.1.

The concept of the Internet of Things is not new. Kevin Ashton and Neil Gross deserve credit for coining the expression. I quote Neil Gross' wonderful explanation of the Internet of Things from his article in *Business Week* in 1999, "In the next century,

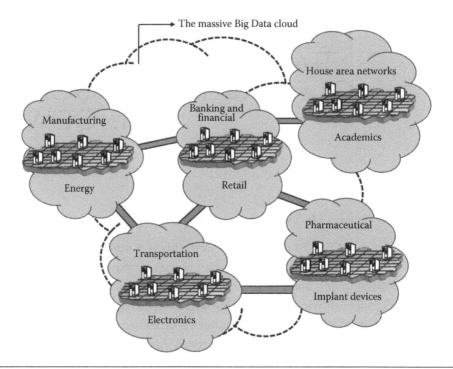

Figure 10.1 The Internet of Things—A galaxy of thousands of clouds connected together. IoT doesn't have a particular shape. It expands dynamically in every direction. Ray Kurzweil will tell you where it's heading.

planet earth will don an electronic skin. It will use the Internet as a scaffold to support and transmit its sensations. This skin is already being stitched together. It consists of millions of embedded electronic measuring devices: thermostats, pressure gauges, pollution detectors, cameras, microphones, glucose sensors, EKGs, electroencephalographs. These will probe and monitor cities and endangered species, the atmosphere, our ships, highways and fleets of trucks, our conversations, our bodies—even our dreams."

Kurzweil's 5th Epoch

The trend and evolution of the Internet of Things amazingly coincides with Ray Kurzweil's evolution theory in his famous book *The Singularity Is Near* as shown in Figure 10.2.

He classified evolution into six epochs. He was right when he said "Evolution is a process of creating patterns of increasing order." It seems that we are at the very beginning of Epoch 5, which is "The Merger of Human Technology with Human Intelligence." We are not there yet, but the Internet of Things phenomenon seems to follow Epoch 5 pattern, by bringing informatics, machines, and people into one convergence.

The impact on the Internet was phenomenally beyond any expectation. Predicting the future of the Internet has been very elusive. Even the fathers of the Internet could not see the end of the tunnel of Big Data or Internet of Things. I give Ray Kurzweil all the credit for making us aware of the concept of singularity and combining human intelligence with artificial intelligence. As a result, the Internet workload has increased exponentially

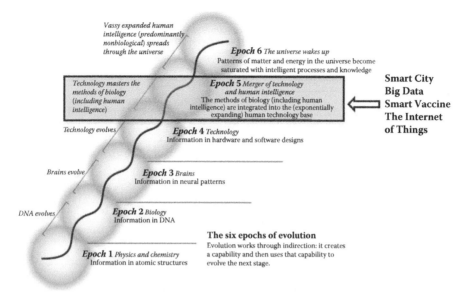

Figure 10.2   Kurzweil's theory of technology evolution. Smart City, Big Data, Internet of Things, and even the Smart Vaccine will be part of Epoch 5.

or even logarithmically, and we are going to hit the wall pretty soon with the IP address (IPv4), which gives us only a total of 2^{32} (about 4.3 billion) possible addresses. We have already reached the ceiling with 96% capacity as of last May 2014. Most users have no idea what it means. Luckily, the Internet Engineering Task Force (IETF) in 1998 had formalized the successor protocol. Internet protocol version 6 (IPv6) is coming to the rescue. IPv6 will offer greater scalability and should be enough for a while.

IPv6 uses a 128-bit address, allowing 2^{128}, or approximately 3.4×10^{38} IP addresses, or more than 7.9×10^{28} times as many as IPv4. IPv4 and IPv6 protocols are unfortunately not upward compatible or even interoperable, complicating the transition to IPv6. However, several IPv6 transition mechanisms have been devised to permit communication between IPv4 and IPv6 hosts.

As of now, Forrester Research estimates that there will be 25 billion smart devices and intelligent systems "things" connected to IoT around the world by 2020. Simplistically, it means 25 billion new IP addresses will be assigned to all these smart devices, which will consume a substantial reserve from the remaining IP available addresses.

Architecture of the Internet of Things

Because of the massive volume of data that IoT threatens to produce, the recent trend toward clustering applications per sector becomes more logical and cost effective. Smart cities will have to utilize smart *infrastructures* threaded with smart grids as the main highways to secure the transfer and exchange of information among applications. Advances in embedded sensors, processing, and wireless connectivity are bringing the power of the digital world to objects and places in the physical world.

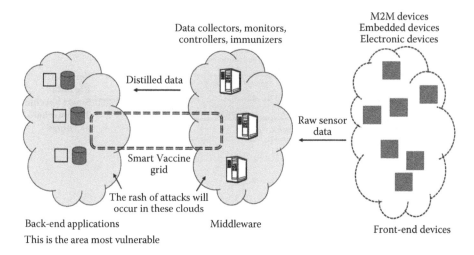

Figure 10.3   A view topology of the Internet of Things (IoT). Embedded systems are at the consumer side, then data gets distilled, and end up in the sanitized data warehouses (on the left). The new disruptive technology is around the corner. It is called "Edge Technology," which empowers the consumers more and more. Basically, all computing in EC takes place at the consumer site.

Despite its gargantuan landscape and complexity, the Internet of Things is becoming a true marvel of integration and polymorphism. IoT is a true kaleidoscope with intricate geometry and fabric. It will have a tremendous impact on all sectors of the economy and home. Services will be grouped by application and will be securely bundled with intelligent security layer offered by Cognitive Early Warning Predictive System (CEWPS) and the Smart Vaccine (SV).

Basically, the Internet of Things has a very simple concept, as shown in Figure 10.3. There are three clouds that constitute the Internet of Things, which are as follows:

1. *First cloud*: The front-end devices, which are the data-generating cloud. All censored data will be transmitted to the second cloud.
2. *Second cloud*: This is where all the raw data get collected and distilled and condensed. This cloud is referred to as the middleware cloud.
3. *Third cloud*: It contains all the applications that generate the end reports to the consumer.

The Smart Vaccine grid (SVG) plays a critical role in eradicating all the attacks on the middleware and the application clouds. SVG is the best security defense for the clouds. Digital Immunity (DI) will guarantee to offer the best shield.

Here are some of the most promising networks of IoT that will enhance the quality of our smart cities:

Category 1

A *home area network* (*HAN*) is a new emerging technology that connects everything at home as one network with IoT service providers. This is an awesome technology with several tangible benefits. A home area network is the communication technology that will allow smart devices in the house to operate autonomically and responsibly. Call it the house of the future. The demand for HAN-enabled smart devices is growing quickly. I expect every modern house will be HAN-enabled. The price of smart devices will go down, and the household will become smart. Whirlpool has stated that 100% of their home appliances will be smart grid compliant by 2017, and in a recent survey by General Electric, 82% of Americans believe that smart meters and smart appliances are the future, and 88% are willing to use smart devices.

The main incentive will be economic. Utility companies will be pushing for HAN because it will simplify their infrastructure maintenance. It has to be a plug-and-play type of a deal. Instead of selling individual products, some service providers have begun offering complete and externally managed home automation and home security solutions that lease networked systems of devices in a subscription model together with externally managed services. Smart grid technology and networking market a powerful and comprehensive suite of critical infrastructure networking solutions. Utility companies and cities in the United States and worldwide are trying to partner with HAN companies, as technology intermediaries offer homes a complete suite of applications, which cover advanced metering, outage detection, voltage monitoring, demand response, network management, and even offer seamless Web services to utility's back office applications as shown in Figure 10.4.

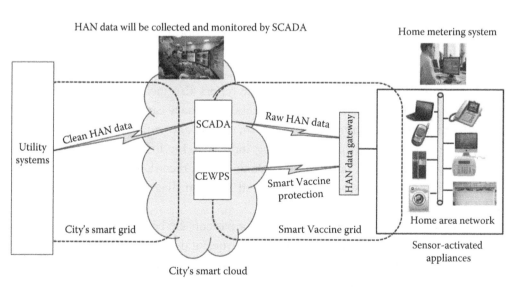

Figure 10.4   Category 1: Homes will have smart devices and appliances connected to a home area network. The convenience, availability, and reliability of externally managed cloud-computing resources will continue to become an appealing choice for many home dwellers without interest or experience in IT.

Some of the smart appliances that will be connected to HAN are as follows:

- *HVAC*: An integrated thermostat for air conditioning and heating
- *Smoke/CO detectors*: Reliable rejection with actual screen reading
- *Garage door and gate openers*: With smart program to recognize incoming automobiles
- *Lighting*: Smart programs to advise household on consumption and usage
- Wireless program-activated smart devices
- TV cable
- Telephone
- TV entertainment
- House alarm

Category 2

Health care wearable devices networks: Health care is one of the most crucial sectors that could benefit from the Internet of Things. As a matter of fact, health care has been a troublesome area for the government. California Health Care Almanac (July 2014) report describes the health care situation: "Even with the slow growth in national health spending in recent years, the U.S. continued to spend a greater percentage of its wealth on health care than any other industrialized nation. In 2012, the U.S. spent an average of $8915 per person on health care, reaching a total of 2.8 trillion dollars."

The U.S. Department of Health has just released a report on the health of Americans, entitled appropriately *Health, United States, 2003*, http://www.cdc.gov/nchs/data/hus/hus03.pdf.

It is available in print and online. The online version is periodically updated and revised. It is worth reading. The report is full of both good news and bad. The good news is that the life expectancy of Americans has reached an all-time high. But the bad news is that, during the last 5 years, the report also includes preventive care to treat obesity, smoking, vaccination, and access to primary care.

With the potential to improve the health, safety, and care of billions of people, health care is one of the most promising industries for IoT. With Wi-Fi-enabled medical tools and devices, hospitals are able to collect, record, and analyze data faster and more accurately. This helps medical staff perform diagnosis and treatment and undoubtedly improve standards of care.

Health monitoring and wearable devices for patients are becoming extremely popular, as they are able to transmit a patient's real-time, vital-sign data from their home to medical staff. Such Wi-Fi-powered devices include *things* such as glucometers, scales, heart rate, and ultrasound monitors. Furthermore, wearable devices are gaining attention among the elderly and those with chronic illness. With the push of a button, a person is able to alert the medical staff of an emergency situation.

The Magic of a VeriChip Implant

In 2002, Applied Digital Solutions manufactured the *VeriChip*, which is an injectable identification chip that can be inserted under the skin of a human being to provide biometric verification. VeriChip is about the size of a grain of rice. It holds an identification number, an electromagnetic coil for transmitting data, and a tuning capacitor; the components are enclosed inside a silicon and glass container that is compatible with human tissue. The chip, which uses an RFID (wireless transmission) technology similar to the injectable ID chips used by animal shelters to tag pets, can be read by a proprietary scanner up to 4 ft away. Unfortunately, like anything ahead of its time, certain privacy advocates have raised concerns regarding potential abuse of the VeriChip, with some warning that adoption by governments as a compulsory identification program could lead to erosion of civil liberties. VeriChip needed further enhancements of its security features, which made it susceptible to cloning, which could present a risk of identity theft. VeriChip could have played a major role in identity theft protection (Figure 10.5).

Additionally, fitness bands such as the Nike FuelBand or Fitbit measure whole-body movement throughout the day—transmitting the data wirelessly to the user's computer, tablet, or smartphone. This trend also has the potential to impact the way health insurance companies operate.

A large part of the impact of IoT technology will be where health care data exist in a lot of fragmented areas, including equipment, electronic medical records, along with

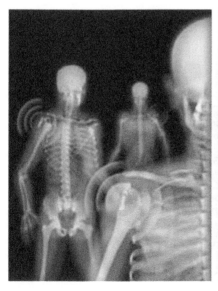
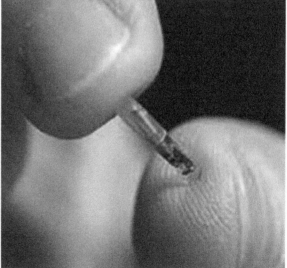

Figure 10.5   The VeriChip implant will be as ordinary as getting an airline ticket. It is like any disruptive technology, it has to show the benefits first. The Associated Press on October 13, 2004, published an article that highlighted "The Food and Drug Administration said Wednesday that Applied Digital Solutions of Delray Beach, Florida, could market the VeriChip, an implantable computer chip about the size of a grain of rice, for medical purposes."

the handling of patient data, tracking admissions, and managing best practices. It also shows how connecting and funneling data can help make better-informed decisions.

With all the rumbling and brouhaha about IoT in health care, the federal Health Insurance Portability and Accountability Act (HIPAA) of 1996 reminds everyone that the primary goal of the law is to make it easier for people to keep health insurance, protect the confidentiality and security of health care information, and help the health care industry control administrative costs.

So keeping the patient's health records private and secure (in the order) should be the goal of IoT and not embracing technology for the sake of technology, as many vendors believe. The fact that medical records are still vulnerable and not perfectly secure raises a major concern about the real objective of medical technology vendors (Figure 10.6).

Hacking medical records is a profitable business. There are thousands of crime service providers (CSP) who specialize in identity theft of medical records. Even insurance companies resort to their services to collect evidence on insurance fraud from subscribers.

MIT Technology Review Journal, in its December 23, 2014 issue, published an alarming article titled *2015 Could Be the Year of the Hospital Hack*. The article gives a reason for the hospital invasion "The cause of the uptick isn't hard to diagnose. Medical organizations across the world are switching to electronic medical records, and computer security is not always a high enough priority during the process, says Leonard the security manager from Websense. Besides that, he says, easy and fast access to medical information often trumps security."

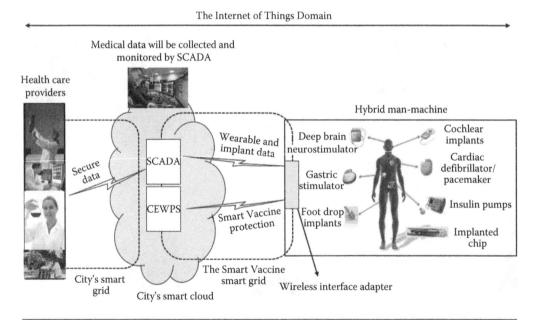

Figure 10.6 Category 2: Smart wearable and implant medical devices will be securely collected and monitored by SCADA and the gracious support of CEWPS/Smart Vaccine. The integrity and security of the medical data will be one of the biggest advantages of the Internet of Things. Digital Immunity (DI) will be the Holy Grail. HIPAA will eventually recommend DI as a mandatory requirement for the health care industry. Do not be surprised!

Software vendors usually release patches to plug the holes in their antivirus systems, but still hundreds of thousands of systems are likely still vulnerable. Though there are many other ways that malware authors can infiltrate networks and steal sensitive information, "the massive number of systems that are susceptible to this vulnerability is unique," says Websense's Leonard.

The Heartbleed security bug, disclosed in April 2014 in the OpenSSL cryptography library, caused so many hospitals to be attacked, and their private patient records were compromised and stolen for identity theft purpose.

It is becoming evident that the present Antivirus Technologies (AVT) have not been able to eradicate cybercrime in the financial and health care domains. The reason could be very obvious: AVT companies have higher financial incentives to market Trojans and viruses to cyber lords and crime service providers. After all, AVT companies are profit organizations and willing to market their virus services to foreign crime organizations and their (AVT) products to the general public. The fact that cyberattacks have been on the rise in the United States and over 60% of the health care systems in the United States are still vulnerable raises eye brows, and whistle blowers have been away on a wild-goose chase.

Zombies Are Made in China

China is the fourth biggest country in the world, but when it comes to cybercrime, it is second to none. For years, intelligence agencies and private security experts have warned that Chinese hackers are trying to steal western corporate secrets. The cries have grown even louder as the attacks have become bolder and signs of government involvement have surfaced. In a forthcoming book, Eric Schmidt, the executive chairman of Google, reportedly brands China "the most sophisticated and prolific" hacker of foreign companies.

The Chinesed target health care because they knew that hospital system lack tight security. The Chinese Black Hatters went after companies such as HCA and CYH who operate large networks of health care facilities. For example, the Nashville-based HCA is the nation's leading provider of health care services, managing about 165 hospitals and 115 freestanding surgery centers in 20 states and England and employing approximately 204,000 people. Approximately 4%–5% of all inpatient care delivered in the country today is provided by HCA facilities. The Franklin, Tennessee-based Community Health Systems (CYH) manages a network of 206 hospitals providing general and acute care services in 29 states. These are the networks that the Chinese hackers are targeting to steal patient names, social security numbers, physical addresses, birth dates, and telephone numbers. This critical information, which is often used as currency among shadowy international hacker groups, is almost always stolen for the purpose of identity fraud, allowing thieves to open bank accounts and credit cards on the victim's behalf.

CEWPS brings a new type of security layer to support the information assets of public and private institutions, as well as SCADA systems that monitor critical infrastructure systems. Here is how it works.

People who have implants and wearable devices will be connected via secure Wi-Fi to City Smart Grid and Smart Vaccine Grid. Pretty much like at home, where we have wireless router connected to a modem and to a cable or to an Internet service provider (ISP). The modem is actually a node on the Smart Vaccine smart grid, which provides immune security for all the devices worn or implanted in the person.

Category 3

Machine-to-Machine Networks (M2M): This is going to be the most influential paradigm shift that the Internet of Things would offer. As a matter of fact, there is a little confusion about the similarity of M2M and IoT. Simply put, Machine-to-Machine is where *machines* use a network or the City Smart Grid to communicate with remote applications that monitor and control, either the *machine* itself or its surrounding environment. The potential interconnection of smart objects and the way we interact with the environment is what the Internet of Things is envisioned to be, where the physical world will merge with the digital world.

M2M is what provides the Internet of Things with the connectivity that enables capabilities, which would not be possible without it. M2M with Internet protocols could be considered a subset of the Internet of Things and understood from a more vertical and closed point of view. On the other hand, the Internet of Things encompasses a more horizontal and meaningful approach where vertical applications are pulled together to address the needs of many people.

We define M2M as the communication between a machine or device and a remote computer. M2M is about connecting a device to the cloud, managing that device, and collecting machine and sensor data. In essence, M2M is about connecting and communicating with a *thing*, where a thing can be a machine, device, or sensor, basically anything that can send data.

The rise of objects that connect themselves to the Internet—from cars to heart monitors to stoplights—is unleashing a wave of new possibilities for data gathering, Predictive Analytics, and IT automation. It is the beginning of a new epoch. But let's think as engineers and not like entrepreneurs. We are creating a complex galaxy of clouds where everything is connected to everything. Complexity requires reliable monitoring and management. Often, complex systems tend to oppose their own proper functions and exhibit unexpected behavior. Ask any engineer and he/she will tell you that systems often tend to malfunction conspicuously just after their greatest triumph. So, the corollary of this systemantics is to collect reliable data during testing and adjust the design. As the authors of the excellent *Trillions: Thriving in the Emerging Information Ecology* put it, "The data are no longer in the computers. We have come to see that the computers are in the data."

The Anatomy of Machine to Machine

A point worth stressing is that data transfer patterns in the M2M-driven Internet of Things will differ fundamentally from those in the classic *human-to-human* (H2H)

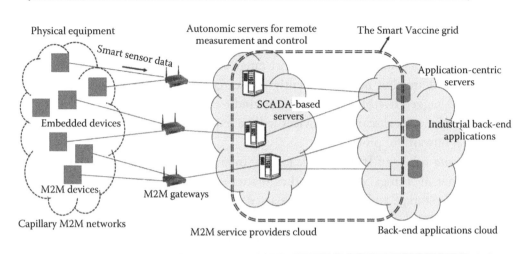

Figure 10.7 Category 3: Topology of the Machine-to-Machine (M2M) Internet of Things. You notice that the Smart Vaccine Grid is always on the alert, by offering Digital Immunity, to protect the M2M service providers and the back-end application clouds.

Internet. M2M communications will feature orders of magnitude more nodes than H2H, most of which will create low-bandwidth, upload-biased traffic. Many M2M applications need to deliver and process information in real time, or near-real time, and many nodes have to be extremely low-power or self-powered (e.g., solar powered) devices. Figure 10.7 shows the topology of M2M. The following is a partial list of M2M categories:

Appliances: The *things* in the IoT, or the *machines* in M2M, are physical entities whose identity or state (or the state of whose surroundings) is capable of being relayed to an Internet-connected IT infrastructure. Almost anything to which you can attach a sensor—a cow in a field, a container on a cargo vessel, the air-conditioning unit in your office, a lamppost in the street—can become a node in the Internet of Things.

Interface sensors: These are the components of *things* that gather and/or disseminate data—be it on location, altitude, velocity, temperature, illumination, motion, power, humidity, blood sugar, air quality, soil moisture, etc., you name it.

Communications: All IoT sensors require some means of relaying data to the outside world. There is a plethora of short-range, or local-area, wireless technologies available, including RFID, NFC, Wi-Fi, Bluetooth, and Wireless M-Bus. For long-range or wide-area links, there are existing mobile networks (e.g., using GSM, GPRS, 3G, LTE, or WiMAX) and satellite connections. New wireless networks such as the ultranarrowband Sigfox and the TV white-space NeulNET are also emerging to cater specifically for M2M connectivity. Fixed *things* in convenient locations could use wired Ethernet or phone lines for wide-area connections.

Server (on premises): Some types of M2M installation, such as a smart home or office, will use a local server to collect and analyze data—both in real time and episodically—from assets on the local area network. These on-premise servers or simpler gateways will usually also connect to cloud-based storage and services.

Local scanning device: *Things* with short-range sensors will often be located in a restricted area but not permanently connected to a local area network (e.g., RFID-tagged livestock on a farm, or credit-card-toting shoppers in a mall). In this case, local scanning devices will be required to extract data and transmit it onward for processing.

Storage and analytics: If you think today's Internet generates a lot of data, the Internet of Things will be another matter entirely. It will require massive, scalable storage and processing capacity, which will almost invariably reside in the cloud—except for specific localized or security-sensitive cases. Service providers will obviously have access here, not only to curate the data and tweak the analytics but also for line-of-business processes such as customer relations, billing, and technical support.

This is because the concept applies to and has grown from a wide range of market sectors.

In this chapter, we are going to introduce another concept that has never been addressed or discussed earlier. We are going to discuss how we can create a hybrid system that tightly couples two versatile systems together. The supervisory control and data system (SCADA) is widely used in the manufacturing and power industries as the nerve center to critical processes. Also, SCADA is used as the data collection and supervision in power plants and for the management of the critical infrastructures in large metropolitan cities.

SCADA is the *de facto* of the control (analog–digital) systems. In the olden days, we had IBM 1800. But when new chips and operating systems emerged it was no more used. One should remember that SCADA is a generic name. There are over a dozen SCADA brands with a variety of features, which are grouped by industry, by technology, and, of course, by cost. Take, for example, the Siemens SCADA that is known for its versatility. We could add Digital Immunity (DI) to its performance, which would definitely offer the customer the best of two worlds.

Digital Convergence of the Internet of Things, SCADA, CEWPS, and Big Data

What Is Digital Convergence?

Digital Convergence (DC) is what I call *cooperative engineering* because it is an additive process that combines the strength properties of all converged elements. It is different from *fusion*, which trickled from the Latin word *fundere*, meaning melt, where all the elements involved will melt together and form one new element. Digital Convergence creates a multifaced platform that provides higher performance and greater economies of scale.

In a cloud-based environment, DC will offer near-real-time visibility, more responsive control, better Predictive Analytics of assets, and more importantly, workforce enablement via remote collaboration tools. We are going to show how four emerging technologies have to converge onto one cloud-based environment: Information Technology (IT), Consumer Technologies (CT), Operational Technologies (OT), and Infrastructure Technologies are subsets of the Internet of Things. All these technologies will be protected by the Smart Vaccine Grid (SVG), which is the security backbone of the Smart City. We added the Critical Infrastructure Technologies (CIT), which is the most crucial ingredient of the Smart City. It will also be protected by the Smart Vaccine cognitive grid. At the same time, Big Data is in the background.

Emerging Technologies: The Big League Players

Figure 10.8 represents how the mega-Digital Convergence abstraction framework is going to shape up. We see how the four technologies are going to coexist and interconnect. Big Data, *the mother of all clouds*, will be hovering in the background. IT, OT, CT, and the infrastructure technologies will prevail as the four major clouds in the Smart City. These four technologies will be plagued with constant Virus Rains and storms unless they are connected to an intelligent grid that would monitor and alert nearby system. Any attack on one of the IoT technologies (listed earlier) will proliferate and becomes pervasive and even uncontrollable. CEWPS/Smart Vaccine runs on its own cognitive smart grid (CSG), like the human nervous system supporting the immune system. The need for this intelligent grid is a matter of life and death. We will describe later how it will function and offer its security services (Figure 10.8).

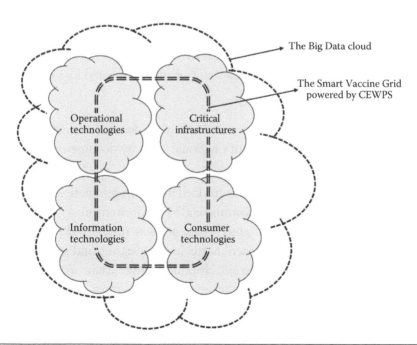

Figure 10.8   The megadigital convergence abstraction framework of emerging technologies. The Smart Vaccine will be one of the big players offering Digital Immunity to the other technologies that make up the Internet of Things.

Group 1: Information Technology (IT)

It traditionally comprises resources and connectivity for processing and managing data to support business functions and transactions. Its goal is to ensure the confidentiality, integrity, and availability of data and systems. IT includes solutions such as enterprise resource planning, HR management, customer service, transaction processing, financial reporting, and corporate collaboration.

Group 2: Consumer Technology (CT)

It encompasses the products and services that companies provide to end users or customers. It includes smartphones, tablets, health- and fitness-monitoring devices, location-aware services, and gaming networks, to name just a few. Ubiquitous connectivity and advanced mobility, combined with the boom in cloud-based services, have further fueled the surge of consumer products. Technologies such as near field communication (NFC), radio frequency identification (RFID), and Bluetooth low energy are enabling a new wave of products like digital wallets and personal health monitors.

Group 3: Operational Technology

It is typically defined as systems and related automation assets that monitor and control physical equipment and events such as supervisory control and data acquisition (SCADA) systems or systems that support the creation and delivery of products and services. Physical control of a process or any component of the critical infrastructures, as described in the book, is the most critical part of OT. Historically, operational systems have been managed and maintained separately from IT. That's continuing to change as businesses begin to mesh OT and IT and connect the two public and private clouds. OT includes another category of systems such as environmental control, plant management, integrated facility management, air traffic control, and automated logistics operations.

Group 4: Critical Infrastructure Technologies

The critical infrastructure sectors are defined in Federal Costumer Identification Program Policy based on the President's national strategy documents and Homeland Security Presidential Directive 7.

1. *Agriculture*: Includes supply chains for feed and crop production
2. *Banking and finance*: Consists of commercial banks, insurance companies, mutual funds, government-sponsored enterprises, pension funds, and other financial institutions that carry out transactions, including clearing and settlement
3. *Chemicals and hazardous materials*: Produces more than 70,000 products essential to automobiles, pharmaceuticals, food supply, electronics, water treatment, health, construction, and other necessities
4. *Defense industrial base*: Supplies the military with the means to protect the nation by producing weapons, aircraft, and ships and providing essential services, including information technology and supply and maintenance

5. *Emergency services*: Includes fire, rescue, emergency medical services, and law enforcement organizations

6. *Energy*: Includes electric power and the refining, storage, and distribution of oil and natural gas

7. *Food*: Covers the infrastructures involved in postharvest handling of the food supply, including processing and retail sales

8. *Government*: Ensures national security and freedom and administers key public functions

9. *Information technology and telecommunications*: Provides information processing systems, processes, and communications systems to meet the needs of businesses and government

10. *Postal and shipping*: Includes the U.S. Postal Service and other carriers that deliver private and commercial letters, packages, and bulk assets

11. *Public health and health care*: Consists of health departments, clinics, and hospitals

12. *Transportation*: Includes aviation, ships, rail, pipelines, highways, trucks, buses, and mass transit that are vital to our economy, mobility, and security

13. *Drinking water and water treatment systems*: Includes about 170,000 public water systems that rely on reservoirs, dams, wells, treatment facilities, pumping stations, and transmission lines

There are a number of cybersecurity technologies that can be used to better protect critical infrastructures from cyberattacks, including access control technologies, system integrity technologies, cryptography, audit and monitoring tools, and configuration management and assurance technologies. In each of these categories, many technologies are currently available, while other technologies are still being researched and developed. The following list summarizes some of the common cybersecurity technologies, categorized by the type of security control they offer:

1. *Access control*: Boundary protection firewall controls access to and from a network or computer.

2. *Content management*: Monitors Web and messaging applications for inappropriate content, including spam, banned file types, and proprietary information.

3. *Authentication biometrics*: Uses human characteristics, such as fingerprints, irises, and voices, to establish the identity of the user.

4. *Smart tokens*: Establish identity of users through an integrated circuit chip in a portable device such as a smart card or time-synchronized token.

5. *Authorization*: User rights and privileges. Allow or prevent access to data and systems and actions of users based on the established policies of an organization.

6. *System integrity*: Antivirus software provides protection against malicious code, such as viruses, worms, and Trojan horses.

7. *Integrity checkers*: Monitor alterations to files on a system that are considered critical to the organization.

8. *Cryptography*: Digital signatures and certificates use public-key cryptography to provide (1) assurance that both the sender and the recipient of a message or transaction will be uniquely identified, (2) assurance that the data have not been accidentally or deliberately altered, and (3) verifiable proof of the integrity and origin of the data.

9. *Virtual private networks*: Allow organizations or individuals in two or more physical locations to establish network connections over a shared or public network, such as the Internet, with functionality that is similar to that of a private network using cryptography.

10. *Intrusion detection systems*: Detect inappropriate, incorrect, or anomalous activity on a network or computer system.

11. *Intrusion prevention systems*: Build on intrusion detection systems to detect attacks on a network and take action to prevent them from being successful.

12. *Security event correlation tools*: Monitor and document actions on network devices and analyze the actions to determine if an attack is ongoing or has occurred. Enable an organization to determine if ongoing system activities are operating according to its security policy.

13. *Computer forensics tools*: Identify, preserve, extract, and document computer-based evidence.

Cybercrime Hitting the Internet of Things with Virus Rain

What Is Virus Rain?

We coined the term *Virus Rain* to describe a massive surprise attack hitting a targeted Smart City with a rain of vicious viruses. Another term that we coined in 2001 is the *Electronic Pearl Harbor*. It is like a rapid epidemic that spreads a large quantity of infectious diseases to a large number of people in a given population within a short period of time. The Virus Rain is a tsunami of thousands of stealth-active viruses ready to damage all the systems that control the critical infrastructures in any congested metropolitan areas, including smart cities.

How is the Virus Rain created? Figure 10.9 shows the global manufacturing of the Virus Rain. Many crime organizations collaborate and prepare the attack from different locations on the globe, which make it difficult to trace. In Chapter 13, we discuss the Electronic Pearl Harbor attack.

A hard look at the reality of things reveals that the Internet of Things has some real security concerns that need to be addressed. Cyberspace belongs to everyone, and no one owns it. All these wonderful emerging technologies including the Internet of Things do not have a formal custodian or an administrator that imposes governance and policy rules. Pervasive integration and this massive convergence of information, operational, and consumer technology ecosystems will transform the very nature of security risks. It will also open new opportunities for new breed of cyber thieves who will introduce new crime techniques and attacks that can have serious consequences on business

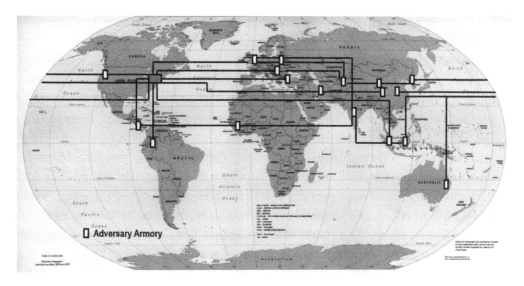

Figure 10.9 How the Virus Rain is launched against the northeastern region of the United States. Virus Rain is being packaged and assembled throughout the world from different adversary locations. Cyberterrorism comes in many different flavors. Basically, the Virus Rain is a massive cyber invasion from different fronts. It is the ultimate surprise attack with a huge variety of untraceable payloads.

operations, public health and safety, and consumer confidence. The convergence of technologies is already well under way, and connected devices will continue to proliferate and evolve in ways that are impossible to predict. So, too, will security risks. Organizations that want to get ahead of the convergence curve should take action now to formulate a strategic approach to integrated security, one that balances the security objectives unique to information, operation, and consumer technologies. This is easy to say. But here is the big problem: companies will hire consulting firms and spend hundreds and days at millions of dollars, preparing a security strategic plan. For what? It will not go anywhere. How could it be implemented? And what are the technologies that will be incorporated in the development of this plan? Planning a security plan is an excellent corporate exercise, but implementing the plan is very challenging and often it becomes outdated the moment it rolls out for production.

Security is a critical operating necessity that should be incorporated in the design of things. Unfortunately, security trailed behind innovation and the technology curve. The Department of Homeland Security (DHS) recently announced that a hacker group had successfully infiltrated a U.S. public utility, which is part of the critical infrastructures, via Internet *cyber tunnels*, and compromised its control system network. While no damage was done, the incident underscores the fact that threats to critical infrastructure providers are very real. They are also on the rise. In 2013, the DHS Industrial Control Systems Cyber Emergency Response Team (ICS-CERT) responded to 256 cyber incident reports, an increase of 86% over 2012.

And here is another example, consider, for instance, the introduction of consumer products and services in the health care industry. A new wave of implantable devices such as pacemakers and glucose monitors are being deployed to monitor and wire-lessly report patient health status to doctors and hospitals. Hackers have demonstrated that they can infiltrate these connected medical devices, a capability that could result in not only serious health and safety risks but also data-privacy concerns and legal exposure. These types of technologies have been deployed before their risks are fully understood, and only few health care providers are prepared to manage these risks.

The U.S. National Institute of Standards and Technology (NIST) has published a comprehensive cybersecurity framework (http://www.nist.gov/itl/csd/launch-cybersecurity-framework-021214.cfm) that aims to reduce cyber risks related to critical infrastructure. The framework provides risk-based cybersecurity guidelines that, while voluntary, will in effect set a standard for cybersecurity that may be used in legal and regulatory investigations. As a result, security organizations may need to adapt to new regulatory, compliance, and safety requirements. For many, operational and consumer technologies will be a particular challenge because organizations may not have a holistic understanding of threats and an integrated approach to manage risks.

Design of the Intelligent Grid, the New Digital Immunity

When the movie *The Terminator* was released in 1984, it was about a cyborg assassin pro-grammed to kill with his robotic emotionless might. The movie was apocalyptic and sin-ister because it shows how technology was gone haywire mastered by AI-actuated robots that looked human. The most fascinating feature in the movie was that the Terminators became indestructible and were able to spawn life autonomically in themselves. The movie leaves you in awe and suspense. The moral of the story is that cybercriminals are real ter-minators who are like programmed cyborgs who would like to control the cyber world.

The Smart Vaccine Grid (SVG) with its army of vaccinators and paramedics will protect the city's smart grid from cyber evil. SVG is powered with nondestructive residual memory leading to an enhanced response to subsequent attacks. The vaccina-tion mechanism is the kinetic energy that constantly keeps the critical components of the smart city protected from preempted and persistent attacks.

Albert Einstein once said, "We cannot solve our problems with the same think-ing we used when we created them. No problem can be solved from the same level of consciousness that created it. If I had an hour to solve a problem I'd spend 55 minutes thinking about the problem and 5 minutes thinking about solutions."

Einstein said it right. He had great power of causality reasoning and common sense. Antivirus Technology (AVT) vendors did not think out of the box. Cybertechnology is in its fourth generation and yet AVT traders are spinning in their own revolving doors. Cybercrime industry has leapfrogged AVT. The Darth Vaders of cybercrime can shake the world from its roots. To overcome the accelerating cybercrime, we need to outrun it with different thinking and skill set.

President Obama has said early on in his tenure as president, "It's the great irony of our information age, the very technologies that empower us to create and to build also empower those who would disrupt and destroy." But cyberterrorism is a giant force that no one could arm wrestle with. Conventional military hardware is futile.

There are two Critical success factors that need to be satisfied in order to win the battle against cyberterrorism. The first factor is to predict the time of attack. The second factor is initiate the attack with better fighting skills. In other words, imitate the approach of the Human Immune System's *defense by offense*. The Smart Vaccine replicates this approach, which gives it the upper hand in every battle.

The Smart Vaccine grid is equipped with a tremendous resilience and scalability. Its framework is reinforced with spectrum of technologies that dominates the twenty-first century: on-demand computing, autonomic computing, AI grid computing, Big Data computing, and cloud computing. To remove any confusion about overlapping terms, between the Smart Vaccine and the Smart Vaccine grid, the Smart Vaccine is the AI-based commander that manages all the vaccination and paramedic services to critical systems that are of the city's smart grid, while the Smart Vaccine grid is the grid that the Smart Vaccine uses to deliver its vaccination services. The Smart Vaccine resides on its SVG. The best analogy is the relationship of the locomotive and the rails. In this chapter, we will discuss the design of the SVG and how it works. The following are a list of the services performed Smart Vaccine grid:

- *Grid identification services*: Determine the destination grid and its content.
- *Alert services*: Created by the alert server commander and sent to CEWPS commander.
- *Smart Vaccine support*: It helps the Smart Vaccine commander locate infected systems.
- *Attack/virus services*: Collect information on the attack and nature of the pay-load (virus) used.
- *CEWPS services*: Dispatch the alert to the grid commander.
- *Grid directory services*: Prepares information about the system on the grid.
- *Grid broker services*: Determines the best route for the vaccination of the critical system.
- *Grid scheduler services*: Determines the best time to instantiate the vaccination services.
- *Grid state services*: Keep track of the state of vaccination services.
- *Grid vaccination services*: Instantiate vaccination services.
- *Grid documentation services*: After the vaccination to save the vaccination and the attack episode.

Panoramic View of How SVG Fights to Defeat Cyberattacks

Let's talk for a minute about the nature of the vaccination services.

It is a software component that communicates using pervasive, standard-based Web technologies including HTTP- and XML-based messaging. The vaccination services are available anywhere on the Smart Vaccine grid, and it can service any kind of critical system at any time.

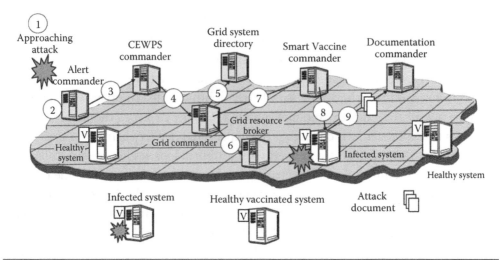

Figure 10.10 All critical systems are connected to City's Smart Grid and to the Smart Vaccine Grid. When the attack is already on the grid trying to infect systems, a convoy of SV paramedics and vaccinators rushes to the battlefield, and the fighting starts. Vaccinators go to work, and damage control is activated. The attacking virus is captured and destroyed before it mutates and multiplies. The SV commander is directing the battle and in constant communication with CEWPS and City Grid Commanders. Once the battle is over, it will be documented and stored in the Attack Knowledge Base.

Smart Vaccine services (SVS) are dynamic with its code reuse feature, which offers the positive side effect of vaccination services, interoperability, and flexibility. One service might be utilized by several systems that are working together to defeat the attack (Figure 10.10).

The Smart Vaccine grid will conduct the following services during an attack:

1. The approaching attacks have been noticed.
2. Tracked and analyzed by the early warning component of CEWPS.
3. The alert commander gives all the details to the Central Coordination Center (CCC).
4. The CEWPS commander relays all this information to the grid commander.
5. The grid commander queries the directory (registry) for the proper vaccination services.
6. The grid resource broker determines the right resources and the required services.
7. The information is dispatched to the Smart Vaccine commander for execution. All healthy systems on the grid also get vaccinated before they are hit with a distributed attack.
8. The Smart Vaccine commander instantiates the vaccination services at the infected system.
9. The details of the attack are being documented and sent to documentation commander who will store the episode at the knowledge engine.

CEWPS/Smart Vaccine was designed to protect grid-centric infrastructure critical systems. The grid has many topologies and designs. CEWPS cognitive Smart Vaccine grid was developed to offer, like the human body, quick response for all the systems on the grid. The focus in the Smart Vaccine grid is not system virtualization or computing ubiquity, or processing scalability or parallel processing. The Cognitive Smart Vaccine grid was solely designed to expedite the delivery of vaccination services to critical systems.

Digital Immunity Is the Holy Grail of Smart Cities

Take, for example, the following scenario: your finger accidently received a small cut by a rusty nail. There was some bleeding, which stopped with the help of some alcohol and iodine tincture. A couple of days later, you developed a stiff jaw, followed by a stiff neck, fever, and then muscular stiffness and spasms throughout the body. Other symptoms include difficulty in swallowing accompanied with headache and sluggish movement. The body goes into war and all defense armies (B cells) are mobilized, using the theme defense by offense, to eliminate the attacking germs (pathogens).

The nail was dirty and infected with tetanus bacteria. You vaguely remembered that a month ago you had taken a tetanus shot, which saved your life. The tetanus vaccine helped your white blood cells (B cells) to defeat the tetanus pathogen, and a few days later, you recovered. What really happened is a true biological miracle: the vaccine created fictitious battle (as an exercise) in the body, and the B cells developed the strength and knowledge to fight the tetanus bacteria. Our body's immune system would learn about the nail accident and an army of B cells and killer B cells would fight with better weapons and artillery (antibody) to bring victory to the body. Had our body did not have the immune system that memorized the tetanus shot, the bacteria would have multiplied and brought eminent death.

Now, let's assume that we installed CEWPS system and its Smart Vaccine grid in smart city loaded with hundreds of critical systems on its smart grid. Once we couple SVG with the city's smart grid, all these critical systems would be immunized with an army of aggressive Smart Vaccine. Digital Immunity took over and the city can sleep comfortably. All the city's critical systems would be monitored real time by SVG. If one of these critical systems, intentionally or unintentionally, suffered a backdoor worm attack (the detection system was sleeping on the job), then SVG would know about it and would issue an alert before the worm multiplies and infect the other critical systems.

Like in the human body, there would be a two-stage respond to the attack: the first stage is to *identify* the attacking virus, and the second stage is to learn the *anatomy* of the virus before it gets dismantled and its main parts would be saved for the next attack. The Smart Vaccine army would follow the same immunological response by isolating the infected system first; learn more about its attack vector, payload, and impact; and preserve its structure to build more robust vaccine for the next attack. The infected system was repaired, and it acquired a big dose of Digital Immunity.

Digital Immunity is the greatest paradigm shift. SVG is the immune system of smart cities. It is a contiguous living *superorganism* that we humbly call the Holy Grail of smart cities.

Figure 10.11 shows the systematic sequence of the vaccination services.

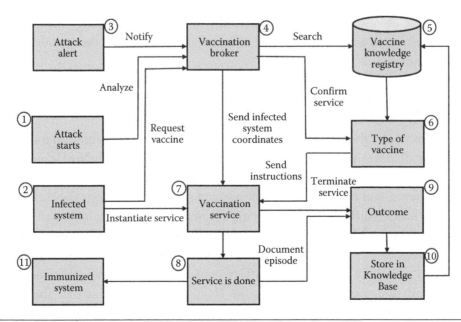

Figure 10.11 The systematic sequence activities starting with the attack, how it was recognized matched with the specific vaccine (antidote), followed by the vaccination treatment, and finally storing the attack episode in the Knowledge Base.

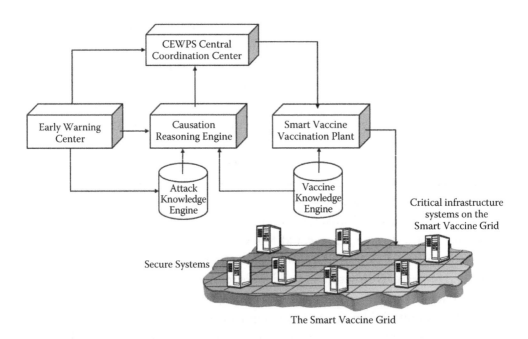

Figure 10.12 CEWPS represented as a manufacturing plant showing how all the engines work in sync to deliver Digital Immunity to infrastructure critical systems.

The SVG vaccination services are in fact part of the Web services family; we believe that VS are of industrial strength because they are cognitive and autonomic. It raised the technology bar of the Web services (Figure 10.12).

Glossary: SCADA System

Access control list: List of all access permissions for a particular resource.

Access protection: Measures that authorize or limit access to plant elements according to business and security aspects.

Antivirus software (virus scanners): A program for identifying and eliminating malware on computer-based systems and in networks.

Authentication: Process of verifying the identity of a user, process, or device. It is often a prerequisite for access to resources of an information system.

Authenticity: Genuineness of an object.

Authorization: Access right to system resources.

Backdoor: Covert, undocumented method for accessing a computer system. A backdoor is a potential security risk.

Bot: Short for *robot*; a program used for specific tasks, such as sending spam messages or sending an endless number of data packets in denial-of-service attacks.

Botnet: A large group of infected computers that can be used to mount coordinated attacks.

Boundary protection: A method for protecting an industrial control system (ICS) and for separating it from office IT systems and the Internet.

Bounds checking: Check to determine whether input parameters are within expected bounds. Helps to prevent buffer overflows.

Buffer overflow: If more data are transferred to an input interface than the input buffer holds, this may cause data in other areas to be overwritten. Attackers use this method to crash a system or to introduce malicious code and take control of the system.

Certificate revocation list (CRL): List of certificates that the certification authority classifies as no longer valid.

Certification authority (CA): Institution that is regarded by one or more users as trustworthy for creating and assigning public key certificates.

Computer Emergency Response Team (CERT): A group of IT security experts that evaluate current and potential security incidents and publish prompt warnings and countermeasures.

Configuration control: Monitoring of hardware, firmware, software, and documentation in order to protect the system from nonpermissible changes before, during, and after system implementation.

Control center: A central location according to ISA-99 from which a resource group is managed. Industrial infrastructures typically use one or more control centers to monitor and coordinate operation. In more complex plants, these are generally linked via a wide-area network (WAN). A control center includes the SCADA host computer, the associated operator displays, and auxiliary systems such as archive servers.

Control network: Security-critical networks that connect multiple control devices or operator control facilities of automation systems. A control network can be subdivided into multiple zones. At the same time, a company can have multiple control networks.

Control server: A server on which the overall control system is installed—typically, a commercially available application for a DCS or SCADA system.

Control system: A system for targeted specification of certain variables. Control systems include SCADA systems, DCS, PLC, and other forms of industrial instrumentation and controls.

Countermeasures: Actions, devices, procedures, or other measures that reduce the vulnerability of control systems.

Cyberattack: Malicious, unauthorized access to networks, computers, and controllers, the objective of which is to steal, modify, or delete data or manipulate processes.

Distributed control system (DCS): A control system whose distributed elements are connected for overall operation. Distributed process control systems are mostly used for continuous processes, such as oil refining, chemical production, and papermaking. However, they are also used in batch processes (manufacturing, packaging, and shipping of mechanical goods).

Defense in depth: Defense in depth is a graduated protection concept for computer networks. If one protection mechanism does not succeed, others can thwart the attack at another location.

Denial of service (DoS): The attempt to prevent authorized access to a resource or to limit the operability of a system.

Digital signature: A type of electronic signature that guarantees the identity of a person or device or the integrity of data.

Directory traversal: Directory traversal is a security gap that arises when invalid directory paths are input. While they typically occur with Web applications, all application types can be affected. Directory traversals result when an application uses external inputs to create a file or a directory name. If the application involved has not taken suitable precautions, protected content can be accessed by inputting control characters.

Demilitarized zone (DMZ): A demilitarized zone (DMZ)—also called a perimeter network—is a network area located between the network to be protected and an external network (usually the Internet). DMZs enable the configuration of a shell-type security model in which they act as intermediaries between the two networks. They guarantee secure transfer from a secure source to an unsecure destination or vice versa.

DNS cache poisoning: Manipulation of data of a domain name server so that users calling up one website are redirected to another fraudulent site.

Ethernet: The most commonly used LAN technology to combine multiple devices into a network.

Firewall: According to ISA-99, a firewall is an integral part of the connection between two networks and regulates the data communication between them. A firewall can be either an application installed on a suitable computer or a separate device that forward or rejects data packets in a network. It enables or blocks access to certain ports based on defined rules.

Fuzzing or fuzz testing: A test method for software that analyzes the input behavior using random data. This method attempts to run code by providing random parameters (so-called fuzz) outside the usual area. In this way, it is possible to identify points in the program code that do not correctly process input data outside the expected area.

Hacktivism: Politically or ideologically motivated vandalism, for example, in the form of manipulated websites.

Hardening: Security measures that reduce the number of possible attack points of a system.

Honeypots: Devices or techniques designed to detect and monitor malicious code and to track its activities in a secure environment.

ICS-CERT: The Industrial Control Systems Cyber Emergency Response Team (ICS-CERT) concentrates on security aspects of control systems. It collaborates closely with the US-CERT to analyze and respond to incidents that are relevant to control systems.

Identification: Verification of the identity of a user, process, or device; typically required for access to resources of an IT system.

Identity provider: Device that sets up, maintains, and manages identities.

Identity theft: Generating a false identity using stolen identification data (e.g., name, date of birth, address).

Incident: A situation that endangers confidentiality, integrity, or availability of data, systems, or security guidelines. These can be caused intentionally or by accident.

Incident response plan: A defined procedure for detecting, reacting to, and limiting the possible damage from cyberattacks.

Industrial automation and control system (IACS) or industrial control system (ICS): The combination of personnel, hardware, and software as a whole that can influence secure and reliable operation of industrial processes.

Industrial security: Industrial security describes measures to increase the industrial security standards of a plant for protection against cyberattacks and unauthorized access to overall control systems, industrial controls, and PC-based systems of the plant.

Information asset: Knowledge or data that are valuable to a company.

Information security: Guarantee of confidentiality, integrity, and availability of information.

Information security event: Identified system, service, or network incident that indicates a possible violation of information security or a loss of control.

Information security management system (ISMS): Part of the higher-level management system; the aim of which is to ensure information security in every respect.

Information security risk: Probability that a vulnerability in the IT infrastructure and plant infrastructure will be exploited and cause damage to the company.

Integrity (data integrity): The certainty that data have not been modified by unauthorized persons. Data integrity pertains to the storage, processing, and transport of data.

Intrusion detection system (IDS): A security function that monitors networks and systems and looks for unauthorized accesses in order to issue timely warnings.

Intrusion prevention system (IPS): A system that detects unauthorized intrusions and attempts to defend against them.

IPSec: Short for *IP security*; a group of protocols that were developed by the Internet Engineering Task Force for the purpose of supporting exchange of data packets at the IP level. IPSec is an essential component of VPN. It provides two types of encryption: transport and tunnel. The transport mode encrypts only the payload and not the header. The more secure tunnel mode encrypts both the header and the payload. At the receiving end, an IPSec-capable device encrypts every packet.

ISA-99: ISA-99 is an international committee that specifies cybersecurity standards.

IT security: Protection of nonphysical, computer-related goods such as software applications, process programs, and personnel data.

Key logger: Program for covert recording of keyboard inputs. It is used to intercept passwords.

Least privileges: The principle that authorizations for certain functions are only granted to those who actually need them. Thus, many users may be authorized to query a database without also being granted permission to delete entries.

Logic bomb: A malicious program that is executed only under certain conditions, for example, deletion of data records if the name of an employee is no longer listed on the payroll.

MAC address: A globally unique identification number for each network-capable device.

Malicious code: See *malware*.

Malware: A program that is installed covertly on a computer and that jeopardizes the confidentiality, integrity, and availability of data and applications on this computer.

Man-in-the-middle (MitM) attack: An attack on authentication processes in which the attacker is positioned between the requester and the authentication point, thus allowing the attacker to intercept and manipulate the data communication.

Network segmentation: Division of a network into subnets, each of which represents a network segment or network layer. Network segmentations can increase the performance and security of networks.

Password: A character string consisting of letters, numbers, and other symbols that a user uses to identify himself/herself or to gain access to a system.

Patch: Software used to eliminate known problems.

Patch management: Measures for providing, checking, and installing multiple patches on multiple computers.

Payload: Unauthorized activities of a malware.

Penetration test: Test of the vulnerability of computer systems using hacker tools.

Pharming: Redirection of data traffic from one website to another through interventions in the domain name system (e.g., as a result of DNS cache poisoning).

Phishing: The attempt to obtain confidential access information of a user. E-mails that appear to be authentic are used to lure users to a website where they are requested to enter their access data.

Port: The physical and/or logical interface of computers via which they communicate with other devices.

Port scanning: Automated examination of a computer with the goal of finding open ports and thus possible attack points.

Private key: A cryptographic key that is used in combination with a public key to decrypt and encrypt data. In contrast to the public key, the private key is kept secret.

Programmable logic controller (PLC): User-programmable controls—as opposed to hard-wired controls—that are used as the core for implementing industrial automation systems.

Protocol: A set of specifications (e.g., formats, procedures) that regulate the communication between devices.

Protocol analyzer: Software or a device that analyzes communication within a network in order to check its operability.

Public key: A cryptographic key that is used in combination with a private key to decrypt and encrypt data. In contrast to the private key, the public key is not kept secret.

Public key certificate: A data record that identifies a person or application uniquely. It contains the public key and is digitally signed by a trustworthy institution.

Public key infrastructure: A framework that enables issuing, managing, and revoking of public keys.

Role-based access control (RBAC): Role-based access control is one of certain functional roles, and thus, certain authorizations are assigned to the users of a computer or network.

Rootkit: A collection of programs that a hacker uses to disguise his attack and to obtain administrator rights for a computer or a network.

SCADA: Supervisory control and data acquisition; refers to the monitoring and controlling of technical processes using a computer system.

Scavenging: Searching discarded lists, source codes, and storage media for passwords and access information.

Security cells: The subdivision of an industrial network into individual, well-organized, and maintainable segments produces so-called secure automation cells. The cells are structured as logical segments based on spatial or functional aspects. They are protected with all required safety functions and operate fully autonomously. The data traffic and personnel traffic between the cells are subject to clearly defined controls and are monitored.

Security incident: One or more undesired and unexpected events that can interfere with company operation or jeopardize information security.

Security incident management: Procedures for detecting, announcing, and reacting to security incidents.

Social engineering: A nontechnical attack on the security structure. Attempt to obtain critical access data from employees through false pretenses.

Spoof: Forgery of an authorization for the purpose of executing unauthorized actions.

Spyware: Covertly installed software for collecting information about the user, the computer, or the associated company.

SQL injection: The attempt to gain control over a computer by transferring special characters to a SQL application on the computer.

Stuxnet: Stuxnet is a malware that appeared publicly for the first time in July 2010 and operates using zero-day exploits, stolen certificates, and other components. It attacks Windows PCs on which a particular Siemens automation software is installed. After successful infection of the PC, Stuxnet attempts to obtain information about the system and to download blocks of code to the PLC. Stuxnet is directed toward very specific plant configurations.

Trojan: A computer program that provides functions that appear to be useful but that also contains malicious functions, for example, utilization of the authorization of the calling system part.

Trusted channel: A secure communication channel for data communication between two security zones.

US-CERT: A project between the U.S. Department of Homeland Security and public and private institutions with the goal of protecting the Internet infrastructure of the United States. US-CERT coordinates the national defense against cyberattacks.

Virtual private network (VPN): An encrypted connection of computers or networks via the Internet. It enables exchange of confidential data over public networks.

Virus: Software with functions that are normally malicious and goal of which is to infect other programs or systems. Viruses typically require an interaction of the user to disseminate. This distinguishes the computer virus from the computer worm, which is able to disseminate on its own.

Wardriving: Systematic search for wireless access points in which a person drives past houses and buildings while using a notebook to scan for unsecured WLAN. The goal is to gain unauthorized access to a computer or a plant controller.

Whitelisting: A measure that uses a positive list to limit access to certain resources and to prevent execution of unknown programs. Its main purpose is to protect computers and networks from malware and to prevent unnecessary wasting of resources.

A whitelist lists all applications that are permitted to be executed by a user or administrator. Before an application is started, a check is made to determine if it is on the list. An integrity check (e.g., using hash codes) ensures that the application is in actuality the released application and not another program with the identical name.

Worm: A program that runs independently and can replicate itself in networks. Its dissemination ties up resources. Functionally speaking, worms may contain malicious code. It is typical for worms to have a more or less aggressive dissemination function that they can execute without a user.

Zero-day attacks: A zero-day attack is an attack that exploits previously unknown security gaps (so-called zero-day exploits).

Websites

http://blog.econocom.com/en/blog/smart-city-a-whole-ecosystem/ Smart City.
http://en.wikipedia.org/wiki/Siberian_pipeline_sabotage.
http://en.wikipedia.org/wiki/Stuxnet.
http://spectrum.ieee.org/telecom/security/the-real-story-of-stuxnet.
http://www.businessinsider.com/nsa-firing-sysdadmins-2013–8#ixzz3NKnwJLPV.
http://www.nist.gov/cyberframework/upload/cybersecurity-framework-021214-final.pdf.
http://www.symantec.com/connect/blogs/stuxnet-05-disrupting-uranium-processing-natanz.
http://www.wired.com/2011/07/how-digital-detectives-deciphered-stuxnet/7/ stuxnet great.

11

Convergence of SCADA, CEWPS Dashboard, and Predictive Analytics

SCADA & CEWPS: The Best Techno-Solution for Smart Cities

The challenging issues for SCADA systems and projects today are not the same as they were a few years ago. Today, there is much more importance placed on integration, use of new communication and network technologies, and of course, security against hacking and cyberterrorism. We are using the German SCADA Siemens (SIMATIC WinCC) in our examples because we are familiar with this system and we could explain its operation in simple terms. The SIMATIC WinCC (SIMATIC *stands for Siemens* and TIC *stands for Automatic*) system is a modified version of Microsoft Windows, customized to fit the industrial environment. WinCC is written for Microsoft Windows operating system. It uses a relational database engine and Microsoft SQL Server for logging, and some additional components written in VBScript and ANSI C, plus application programming interface (API) plugs to facilitate integration. It is an open system that accepts products from different vendors and different platforms.

The idea of coupling SCADA with CEWPS, as shown in Figure 11.1, would be a double-barrel solution for safer smart cities. With SIMATIC, Siemens could offer smart cities with a state-of-the-art system featuring a big variety of high-performance functions for monitoring automated processes with total production transparency.

The statement "success of smart city is in its smart grid" is not totally accurate, because a grid is smart if it satisfies two critical conditions. The first condition is to bundle the grid with a cognitive system to control the dynamics of every signal on the grid. SIMATIC WinCC would definitely be the best nerve center to maintain steady optimum grid operation. The second condition is to couple the smart grid with a cognitive security grid (layer) using the innovative concept of Digital Immunity (DI). The Cognitive Early Warning Predictive System (CEWPS) is the culmination of AI defense mechanism to put an end to cyber vandalism and hooliganism that are plaguing all systems around the world. Organized cybercrime starts with a small organization and proliferates throughout the Smart City. Traditional ant-killing bait stakes from your friendly AVT vendor does not work for smart city cyber violence. CEWPS is a different type of weapon that The Smart City could rely on. Immunizing

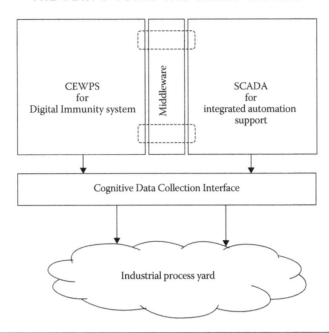

Figure 11.1   The loose coupling of CEWPS and SCADA offers a computing environment from the best of two worlds. The two systems are the state-of-the-art computing technology. The middleware slate is the medium that transfers messages and commands between the two systems. The industrial computers are connected to a multipurpose information bus that manages the traffic of collected data from the process and orchestrates the vaccination services.

the critical systems of smart city infrastructures is the most effective security shield, inspired by the two immunization pioneers Pasteur and Jenner. Combining the strength of CEWPS and SCADA will provide an incomparable immunity shield against any vicious attack on the City Smart Grid (CSG) empowered by the Smart Vaccine Grid (SVG), illustrated by Figure 11.2.

SCADA systems, by design, tie topographically several decentralized facilities such as power plants and stations, oil refineries, water distribution, and wastewater treatment systems. The move from proprietary *black box* technologies to a more open platform, has facilitated connectivity and interoperability with SCADA systems, office,

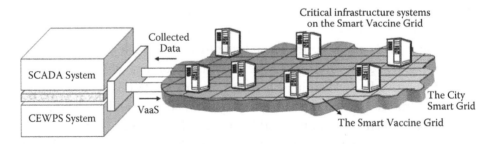

Figure 11.2   SCADA and CEWPS hybrid configuration. While SCADA is responsible for the data collection and process management, the CEWPS/Smart Vaccine makes sure that all critical systems are immunized and safe from any malware. The City Smart Grid (CSG) is coupled with the Smart Vaccine Grid (SVG). The SCADA collects the city's performance data for predictive analytics from the critical systems.

and the Internet, but unfortunately it makes SCADA a big attraction for cyberterrorism. The U.S. Computer Emergency Readiness Team (US-CERT) released a vulnerability advisory document cautioning users to observe strict access management. Consequently, the security of some SCADA-based systems has come into question as they are seen as potentially vulnerable to cyberattacks.

The creation of a hybrid *loosely coupled* SCADA/CEWPS configuration for the protection of smart cities would reinvent the concept of cybersecurity. Integrating human brainpower and knowledge in immunity and causality reasoning would bless smart cities with a cognitive and autonomic *secure sphere* ushering the acceptance of Digital Immunity. It would definitely make hackers think twice. CEWPS intelligent structure includes a reverse engineering engine that can dismantle any virus and reveal its genetics. Knowing thy enemy is the best way to defeat it. With the Internet of Things (IoT) becoming the new cyber fabric, the need for Digital Immunity could not be more timely and vital.

Merging SCADA and CEWPS

SCADA and CEWPS are two complementary systems that could easily achieve an optimum *economies of scale*. SCADA systems are in fact a special system designed with analog/digital conversion feature to manage, monitor, and collect process data from complex industrial plants, including those of manufacturing, production, power plants, and refineries. SCADA's umbrella also covers all public and private infrastructure processes.

CEWPS is a different creature with different purposes in life. First of all, it comes with highly trained commanders in counterattack and counterterrorism. The Early Warning Predictive System (EWPS) is like the RADAR of Air Traffic Control, built with great cognitive and reasoning power. The Smart Vaccine Commander (SVC) has an army of vaccinators (Smart Vaccine troops), an army of aggressive virus cannibals, an army of Smart Vaccine paramedics to repair the infected systems, and forensic agents to identify the anatomy of the attackers and their tools. CEWPS is equipped with smart knowledge engines to store battle episodes, a registry of attacks and viruses (Attack Knowledge Base), matched with a registry for all new and past vaccines ready for the next battle (Vaccine Knowledge Base). All CEWPS components are equipped with autonomic features, which include self-configuring, self-healing, self-navigating, and self-protecting. The vaccination team follows the orders of the Smart Vaccine Commander.

Both SCADA and CEWPS communicate with each other in real-time mode. They have their own dashboards, displaying interactively common information from each other. Let me put it this way: SCADA controls the process and CEWPS secures SCADA.

Anatomy of the CEWPS Dashboard

The dashboard is considered a cognitive *magnifying glass* that stretches our span of control over the performance of the system. CEWPS dashboard comes with two modes.

The first mode is the real-time visualization section, which displays immediate information about the critical system. The second mode shows temporal *historical* data, trends, and variances against preset thresholds.

Mode 1: Real-Time Visualization Dashboard

The CEWPS real-time dashboard (CRD) is the most efficient way to check the pulse of the system. The dashboard is located at the Central Coordination Center and administered by authorized personnel only.

The "touch screen" dashboard allow administrators to modify dynamically necessary to adjust key operational variables. The dashboard is refreshed dynamically with incoming real-time data from the real world. Figure 11.3 shows the main screen of the dashboard. CRD will also give you the ability to interrogate the system to make sure the readings are right. Sophisticated attacks could hijack the dashboard or internally modify the data while the screen indicates normal operation.

The dashboard is a live window: The intelligence of CEWPS is reflected in all the components including the dashboard. The cognitive features in the system can detect any abnormal situations, particularly if any of the critical systems on the grid is getting compromised. Since the system is fully autonomic, it has the cognitive ability to locate an attack on the grid, correct the incoming data to the dashboard back to the preset parameters, and alert the administrators. Autonomic computing in CEWPS is not an option but the main ingredient which was incorporated in all the smart systems, particularly in the early warning prediction and the vaccination mission.

The Cognitive Early Warning Predictive System

The Dynamic Dashboard Main Menu

Monday, January 05, 2015 10:04:05 AM

User ID   Password

Grid Activities	Smart Vaccine Performance
Critical System Parameters	Vaccination Services
Attack Status	Attack Forecasts
Early Warning Alerts	CEWPS Utilization
Reverse Engineering	Attack Forecasts
Payload Analysis	Reporting Systems
Historical Reports	Knowledge Engines

Exit   Main Menu

Figure 11.3 The main dashboard of CEWPS: It is fully autonomic and located at the Central Coordination Center (CCC). All CEWPS screens are touch screens, and the fields (buttons) can be moved around to the taste of the administrator, who can add new functions (buttons) if needed.

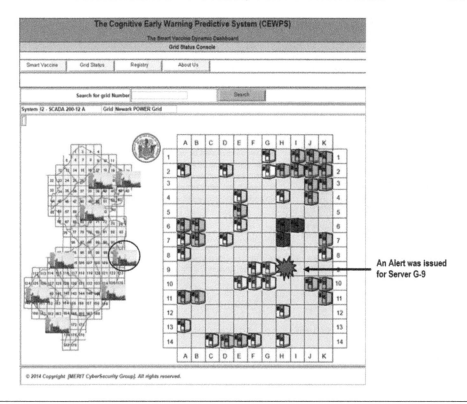

Figure 11.4 The state of New Jersey as represented in a critical infrastructure smart grid. The power grid computers for the metropolitan areas of Jersey City, Newark, Trenton, Atlantic City, and Camden are shown. These areas are the most critical areas for CEWPS to secure. A blinking alert was issued for G-9. The cognitive system will show the cause and the recommended action.

The Smart Vaccine Grid: Figure 11.4 shows one of the interesting features of CEWPS. The real-time screen shows the Smart Vaccine Grid (SVG) covering the whole region. In this example, we took the state of New Jersey (shown on the left of the screen). Every critical system is recognized by its coordinates. If a specific server, say, G-9 (right side of the screen), starts to blink, then the administrator can click on it and a blowout screen will come up showing the details of the server and what causes the blinking. Action will be taken immediately.

The quick response: Now, the Early Warning Predictive (EWP) system tries to locate the origin of the attack and checks with the Honeynet if the attack tried to penetrate the trap. The EWP activates heavy-duty tracking systems to find out more about the attack vector and its payload. EWE will activate a series of queries to the Virus Knowledge Base (ViKB) to get more information on the virus. Also, a request was instantiated to query the Vaccine Knowledge Base (VaKB) for the proper vaccine. Another request was instantiated to query the Documentation Knowledge Base (DKB) to select matching attack episodes.

Figure 11.5 shows an alert status screen giving the operator additional information. CEWPS responds quickly and the Smart Vaccine Commander takes charge.

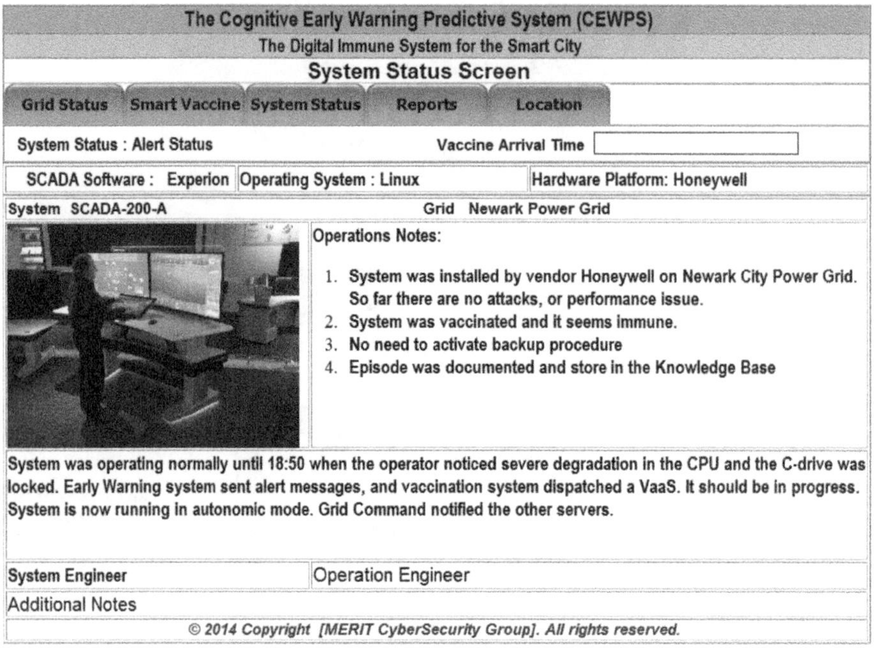
The Cognitive Early Warning Predictive System (CEWPS)
The Digital Immune System for the Smart City
System Status Screen
Grid Status
Smart Vaccine
System Status
Reports
Location
System Status : Alert Status
Vaccine Arrival Time
SCADA Software : Experion
Operating System : Linux
Hardware Platform: Honeywell
System SCADA-200-A
Grid Newark Power Grid
Operations Notes:
1. System was installed by vendor Honeywell on Newark City Power Grid. So far there are no attacks, or performance issue.
2. System was vaccinated and it seems immune.
3. No need to activate backup procedure
4. Episode was documented and store in the Knowledge Base
System was operating normally until 18:50 when the operator noticed severe degradation in the CPU and the C-drive was locked. Early Warning system sent alert messages, and vaccination system dispatched a VaaS. It should be in progress. System is now running in autonomic mode. Grid Command notified the other servers.
System Engineer
Operation Engineer
Additional Notes
© 2014 Copyright [MERIT CyberSecurity Group]. All rights reserved.

Figure 11.5 The alert screen coming alive. Response will become fully autonomic and will trigger a family of predefined workflows to help the operator supervise the autonomic operations in case an override becomes necessary.

Critical System Parameters: The main dashboard has several screens that allow the administrator to see the key performance indicators (KPI) of the critical systems on the grid, before he can evaluate the situation and take necessary action. The KPI indicate the performance of the system in normal situation, the safety threshold, the workload, and the utilization of the resources.

CEWPS real-time operating features show the "live" readings of every section of the system. Here is the list of the critical parameters that have to be watched and regulated if necessary:

- Utilization of channel between SCADA systems on the grid and CEWPS
- Number of SCADA performance readings sent to CEWPS
- CEWPS readings
- Utilization of the Vaccine Knowledge Engine
- Utilization of the Virus Knowledge Engine
- Number of the attack documents stored
- Number of Smart Vaccine vaccination services per hour
- Average turnaround time of the vaccination service
- Average turnaround time of the vaccine fabrication time
- Average turnaround time of reverse-engineered attack
- CEWPS information exchange with other smart city systems
- Number of attack attempts per hour
- Number of early warning alerts per hour

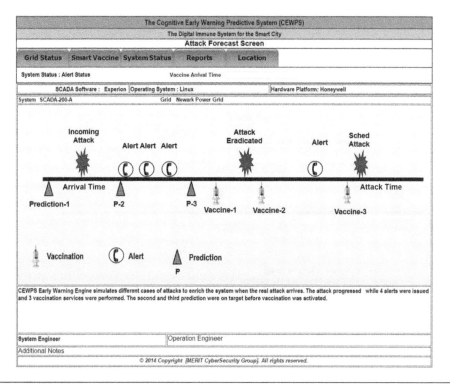

Figure 11.6 This screen shows exactly what happens in the vaccination battlefield: Prediction-1 said the attack is coming. Prediction-2 was triggered and succeeded with three alerts. The Smart Vaccine did not respond. Prediction-3 was instantiated and the Smart Vaccine started its vaccination services. When the attack arrived to the grid, it was eradicated. The attack was supposed to unleash its payload, but successive vaccinations and another alert did help. The attack was memorized and saved in the Document Knowledge Base (DKB).

- Number of analyzed attacks
- Number of reverse-engineered viruses
- Number of successful attacks on the grid

Attack Status: One of the unique screens of CEWPS (Figure 11.6) shows how a virus is attempting to penetrate a system and how the Early-Earning Engine is predicting the arrival time. Simultaneously, alarms go off and vaccinators are ready to inoculate the system. It is a tug-of-war scene. The attack is never materialized. The first three alerts were timely, and the attack was eradicated. The scheduled attack is never materialized. The Smart Vaccine Commander dispatches the vaccination service on time, Vaccine-1 missed the attack, but it was attacked by Vaccine-2. No system could watch the battle field real time from the headquarters (CCC) like this one!

Early Warning Alerts: The big challenge in the world is to see the future. In the world of cyberattacks, we try to eliminate any attack before it spills its payload and creates its planned pervasive devastation. Earlier, we mentioned the formula of defeating the attacker, which is as follows:

- *First condition*: Know the attacker's weapons and time of attack
- *Second condition*: Have better weapons and higher skills

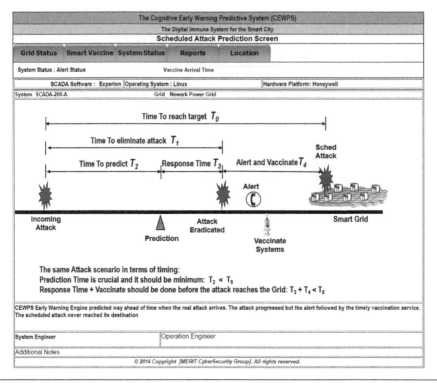

Figure 11.7   The uniqueness of CEWPS comes in its accurate prediction. As soon as the virus reaches the grid, the Smart Vaccine army will be ready to protect the critical system. The cognitive Smart Vaccine Grid (SVG) is of paramount importance in the victory.

If we apply it to cyberattack, our formula becomes as follows:

- *Know the Arrival Time of the Virus to the Grid*: This is a very difficult task to accomplish, as we resort to forsaking prior attack data. The time the alert was broadcast gives us a good estimate of the arrival of the virus to the grid.
- *Get the Smart Vaccine army ready for the fight*: We can assume the worst case when the captured virus had already created its own clones and they are on the grid. The Smart Vaccine had already vaccinated all the systems, and the army, the paramedics, and the virus killers have been mobilized and are prepared for the virus clones to show up (Figure 11.7).

The main dashboard at the Central Coordination Center (CCC) has a chain of dynamic screens to check the pulse of the grids. Figures 11.8 and 11.9, for example, show the grid elements, location by coordinates, type of system, the industry, criticality, the customer base, and the present and maximum load (the red zone) that can be handled.

> *Status of the Reverse Engineering Module*: This is one of the most sophisticated components of CEWPS. It functions like the medical MRI to show how the malware software was intended to work. CEWPS is equipped with a versatile debugger and an interactive disassembler to decompose the attack and rebuild

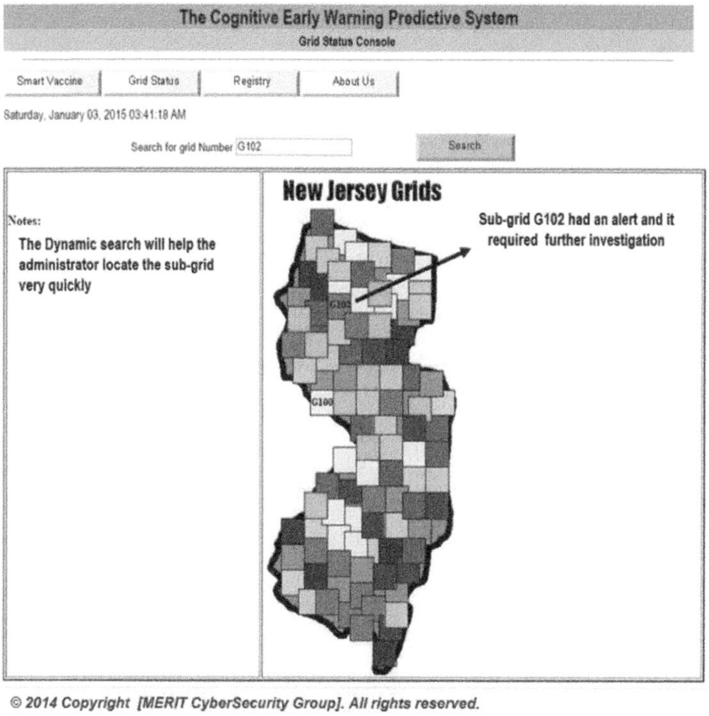

Figure 11.8 In order to use CEWPS and its Smart Vaccine Grid, we need to establish the grid first. Then we need to identify all the critical systems by coordinates in the region (in this case we selected the state of New Jersey). Then we need to store the characteristics of each system: the industry, the risk involved, and its contingency plan. A review of its past history is also valuable.

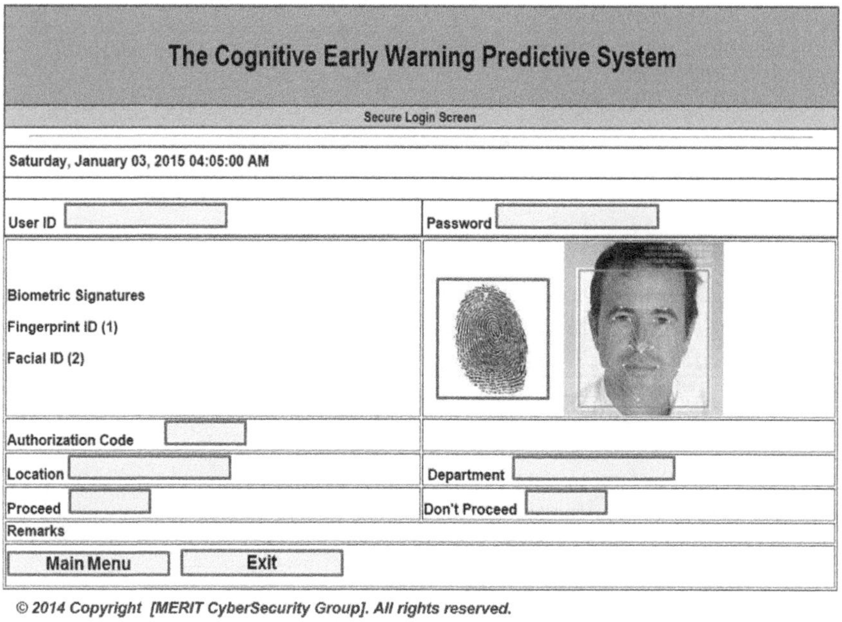

Figure 11.9 Screen-1 CEWPS is equipped with advanced biometric component for secure login to authorize and authenticate users and system administrators. All users have to be in the active user registry.

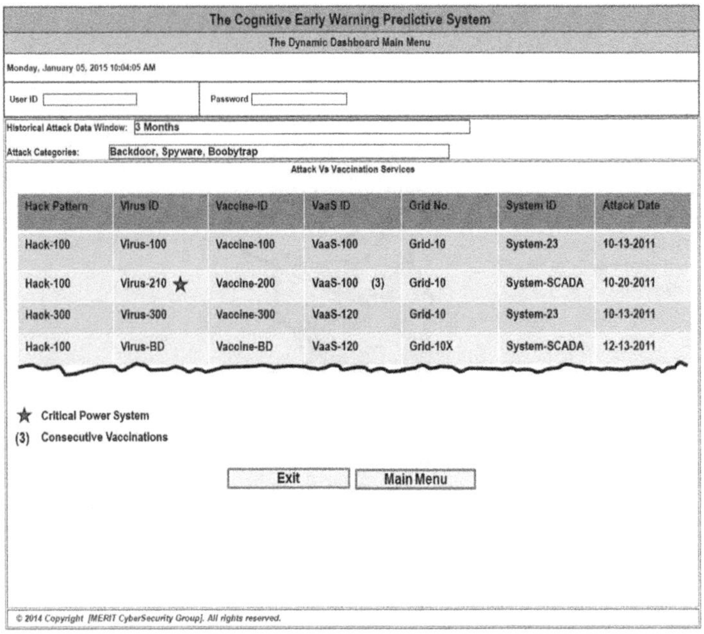
The Cognitive Early Warning Predictive System
The Dynamic Dashboard Main Menu
Monday, January 05, 2015 10:04:05 AM
User ID | Password
Historical Attack Data Window: 3 Months
Attack Categories: Backdoor, Spyware, Boobytrap
Attack Vs Vaccination Services

Hack Pattern	Virus ID	Vaccine-ID	VaaS ID	Grid No	System ID	Attack Date
Hack-100	Virus-100	Vaccine-100	VaaS-100	Grid-10	System-23	10-13-2011
Hack-100	Virus-210 ★	Vaccine-200	VaaS-100 (3)	Grid-10	System-SCADA	10-20-2011
Hack-300	Virus-300	Vaccine-300	VaaS-120	Grid-10	System-23	10-13-2011
Hack-100	Virus-BD	Vaccine-BD	VaaS-120	Grid-10X	System-SCADA	12-13-2011

★ Critical Power System
(3) Consecutive Vaccinations
Exit | Main Menu

Figure 11.10 The Early Warning Engine is equipped with an online analytical processor (OLAP), a data-mining engine that generates analytical reports on vaccination services, and predictive reports for future viral attacks. Some of these soft reports are self-generated.

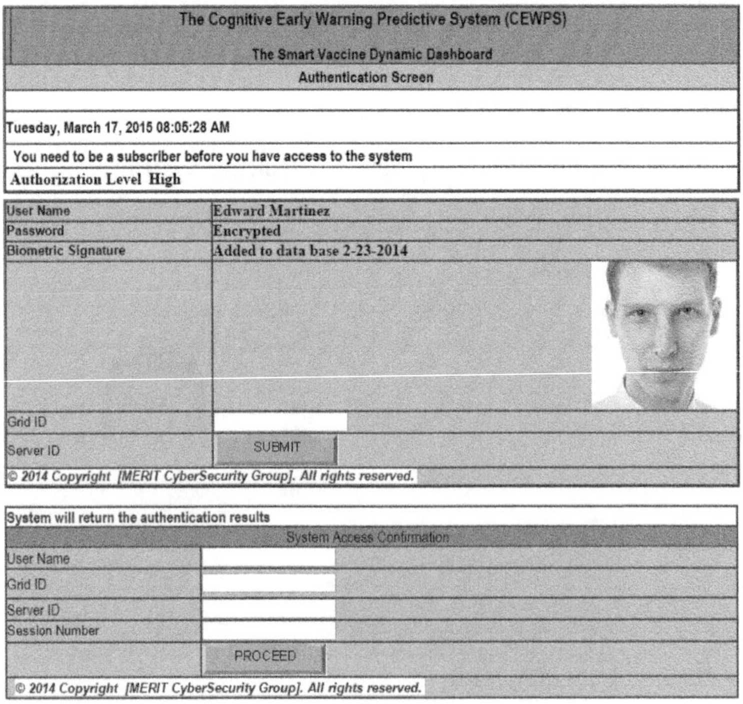
The Cognitive Early Warning Predictive System (CEWPS)
The Smart Vaccine Dynamic Dashboard
Authentication Screen
Tuesday, March 17, 2015 08:05:28 AM
You need to be a subscriber before you have access to the system
Authorization Level High
User Name: Edward Martinez
Password: Encrypted
Biometric Signature: Added to data base 2-23-2014
Grid ID
Server ID
SUBMIT

System will return the authentication results
System Access Confirmation
User Name
Grid ID
Server ID
Session Number
PROCEED
© 2014 Copyright [MERIT CyberSecurity Group]. All rights reserved.

Figure 11.11 Screen-2 CEWPS takes security very seriously. The system people of the city's system could access some of the CEWPS screens. They have to be authorized and then authenticated, in this order, and reviewed frequently by the Central Coordination Center (CCC).

the matching vaccine. A whole book could be written on this subject. That is why this module was designed by a team of reverse engineers.

Analysis of the Attack Payload: This is one of the most challenging parts of computer science. It is comparable to defusing a bomb. It requires specialized experience in binary and assembly languages. The reverse engineers use very sophisticated tools such as interactive disassembler (IDA), which generates assembly language source code from machine-executable code. Also, OllyDbg is heavily used by our CEWPS reverse engineering team, which is an x86 debugger that emphasizes binary code analysis. It is often the primary tool because of its ease of use and availability.

Virus Analysis: This information is vital for the fabrication of the matching vaccine. Again, it is like in the human body, no vaccine could be built without knowing the structure of the virus code. Some virus code runs very low down to the operating system level and building a matching vaccine would be very challenging. It would get very problematic if the attacking virus modified the operating system (since now Windows become open code and available to programmers).

Once the virus structure is known, it will be documented and stored in the Virus Knowledge Engine (ViKE) for future referral. Similarly, the matched vaccine would also be documented and stored in the Vaccine Knowledge Engine (VaKE).

Access Control and Management: For a complex system such as CEWPS, Access Control and Management is an operating necessity. Cyberterrorists and professional hackers will test their skills by trying to penetrate through the Smart Vaccine Grid to the city's smart grid and compromise some of the critical systems. CEWPS designers instituted a strict Access control & Management systems to perform authorization identification, authentication, access approval, and accountability of entities through login credentials including passwords, personal identification numbers (PINs), biometric scans, and physical or electronic keys. AI technologies were used to add a cognitive layer to the security system. All CEWPS users credentials are stored in the User Registry. Figure 11.9 through 11.11 shows some access screens.

Vaccination Services: This is another form of useful information that tells the administrator the activities of the vaccination services that are being serviced at the time of the display. CEWPS Central Coordination Center (CCC) is the traffic control tower of the Smart Vaccine Grid (SVG). The dashboard reflects the real-time logistics and status of each vaccination service (routine and emergency). A real-time snapshot screen is shown in Figure 11.12.

Attack Forecasts: The main principle of forecasting is to find the model that will produce the best attack forecasts. We rely on historical attack episodes to acquire complementary knowledge. We copied this concept from the Human Immune System that collects previous body attack. Once the patient is immunized, the body know the identity of the pathogen and the corresponding antidote. One of the most versatile components of CEWPS is its Reasoning Engine. It is a

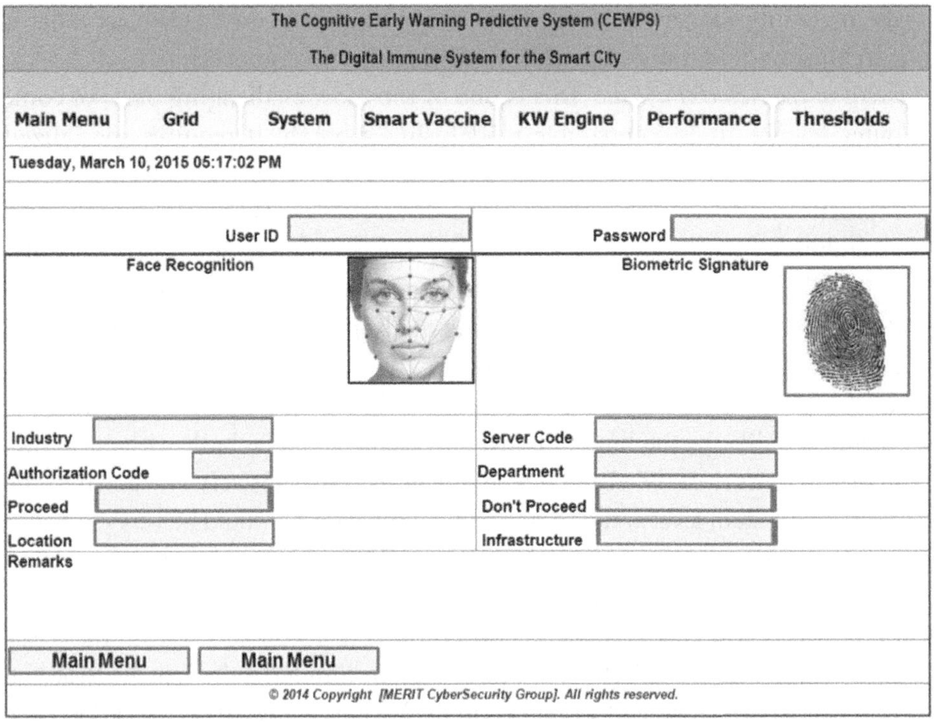

Figure 11.12 Screen-3 All users of the Smart City critical systems have been registered and fingerprinted with their images in the city's employee register (revised weekly). The position of the user dictates the authorization level. Users have to be authenticated before they can access the system.

formidable predictor and causality model that calculates the discovery of attack causes. Prediction follows common sense. If historical data of (a priori) previous attacks were retrieved from the Attack Knowledge Base (AKB), and if a relationship is established with joint and conditional probabilities among these past attacks, then the Reasoning Engine with predefined logic rules could generate a reasonable forecast for similar future (posteriori) attacks.

Mode 2: Smart City Predictive Analytics Dashboards

In this mode, we show the Predictive Analytics reports for the Smart City. Again, we calculate the probabilities of incoming attacks and their impacts on the critical systems. Predictive Analytics reviews the past and the present attack data and extend it to the future. The Inference Engine applies predefined logical rules to the data and deduces new knowledge as shown in Figure 11.13.

CEWPS Performance

We track CEWPS performance, as a system, and make sure that the major components are operating without degradation, and determine the bottlenecks. Also, we

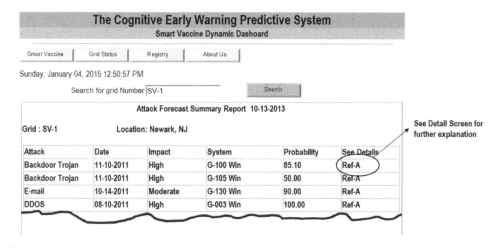

Figure 11.13 Einstein said once "The only source of knowledge is experience." Prediction is the science of extracting future virtual realities from current and historical facts. CEWPS stores current and historical attacks, which make prediction feasible (not necessity optimum). In this screen, we have four predictions with one showing 100% probability that an attack will occur soon. The attack hit the city grid after 6 hours, but alerts and vaccination services nullified the DDOS.

need to look at the capacity planning that evaluates if the system can handle the future growth. We know that the smart grid is going to have more systems attached to it, and the city has to provide the growth data in order to produce a credible capacity plan.

Attacks: The Documentation Knowledge Base has all the historical episodes, and the system can generate a report showing the most frequent attacks on the grid. It also shows the type of payload, attack vectors, and the time of attack and how long it took. These are very significant information about the profile of the attacks on the grid.

Viruses: A detailed analysis on the profile of the viruses, the forensics' report, the code, and the strategy are involved in the attack.

Vaccines: Like the profile of the attacks, this information is the detailed analysis on the type of vaccine used for a particular attack, the time to produce the vaccine, how the Smart Vaccine commander is handling the vaccination, and all the data relevant to the vaccination itself, as shown in Figures 11.14 and 11.15.

Smart City Predictive Analytics

No one has the ability to capture and analyze data from the future. However, there is a way to predict the future using the data from the past. It is called Predictive Analytics, and organizations do it every day.

Predictive Analytics is the process of using a set of sophisticated analytic tools to develop predictive models and estimations of what the environment will do in the future. Predictive Analytics for The Smart City differs from PA for the smart grid, which also differs from the PA of CEWPS.

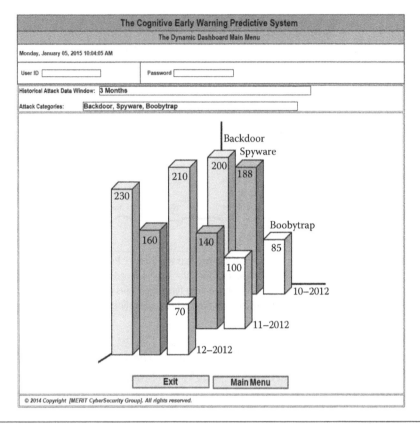

Figure 11.14　CEWPS also generates a large variety of graphical reports and pie charts from all the Knowledge Bases. The city examines these reports and studies the risks involved, and then takes action.

The following are three primary categories of concern in conducting PA for The Smart City:

Category 1: Systems

City Smart Grid: The backbone of the city. Its incremental growth with the infrastructures, IoT workload, the city smart cloud.

CEWPS: Performance in the next 2 years. Reliability of the hardware and the software component. Capacity planning to make sure CEWPS can handle the workload. Interfacing with SCADA systems.

Vaccine Smart Grid (VSG): This is the backbone of CEWPS in managing the logistics of vaccination services. The response time to complete the VaaS. The performance of the paramedics in repairing the infected servers. Any bottlenecks while interfacing with the city smart grid (CSG). What is the saturation limit of the grid?

SCADA Systems: It is not the responsibility of CEWPS. However, the Smart Vaccine protects the communication links.

City Smart Cloud (CSC): Future scalability and performance during the VaaS. Any degradation areas that need to be monitored.

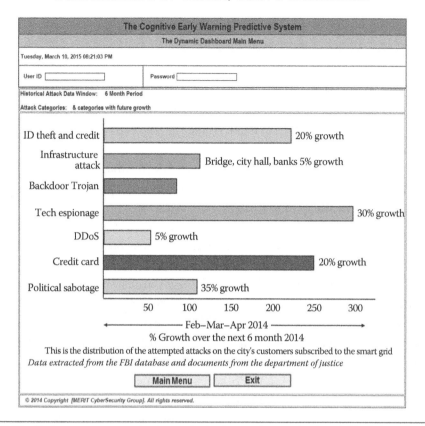

Figure 11.15   Performance management and capacity planning were two prominent specialties that saved enterprises' computing operating costs. The same techniques apply to malware prediction. Data mining is another valuable technique incorporated in the early warning subsystem. The city commander can learn a lot from this screen.

Category 2: People

Growth of the Subscribers: They are the customers of the city grid, and one of the PA objectives is to gauge the affinity of customers toward being *connected* to the grid or to the cloud. It is one of the most critical metrics. Also, customer growth influences the traffic on the grid, which requires close performance management.

People Preferences: The Internet of Things is in full swing. Machine to machine is a great convenience to the populace. ABI research predicts that a holistic migration of people to infrastructure is the new wave. Research companies are rigging fancy estimates of PA that more than 30 billion devices will be wirelessly connected to the Internet of Things by 2020. A study done by Pew Research Internet Project has also an eye-popping survey: "a large majority of the technology experts and heavy Internet users who responded—83%—agreed that the Internet/Cloud of Things, embedded and wearable computing will proliferate and reap beneficial effects by 2025!"

Power Consumption Growth: A very critical metric that needs a thorough predictive analysis. Obviously, this *sheep dip* into the cybersphere-of-everything will create a tremendous strain on utility companies. Blackout is the bugaboo that makes the utility companies sweat a lot. The smart grid is smart enough to buffer high spikes of power consumption.

Category 3: Predictive Analytics for Attacks

Attack Distributions: Once the vaccine smart grid is in full operation, the Attack Knowledge Engine (AKE) can determine the necessary statistics on the types of the grid attacks.

Attack Duration: AKE stores all the past (a priori) attack episodes. Queuing mathematical models (we have some samples in Chapter 9) can predict the times of attacks and early warnings.

Attack Growth: Adding more infrastructure nodes (critical systems) to city's smart grid will correlate with the growth of attacks on vulnerable systems in terms of frequency and sophistication.

Attack Impact: Attack impact (financial damages and system breakdowns) correlates with the growth of attacks. A very scary metrics.

Areas Most Damaged: The city smart grid will keep statistics on the city areas where damage was noticeable in terms of confusion and car gridlocks and delayed public transportation.

Smart Vaccine Performance: CEWPS keeps real-time data on the status of vaccination services and how the Smart Vaccine commander is managing to protect the critical system and the treatment of the attacked systems. All the statistics are available in the Vaccine Knowledge Engine.

Virus and Vaccine Distribution: Along with the performance of the vaccination service, CEWPS keeps real-time statistics on the types of attacks and how on the response of the Smart Vaccine.

Websites

http://www.fbi.gov/about-us/investigate/cyber.
http://www.fbi.gov/about-us/cjis/ncic.
http://www.fbi.gov/about-us/investigate/cyber/ncijtf.
http://hackmageddon.com/tag/denial-of-service-attack/.
http://www.pcmag.com/article2/0,2817,2372364,00.asp?obref=obnetwork.
http://www.state.nj.us/nj/safety/.

12

CEWPS KNOWLEDGE ENGINES

Introduction to Causal Discovery and Bayesian Networks

Democritus once said that he would rather discover a single cause than be the king of Persia "Beyond such discarded fundamentals as 'matter' and 'force' lies still another fetish amidst the inscrutable arcana of modern science, namely the category of cause and effect."

The Cognitive Early Warning Predictive System is equipped with four knowledge engines that support the causal Reasoning Engine that is based on Bayesian network model as shown in Figure 12.1.

A simplistic analogy may help jump-start our introduction to Bayesian networks: in the same way, one can use a phone book, without having to memorize all the names and numbers, and one can deliberately (and correctly) reason with the domain knowledge contained in a Bayesian network, without having to become a domain expert.

Over the past 25 years, Bayesian networks have emerged as a practically feasible form of knowledge representation, primarily through the seminal works of UCLA Professor Judea Pearl. With the ever-increasing computing power, Bayesian networks are now a powerful tool for deep understanding of very complex, high-dimensional problem domains. Their computational efficiency and inherently visual structure make Bayesian networks attractive for exploring and explaining complex problems.

However, Bayesian networks are somewhat of a disruptive technology, as they challenge a number of common practices in the world of business and science. So, beyond the world of academia, promoting Bayesian networks as a new tool for practical knowledge management and reasoning still requires significant persuasion efforts. In the opinion of many AI researchers, Bayesian Network (BN) is the most significant contribution in AI in the past 10 years. They are used in many applications, for example, spam filtering, speech recognition, robotics, diagnostic systems, and even syndromic surveillance. The key benefits of Bayesian networks in prediction attacks are threefold:

1. Knowledge unification
2. Knowledge representation and communication
3. Reasoning the occurrence of the attack

Short Course in Probability as Related to Predicting Incoming Cyberattacks

A probability is a number between 0 and 1 (including both) that represents a degree of belief in a fact or prediction. The *value 1 represents certainty that a fact is true* or that a

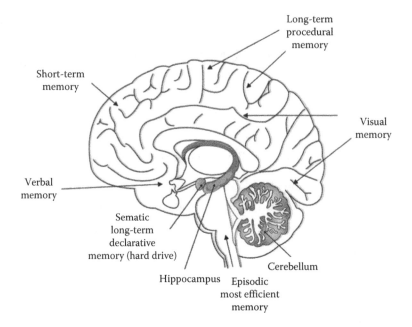

Figure 12.1 Associative memory puts it all together. "Green" means "go," but what does "red" mean? Just about everybody says "stop." Traditional memory stores data at a unique address and can recall the data upon presentation of the complete unique address. Associative memories are capable of retrieving a piece of data upon presentation of only partial information from that piece of data. They are used in AI and CEWPS.

prediction will come true. The *value 0 represents certainty that the fact is false. The value 0.5 means that a predicted outcome is as likely to happen as not.*

Conditional Probability is a probability based on some background information. This is the reason CEWPS collects historical attack episode, so they can be used for future attack forecasts.

p(Attack A|Damage B): denotes the conditional probability of an Attack A occurring, given that Damage B has already occurred.

Conjoint Probability is the probability that two things occurred at the same time. I write p(Attack A and Attack B) to mean the probability that Attack A and Attack B by accident occurred at the same time. But Attack A and Attack B are not connected to each other.

But this formula p(Attack A and Attack B) only works because in this case Attack A and Attack B are independent; that is, knowing the outcome of the first Attack A does not change the probability of the second Attack B. Or, more formally, $p(B|A) = p(B)$.

Bayes' Theorem

At this point, we have everything we need to derive Bayes' theorem. We will start with the observation that conjunction is commutative, that is,

$$p(\text{Attack } A \text{ and Attack } B) = p(\text{Attack } B \text{ and Attack } A)$$

for any Attack *A* and Attack *B*. Next, we write the probability of a conjunction:

$$p(\text{Attack } A \text{ and Attack } B) = p(\text{Attack } A) \, p(\text{Attack } B | \text{Attack } A)$$

If we do not know anything about the nature of Attack *A* and Attack *B*, then we can say they are interchangeable. Interchanging them yields

$$p(\text{Attack } B \text{ and Attack } A) = p(\text{Attack } B) \, p(\text{Attack } A | \text{Attack } B)$$

If I need to know the probability of Attack *A* and Attack *B* occurring at the same time, then it is equal to the probability of Attack *B*—in the future multiplied by the probability of Attack *A*—from the past & Attack *B*

$$p(\text{Attack } A \text{ and Attack } B) = \frac{p(\text{Attack } A) \, p(\text{Attack } B \text{ and Attack } A)}{p(\text{Attack } B)}$$

And that is Bayes' theorem! It might not look like much, but it turns out to be surprisingly powerful.

CEWPS Works Like a Brain

Generally speaking, an expert system is an artificial intelligence (AI) computer program designed to hold the accumulated knowledge in a specialized domain. The human brain holds information in the form of electrochemical and electrical impressions. Researchers have been able to trace memory down to the structural and even the molecular level in recent years, showing that memories are stored throughout many brain structures in the connections between neurons and can even depend on a single molecule for their long-term stability.

There are three basic types of memory:

1. *Very-Short-Term Memory* (*the sensory register*): This comes in visual and auditory blips. We receive brief glimpses (1–2 seconds visually, may be 3–4 seconds aurally) of experiences, like looking out a window then shutting your eyes and seeing the brief *afterimag*e of the *window. Neurons are firing very quickly to capture the experience.*

2. *Short-Term Memory* (*working memory*): This is the memory that you are aware of and can retrieve rather quickly. A helpful computer analogy is the term random-access memory (RAM), a limited form of memory that runs the programs of thinking and imagining—which is unlike accessing the hard drive.

3. *Long-Term Memory* (*the hard drive*): Those experiences and associations of experiences that we have been exposed to over the course of our lives make up long-term memory (especially 2–5 or more years and the early, impressionable years of our lives). Repeated experiences strengthen the neural pathways by developing more sensitive cell receptors; this process is known as *long-term potentiation*. There are two types of long-term memory—declarative and procedural (Figure 12.1).

The hippocampus takes simultaneous memories from different sensory regions of the brain and connects them into a single *episode* of memory, for example, you may have one memory of a dinner party rather than multiple separate memories of how the party looked, sounded, and smelled. As memories are played through the hippocampus, the connections between the neurons associated with a memory eventually become a fixed combination, so that if you hear a piece of music, for example, you are likely to be flooded with other memories you associate with a certain episode where you heard that same music.

In a brain scan, scientists see these different regions of the brain light up when someone is recalling an episode of memory, demonstrating how memories represent an index of these different recorded sensations and thoughts. The hippocampus helps solidify the pattern of connections that form a memory, but the memory itself depends on the solidity of the connections between individual brain cells, according to the research from McGill and from New York University.

Information processing starts with the input from the sensory organs and transforms physical stimuli such as touch, heat, sound waves, or photons of light into electrochemical signals. The sensory information is repeatedly transformed by the algorithms of the brain in both bottom-up and top-down processing.

What Is an Expert System?

In artificial intelligence (AI), an expert system is a computer system designed to act like a human expert. CEWPS can analyze complex situations with the same skill and experience as a human expert. We have to admit that one day, computers will be able to reason faster than humans according to Dr. Ray Kurzweil in his famous book *The Singularity Is Near*. For now, CEWPS has the skills of a crime expert, experienced software forensician, military planner, software and hardware engineer, and finally a system paramedic. In sum, we put together an AI system, embedded with smart rules and decisions trees that replicate the human immunity.

Figure 12.2 shows the expert components of CEWPS. These are the vital organs of the Digital Immune System. We start with the Central Coordination Center, the Early Warning Center, the Knowledge Bases, the Smart Vaccine Center, the Inference Engine, and let's not forget the domain expert who will add more crime knowledge and attack cases to the database. Let's talk about the Knowledge Bases.

> *CEWPS main* Knowledge Bases: These are massively scalable Amazon-like fulfillment centers with an army of Kiva robot drive units (metadata) working around the clock to meet the heavy workload of CEWPS. CEWPS Knowledge Bases store groups of similar entities linked together to form what we call a *knowledge model*. CEWPS has four Knowledge Bases; each one stores one facet of crime domain. Figure 12.2 shows the topology of the Knowledge Bases.

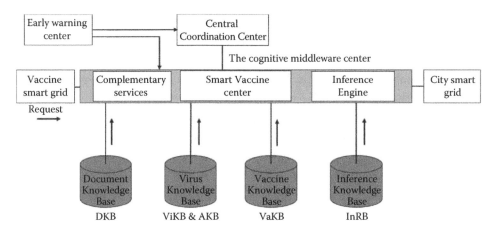

Figure 12.2 CEWPS Knowledge Databases are considered *fulfillment centers* during attack/vaccination cycles. They work like the cylinders of a Ferrari during a quick response. When the Vaccine Smart Grid needs service, all the KB respond on time to the Smart Vaccine Commander.

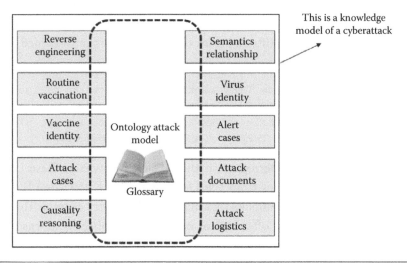

Figure 12.3 The purpose of ontology is to create a knowledge model from the attributes of an object. A cyberattack ontology, in the diagram, has 10 subject classes that are tied together to represent a cyberattack.

Virus Knowledge Base (AKB): It is part of the Attack Knowledge Base (AKB). It is considered the morgue of CEWPS especially after the battle. This deep repository stores the attack episodes with the captured viruses. The virus profile information, their anatomy, and the reverse engineering data are stored in the database as organized relational tables with an index for fast retrieval. AKB contains two types of entities: the *Attack Patterns* and the *Attack Ontology Models* (also called Cyberattack Data Models) (Figure 12.3).

Vaccine Knowledge Base (VKB): Consider it the medical center of CEWPS, where each vaccine corresponds to a virus and attack. Vaccinators know the vaccination process, and the adaptive vaccine is injected into the infected system. The paramedics know how to revive the damaged system.

Documentation Knowledge Base (DKB): Considering the library of CEWPS, the collected data about previous attack episodes are truly precious attack savings. In the Human Immune System, the T cells keep part of the virus and the antigen that mobilized the B cells. Each document record describes how the attack occurred, the strategy of the attack, and tools used. The city grid will receive several hundred attacks as the statistics shows in Chapter 11. The Vaccine Commander has access to the DKB to determine the strategy of similar attacks.

Inference Rules Base (InRB): This is the center of the defense reasoning. We can say that one of the features of CEWPS is that it relies on rules to do its inference. The rules define the behavior of an attack and its vector while the Inference Engine executes the rules. The format of rules is usually the following:

```
IF < antecedent > THEN < consequent >
IF < attack > THEN < outcome >
IF < virus > THEN < quarantine >
```

So the rules collection of facts about the crime domain. The inference performs its causational interpretation and evaluates the facts in the Knowledge Base in order to provide an answer. Here are additional rules that are used by the Inference Engine for causal reasoning:

```
IF< Attack on the system > THEN <Intrusion Detection failed >
IF< Attack on the grid > THEN <Smart Vaccine was late >
IF< vaccine is not available > THEN< virus is not caught >
IF< Substation is down > THEN < SCADA did not respond>
```

The security specialist will interrogate in the Attack Knowledge Base (AKB) and retrieve specific attacks episodes from the Documentation Knowledge Base (DKB). The specialist will evaluate the attacks that met his or her query criteria. The Inference Engine with specific rules will offer him or her the best probabilistic reasoning solution. It is a two-way iterative process. The specialist will store some of his or her experience and knowledge in the Inference Knowledge Base (IKB). Over time, IKB will become more mature and will make the reasoning more accurate (Figure 12.4).

CEWPS is much more than an expert system. It is a cognitive system. It has the capability to think, reason, and remember incidents and episodes. CEWPS knowledge augmentation is caused by the challenging vaccination missions of the Smart Vaccine. All vaccination episodes contribute to the intelligence and cognition amplification of CEWPS. One important note: the Knowledge Base has to be populated (before it could be instrumental) with semantic structures such as Attack Patterns, honeypot traps, virus program logic, vaccine prescriptions, and most importantly vaccination episode documents. These documents are dynamically used in the Inference Engine to generate attack predictions and forecasts.

Semantics: One word on semantics: It is very useful in argumentation and studying the relationship between words that share something in common. It is like a large family with many siblings, children, and grandchildren. All the family members are

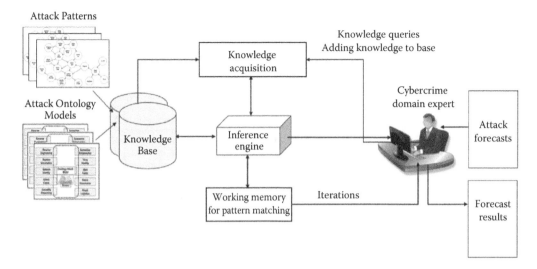

Figure 12.4 An expert system consists of a Knowledge Base and an Inference Engine. The Knowledge Base will contain two types of records: the Attack Patterns and the Attack Ontology Models. The domain expert will interrogate the system and check specific attacks from the past. Then he will select the attacks that meet his query criteria. The Inference Engine will offer him the best probabilistic solution. We can say that CEWPS is an expert system.

tied to the father. Some members belong to the first generation, and others belong to the second or later generation. We can pick any member from the tree that could lead us back to the head of the family.

When we talk about a cyberattack, there are many words that can be linked to the word cyberattack, and by means of reasoning and backward chaining, we could learn more about in question. Figure 12.5 represents two crucial subjects that are integrated

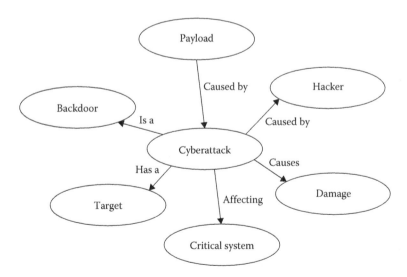

Figure 12.5 This is an ontology of a cyberattack. We can say that ontology represents an attack as a knowledge model. In this example, an attack has six objects that are tied with a relation to the cyberattack. Therefore, we have a cyberattack knowledge model (CKM). During the reasoning process, these objects will be part of the rules used by the Reasoning Engine that computes a probabilitic forecast for future attack.

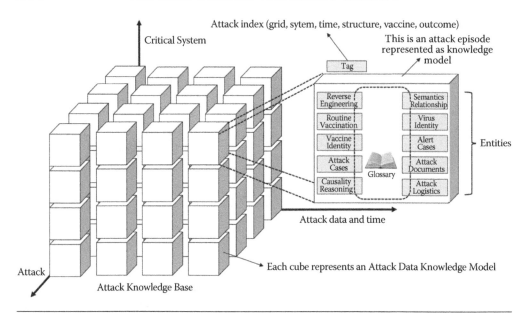

Figure 12.6 The Attack Knowledge Base (AKB) stores the cubes that represent the cyberattack knowledge model (CKM). The meta-engine will store the location (index) of the cube in the attack knowledge base. To retrieve the whole knowledge model of an attack, we use the tag. It's like the phone book, we use the index at the top to get the page of the desired number.

in the design of CEWPS knowledge engines: Ontology and Semantics. Ontology represents cyberattack as a knowledge model. Semantics collects all the words that are related to a subject, in our case it is a cyberattack. So, Ontology relies on Semantics for the development of an attack knowledge model.

Figure 12.6 shows the *cyberattack knowledge model* as the building block of the Attack Knowledge Base. The Cyberattack Knowledge Model has 10 distinct entities (objects) that describe the cyberattack. A cyberattack knowledge model can be represented numerically as the collection of relations, number of entities, and all related axioms.

$$\text{Attack Data Model} = \sum \text{Entities (Relations, Instances, Axioms)}$$

In addition, the metadata engine adds an index to all the Cyberattack Knowledge Model (CKM) records before they are stored in the Attack Knowledge Base. Figure 12.7 shows the colossal Knowledge Base in CEWPS.

The cubes are aggregated and stored in the master CEWPS Knowledge Base. They are instances from the virus domain, vaccine domain, and memory domain.

Domain: It is defined as an open space that contains similar objects of the same nature. We can say that the cyberattack domain contains the cyberattack occurrences. The Cyberattack Knowledge Base is the repository of all the cyberattack knowledge models. Mathematically, we can represent the relationship between the cyberattacks and their knowledge model.

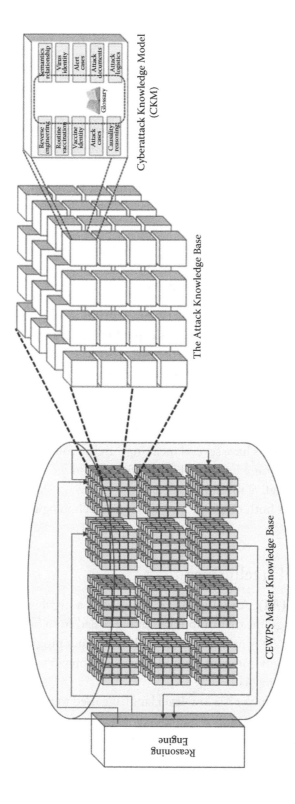

Figure 12.7 The CEWPS master knowledge engine stores four different types of knowledge instances: 1, the Attack KB; 2, the Virus KB; 3, the Vaccine KB; and 4, the History KB. A sample attack is referred to as (a knowledge model) which is developed with ontology techniques. The knowledge model will be used by the Reasoning Engine for prediction.

Domain------=-¶ $\sum$ Knowledge Model¶
Cyber--Attacks¶   Cyber-Attacks¶

Relationship between semantics and ontology: Finding simple definitions for the terms semantics and ontology is truly challenging. Most dictionaries copied the same definition over and over. Take, for example, the word *semantics*: everyone without exception copied the following explanation: *is the study of meaning*. As for ontology, everyone offered the same definition: *An ontology is a formal specification of a shared conceptualization.*

We have yet to find a down-to-earth explanation of these two terms. We have searched hundreds of presentations from seminars, academic textbooks, and research papers, but we could not find the straightforward and simple terms that made us comfortable. So, we decided to offer our own explanation.

Semantics and Ontology Relationship to CEWPS

There is a very attractive relationship between semantics and ontologies. Again, ontology is the technology to organize knowledge. Our main focus in ontology is to facilitate the construction of a model to represent cyberattacks, which can be used in our probabilistic reasoning to predict future malware events. To build this data model, we need to capture all the necessary components (ingredients) such as concepts and actual instances from the world of cybercrime.

Semantics engineering is the study of the relationship between words and their meanings. Words will always have several meanings. In the context of cybercrime and terrorism, the term *cyberattack* becomes highly critical, and we need to tie the term "cyberattack" to all its relative meanings.

CEWPS incorporates both ontology and semantics technologies in its knowledge engines.

Glossary: Artificial Intelligence

Artificial intelligence (AI): Although originally seen as a highly ambitious concept of computer programs that cannot be distinguished from human beings (as in the Turing test), AI is now used to describe computer programs that *learn and adapt* using the environment around them. The previous view of AI is now referred to as strong AI.

Assembly language: Assembler is a low-level language used to program microprocessors directly. It is essentially a human readable form of machine code and can therefore be very efficient, but very difficult, to program with.

Automated theorem proving: Automated theorem proving (ATP) is the autonomous proving of mathematical theorems by a computer program. Logic programming was developed as a side effect of research into ATP, with lots of work being done in inference rules to simplify logical sentences. "E" and "Otter" are examples of high-performance theorem proofs, "E" using purely equational calculus, while the latter makes use of the resolution principle in first-order logic.

Backtracking: Backtracking is a feature of many languages developed when computers had highly limited memory size and were therefore unable to store previous computations or a large amount of state information about a running program. Backtracking means that the interpreter exhausts a possibility in the search tree and then backtracks to the last choice point, where it carries out its work along any unvisited paths so far. Algorithms featuring backtracking for traversing trees include depth-first search and breadth-first search.

Backward chaining: Backward chaining starts with a list of goals and works backward to see if there are data available that will support any of these goals. An inference engine using backward chaining would search the inference rules until it finds one that has a then clause that matches a desired goal. If the if clause of that inference rule is not known to be true, then it is added to the list of goals.

Boolean connectives: Boolean connectives are used to join atoms together to form a formula. The primary connectives are NOT ($\neg$), AND ($\wedge$), OR ($\vee$), IMPLIES ($\rightarrow$), IF-AND-ONLY-IF ($\leftrightarrow$), T (truth), and $\perp$ (falsity).

Clausal form: Clausal form is one of the normal forms in which a formula can be represented. A formula in clausal form can take up a lot more space than in a simplified form, but will ultimately contain no quantifiers and therefore be operable on by the resolution rule.

Clause: A clause is a disjunction of literals, interpreted as a conditional statement.

Compiler: A compiler is used in many languages to translate the source code written by the programmer into machine code, executable by the computer. There are often intermediate stages of compilation (e.g., assembler and Java bytecode), but most logic-programming languages are interpreted rather than compiled.

Concurrent programming: Concurrent programming involves one or more threads running simultaneously. The advantage of concurrent programming is in multiprocessor environments, which can be substantial when it increases in speed.

Constraint programming: Constraint programming is where relationships between data are described in terms of constraints. Instead of specifying steps to follow (i.e., an algorithm), only properties of solutions are specified.

Control structure: The control structure is the data structure used by a programming language to store the current state of the computation and how it is traversed.

De Morgan laws: The De Morgan laws (equivalences) expressed in logic are

$$\neg(P \wedge Q) = (\neg P) \vee (\neg Q)$$

$$\neg(P \vee Q) = (\neg P) \wedge (\neg Q)$$

These laws provide a simple way to push negations inside closed expressions and are required when reducing a formula to negation normal form.

Declarative paradigm: Declarative programming has two different meanings:

1. Programs that describe what something is, not how it is created, for example, webpage code that describes what the page should look like but not how to display it
2. Programs that are written in a functional, logical, or constraint programming language

Depth-first search: Depth-first search (DFS) is an algorithm for traversing or searching a tree, tree structure, or graph. The algorithm extends the current path as far as possible before backtracking to the last choice point and trying the next alternative path.

First-order logic: First-order logic is a powerful extension of propositional logic. This logic introduces quantifiers. The two quantifiers are the existential quantifier ($\exists$) and the universal quantifier ($\forall$). $\exists x$, $f(x)$ says that there exists an x, such that $f(x)$ is true. That is, f is satisfiable. On the other hand, $\forall x$, $f(x)$ says that under no circumstances f is false. That is, f is valid.

Formula: A formula is essentially the *if test* in propositional calculus. Formulas are made up of atoms joined together by Boolean connectives. Formulas can be represented as formation trees, in which the nodes are atoms or connectives. Brackets are used to disambiguate the meaning of formulas, and binding conventions apply to the relevant connectives. Formulas take on a Boolean value. Recursively, a formula can be defined using the following rules:

1. Letters of the alphabet are formulas.
2. If f is a formula, $\neg f$ is also a formula.
3. If $f1$ and $f2$ are formulas, then $f1 \sim f2$ is a formula, where $\sim$ is a Boolean connective.
4. Nothing else is a formula.

Forward chaining: Forward chaining starts with the available data and uses inference rules to extract more data until an optimal goal is reached. An inference engine using forward chaining searches the inference rules until it finds one where the if clause is known to be true. When found, it can conclude, or infer, the then clause, resulting in the addition of new information to its dataset.

Functional paradigm: The functional programming paradigm treats computation as the evaluation of mathematical functions. No state information is held during execution unlike procedural programming that relies on the execution of sequential instructions.

Fuzzy sets: Fuzzy sets form part of fuzzy logic and deal with the *member of* relation in set theory. Unlike classical set theory, fuzzy sets allow different degrees of membership using a scale ranging from 0 to 1, that is, nonmember to full member.

Goal: A conclusion in a logic-programming query, which if made true allows the language interpreter to return success for the query. Goals are the same as subgoals, which are the "then" clauses of an "if... then..." query. If all the subgoals of a query can be proven true, then so can the antecedent.

Ground term: A ground term is a term that does not involve a variable.

Higher-order functions (metaprogramming): Higher-order functions are often added to programming languages to reduce coding for programmers and help prevent repetitious blocks of code occurring. They take one or more functions as input and another function as output. In logic programming, these are referred to as metaprograms since they deal with programs rather than functions.

Horn clause: A Horn clause is a clause with at most one positive literal. If a Horn clause has exactly one positive literal, then it is known as a definite clause. Similarly, a Horn clause with no positive literals is referred to as goal.

Imperative paradigm: The imperative programming paradigm takes on the "Do this, do that" approach, forming a sequential statement list in the code. Unlike logic programming, imperative languages state *how* the computation is to take place, rather than *what* is to be computed.

Implementation constraint: An implementation constraint puts limits on coding or construction, for example, required standards, platform, or implementation language.

Indeterminacy: Indeterminacy means that in a sequence of events, it is down to chance which event will occur next. This occurs in the concurrency of mathematical logic–based logic programming where the concurrency is implemented using message passing systems. These messages arrive in random order, and therefore, indeterminacy results in the order of execution.

Inference engine: An inference engine is a computer program that controls how "if... then..." rules are applied to the Knowledge Base (facts and relationships) of a database in order to conclude (infer) new facts or relationships.

Inference rules: Inference rules are logical rules that allow new logical formulas to be derived from existing ones, usually in pursuit of a conclusion. There are many rules that can be replaced by the rule of resolution provided the formulas are in clausal form.

Interpreter: An interpreter is a program that itself runs other programs. Unlike a compiler, the interpreter will *interpret* the source code directly without first translating the source code into machine code.

Literal: A literal is either an atom or a negated atom.

Logical consequence: Logical consequence is the relation that holds between a set of sentences and a conclusion that can be drawn from them. If the set of sentences A, ..., A_n can be used to show R, then, we say A, ..., $A_n|R$.

Logic-programming paradigm: Logical languages deal with the extraction of knowledge from basic facts. Logic programming makes use of pattern-directed invocation of procedures from assertions and goals. They answer queries via searching. Searching is done via forward chaining and backward chaining.

Logical sentence: A sentence is a formula with no free (i.e., unbound) variables. Since all the variables in a sentence must be bound, sentences always have a Boolean value in a given structure.

Modal logic: Modal logic is an extension to standard logic that allows modalities to be expressed in three ways. A sentence is either *possible, necessary, or contingent.* These classifications have much in common with propositional validity but are not used as a basis for logic programming.

Natural language processing: Natural language processing (NLP) is the study of computer understanding and generation of natural human languages.

Negation normal form: Negation normal form is a normalization for formulas where negation occurs only immediately above propositions. This can be brought about using equivalences and the De Morgan laws. Negation normal form is a step toward clausal form of disjunctive normal form.

Nondeterminism: Nondeterminism refers to a computational property that may have more than one result.

Object-oriented paradigm (OOP): OOP is a relatively new paradigm that emphasizes modular programming and data separation. The primary concept of OOP is breaking a large problem down into smaller problems, which are solved and then called by other methods within the program.

Perfect play: Perfect play is an idea of game theory, in which the behavior of a player is that which leads to the best possible outcome for that player.

Predicate calculus: See first-order logic.

Procedural paradigm: The procedural programming paradigm is where code is separated up into functions or methods that can be called individually. This prevents code duplication in moderately complex programs and makes layout easier, allowing for modular coding. Procedural programming is also used as a synonym for imperative programming.

Propositional atom: A propositional atom is simply a variable, as in math, which can take on either true or false as its value. Atoms cannot be separated into *subatoms*; they are atomic.

Propositional calculus: Propositional calculus (logic) is a subset of first-order logic. It can be referred to as "the study of if tests." That is, we can express atomic statements in terms of if something is true, then do something else. Boolean connectives are used to expand on this, creating a final statement (formula) with a true or false value. The three *ingredients* in propositional calculus are atoms, Boolean connectives, and punctuation. Propositional calculus is a deduction system on objects (propositions) that can be used to prove propositional relations.

Prune: The act of removing parts of a search tree in order that they would not be computed.

Resolution: Resolution is an inference rule that can be used in place of the other inference rules provided the formulas in question are in clausal form. Resolution takes two clauses (a clause being a disjunction of literals) and produces a new one from them by eliminating atoms whose complement appears in one of the original formulas.

Scientific community metaphor: The scientific community metaphor is used as a metaphor to employ systems displaying certain traits mirrored in the scientific community.

Search tree: A search tree is a data structure used by many logic-programming interpreters to find solutions to a query. Since all data structures can be represented as a tree, this is a logical and efficient way to retrieve data.

Semantics: Semantics essentially means *meaning*. The semantics of a logic describes the meaning of it.

Skolem normal form: Skolem normal form applies to first-order logic in which all existential quantifiers ($\exists$) are removed and replaced in some way by universal quantifiers ($\forall$). To Skolemize a formula, the following second-order equivalence is used as the main principle of converting to Skolem normal form:

$$\forall x \exists y R(x, y) \Leftrightarrow \exists f \forall x R(x, f(x))$$

Stable model semantics: Stable model semantics is a tool used to add negation to many logic-programming languages. Rather than mirror the mathematical view of negation, it assumes that all atoms not held as true by a program are therefore false. Stable model semantics also goes on to define a family of models of a logic program.

Terms: Terms are constants or variables used to name objects. A special term, known as a ground term, is one that does not involve a variable.

The Turing test: The Turing test is a simple test to determine the effectiveness of the conversational ability of a machine with humans. If a human cannot tell the difference between a conversation with a machine and with another human, then the machine will pass the test.

Type system: A type system in a programming language is a way of classifying different data structures or elements. This classification can then be used as a code check in order to ensure that various data types match where appropriate.

Unbound variable: A variable in a logic-programming language that is initially undefined but that may get bound to a value or another logic variable during unification of the containing clause with the current goal.

Validity: The validity of a formula gives some insight into when the formula is true. *A* valid formula is always true, $A \lor \neg A$, for example, *A* satisfactory formula is true in some, but not all, situations.

References

Allen, B.D., *Think Bayes*. O'Reilly, Sebastopol, CA, September 2013. Judea, P., *Causality, Models, Reasoning and Inference*, 2nd edn. Cambridge University Press, Cambridge, U.K., 2009.

Stephen, L. and Danny, K., *Artificial Intelligence in the 21st Century*. Mercury Leaning and Information, Dulles, VA, 2013.

Websites

http://ftp.cs.ucla.edu/pub/stat_ser/r350.pdf
http://home.agh.edu.pl/~wojnicki/phd/node38.html.
http://methodology.psu.edu/ra/causal

13

THE NEXT CYBER WAR: THE EVIL FIGHT WITH THE GOOD!

The Different Scenarios of Massive Cyberattacks

One of the marvels of the Human Immune System is that no backdoor virus or Trojan can sneak into the body, from anywhere, without its knowledge. This is because the white blood cells (Leukocytes) are the cells of the immune system that are involved in protecting the body against both infectious disease and foreign invaders. These cells are the defending army and are running in the streams of blood like a nebulous grid watching over every cell on the body. Now you got the picture why grids are the best mechanism to protect systems.

Another hole in system security is when a system administrator is dismissed *fired* without changing the passwords on systems. This is a fatal mistake that companies often ignore. The National Security Agency, hit by disclosures of classified data by former contractor Edward Snowden, said it intends to eliminate about 90% of its system administrators to reduce the number of people with access to secret information. This computer security flaw does not work in the human immune environment because once cell becomes inactive (dead), it is kicked out of the body permanently and loses all its living privileges. It cannot masquerade into a living cell.

Another major hole in computer security is that computers are not capable of remembering any previous attacks, like the M cells of the human body. This is a fundamental feature in the Human Immune System caused by vaccination.

So, we have incorporated in the Cognitive Early Warning Predictive System (CEWPS/Smart Vaccine™) with similar functionalities to the Human Immune System. The result is that Digital Immunity offers an autonomic and cognitive protection to systems, all because of the superfast connectivity and response of the grid. We will demonstrate the versatility of CEWPS/Smart Vaccine with three high-profile cyberattacks.

The Pearl Harbor Attack

On Sunday, at 7 AM on December 7, 1940, at Opana Radar Site, two privates, George E. Elliott Jr. and Joseph L. Lockard, detected what they called on CR-270B Radio Direction Finder, a primitive form of radar, "something completely out of the ordinary."

In fact, it was so out of the ordinary that the inexperienced watch officer assumed it must be friendly airplanes and told them to just forget about it. Then all hell broke loose. Within 2 hours, 5 battleships had been sunk, another 16 damaged, and 188 aircraft destroyed. Only chance saved three U.S. aircraft carriers, usually stationed at Pearl Harbor but assigned elsewhere on the day. The attacks killed under 100 Japanese but over 2400 Americans, with another 1178 injured. A date which will live in infamy.

George Santayana was right when he said "Those who cannot remember the past are condemned to repeat it." It just happened again, but this time it was a different kind of attack at a different place.

We're presenting three attack scenarios, plotted and executed by politically motivated cyberterrorists. They are members of a reputable Crime Service Provider. The malware technologies are available on the market, which make these attacks easy to happen.

Scenario-1 The Electronic Pearl Harbor Attack

On August 24, 2005, the northeastern region of the United States was hit by an unusual type of a massive cyberattack that is called "The Virus Rain™." The attack caught the region and the country by surprise, and hundreds of incident response teams scrambled to catch up with the attack (Figure 13.1).

Systematically with a progression of 1-minute interval, the heavy Virus Rain spread very rapidly and hit the whole region like a hurricane bringing down the electrical grid, followed by the metro rail system, the hospital systems, government systems, the ATMs and banking systems, the metropolitan traffic control systems, bridge tolls systems, and even airport control tower systems. The national Cyber Emergency

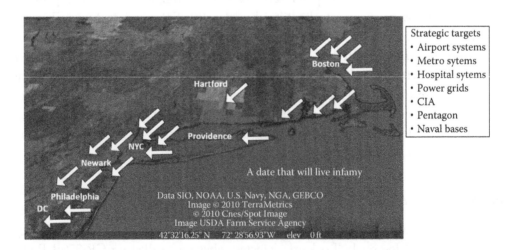

Figure 13.1 The electronic Pearl Harbor exemplified by the Virus Rain massive attack, as envisioned by the author.

Response Team (CERT) estimates that over 500,000 different types of *mutating* viruses have been unleashed to paralyze the region. Later, the attack was referred to as "The Electronic Pearl Harbor 2™"!

The Virus Rain is a fictitious massive cyberattack, but it may become a reality soon. All the technologies of the attack are present today, but more importantly, it will be fueled with anti-American sentiment. The Virus Rain was designed and launched from several remote stealth cyber launch pads. It hit the heart of New England with its payload of remote control viruses, mutating stealth-smart bombs, backdoor hemorrhoid zombies, and autonomic heart attack, and kamikaze agents. It was like the four horsemen of the apocalypse or the final battle of Armageddon. All this will be executed from the Internet, from anywhere in the world! Stuxnet was a tiny show.

It is a simulated scenario that could happen, but it is not probable but possible, simply because the new enabling technologies would let this calamity to happen. The Cognitive Early Warning Predictive System (CEWPS/Smart Vaccine) will definitely be the best techno solution to stop the Virus Rain. Grid technology is the only way to offer the fastest response of the Smart Vaccine services.

All massive attacks are preplanned and rehearsed and have determined targets. There's a new service on the block called *Crime as a Service* (CaaS) which is managed by global *franchised* organized crime providers. Figure 13.2 shows a fraction of the malware network. By the way, we're not counting the anonymous and invisible "Deep Web" which is another universe of malware. According to *Fortune* magazine (September 14, 2014), the article "Fortune 5: The Biggest Organized Crime

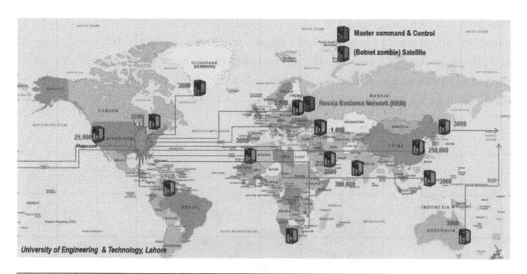

Figure 13.2 This is how the world runs today: Premeditated terrorism is *shock and awe* and is the most fearsome event but can be predicted and defeated. We simulated this scenario and how the Smart Vaccine provided Digital Immunity just in time.

Groups in the World" uncovers the five most contagious cyber Mafia in the world (Figure 13.2):

1. *Yamaguchi Gumi*—Revenue: 80 billion dollars, Japanese
2. *Solntsevskaya Bratva*—Revenue: 8.5 billion dollars, Russian
3. *Camorra*—Revenue: 4.9 billion dollars, Italian American
4. *'Ndrangheta*—Revenue: 4.5 billion dollars, Italian
5. *Sinaloa Cartel*—Revenue: 3 billion dollars

But the world is heavily sprinkled with 3,000 organizations that hosts over 1,000,000 servers with an awesome number of zombie botnets referenced in *Cyber Warfare* book from O'reilly. A study done at University of California, Berkeley in 2001 suggests that the Deep Web is 85% of the the surface Web.

The Magic Smart Grids

Let us talk about smart grids: Our body has two cognitive grids that help us to survive. The first one is the nervous system; we call it neurogrid. The second is called immunogrid. These two grids are tightly coupled and work together.

CEWPS is also geared with a cognitive immune system that we call the Smart Vaccine Grid. Now the only way to protect the northeastern region from attack avalanches is to build a smart grid for the region to deliver the Smart Vaccine Services.

Scenario-2 The California Power Plant Attack

The target scene: The scenario belongs to California's electric power and distribution grid that is managed by the California Independent System Operator (CAISO) company. There are 12 computerized consoles within the main CAISO control room in Folsom. In case of a natural disaster or other emergency, there is another control room and mapboard in Alhambra, in southern California, that serves as a backup for the Folsom facility (Figures 13.3 and 13.4).

Figure 13.3   The California ISO company manages the power generation and distribution of the three major electric companies in California: PG&E, SCE, and SDG&E. Operators who work 7 × 24 in this control room monitor and manage 85% of California's power needs and resources. The control room monitors 25,526 circuit miles with distributed computers.

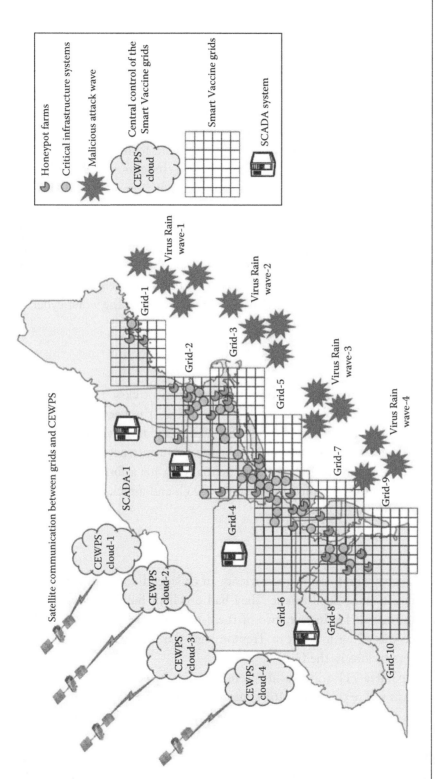

Figure 13.4 The 10 interlinked Smart Vaccine grids in New Jersey state will not allow any Virus Rain to attack the critical systems. The city smart grids are the nervous system and the vaccine smart grid is the immunity grid. We're also assuming that some of the customers are on the cloud, and they will get prompt VaaS. All the grids will be communicating with each other and share information with the State Security Command. If any of the Virus Rains reaches the grids, the honeypots on the grids will catch the attacking virus and an antidote will be packaged and dispatched to all four Smart Vaccine Commanders. It works. Today, none of the cybersecurity and antivirus companies have a system with the sophistication described in this chart.

Scenario-3 The Newark 4th of July Cyberattack

This is another scenario of not only how international terrorists can inflict damage to the critical infrastructures of a very busy city like Newark, New Jersey, but it also created trauma in peaceful citizens who learned to trust the government system. More than 100,000 people commute to and from Newark on weekdays, making it the state's largest employment center with many white-collar jobs in insurance, finance, import–export, health care, and government. As a major courthouse venue including federal, state, and county facilities, it is home to more than 1000 law firms. The city is also a *college town*, with nearly 40,000 students attending the city's universities and medical and law schools. Its airport, maritime port, rail facilities, and highway network make Newark the busiest transshipment hub on the East Coast in terms of volume.

The New York blackout of 2003 affected 50 million people and cost over 10 billion dollars (no one knows the true figures). It may cost 10 million dollars per mile to set up the cognitive Smart Vaccine grid, but it is worth the implementation. The next blackout will be even worse because the Virus Rain wave will be the worst cyber tsunami the United States will encounter (Figure 13.5).

How the Attack Was Planned

The team rented for the duration of 2 months, an apartment close to the campus of New Jersey Institute of Technology (NJIT). They had all the necessary equipment to do the attack which came from Albania. They visited the targeted sites and timed each dry run. The plan was to attack some of the critical infrastructures and hack the government computers and steal all the confidential data for a foreign government. They had a plan to go to the capital Washington, D.C. and attack the computers of the Pentagon and the State Department.

Cyberterrorists

They were five people who became good friends in college. There were all graduates of NJIT computer science department. They had excellent hands-on experience in programming and networks. In fact, two of them had been accepted at the CIA in Virginia and one was going to work in Trenton with the NJ government, the other two accepted overseas jobs in the Gulf.

The agency operates 711 trains aside from Amtrak, which is a federal agency. New Jersey Transit rail network has 161 stations, providing nearly 223 million passenger trips each year, with more new technologies to improve the customer experience. Real-time information services became available for rail customers on their handheld devices and desktop computers. Google Wallet's contactless payment system allows rail and bus customers to use their smartphones to tap and pay for transportation tickets at select ticket vending machines.

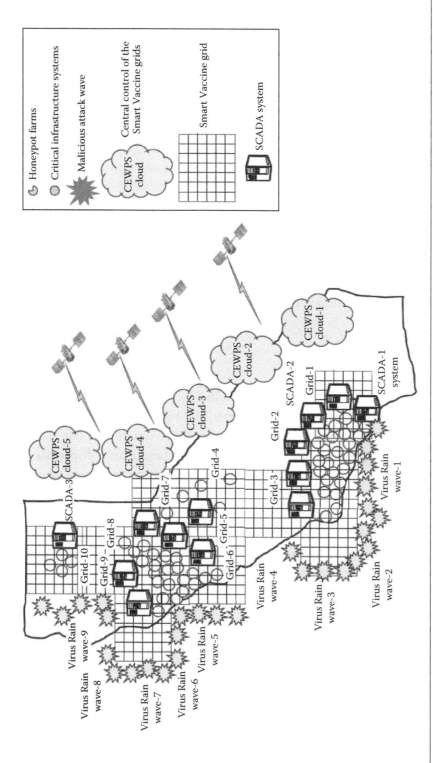

Figure 13.5 The 10 interlinked Smart Vaccine grids in New Jersey state will not allow any Virus Rain to attack the critical systems. The city smart grids are the nervous system and the Vaccine Smart Grid is the immunity grid. We're also assuming that some of the customers are on the cloud, and they will get prompt VaaS. All the grids will be communicating with each other and share information with the State Security Command. If any of the Virus Rain reaches the grids, the honeypots on the grids will catch the attacking virus and an antidote will be packaged and dispatched to all four Smart Vaccine Commanders. It works. Today, none of the cybersecurity and antivirus companies have a system with the sophistication described in this chart.

The Traction Power System

A traction substation or traction current converter plant is an electrical substation that converts electric power from public utility to an appropriate voltage, to supply railways, with traction current. New Jersey Transit 25 Hz Traction Power System is a traction power grid that allows the trains to operate along the Northeast Corridor (NEC) including 400 miles (362 km) between Washington, DC, New York City and all the way to Boston.

A typical substation includes two to four 138/12 kV transformers and 138 kV air switches that permit the isolation of individual transformers, shutdown one of the two 138 kV feeders, or cross-connection from one feeder to another. The output of the transformers is routed to track catenary via 12 kV circuit breakers and air disconnect switches. Cross-connect switches allow one transformer to feed all catenary lines. Today, about 55 substations are part of Amtrak's network. Substations are spaced on average 8 miles apart and feed 12 kV catenary circuits in both directions along the line. Thus, the catenary is segmented (via section breaks, also called *sectionalizations* by the PRR) at each substation, and each substation feeds both sides of a catenary's section break. A train traveling between two substations draws power through both transformers.

Train Movement Control

New Jersey Transit and Amtrak trains are controlled by the centralized traffic control (CTC) system that is located at the headquarter. All trains are governed by signal protocol that provides movement authority. The computer system will not allow for conflicting authorities between the train operator and the headquarter dispatcher. The dispatcher, who could see all the train movements from his or her screen or on the whiteboard (like traffic controller at the airport tower), will be responsible for issuing the control signals to train operators for train movement.

Figure 13.6 shows how computers interact with the trains. At the headquarter, there are three central systems that handle three distinct operations. The central traffic system is responsible for overseeing the movement of all trains on the tracks. The CEWPS/Smart Vaccine system is responsible for keeping the whole network immunized. SCADA system is responsible for the collection of data in the power lines, the tracks, and the trains. The three computers operate through a secure Ethernet network at the headquarters.

The hackers have lots of opportunities to vandalize the system from different locations:

> *The central transit location*: In the city of Newark, electricity and gas are provided by Public Service Electric & Gas Company (PSEG). PSEG has been named America's most reliable electric utility for the second year in a row. The central traffic center located in Newark has several servers that monitor and control

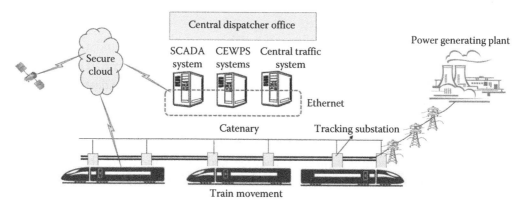

Figure 13.6 The trains are driven by the tracking substation which is controlled by the central computer.

the movement of the trains and the shifting of the rails. The network operations are running in normal mode, until the morning on Tuesday, October 8, 2013, when the train signaling system went erratic and forced the operators to halt service.

New Jersey Transit trains started to run again following a signal problem that halted service on 11 of its 12 lines for about an at least 4 hours. The signals that direct the trains went out. The signal management servers showed on the operator console unexpected error messages indicating the transmitted signals to the trains got scrambled and forced the train operators to switch to emergency mode and stop the trains.

Service was suspended on all trains, and central operations started to receive a deluge of phone calls from the confused train operators. All trains were fully powered while they were not running and crews made regular announcements to the commuters. New Jersey Transit is investigating what caused the computer problem.

Newark Penn Station: Commuters and other riders filled the platforms of the station, but there were no arriving or departing trains. Everyone thought that two locomotives had collided, and no one could explain this mishap.

The train movement: It is not an easy job but it shows that any unexpected action could take place. These terrorists will continue to attack the infrastructures of populated cities. The next one will definitely have casualties in addition to creating havoc in peaceful cities.

How the Attack Was Planned

The team worked for 2 weeks to plan the attack. They visited the targeted sites, and timed each dry run. Wireless public hot spots were used to communicate through obfuscated stealth public blogs. They also used an interactive simulation model to run different scenarios. They had three backup plans in case one of the attacks fails.

The Terrorist Team

The four terrorists were Caucasians who lived in the United States under business or student visas. There was no immigration restriction on them and they had no criminal records. The FBI and CIA did not have any indication of such clandestine activity. They met in April in Beirut, Lebanon, and were advertised by an organized terrorist group from Eastern Europe for 1 million dollars to stop suddenly the trains from Newark Penn Station and cause a head-on crash. They planned the attack and learned how to communicate with one another. They learned the cryptic words that were used to communicate on the underground Internet. The ISP (Internet host server) was located in Sofia, Bulgaria.

The four terrorists arrived to the United States first week of June to New York to attend a technical conference in New York City—as indicated by the immigration officers. The conference was going to be held on June 21–26 in Javits Center. The INS did not verify the authenticity of this information right away. They stayed at the Sheraton in Stamford, Connecticut (away from Newark), as attendees of the conference.

Terrorist Communication Protocol

All the terrorists were university graduates and very experienced in Telecommunication systems. They used an uncensored USENET, which is the great grandfather of the Internet. ARPANET was used solely by DOD. It uses the powerful UNIX protocol UUCP for telecommunication. It requires encrypted access with a very high port (29112—as secret entry into the Internet). Line command was used instead of browser.

All four attackers connected as clients to the stealth server. All audio telecommunications among the team is encrypted with the latest technology. Digital messages used were the new *self-erase* technique.

Mobiles

Four standard unlocked Samsung Galaxy mobiles were purchased from the international airport in Beirut. The mobiles were customized in China to be IP stealth and self-destructive and have self-erase history and detonation trigger. They were subscribed with fake names with the Kepler Telecom (main mobile company in Kazakhstan), which operates global satellite IP telephony named Thuraya.

Designated Target

The terrorist team selected the central train system because most of the trains were on 11 lines and were outside Newark Penn Station. All trains run with an electrification system (third rail system) energized by electric power from a tracking substation. The plan was that two terrorists would be giving instructions to the other hackers through stealth wireless mobiles. Hacker-1 was able to intersect the train signals arriving from the central signal servers. Hacker-2 attacked the central servers to shut the system down. If one train stops, all the other trains on the same rail stops—an order from the headquarter dispatcher. The Vaccine Smart grid 3 recognized the virus that was designed to intercept the train movement signals before they reach the trains. The virus was captured and eliminated from the network. Hacker-3 and Hacker-4 were giving instructions to the other hackers in the field and also paved the way for the escape.

Figure 13.7 shows the scene of the crime, the Vaccine Smart Grids that protected the central systems as well as the clouds. This scenario could happen any time unless a cognitive system like CEWPS is in charge of the Digital Immune System.

The Stuxnet: The New Nightmare for Smart Cities

Good and Evil at the Crossroads

In ontological dualism, the world is divided into two overarching forces: the evil force and the good force. In the Abrahamic religious influence, evil is usually perceived as the dualistic antagonistic opposite of good, in which good should prevail and evil should be defeated. But ever since the creation of man, good and evil have been constantly arm-wrestling and perpetually fighting to defeat each other and control the world.

One of the most haunting questions we face concerns the problem of evil. Why is there evil in the world if there is a God? However, the scriptures make it plain that God did not create the world in the state in which it is now, but evil came as a result of the selfishness of man. We interpret all this by saying that creativity is a two-edge sword. We created the Internet and we brought the good, the bad, and the ugly with it. The truth of the matter is that evil is what motivates us to defend ourselves and build secure defenses around us. Without evil, we do not need antivirus programs, intrusion detection, or penetration testing tools. Technology is purely democratic and is available to everyone. Hacking schizos are in fact the best security virtuosos your money can buy. We consider hacking is a satanic chess game of the highest order, between evil and good. The chess clock is ticking, and the score is still draw. They know the weak cracks and the wet patches of Windows. They use the most intricate tunnels to get to the processing vault. To these goons of cyberspace, hacking is the thrill of a bungy jump!

Stuxnet: The New Cyber War Missile

Sergy Ulasen, a programmer from Kaspersky Lab, was the pioneer who discovered the diabolocal worm Stuxnet in June 2010 (https://eugene.kaspersky.com/2011/11/02/the-man-who-found-stuxnet-sergey-ulasen-in-thespotlight/). It was designed to attack industrial programmable logic controllers (PLCs). Sergey Ulasen said "the complexity of Stuxnet's code and extremely sophisticated rootkit technologies led us

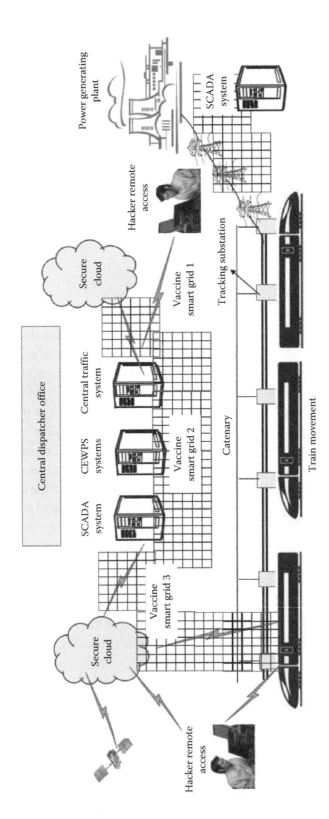

Figure 13.7 A railway electrification system supplies electric power to railway trains and trams without an onboard prime mover or local fuel supply. Hacker 1 was able to intersect the train signals arriving from the central signal servers. Hacker 2 attacked the central servers to shut the system down. If one train stops, all the other trains on the same rail stop—an order from the headquarter dispatcher. The Vaccine Smart Grid 3 recognized the virus that was designed to intercept the train movement signals before they reach the trains. The virus was captured and eliminated from the network. Hacker 3 and Hacker 4 were giving instructions to the other hackers in the field and also paved the way for the escape.

to conclude that this malware was a fearsome beast with nothing else like it in the world and that we needed to inform the infosec industry and community of the details ASAP." It is the tip of the iceberg. Stuxnet was a *politically motivated* cyberattack aimed at the destruction of the nuclear program of Iran. Blessed by the westernized world, Stuxnet ushers the beginning of a new era of cyberterrorism. Stuxnet got its malevolent name from two files found inside it. The first part, "stu," comes from the (.stub) file; and the second part, "xnet," comes from the (MrxNet. sys) file. Stuxnet becomes an overnight celebrity due to its diabolical design and mysterious way to cross the borders of Iran's Natanz nuclear plant critical systems. It is interesting to note that Sergey Ulasen traveled to Iran and helped the Iranians fish out the malware directly from the centrifuges.

Stuxnet Architecture

For the people who have never heard of Stuxnet, it is a worm written in Microsoft assembly language, C and C++. Also, part of the code was custom designed with undocumented language. Some people pointed the finger at Roel Schouwenberg, a senior researcher with Kaspersky's Americas, who could have been involved in the creation of the STUXNET. Stuxnet has three components: a worm that executes all routines related to the main payload of the attack, a stub file that automatically executes the propagated copies of the worm, and a rootkit component responsible for hiding all malicious files and processes, preventing the detection of the presence of Stuxnet.

The worm (Stuxnet 0.5) was at first identified in mid-June of 2010 by the security company *VirusBlokAda* (antivirus software vendor established in 1997 in Belarus). *Kaspersky Lab* experts also confirmed that there were two versions of Stuxnet (0.5 and 1.0) that were on the loose attacking SCADA systems from June 2009 to November 2010. The attack was aimed at two operating systems: (1) the Windows operating system and (2) Siemens PCS 7, WinCC, and STEP7 industrial software for Siemens' programmable logic controllers (PLC is a digital computer used to control industrial electromechanical processes).

In the United Kingdom on November 25, 2010, Sky News reported that it had received information from an anonymous source at an unidentified IT security organization that Stuxnet, or a variation of the worm, had been traded on the black market. A new weapon has been unleashed upon the world, and Stuxnet cannot be stuffed back into Pandora's box.

Stuxnet Strategy of Attack

Stuxnet attacked Windows systems using an unprecedented four zero-day attacks. It is initially spread using infected USB flash drive and then uses other exploits and techniques such as peer-to-peer RPC to infect and update other computers inside private networks that are not directly connected to the Internet. Stuxnet is unusually large at half a megabyte in size and written in several different programming languages (including C and C++), which is also irregular for malware.

Two Attack Strategies

Increase the Rotor Speed

The virus worked by first causing an infected Iranian IR-1 centrifuge to increase from its normal operating speed of 1064–1410 Hz for 15 minutes before returning to its normal frequency. Twenty-seven days later, the virus went back into action, slowing the infected centrifuges down to a few 100 Hz for a full 50 minutes. The stresses from the excessive, then slower speeds, caused the aluminum centrifugal tubes to expand, often forcing parts of the centrifuges into sufficient contact with each other to destroy the machine.

Disturb the Gas Pressure

After painstaking analysis, we can now confirm that the 417 PLC device attack code modifies the state of the valves used to feed UF6 (uranium hexafluoride gas) into the uranium-enrichment centrifuges. The attack essentially closes the valves causing disruption to the flow and possibly destruction of the centrifuges and related systems. In addition, the code will take snapshots of the normal running state of the system and then replay normal operating values during an attack so that the operators are unaware that the system is not operating normally. It will also prevent modification to the valve states in case the operator tries to change any settings during the course of an attack cycle. Natural uranium consists of three isotopes; the majority (99.274%) is U-238, while approximately 0.72% is fissile U-235 and the remaining 0.0055% is U-234. If natural uranium is enriched to contain 3% U-235, it can be used as fuel for light water nuclear reactors. If it is enriched to contain 90% U-235, it can be used for nuclear weapons.

The virus then propagates across the network, scanning for Siemens Step7 software on computers controlling a PLC. In the absence of both criteria, Stuxnet becomes dormant inside the computer. If both the conditions are fulfilled, Stuxnet introduces the infected rootkit onto the PLC and Step7 software, modifying the codes and giving unexpected commands to the PLC while returning a loop of normal operations system value feedback to the users. Here is a little more detail for our advanced readers.

Now that Stuxnet is running without the user's knowledge, it can move on to its targets. The Windows machines in the SCADA system communicate with the PLCs by way of a program called WinCC/PS7, or Step 7. This program essentially translates user commands into useful commands for the PLCs using a set of libraries. When Stuxnet is installed, it targets one of these libraries (s7otbxdx.dll),

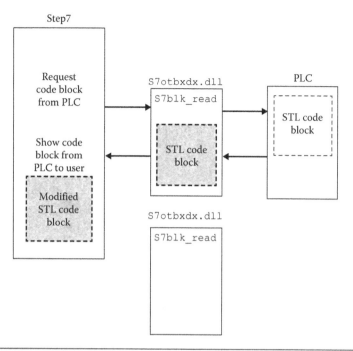

Figure 13.8 Step 7 function after s7otbxdx.dll is replaced by Stuxnet. The original file is renamed and bypassed in favor of Stuxnet's modified version.

which contains the translations for reading and writing new processes for the PLC, among other things. It takes advantage of a zero-day exploit in the WinCC database (a backdoor password that ships with the software) to give itself access to the database's libraries. Stuxnet renames s7otbxdx.dll to s7otbxsx.dll and replaces the original library with a modified version. This modified library contains almost everything present in the original, but some commands are intentionally translated incorrectly (Figure 13.8).

Step7 function after s7otbxdx.dll is replaced by Stuxnet. The original file is renamed and bypassed in favor of Stuxnet's modified version.

Now U-235 is the only variety or isotope of uranium that goes bang. In other words, only U-235 can be used in a nuclear weapon or nuclear reactor. But U-235 and U-238 are chemically identical.

How do you separate them? You combine uranium with the incredibly reactive gas fluorine to make a new gas, uranium hexafluoride. Then you pump this radioactive gas into a centrifuge and spin for week after week after week.

Ever so slowly, the gas with the heavier U-238 gradually gets thrown to the outside wall of the spinning centrifuge, while the gas with the not-so-heavy U-235 is left behind in the center.

But this central gas still has a lot of the heavier U-238 gas mixed in, so you take out that central gas and feed it into another centrifuge, spin it for a few more weeks or months, and repeat over and over.

Of course, to be really efficient, a centrifuge has to spin very quickly, so quickly that it is only a few percent away from self-destruction. The underground uranium centrifuge plant at Natanz in Iran had some 6000 centrifuges up and spinning by April 2008.

The Crack in the Door

The Iranian Natanz centrifuge plant was not connected to the Interweb. So, the makers of Stuxnet instead sent their virus to five specific domains in Iran via the Internet. These domains were somehow associated with the Natanz centrifuge plant. We still do not know who or what these domains were, whether they supplied hardware or software or they were contractors such as electricians, plumbers, or network specialists. But we do know that the Stuxnet virus easily entered the computers at these domains with no trouble at all, because it had four zero-day vulnerabilities and two genuine, but stolen, digital certificates. One or more of the workers at one or more of these domains then broke the air-gap rule. He or she took a USB memory stick that they had used at the domain into the uranium centrifuge plant and used it in a computer there.

Stuxnet was now inside the computers that controlled the ultrahigh-speed centrifuges that, in turn, separated out the desirable U-235, the only isotope of uranium that is used in nuclear weapons or power plants. Once Stuxnet was inside the computers that controlled the spinning centrifuges, it made copies of itself and spread to all the computers on the internal network at the underground centrifuge plant. Then the Stuxnet virus went deeper and looked for motors spinning at 1064 rev/second (it is the normal RPM). It sped up the uranium centrifuges from their normal 1064 rev/second to 1410 and kept them there for 15 minutes. This burst of overspeed created subtle damage in the bearings and structures of the centrifuges, which were already running at a speed close to critical. Over time, this damage would destroy the centrifuges. Then Stuxnet went to sleep for 27 days. This time, when it woke up, it slowed down the centrifuges to an incredibly slow 2 rev/second and kept them at this speed for 50 minutes.

The security of PLC has always been very low, because nobody thought they would be a target. But what if every traffic light, elevator, and water pump in your country suddenly stopped working? What if the tiny valves that let fuel into every petrol and diesel engine suddenly stopped working?

The United States and Israel execution of this plan was astounding. Although Stuxnet failed to satisfy its own standards of success in one regard, according to Sanger, the worm was never intended to travel outside Natanz's isolated, air-gapped networks. But an error in the code caused the worm to replicate itself and spread when an Iranian technician connected an infected laptop computer to the Internet. Fortunately, the worm did not cause widespread damage because it was engineered to affect Iranian enrichment facilities only.

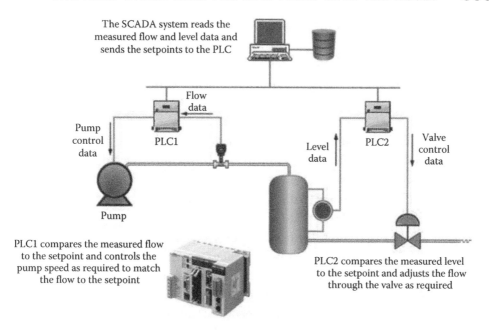

The SCADA system reads the measured flow and level data and sends the setpoints to the PLC

Flow data

Pump control data

PLC1

Level data

PLC2

Valve control data

Pump

PLC1 compares the measured flow to the setpoint and controls the pump speed as required to match the flow to the setpoint

PLC2 compares the measured level to the setpoint and adjusts the flow through the valve as required

Figure 13.9 Simplified configuration showing the pump manipulated by Stuxnet program, which in turn affected the speed of centrifuges of the plant. The attack increased the rotational speed of the motor that drives the pump of the centrifuge, and all hell broke loose. However, the readings on the PLC did not change. That is where the damage was done. Operators did not see anything unusual.

Stuxnet 0.5 tampered with the valves that fed uranium hexafluoride into centrifuge groupings. By triggering the valves to prematurely open and close, there was a change in pressure, which in turn caused the gas to solidify and thus destroy the centrifuges and the sensitive equipment used to develop them (Figure 13.9).

Stuxnet 1.0 was the later version, which took on a completely different strategy. This time, the virus interfered with the computerized frequency converts that controlled the speed of the centrifuges during the enrichment process. By causing the centrifuges to spin at speeds from both extremes, there was permanent damage to key parts of the enrichment process.

Damages

Stuxnet 1.0 was reported to have infected an estimated 100,000 computers, many of which were not even involved with the uranium-enrichment program. Natanz uranium-enrichment plant had approximately 10,000 IR-1 (based on the Pakistani centrifuge called the P1); Stuxnet decommissioned 1,000 centrifuges.

Historical Background

On May 9, 1979, a prominent Iranian Jew, Habib Elghanian, was executed by the new Islamic government shortly after the revolution. He was known throughout Iran at one time as the largest producer of plastic goods, was a successful importer and industrialist with different manufacturing companies, the wealthiest Jew in Iran, and was their community's leader as well as a generous philanthropist to Iranians of all religions. Menachem Begin, the then prime minister of Israel, who was the head of Zionist militant Irgun (which gave birth to the Mossad), took a solemn oath to avenge Elghanian's blood. In May 2009, two representatives of the Mossad visited the Elghanian family in Glendale, California, and delivered document stating that the first Stuxnet will be in honor of Habib Elghanian. The number 19,790,509 in hexadecimal coding was the password that triggered the first step of the infection routine in Stuxnet. June 4, 2008, was the kickoff date of Stuxnet attack. It took 2 years to fabricate in Israel with the blessing of the CIA and the Institute of Terrorism in Israel. According to reliable news coming from the Institute of Terrorism in Philadelphia and Jerusalem, Stuxnet was designed by top-notch team of 4 Israeli cryptographers, 3 Iranian nuclear engineers, 2 German process engineers, and 5 U.S. cyber experts, 3 U.S. and one Israeli experts in intelligence and antiterrorism (a total of 18).

According to the *Jerusalem Post* newspaper (November 20, 2010), the German security expert Ralph Langner reported in his analysis that Stuxnet contained two distinct *digital warheads*, specifically designed to attack the uranium-enrichment plant at Natanz and the nuclear power plant in Bushehr. The Pakistan newspaper *The Nation* (September 25, 2010) also mentioned that "Stuxnet was assembled by a highly qualified team of experts, involving some with specific control system expertise."

The team managed to get detailed information about SCADA from Siemens. They approached Siemens as engineers from Libya (which was very friendly with Iran). Two members of the team claimed that they had permission to visit Bushehr plant. They also secretly got a complete set of the engineering drawings of the Bushehr plant. Three Iranian engineers were executed afterward as spies. Second, the team succeeded in getting reliable contact inside Iran on the uranium-enrichment plant. The team worked in Israel putting and testing Stuxnet for 18 months before they are able to load and hand the USB to the agent inside Iran.

The New Generation of Stuxnet

What lesson do we learn from Stuxnet? Our main concern is that the new generations of Stuxnet will be smarter and will be able to do more damage in smart cities. Like CEWPS, which is a quantum leap into cybersecurity, the next Stuxnet, let's call it Stuxnet 4.0, will be a quantum leap into cybercrime as shown in Figure 13.10.

The diagram highlights the landscape of cybertechnology over 30 years.

1. The trajectory of the Antivirus Technologies (AVT) covering all the work they have done including research. The profile is moderate with no substantial advances in AI or nanotechnologies. It showed progress especially after Microsoft Windows' flaws and security holes. AVT vendors did a

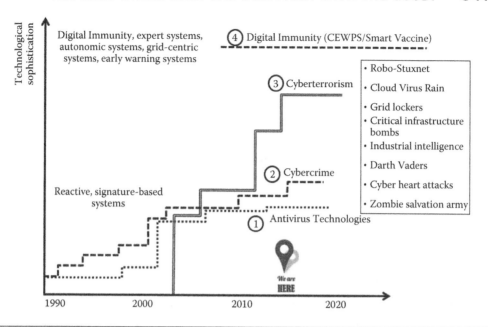

Figure 13.10 Cyberterrorism, although it started late, has surpassed Antivirus Technology in sophistication, but bringing new technology such as Digital Immunity has become a pivotal importance. (From the National Institute of Standards and Technology, Gaithersburg, MD.)

super job putting the pressure on the software giant to patch the holes and fix the bugs.

2. Nonetheless, the Black Hat community outsmarted AVT vendors and took advantage zero-day response from Microsoft and created ingenious attacks to rob data, corporate secrets, and espionage research labs blueprints and stole public records, medical records, military engineering drawings, and even money from banks.

3. Foreign country in collaboration with U.S. underground organizations took a quantum leap into cyberterrorism. They demonstrated that they can do real damage to the United States and western Europe without any fear or hesitation. They mastered all the security tools and tricks and turned the tables on all the security gurus of the industry. They continue to lead in international malware, which has become one of the most prosperous businesses in the world.

4. Digital Immunity engineered by CEWPS/Smart Vaccine is more advanced than the state of the art of cyberterrorism. Smart cities will have to implement Digital Immunity technology in their grids to shield all the critical infrastructures of computer systems from massive attacks (called the Virus Rain) launched by global organized cyberterrorists.

Stuxnet may have won the battle but not the war for sure. But cyber war is starting to become a reality. What is surprising beyond everyone's expectations is that many

East European and Asian countries have undefeatable electronic armies (according to the *New York Times (January 18, 2015)*, the North Korean Electronic Army is made of 6000 hackers) that could hijack any cyber command in the world. The U.S. Cyber Command is not immune from a massive stealth attack.

The migration to smart cities is picking up momentum, and many large metropolitan areas with complex infrastructures will be implementing smart city technologies (SCT). These technologies will achieve smart governance, smart energy, smart building, smart mobility, smart infrastructure, smart technology, smart health care, and smart citizens. Smart cities will offer higher quality of life and, above all, sustainable economic development.

Along this accelerated urban modernization boom and migration to intelligent cities, cybercrime will also pick up the pace and keep up with the latest technologies and will be ready for some real earth-shattering cyberattacks. Figure 13.11 shows a typical sequence of attack:

1. Adversary headquarters, from somewhere in the cloud, decide to retaliate and drum up a malicious attack on a smart city and take them by surprise. The dashboard is already showing the location of the target and ready to kick it off.
2. The dashboard executes a command to upload on the cloud-based Stuxnet type 1 missile, a package containing payload, link file, and rootkit.

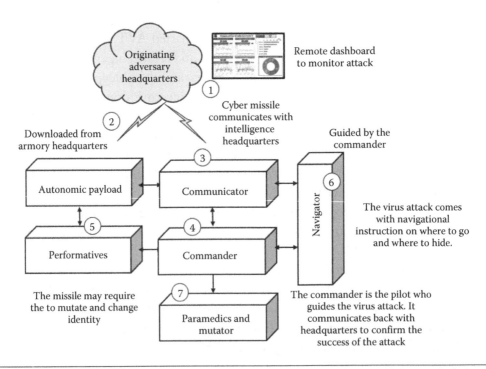

Figure 13.11   The cloud-based Stuxnet (type 1) is a self-contained executable software, guided autonomously from a remote dashboard located on the cloud. Its mission is to penetrate the Smart City power or informational grid. Thousands of these Stuxnets will make the Virus Rain.

3. At the same time, the dashboard is in sync with the communicator, which is the component that will guide the attack. It got all the information needed to copilot with the commander.

4. The commander (colonel) will make sure all components are working together according to the instructions dictated by the dashboard.

5. The instructions are ready to be linked and assembled into performatives and will be under the command of the colonel that guides the missile.

6. The navigator will decide on the best route of the attack. It has to decide the safest way to land into the target machine.

7. In case of alarm, the missile will mutate and hide and wait until the navigator decides to take an alternative route.

In the next few years, cyberterrorism is going to turn to artificial intelligence (AI) and nanotechnology to develop ultrasmart systems that will trigger massive attacks in smart cities. We know that smart cities will be powered by a smart grid that manages energy, water, transportation, public health and safety, and other key services. Also smart cities will also be equipped with soft informational grids to facilitate information ubiquity and links homes to offices, cars, and schools.

The industry of cybercrime has been flourishing and has become global and highly organized. Cloud technologies will pave the way for more sophisticated malware delivery. Let's take, for example, the cloud-based cyber missiles that form the Virus Rain.

Cloud-Based Stuxnet: The Virus Rain Attack

This attack will be organized by an adversary country motivated by counter political incentives. The Virus Rain will originate from a cloud armory and will have 10,000 Stuxnets with different structure and payload. The Virus Rain will hit the smart grid of the metropolitan city like a tsunami. It will create a massive performance slide in every server and network. The smart grid should have an early warning system to handle preemptive attacks such as the Virus Rain. The city's smart grids must have an emergency response mechanism to isolate critical systems from cascaded meltdowns.

Nanotechnology-Embedded Stuxnet (Epoch-5 Nanochip-Stuxnet)

According to Ray Kurzweil's *The Singularity Is Near* book, he systematically explained the six technological evolution epochs. Here is what he said:

Evolution is a process of creating patterns of increasing order. I'll discuss the concept of order in the next chapter; the emphasis in this section is on the concept of patterns. I believe that it's the evolution of patterns that constitutes the ultimate story of our world. Evolution works through indirection: each stage or epoch uses the information-processing methods of the previous epoch to create the next. I conceptualize the history of evolution—both biological and technological—as occurring in six epochs. As we will discuss, the Singularity will begin with Epoch Five and will spread from Earth to the rest of the universe in Epoch Six.

He went on to say the following:

So Singularity will begin with the fifth epoch. It will result from the merger of the vast knowledge embedded in our own brains with the vastly greater capacity, speed, and knowledge-sharing ability of our technology. The fifth epoch will enable our human-machine civilization to transcend the human brain's limitations of a mere hundred trillion extremely slow connections.

Cybercriminals and hell raisers will realize that nanotechnology and artificial intelligence (AI) are two new fields that will be used to develop the new generation of *smart cybercrime*. Governments will also jump on the smart cybercrime bandwagon and will develop secret cyber weapons that will continue the saga of Stuxnet (Figure 13.12).

At present, we do not have human-carrying viruses (HCV) loaded with nanochip and implanted in the arm or shoulder of hackers. Disenchanted employees who would like to retaliate against management would be willing to have a Nanochip-Stuxnet implanted in their shoulder and be ready to smuggle the worm through the company network. At present, we do not have the technologies to detect nanomalware software stored on a chip.

Here is the sequential description of the nano-attack shown in the diagram:

1. An adversary country, from an unknown location, decides to retaliate with a malicious attack on a smart city. This time, new technologies that have never been used before will be deployed for this surprise attack. A microscopic chip

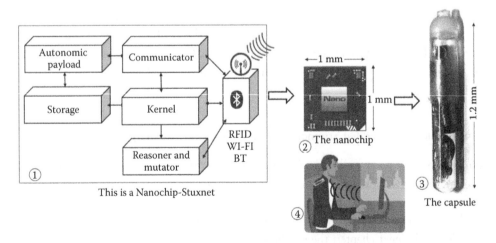

Figure 13.12   The Epoch-5 Implanted Nanochip-Stuxnet (type 2). (1) The structure of the Stuxnet with its RFID transmitter. (2) The nanochip where the Stuxnet is stored. (3) The chip is mounted inside the capsule. (4) The capsule in implanted in the arm of the perpetrator who uses a local or remote computer. The capsule will transmit Stuxnet code into the computer. The rest will be history.

will be used to store the attack software. The chip will be implanted in the shoulder of the hacker. The components of the virus will be all programmed and tested in the lab.

2. The components will be carefully assembled on the (1 mm × 1 mm) wafer of the chip.
3. The chip will be inserted in the capsule and sealed.
4. The chip will be activated by the master control server from the hackers' lab. The chip will remain active during the attack. The hacker will use any PC in the company to upload the malware through Bluetooth or Wi-Fi. Once the worm gets into the network, it will start to execute the instructions that were stored in the storage. The attack is to steal the administrator's password and have access to the central server. Since the worm is in stealth mode, it will not be noticed by the administrator. It will find its way to the system, files directory, and hide for a while to make sure it was not noticed. It will deactivate the antivirus program and hijack the keyboard and then replace few system files and reactivate the keyboard.

Epoch-5 Nanochip-Stuxnet will be the desired weapon for the next cyber war. The terrorist (who carries the implanted Nanochip-Stuxnet) host will allow the chip to start sending Bluetooth messages into target computers either on a network or connected to the grid. Bluetooth technology is robust and reliable, and among other advantages, it is less prone to interference with other protocols.

Digital Immunity Grid Layer

Like the Internet, smart grids will consist of controls, computers, automation, and new technologies and equipment working together to guarantee normal delivery of energy and information. When we talk about grids, most of the time, we refer to power grids. However, there is a new breed of grids that goes beyond the power grid, which is used to deliver information from banks to bank, home to office, home to school, city hall to city hall, and hospital to hospital.

Like in the human body, there are many grids that deliver specific services, but all grids work together, support one another, and exchange information as well. Similarly, smart cities will require several grids functional to deliver specific services and collect service-oriented information.

The Digital Immunity layer will be responsible for providing early warning alerts, vaccination services, and the collection of attack data for better future response.

Smart cities most likely will be a giant crucible for organized cyberattacks. We believe that politically motivated cyberattacks will increase in numbers and in sophistication, and many attacks will be committed by insiders as well as crime service providers (CSPs). The Smart Vaccine grid will be installed in smart cities to shield the critical system from Virus Rain, and Robo-Stuxnets, and Nanochip-Stuxnets (Figure 13.13).

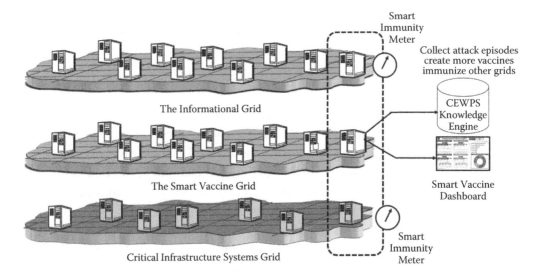

Figure 13.13   The Smart Immunity Meter (SIM) is the new concept that collects real-time information on the immunity level of the grid. It is the barometer of security that sends signals to the Smart Vaccine dashboard that monitors the grids from massive Nanochip-Stuxnet-5 attacks.

The Cognitive Early Warning Predictive System (CEWPS) is the AI system that administers the Smart Vaccine activities including all the vaccination missions. All the knowledge databases will be operating autonomically in real-time basis collecting attack episodes that get converted into knowledge models.

Nobel Laureate Horst Stormer said once: "Nanotechnology has given us the tools... to play with the ultimate toy box of nature—atoms and molecules. Everything is made from it.... The possibilities to create new things appear limitless." The Digital Immunity grid (DIG) is the beginning of a chapter in cybersecurity. In fact, the term *cybersecurity* is an old term with no appeal to it. It should be replaced with the newer term *Digital Immunity*. Digital Immunology would be the new science that will assure healthier urban foundation for smarter economic development.

The Digital Immunity grid (DIG) will introduce two new components:

1. *The smart immunity meter (SIM)*: Conventionally speaking, the term *smart meter* often refers to an electricity meter, but it may also mean a device measuring natural gas or water consumption. In general, a meter is a device to measure *time of use*. In CEWPS terms, SIM is an intelligent real-time device that monitors and determines if a critical system has missed any vaccination for a particular virus. Like the human body, which requires a dozen of vaccination to build its adaptive immunity, critical systems could become vulnerable to cyberattacks unless they have been regularly vaccinated. Smart immunity meters (SIMs) communicate directly with the Smart Vaccine grid dashboard that collects all the meter readings and correlates them with present metrics.
2. *The micro Vaccinebot*: Evolutionary progress looks smooth, but that really is divided into paradigms, specific methods of solving problems. Each paradigm

starts with slow growth, builds to rapid growth, and then levels off. As one paradigm levels off, pressure builds to find or develop a new paradigm. The emergence of artificial intelligence and micro technologies constitutes the new paradigm that has reached cybersecurity. A Vaccinebot is a microscopic self-contained autonomic program that will be installed on a chip that will be programmed to trigger a vaccination service on a grid. It is not easy to comprehend the size of a micro Vaccinebot, but micro engineering is being used extensively in medicine and metallurgy and pharmaceutical industries. Taking the scale down to the nanolevel (1 billionth of a meter) is not unrealistic to have nanoprograms and tools in the cybersecurity domain.

There will be thousands of Vaccinebots that will reside on the grids and will communicate with one another like the human cells and will relay messages to the smart immunity meters. This may sound like a fresh futuristic concept, but it will be part of the new generation of the Smart Vaccine.

The S-Curve Evolution of the Digital Immunity System CEWPS

The Digital Immunity system CEWPS, like other emerging technologies, will follow the "S" evolution curve as exhibited later. It is a major shift from the conventional Antivirus Technology (AVT). The S-curve evolution emerged as a mathematical model and was applied later to a variety of fields including physics, biology, and economics. It describes, for example, the development of the embryo, the diffusion of viruses, and the utility gained by people as the number of consumption choices increases. In the innovation management field, the S-curve illustrates the introduction, growth and maturation of innovations, and the technological cycles that most industries experience.

We have divided the CEWPS S-curve into four milestones to demonstrate some interesting phenomena on the accelerating returns and singularity:

1. *CEWPS-1*: This is the original version that introduced the Digital Immunity concept and vaccination services through the Smart Vaccine. It will be partially adopted by the smart cities.
2. *CEWPS-2*: This is the next generation that will be around 2020. It will be an improved version covering Big Data, the Internet of Things, and the cloud. It will be fully adopted by the smart cities. It will also be accepted by the Antivirus Technology vendors.
3. *CEWPS-3*: It will reach its full maturity, and its Digital Immunity becomes a utility that can be acquired for home and business places.
4. *CEWPS-4*: This is going to be the most crucial version of the Digital Immunity systems. After a decade from the original version, which has brought a new paradigm to the cyber security industry, it will have a great technological impact on Antivirus Technology (AVT) and will go through the accelerating return

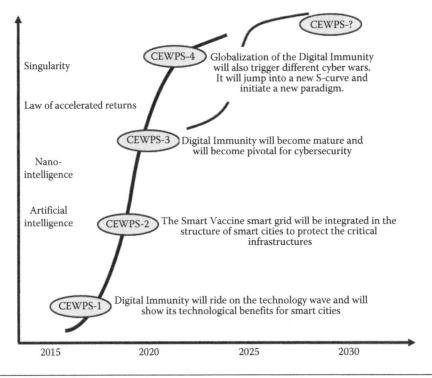

Figure 13.14   The evolution cycle of the Digital Immunity paradigm.

syndrome. New cybersecurity companies will emerge with much more versatile DI platforms. The focus will be on smart cities and how to protect its complex infrastructures. On the other hand, the organized crime service providers and other adversary electronic armies will be very active developing new weapons and more potent attack vectors. It will be time for CEWPS-4 to jump to a new C-curve and shift into a new paradigm (Figure 13.14). Ray Kurzweil's prediction on accelerating returns seems valid as we look at the progress of the Internet and its impact on our societal fabric and life: "An analysis of the history of technology shows that technological change is exponential, contrary to the common-sense 'intuitive linear' view. So we won't experience 100 years of progress in the twenty first century—it will be more like 20,000 years of progress (at today's rate)."

A Closing Word to Open Your Eyes

Duqu 2: The Future Cyber-Espionage Tool

Duqu 2 is a sophisticated piece of malware discovered in 2011; this was used in a number of intelligence-gathering attacks against a range of industrial targets. It had a number of similarities to the infamous Stuxnet worm, leading many to believe it was developed by the United States and Israel. Many prominent security firms claim that the Israeli-linked malware Duqu 2.0 was used to hit very specific targets including the

P5+1 (the six world powers which, in 2006, joined together in diplomatic efforts with Iran with regard to its nuclear program) nuclear talks and the events marking the 70th anniversary event of the liberation of Auschwitz-Birkenau.

The creators of Duqu 2 were so confident that it would never be discovered they decided to attack one of the world's best-known cybersecurity companies directly. The highly stealthy malware would have gone completely undetected while gathering a lot of highly sensitive information before uploading that data remotely to command-and-control servers.

So, what is the anatomy of Duqu 2, who fabricated it, and how it was detected? The Moscow-based firm Kaspersky Lab said it discovered several of its own internal systems had been infected by highly sophisticated malicious malware earlier this year. Furthermore, the cybersecurity firm claims several venues for international negotiations over Iran's nuclear program have been targeted by a surveillance virus, reportedly linked to Israeli intelligence.

Deep forensic and reverse engineering work discovered that the same virus had been used to infiltrate a series of other targets in the West and the Middle East, including, most notably, hotels where the Iranian delegates met with the P5+1 group to discuss Tehran nuclear ambitions.

The investigation described Duqu 2 as "one of the most skilled, Mysterious, and powerful threat actors in the APT (advanced persistent threat World)". The level of complexity of Duqu 2.0 was so high that they believe its use could only be part of "a nation-state-sponsored campaign."

Costin Raiu, Director of Research, said that "The people behind Duqu are one of the most skilled and powerful APT groups and they did everything possible to try to stay under the radar." He admitted that "This highly sophisticated attack used up to three zero-day exploits, which is very impressive – the costs must have been very high."

Costin Raiu explained "To stay hidden, the malware resides only in kernel memory, so anti-malware solutions might have problems detecting it. It also doesn't directly connect to a command-and-control server to receive instructions. Instead, the attackers infect network gateways and firewalls by installing malicious drivers that proxy all traffic from the internal network to the attackers' command and control servers."

Kaspersky didn't name Israel as a suspect, but the previous version of Duqu was very similar to the infamous Stuxnet worm, believed to have been developed by the United States and Israel. Israel all along refused to accept the nuclear talks, and consider the outcome of the talks could have greatly increased Tehran's threats to Israel's security.

The United States decided to lend support to the talks, which upset the Israel–U.S. relations.

In March, Washington directly accused Israeli spies of having snooped on the talks to gather intelligence and used this to fuel opposition to the nuclear deal in the U.S.

Congress. Kaspersky's revelation that the locations where the "P5+1" group met their Iranian governments were targeted had the desired impact.

References

Carr, J., *Inside Cyber Warfare*. O'Reilly, Sebastopol, CA, 2010.

Disrupting uranium processing at natanz. http://www.symantec.com/connect/blogs/stuxnet-05-disrupting-uranium-processing-Natanz.

Kaspersky Lab provides its insights on Stuxnet worm. http://www.kaspersky.com/about/news/virus/2010/Kaspersky_Lab_provides_its_insights_on_Stuxnet_worm.

Kurzweil, R., *The Singularity Is Near, When Humans Transcend Biology*. Viking Penguin Books, New York, 2005.

Langner, R. http://www.langner.com/en/wp-content/uploads/2013/11/To-kill-a-centrifuge.pdf.

Stuxnet: A breakthrough. http://www.symantec.com/connect/blogs/stuxnet-breakthrough

Symantec.com. http://www.symantec.com/connect/blogs/exploring-stuxnet-s-plc-infection-process.

Symantec.com. http://www.symantec.com/connect/blogs/stuxnet-05-disrupting-uranium-processing-natanz.

Vulnerability summary for CVE-2010-2772. http://web.nvd.nist.gov/view/vuln/detail?vulnId=CVE-2010-2772.

Websites

http://articles.mercola.com/sites/articles/archive/2012/09/19/10-amazing-human-body-facts.aspx.

http://en.wikipedia.org/wiki/The_Singularity_Is_Near.

http://people.carleton.edu/~grossea/infection.html.

http://spectrum.ieee.org/telecom/security/the-real-story-of-stuxnet excellent.

http://www.njtransit.com/pdf/rail/Rail_System_Map.pdf.

http://www.symantec.com/security_response/definitions/rapidrelease/detail.jsp?relid=2014–11–14 super.

http://www.zdnet.com/article/kaspersky-duqu-trojan-uses-unknown-programming-language/.

Epilogue

A public lecture was delivered on September 8, 2011, at the Global Security Seminars at UCLA Faculty Club. The topic of this lecture was "Jihadism and Terrorism, our National Security is at Stake."

The goal of this presentation was twofold: first to explain that Jihadism is not Jihad, and second to offer a scientific and philosophical explanation of the anatomy of the multifaceted Jihadism, how it morphed to become terrorism. There is so much bewilderment and emotional disillusion between Jihadism and terrorism mayhem that technology alone cannot disentangle. It is not imperative to understand everything about Islam, but it is obligatory to understand the driving factors that created Jihadism and how it was ingenuously fabricated. Nonetheless, a little historical recital on Islam will be requisite and even enlightening. I did add some updated information relevant to the topic.

According to Islamic Finder (www.islamicfinder.org), a nonprofit organization dedicated to serving Islam on the Internet, the Prophet Muhammad was born on Monday, 12 Rabi Al Awwal, April 22, AD 570. Figure E.1 shows the main events since the birth of the Prophet Mohammed.

We can say Islam started in AD 610, when the Prophet was 40 and received his first revelation delivered by angel Gabriel. Then he started to openly preach the divine revelations. Those revelations were preserved by his close followers (Sahaba) and eventually that collection became the Holy Quran. The Prophet Muhammad received an innumerable number of revelations, most of which are encompassed within the Holy Quran. All we know is that the Holy Quran has 114 chapters that include all the revelations. The prophet would explain the revelations (which are the words of God) to his followers known as Sahaba. All verbal statements or actions of the Prophet Muhammad, his tacit approval or criticism of something said or done in his presence became what is called the *Hadith*. This was unlike the Holy Quran, which went through formal processes of collection and codification, centered around one

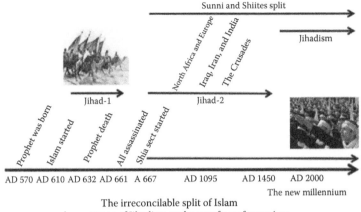

The irreconcilable split of Islam
and emergence of Jihadism as the new face of terrorism

Figure E.1   In Islam, there are three types of Jihad. The first one was during the Prophet Mohammed. The second one occurred after the Prophet Mohammed. The third one is the contemporary one and most troublesome.

overarching principle*: God's words must not in any way be distorted or sullied by human intervention.* There are NO multiple versions of the Quran, only one.

We can say the *Jihad-1* war started with the beginning of Islam, when the Prophet Muhammad started to condemn idol worship and the Meccan forefathers engaged in polytheism. It was the beginning of the armed conflict. The Prophet Muhammad led many successful battles and most of the tribes that initially opposed him converted to Islam. His wisdom and eloquence made him gain political power and magical leadership. Michael H. Hart, in his book "The 100 most influential people," ranked the Prophet Mohammed as the number 1 most influential man in history. Islam, which started with a dozen of his close followers, has spread around the world, and in 2014 it reached 2.08 billion (http://www.muslimpopulation.com/World/).

In AD 632, the Prophet Muhammad passed away and was buried in Medina. With his death, the first Jihad came to an end.

I should mention at this point a crucial milestone in the history of Islam: There was a dispute among the Muslims on who is the rightful successor to the Prophet. The dispute triggered a spiteful split between *Sunnis* and *Shiites*. The Shiites were the followers of Ali, nephew of the Prophet, split from the main stream of Islam and currently account for 10%–15% of all Muslims. Shiites claimed that the Prophet Muhammad had anointed his son-in-law, Ali, as his rightful successor (Khalif). The Shiites believed that successorship *Caliphat* should stay within the family of the Prophet. Unfortunately, the split got wider and wider, even though the Shiites amount to 15% of the Muslim population. The Sunnis, who constituted 87%–90% of the world's Muslim population, are the strict followers of the Prophet Muhammad and the consensus of the people. There has been so much blood between the two sects, and no compromise will be accepted by either sect. All the violence today is the result of that deep-rooted split.

The *Jihad-2* started with the new successor after the death of the Prophet, and lasted almost 823 years, throughout the fifteenth century. During the period of second Jihad, which is considered the golden era of Muslim conquest, Muslims had great armies led by great leaders that continued to spread from Europe through Africa all the way to India. Islam flourished during this period, and the Middle East became the bridge of commerce between the Far East and Europe. The period of second Jihad was the most successful period of Islam after the Prophet. There were many wars but they were fought under the banner of the Holy Quran and the teachings of the Prophet. Yes, there was a lot of violence during the wars, justified to spread Islam and nothing else. We cannot define the *Jihad-2* as terrorism, although, during the period of *Jihad-2*, the power and the leadership struggle of the Islamic community continued for 1348 years until the present.

As shown in Figure E.2, the two sects of Islam were initially headed by the Prophet Muhammad. Then after the split, the Shiites selected Karbala in Iraq as their capital, while the Sunnis kept Mecca as their religious center. The Shiites were divided primarily among Iran, Iraq, and Lebanon, with Alawites (an off-shoot of Shia Islam) in Syria. This area has come to be known as the Shia crescent. The fight still continues and no compromise is in sight. According to a poll by Pew Research, some 40% of Sunnis do not regard Shiites as real Muslims (http:// www.pewglobal.org/topics/muslims-and-islam/).

This conflict planted the first seed of Islamic terrorism that I call "Jihadism." But before we fast-forward into the topic of terrorism, I should say, being a native of Syria, I fully understand the culture of the land and how Islam plays a big role in the geopolitical arena. The West does not understand the genetics of the Middle East, and it never will. I would like to mention candidly that the Jihadism in the

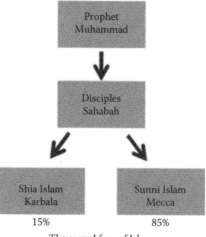

The sacred face of Islam

Figure E.2   The two irreconcilable sects of Islam (the Sunnis and the Shiaas) started after the assassination of Ali in 661 AD, and the Shii'a followers decided to relocate to a new capital Karbala in Iraq.

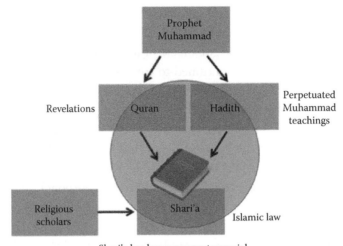

Figure E.3 Shari'a is the Islamic Law, which is the product of Hadith, the Holy Quran, and the religious scholars. The Shari'a is partially applied in most Islamic countries, with the exception of some countries like Saudi Arabia, and ISIS where it is fully applied.

world, and in particular in the Middle East, got more aggressive due the hypocritical intervention of the great powers. The Middle East used to be one land, where all the divine religions coexisted. Look at what we have now, and how many fenced nations we have today.

Now, let's define a very pivotal word in Islam, the *Shari'a*. Shari'a is the Islamic law (Figure E.3). It is the combination of the two major pillars of Islam Quran and the teachings and rulings of the Prophet which is called *Hadith*. Shari'a law itself cannot be altered, but its interpretation is given some leeway by the religious scholars. This is why not all roads lead to Rome, as the saying goes. Shari'a is a complete legal system with the core principle of good on Earth; it also covers the family, the society, crime and punishment, the government, and even the classic meaning of military *Jihad*.

The usual criticisms of Shari'a—that it is very cruel as regards execution, flogging, and cutting off hands—totally ignore all the extenuating circumstances that not applying these penalties would lead to. Islamic terrorism today (e.g. ISIS) ardently practices this, which offends God.

The truth is Shari'a has been controversial. Many Muslim countries fully follow it, while the rest partially follow it. In the strict Muslim countries, Shari'a-prescribed punishments such as beheading, flogging, and stoning continue to be practiced judicially or extrajudicially. Of all legal systems in the world today, Islam's Shari'a law is the most intrusive and strict, especially against women. An interesting feature of Shari'a is that it does not incarcerate the guilty. Nothing like what we have here in the United States.

The word "Jihad" is one of the most troubling, controversial, and abused term in the religion of Islam. In the beginning, it meant a holy war against infidels. Today, *Jihad* and *Jihadism* are not synonymous. These two terms take totally different meanings. The Western world refers to *Jihadism* as Islamic terrorism. Let me articulate on this subject.

Now here is the point, Jihadism followers believe that their holy war against all non-Muslim societies is justified and their recompense will be the paradise. It is prodigious incentive for *martyrdom*. Don't you think so? Interestingly enough, there is no international consensus on the legal definition of terrorism. Also, there is neither an academic nor an accurate legal unanimity regarding the definition of that term. Various legal systems and government agencies use different definitions. Governments have been reluctant to formulate a systematic and legally binding definition. Jihadism is politically and emotionally charged, so is terrorism.

Now let's talk about a couple of interesting points displayed in Figure E.4 the timeline slide. The Russian invasion of Afghanistan in December 1979 gave birth to Al-Qaeda and Taliban. The American invasion of Iraq gave birth to ISIS. The civil war in Syria is in its 5th year. The Russian are pouring kerosene on the fire.

The *Jihad-3* in Figure E.1, I call it *Jihadism* instead, started with Al-Qaeda, through 9/11 until now. Since we are addressing the subject of *Jihadism*, let's talk about the genesis of its sibling *cyber-Jihadism*, its state of the art, and its plans. Of course there are other cyberarmies from China, North Korea, Israel, Iran, and Pakistan that have been launching massive politically driven cyberattacks. *Jihadism* morphed into terrorism. It is a huge mixed bag of human intimidation and disgrace. We would not discuss those armies in this presentation.

If we look at Figure E.5, we can see that terrorists realized that the Internet can be an effective and potent weapon to launch *cyber-Jihadism*. Of course, Jihadi organizations started to recruit professional Internet hackers for the job. Before and during the 9/11 tragedy, there was a tremendous Internet activity, beyond belief. If there hadn't been so much contention and mistrust between the two well-known government

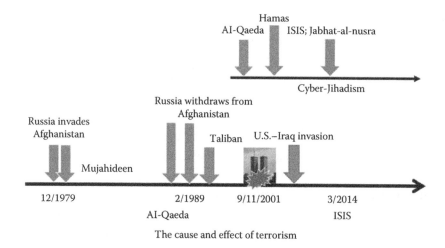

The cause and effect of terrorism

Figure E.4 Timetable of major contemporary events, and how Jihad-3 turned into Jihadism, which is synonymous to (terrorism). Jihadism is used by the radical followers of ISIS.

Figure E.5   International Islamic Jihadi organizations and schools exceeding (3500).

agencies, you know who, the attack could have been eliminated, and the attackers could have been caught before commandeering the planes.

The slide (Figure E.5) is very interesting. It shows the locations of the Islamic organizations and schools around the world that support Jihadism. These organizations are well funded and supported with military and computer science experts. Most of these organizations have websites and are also very active on all the social media sites.

Well, if the Institute of Terrorism and Research reports that there are 3500 Jihadi organizations and schools, then, most likely they have 3500 missile launch websites. Of course, not all of them are invisible. The thing is it is easy to hide or spoof the originating website. The Deep Web has hundreds of cyberarmies anonymously planning to hijack the whole world.

Take, for example, the Syrian Electronic Army (SEA), shown below in Figure E.6, with its website http://sea.sy/index/en, which is an interesting one (they have their own Black Hat Group). It uses the very latest technologies including SEANux, which is an Ubuntu-based Linux with a modified Gnome Shell interface, icons, and GTK theme. It is charged up with penetration testing and privacy tools and other potent missiles. The SEA (Figure E.6) is made up of a group of top-notch computer geeks formed in 2011 to support the government of Syria's president Bashar al-Assad, in collaboration with the Iranians, Chinese, and North Koreans. It uses spamming, website defacement, malware, phishing, and denial-of-service attacks; it has targeted Political opposition groups, western news organizations, human rights groups, and websites that are seemingly neutral to the Syrian conflict. On the outside it looks politically motivated, but in reality, it supports the Shii'a militants. Of course it is the façade of many stealth sites that spy on citizens and spread malware all over.

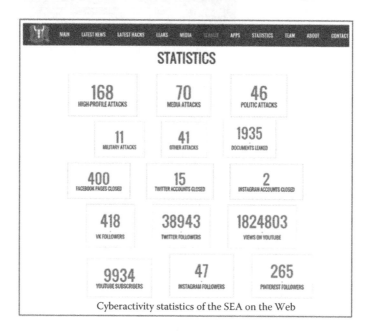

Cyberactivity statistics of the SEA on the Web

Figure E.6   This is a screen produced by the Syrian Electronic Army (Pro Assad) showing all the hacking activities.

The Islamic State of Iraq and Syria also known as ISIS, or The Islamic State of Iraq and Levant (ISIL), with its own site shown in (Figure E.7), has raised the cyberterrorism bar much higher in the name of Sunni Islam. *The New York Times* in its issue of August 27, 2014[2] states "As fighters continue to seize territory, the Islamic State in Iraq and Syria was built. Officers mostly middle-aged Iraqis, including many military officers under Saddam Hussein, are at least 200,000. ISIS is loaded with cash from oil wells, looting and hostage ransoms, but the oil price has crashed, the rapid expansion that made looting so profitable." The *Independent* magazine, Thursday, July 2, 2015 also mentions that "American officials estimated that it was making $2 m a day from oil, and $2 million from ransoms." Not to mention selling women. All the evil acts were carried out in the name of God.

Aside, from the horrific executions of the "infidels" shown on YouTube and BestGore.com, they skillfully managed to penetrate the most resilient sites. But here is

Memri Cyber and Jihad lab

IS Internet defenders video: message to the
servants of the cross

Figure E.7   ISIS is at the top of the cyber-Jihadism iceberg. An example of one of the hacking screens attacking the
Christians.

one final remark from *The Guardian* magazine[3], Sunday, April 12, 2015: "More dangerous everyday items have become hackable too, including cars. Security researchers have proven it is entirely possible for criminals 1500 miles away to seize control of your car when you are driving 65 mph down the highway." Wow, this belongs to the Stuxnet club.

The composite website in (Figure E.7) represents in fact several stealth command centers that are ready to launch cyber missiles. They have recruited the best professionals to design them, foolproof, with the latest technologies of cyber war. No more ISIS talk.

It is becoming a maxim of reality, that hackers (and I hate this term), cyber warriors, have meticulously and scrupulously learned all the kinks of cyber war. The truth is that hacking a system is more fun than securing a system. Hackers are more innovative and creative than chief security officers. That is why these cyber warriors have been winning the game. Jihadi militants believe they are blessed by God and will be awarded the paradise.

Figure E.8 shows the overwhelming proliferation and globalization of Jihadism within short time. These charts were compiled in late 2010 and most likely, the numbers have exploded by orders of magnitude. I could generalize and say that every major city in the world (East, West, and Middle) has Jihadists who are cruising on the information highway to get to their destination. There are no checkpoints, no highway patrol cruisers, no radar. Martyrdom is the ultimate award that lights the fire of all Jihadists. The fast lane to the paradise offers life as a token of loyalty to Islam. It is every Jihadist's dream, whether Sunni or Shi'a. No Marine's Semper Fidelis comes close to Jihadism.

Figure E.8 Islamic Jihadism is a global phenomenon.

Oh, I deliberately left the United States from the charts and put it on another detailed chart (Figure E.9). An incredible number of Islamic/Arab organizations actively operate in the United States. Most of the communications with their global networks are done with highly complex cyphertext, using RSA public-key cryptosystems with certificates signed by secret certificate authorities. Also, there is so much laundering of funds, whose illegality is very hard to prove.

Looking at Figures E.10 through E.13, we can see the devotion of the radical Muslims to Jihadism. Again, a small percentage of the Muslim population believe in Jihadi martyrdom. Most of the rest are peace loving and truly dedicated to the Quran and the Hadith.

Figure E.9 Islamic Jihadism network in the United States. (From U.S. Congress Senate Judiciary Subcommittee on Terrorism, 2009.)

The idea of martyrdom captivates their will to go to heaven

Figure E.10   Excerpts of the devotion of Islamic radicalism. Children are nurtured into violence.

Figure E.11   Every Jihadi suicide bomber is considered a martyr and receives a diploma for his achievement.

Islam promises paradise to all faithful Muslims. It is the sublime reward and every devout Muslim dreams of the paradise. The Quran promotes fighting the infidels and killing them if they refuse to convert to Islam. In fact, the Quran states that Muslims may "Fight in the cause of God against those who fight against you, but do not transgress limits. Lo! God loves not aggressors…" (2:190). Jihadism took this verse and distorted it. This is considered blasphemy and against the teachings of the Prophet Muhammad and the Quran. Period.

Jihadi suicide bombing is a disgrace to the Holy Quran. The notion that Jihadi suicide bombers are martyrs and that the Almighty God conferred upon them a place

Figure E.12 Amazing devotion to Sayed Hassan, leader of Hezbollah, a political religious organization (Shii'a organization loyal to Iran). The title "Sayed" is a religious rank, the highest is Ayatollah.

Figure E.13 Amazing devotion to Abu Baker Al-Baghdadi (Khalifa of ISIS), ex-officer of Saddam.

in Heaven is the most misunderstood interpretation of true Islamic scriptures. It is a derailed fantasy. And awarding every Jihadi suicide bomber a diplomat is definitely the most barbed sacrilege to humanity and the Muslim communities.

Now, the big question is how to prevent Jihadi terrorism. May be I should rephrase my question as follows: Can we extinguish the fire of Jihadi terrorism? Or even a more complex and enigmatic question: Can we predict any of the cyberattacks?

Let's take for a moment the classic plagiarism in academia. Before we pretend that we can eliminate plagiarism, let's focus on predicting it first. The traditional academic methods are unfortunately not working. Academia is adopting new technologies, but when it comes to plagiarism, academia hits the wall. I think if academia wants to eliminate exam plagiarism, they could eliminate the exam altogether and look for other metrics to evaluate the level of knowledge and aptitude of the student. Another method is to allow the student to select a legitimate and pre-approved exam. No school will do that. One way to eliminate plagiarism is to allow the student to select pre-approved projects and earn a *Certificate of Authenticity of Evidence of Work.* Another solution is to scan the profile of each student and his academic history as a priori "plagiaristic" data and conduct probabilistic reasoning analyses to determine the causality of troubles for the student (criminals have a historical profile, why not students?). So every teacher will have the historical profile of students, and with the help of cameras in the classrooms, plagiarism can be controlled partially. Plagiarist students are either very dumb or very innovative. The latter category of students will resort to hi-tech to cheat. For example, Google Glasses (Figure E.14) can be a way to receive answers from the outside. Apple is another means to receive answers in the blink of an eye. Amazing!

Now let's go back to the Jihadi terrorism issue. The world is plagued with Jihadism. It is exponentially problematic, simply because it is driven by politics, and most importantly by Islamic fundamentalism, which encroached all over the world—not just one country or region. Bombing can be executed by car, by self, remote control, or even with an electromagnetic device (Figures E.15 and E.16). But most Jihadists prefer to carry the bomb and detonate themselves. It is considered the ultimate martyrdom!

Figure E.14   Techno-cheating with Google Glass and Apple Watch, which will eventually lead to cyber-Jihadism.

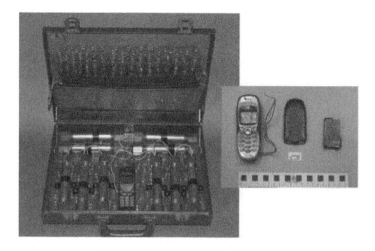

Figure E.15 Cell phones can be used as detonators in bombs of mass destruction as seen below, the ringer is hooked up to the ignition device so that when the phone is called, the bomb will detonate.

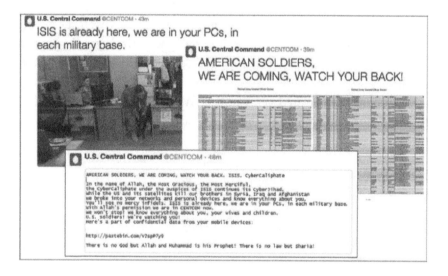

Figure E.16 Hacking the Pentagon has drawn amazement as well as embarrassment.

Let's go back now to *cyber-Jihadism*, which has morphed into a new paradigm. ISIS knows that *cyber-Jihadism* could be staged anywhere in the world without notice. Those ISIS militants who are definitely on the payroll of the Devil have the long end of the stick. This is the greatest advantage that Jihadi terrorists have. They can attack critical infrastructure systems such as computers that control power grids, steal personal information assets, and hack into strategic military intelligence, commandeer airplanes, and even nuclear plants (Stuxnet).

It is not rocket science to realize that cybercrime is now winning the battle and the war. *Cyber-Jihadism* is an active member of the Dark Web and can obtain cyber explosives the moment they are available. In my estimations, there are four technologies that can be combined to build a robust defense against cyberterrorism.

I have highlighted this in my book six advanced technologies that were used to build the Digital Immune System using the CEWPS/Smart Vaccine: Autonomic Computing, Artificial Intelligence, Grid Computing, Honeypot Technology, Cognitive Reasoning, and Knowledge engines. Like the human body, all systems operate independently, concurrently, interoperatively, and all pipes end up in the brain.

Using these technologies, we can build a Digital Immune System for the critical systems per industry. For example, all health care systems will have their own health care grid. All the Government systems will have their own grid. The Power systems will be connected to a dedicated grid and so on. It might be prohibitively expensive, but we start with a candidate industry such as the power grid. Figure E-17 shows the configuration for a typical industry sector that combines the five technologies.

The honeypot moat will be like the medieval times, creating chaos among the attackers. It is the first line of defense and it does its job very well. For cyberterrorism, first, we need to build a smart grid that ties all the critical systems physically and logically together. If one system gets compromised, the other systems on the grid will be protected.

Figure E.18 shows the layered version of CEWPS. Each industry would have its own virtual grid with honeypots and the Smart Vaccine Grid. For illustration purpose,

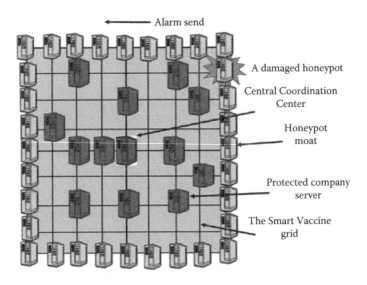

Figure E.17 Traditionally, a moat circling the city would be the safest way against preemptive attacks. If each industry (such as health care) could have its own grid, then we could surround it with a honeypot moat trapping malware. When one of the honeypots gets attacked, it will alarm the rest of the honeypots, and the critical systems of that industry will go on alert. This is where the Smart Vaccine comes in.

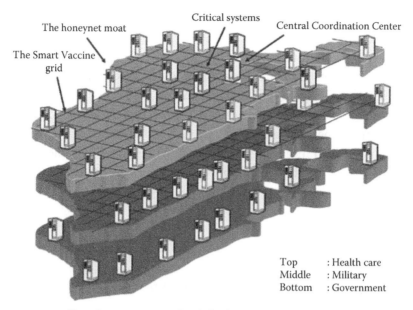

The honeynet moat

Critical systems

Central Coordination Center

The Smart Vaccine grid

Top   : Health care
Middle : Military
Bottom : Government

Three honeynet protected grids for three critical infrastructures

Figure E.18 Each sector will be on a dedicated grid. All the grids will be connected to the Central Coordination Center (CCC).

we're showing three virtual grids for health care, military, and Government critical systems. The three grids are connected to the dashboard of the Central Coordination Center (CCC). Also each grid is connected to the Smart Vaccine Grid (SVG) for vaccination response. The honeynet will also be powered with the five technologies and be as smart as the Smart Vaccine. We can say that honeynets are deployed to fool the attacker and trap them and learn more about the attack. So our moat will have very crucial duties starting with trapping attackers and limiting their actions. Once the attack is apprehended, the CCC will be notified and an alert will be dispatched to all the systems on the grid. Most likely, the attacker will fire several cyber missiles to compromise the other systems. The moat will be ready for all subsequent attacks. At the same time, the CCC will notify the Smart Vaccine for response vaccination. A profile of the attack will be sent to the Cognitive Reasoning Engine (CRE) to be stored for the next attack. The Honeynet will perform trend analysis that will also be sent to the CRE for further digging into the origin of the attack and the expected damage.

Finally as I mention in the book, cybersecurity needs an overhaul because it has reached a midlife crisis. Gartner forecasts that the total cost of information security is expected to reach $76.9 billion! I have presented my views and time will tell if I will get credit when Digital Immune Systems become the de facto of the security industry.

The scenario that I described has a purpose to demonstrate the necessity of a smart grid to defend our critical systems with the new paradigm that we call *vaccination*.

We can say that a smart grid is a mesh of many information buses that work together, like an LA freeway interchange. Some avid computer folks prefer to use the term *information bus*, which is totally agreeable.

A couple of notes worth mentioning: First, when Stuxnet worm was launched, it infected 30,000 IP addresses in Iran due to mutation. Stuxnet designers know now how to package similar missiles and launch them upon requests. Flame and Duqu are even more potent that Stuxnet. Wow! Second, Kaspersky discovered that Stuxnet uses Flame as a lunching pad which means both worms can be remotely controlled. Together, all this sets a new record of Bob Beamon caliber* and definitely merits mentioning.

Thank you.

Websites

http://www.economist.com/blogs/economist-explains/2015/01/economist-explains.

http://www.nytimes.com/2014/08/28/world/middleeast/army-know-how-seen-as-factor-in-isis-successes.html.

http://www.theguardian.com/world/2015/apr/12/isis-cyber-caliphate-hacking-technology-arms-race.

---

* On October 18, Beamon set a world record for the long jump with a first jump of 8.90 m (29 ft. 2 1/2 in.), bettering the existing record by 55 cm (21 3/4 in.). For 40 years, the record was unreachable.

Appendix A: CEWPS Development Team

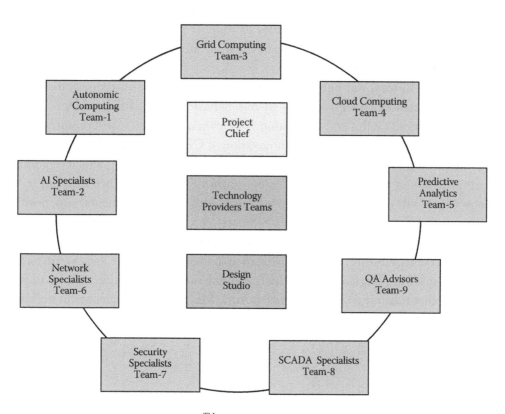

CEWPS/Smart Vaccine^{TM} Team Members Organization

I want to put a ding in the universe.

Steve Jobs (1955–2011)

No more of the old organizational chart that glorifies the rusty bureaucratic high-rise of projects. CEWPS/Smart Vaccine engineering is an icon of innovation, creativity, and most importantly human productivity. CEWPS/Smart Vaccine will certainly put a ding in cybersecurity universe. Everyone on the project works for the whole and is accountable for the whole. All team members are active players in the design ring, and they all share equal authority and respect. They are proud to be chosen for the first system, like Armstrong walking on the moon. CEWPS/Smart Vaccine is the crucible of many technologies that interweave together to create a cohesive of a kind system.

CEWPS/Smart Vaccine is a thinking machine with tremendous computing muscles and an infallible memory. Its knowledge engines store valuable historical attack episodes for future cyber raids. CEWPS/Smart Vaccine is an intelligent autonomic system with sophisticated reasoning rules to support the defense of the critical systems. The uniqueness of the system lies in the innovative approach to digital vaccination. No one has ever done it before.

Throughout history, the human element is the most crucial success factor of any endeavor. Human brittleness resides in our behavior. CEWPS introduces a new approach in system design and fabrication. The team organization will produce maximum creativity and productivity. The innovation of CEWPS/Smart Vaccine ushers in a new dimension in intelligent cybersecurity. It combines singularity, which represents the culmination of the merger of our biological thinking and existence with our technology which will transcend human intelligence with accelerated mental superiority.

There will be a time when CEWPS/Smart Vaccine will be a hybrid thinking machine that will have an edge over the criminal mind and evil-minded meatbags. One day in the near future, we will be able to upload our knowledge and experience to a thinking machine "digital mind," which will enhance our cognitive abilities to reason and predict incoming offensive cyber storms. Maybe then we can outrun malware and bring peace to our smart cities.

Appendix B: The 10 Most Dangerous Botnets*

(roBOT NETwork) Also called a "zombie army," a botnet is a large number of compromised "enslaved" computers that are networked together and used to generate spam, relay viruses or flood a network or Web server with excessive requests to cause it to fail (see denial-of-service attack). The computer, where the owner is not aware of the subtle attack, is compromised via a Trojan that often works by opening an Internet Relay Chat (IRC) channel that waits for commands from the person in control of the botnet. There is a thriving botnet business selling lists of compromised computers to cybercriminals, offensive spammers, and identity thieves.

Botnet attacks are increasing, as cybercrime gangs hijack and commandeer computers for a wild ride. Bot herders use hostage computers to send spam, steal personal data, perpetrate click fraud, and clobber websites in denial-of-service attacks. Here is the list of US 10 most wanted botnets, based on an estimate by security firm Damballa of botnet size and activity in the United States.

No. 1: Zeus

Compromised U.S. computers: 3.6 million
Main crime use: The Zeus Trojan uses keylogging techniques to steal sensitive data such as usernames, passwords, account numbers, and credit card numbers. It injects fake HTML forms into online banking login pages to steal user data.

---

* Courtesy of https://www.damballa.com/.

No. 2: Koobface

Compromised U.S. computers: 2.9 million
Main crime use: This malware spreads via social networking sites MySpace and Facebook with faked messages or comments from "friends." When a user is enticed into clicking on a provided link to view a video, the user is prompted to obtain a necessary update, like a codec—but it is really malware that can take control over the computer.

No. 3: TidServ

Compromised U.S. computers: 1.5 million
Main crime use: This downloader Trojan spreads through spam e-mail, arriving as an attachment. It uses rootkit techniques to run inside common Windows services (sometimes bundled with fake antivirus software) or in Windows safe mode, and it can hide most of its files and registry entries.

No. 4: Trojan.Fakeavalert

Compromised U.S. computers: 1.4 million
Main crime use: Formerly used for spamming, this botnet has shifted to downloading other malware, with its main focus on fake alerts and rogue antivirus software.

No. 5: TR/Dldr.Agent.JKH

Compromised U.S. computers: 1.2 million
Main crime use: This remote Trojan posts encrypted data back to its command-and-control domains and periodically receives instruction. Often loaded by other malware, TR/Dldr.Agent.JKH is currently used as a clickbot, generating ad revenue for the botmaster through constant ad-specific activity.

No. 6: Monkif

Compromised U.S. computers: 520,000
Main crime use: This crimeware's current focus is downloading an adware BHO (browser helper object) onto a compromised system.

No. 7: Hamweq

Compromised U.S. computers: 480,000
Main crime use: Also known as IRCBrute, or an autorun worm, this backdoor worm makes copies of itself on the system and any removable drive it finds—and anytime the removable drives are accessed, it executes automatically. Hamweq, an effective

spreading mechanism, creates registry entries to enable its automatic execution at every start-up and injects itself into Explorer.exe. The botmaster using it can execute commands on and receive information from the compromised system.

No. 8: Swizzor

Compromised U.S. computers: 370,000
Main crime use: A variant of the Lop malware, this Trojan dropper can download and launch files from the Internet on the victim's machine without the user's knowledge, installing an adware program and other Trojans.

No. 9: Gammima

Compromised U.S. computers: 230,000
Main crime use: Also known as Gamina, Gamania, Frethog, Vaklik, and Krap, this crimeware focuses on stealing online game logins, passwords, and account information. It uses rootkit techniques to load into the address space of other common processes, such as Explorer.exe, and will spread through removable media such as USB keys. It is also known as the worm that got into the International Space Station in the summer of 2008.

No. 10: Conficker

Compromised U.S. computers: 210,000
Main crime use: Also called Downadup, this downloader worm has spread significantly throughout the world, though not so much in the United States. It is a complex downloader used to propagate other malware. Though it has been used to sell fake antivirus software, this crimeware currently seems to have no real purpose other than to spread. Industry watchers fear that a more dangerous purpose will emerge.

Index

Printed and bound by CPI Group (UK) Ltd, Croydon, CR0 4YY

23/10/2024

01777691-0009